Pro Android Flash

Stephen Chin
Dean Iverson
Oswald Campesato
Paul Trani

Apress®

Pro Android Flash

ISBN-13 (pbk): 978-1-4302-3231-5

ISBN-13 (electronic): 978-1-4302-3232-2

President and Publisher: Paul Manning
Lead Editor: Steve Anglin
Development Editor: Tom Welsh
Technical Reviewer: James Bucanek
Editorial Board: Steve Anglin, Mark Beckner, Ewan Buckingham, Gary Cornell, Jonathan Gennick, Jonathan Hassell, Michelle Lowman, James Markham, Matthew Moodie, Jeff Olson, Jeffrey Pepper, Frank Pohlmann, Douglas Pundick, Ben Renow-Clarke, Dominic Shakeshaft, Matt Wade, Tom Welsh
Coordinating Editor: Jennifer L. Blackwell
Copy Editor: Mary Ann Fugate
Compositor: MacPS, LLC
Indexers: BIM Indexing & Proofreading Services
Artist: April Milne
Cover Designer: Anna Ishchenko

Distributed to the book trade worldwide by Springer Science+Business Media, LLC., 233 Spring Street, 6th Floor, New York, NY 10013. Phone 1-800-SPRINGER, fax (201) 348-4505, e-mail orders-ny@springer-sbm.com, or visit www.springeronline.com.

For information on translations, please e-mail rights@apress.com, or visit www.apress.com.

Apress and friends of ED books may be purchased in bulk for academic, corporate, or promotional use. eBook versions and licenses are also available for most titles. For more information, reference our Special Bulk Sales–eBook Licensing web page at www.apress.com/bulk-sales.

The source code for this book is available to readers at www.apress.com.

To my loving wife and daughter, who supported me in completing this book, with full knowledge that they would be without a father for several months.

Stephen Chin

To my mother, who always made sure our house was full of books.

Dean Iverson

To my parents.

Oswald Campesato

To my father, who loves me regardless of how much I try to impress him.

Paul Trani

Contents at a Glance

Contents

About the Authors

 **Stephen Chin** is a technical expert in RIA technologies, and chief agile methodologist at GXS, where he led a large-scale lean/agile rollout and pioneered the practice of Agile Portfolio Kanban Planning. He coauthored the Apress *Pro JavaFX Platform* title, which is the current leading technical reference for JavaFX. In addition, Stephen supports the local developer community by running the Flash on Devices and Silicon Valley JavaFX user groups. Finally, he is a Java Champion and an internationally recognized speaker, featured at Devoxx, Jazoon, and JavaOne, where he received a Rock Star Award. Stephen can be followed on Twitter (@steveonjava) and reached via his blog: http://steveonjava.com/.

 **Dean Iverson** has been developing software professionally for more than 15 years. He is currently employed by the Virginia Tech Transportation Institute, where he works with various rich client technologies that organize and visualize the large amount of data collected from the research projects at the Institute. He also has a small software consultancy, Pleasing Software Solutions, which he cofounded with his wife.

Oswald Campesato is a cofounder and CEO of a stealth-mode Web 2.0 company in the social media space. He has worked for various companies, including JustSystems of Japan, Oracle, AAA, and several startups. He is the author/coauthor of four other books.

 **Paul Trani** is really just a six-year-old in a man's body. He has kept his sense of wonder and passion for creating and has inspired countless others around the world as an Evangelist for Adobe Systems, Inc. Prior to joining Adobe, Paul spent ten years as an Adobe Certified Instructor, and he has worked for a handful of award-winning creative agencies in the Denver area, focusing on interactive technologies. He is also a best-selling author on Lynda.com. But don't let him fool you. He's still a kid that thinks Play-Doh is the best mobile interactive technology out there.

About the Technical Reviewer

 **Kunal Mittal** serves as an executive director of technology at Sony Pictures Entertainment, where he is responsible for the SOA, Identity Management, and Content Management programs. He provides a centralized engineering service to different lines of business and leads efforts to introduce new platforms and technologies into the Sony Pictures Enterprise IT environment.

Kunal is an entrepreneur who helps startups define their technology strategy, product roadmap, and development plans. With strong relations with several development partners worldwide, he is able to help startups and even large companies build appropriate development partnerships. He generally works in an advisor or consulting CTO capacity, and serves actively in the project management and technical architect functions.

He has authored and edited several books and articles on J2EE, cloud computing, and mobile technologies. He holds a master's degree in software engineering and is an instrument-rated private pilot. You can reach him here: kunal@kunalmittal.com or www.kunalmittal.com/.

Acknowledgments

We would like to thank Aaron Houston, Adobe Community Manager and long-time friend, for his unbridled support of the author team. He provided essential, up-to-date information on the evolving technology, enabled us to participate in the Adobe pre-release programs, and ensured we had the latest software and licenses to continually make progress.

We are also heavily indebted to James Ward and Duane Nickull for advice and feedback on the technology. They volunteered time from their busy schedules as Adobe Technology Evangelists to answer floods of questions from a very inquisitive set of authors.

It is also impossible for us not to acknowledge the dedication and work that went into building an amazing mobile platform by the entire Adobe Flash and Flex development staff. Arno Gourdol, director of engineering for the Adobe Flash Platform, deserves special mention for driving the engineering teams to hit a very aggressive schedule and providing insight into the future direction of technology with respect to platforms and performance.

Finally, this book would not have been possible without the hard-working folks at Apress—in particular, the foresight and guidance of Steve Anglin in conceiving this title, the insightful comments and commentary from Tom Welsh, and the tactful pressure and organization of Jennifer Blackwell.

Foreword

As developers, most of us have had things pretty easy for the past ten years. Building web applications is a pretty straightforward matter. One of the hardest things used to be deciding what web framework/technology to use. But no matter which one we chose, we were still deploying apps to desktops and laptops through the browser. There was little variety with where and how our applications ran. Those days are over. As mobile devices and tablets have rapidly become more prevalent, we are now faced with having to build applications for a gigantic variety of platforms, devices, screen resolutions, input capabilities, and integration APIs. We must simplify our development tool chain in this ocean of change.

By combining two great platforms, Flash and Android, developers can anchor themselves to a simple and proven technology stack. With its ties to the designer community, Flash is certainly the leader in interactive experiences. Flex provides the bridge between the world of interactivity and the world of testable, maintainable, and object-oriented code. Android continues to proliferate as the platform of choice across mobile devices, tablets, TVs, and more. With Flash, Flex, and Android, developers can easily build beautiful apps that over 100 million Android users can run on their devices.

The fact that it's easy doesn't mean there isn't anything new to learn. Developers must get up to speed on the tool chain and development process. Building mobile and tablet apps provides a whole new set of things to think about. For instance, how do you make a button the same physical size across devices so that a statically sized finger can always press it? With widely varying screen resolutions, how can you keep images looking crisp no matter the output size? What are the typical navigational paradigms used in mobile apps? How do those paradigms change with tablet apps? How is state managed? What happens when the user rotates the device?

There is plenty to learn! But I'm confident that in this book Stephen Chin, Dean Iverson, Oswald Campesato, and Paul Trani will guide you smoothly through the unfamiliar terrain! With their first-hand experience and knowledge, they are the perfect guides to lead you to this new land. And when you arrive, it will be just as easy (if not easier) to build amazing mobile apps with Flash, Flex, and Android as it was to build web apps!

James Ward
www.jamesward.com

Introduction

Our goal in writing this book was to open up the amazing world of mobile and device development to every single developer. You no longer need to learn a custom mobile programming language or be an expert in mobile application design to write good-looking, professional business applications. We believe that in the future, handsets and tablets will just be another deployment target for application developers—and with mobile Flash and Flex technology, that future is now.

For Those New to Flash

This book starts out with a gentle introduction to the Flash tool chain and underlying technologies, and teaches the programming concepts by example. If you have experience in another C-based language, such as Java, JavaScript, or Objective-C, the pacing of this book will allow you to learn ActionScript and MXML while you are being introduced to Flash and Flex mobile concepts and APIs.

For Those New to Android

The Flash and Flex platform takes advantage of all the great features of Android, while insulating the programmer from having to deal with the complexities of the Android APIs and programming model. This means that with simple end-user knowledge of Android, you can be up and running as an application developer, publishing your very own Flash-based applications to Android Market.

For the Rock Star Developers in All of Us

Let's face it—you didn't pick up this book to be just another mobile developer. You want to stretch the limits of the platform, tap into features and capabilities that go beyond the average, and build apps that are impossibly cool.

We are there with you, which is why we pushed the technology to its limits in developing this book. In the later chapters of this book, you will learn how to tap into native Android features, profile and tune your application for optimal performance, and deploy to a variety of different devices beyond simple handsets.

Written by Your Team

We are not your average, faceless authors who write books for a living. We are application developers and technology geeks just like you. We are invested in the technologies we discuss, the future of mobile development, and, most importantly, your success as a future Flash platform developer.

All of the authors have a visible online presence with heavy community involvement, including leading Adobe user groups and technology evangelism. We are excited about the technology and accessible to questions, inquiries, and conversations. Rather than being just another author team, we are your own personal Flash development team.

You will learn a lot from reading this book and coding the exercises, but don't stop there. Start dialogs with other readers and Flash developers. Join a technology user group that specializes in Flash and Flex technology. Reach out to us, the authors, with questions, ideas, concepts, and conjectures.

Most importantly, make the technology your own.

Chapter 1

Introducing Mobile Flash

This book, Pro Android Flash, is the definitive guide to building rich, pervasive user experiences on mobile devices using the ubiquitous Flash Platform. We will show you how to leverage the powerful and mature technologies, frameworks, and tooling that make up the Flash Platform to build highly customized applications that take full advantage of all the mobile features that users demand from their devices. In reading this book, you will gain essential knowledge specific to targeting mobile Android devices, including device density, hardware inputs, native integration, and performance optimization.

Why Android?

There are many different mobile platforms to choose from and a plethora of mobile and tablet devices that are offered as options to consumers. Unlike the desktop, where there has been a considerable amount of consolidation and entrenchment, the mobile market is constantly evolving, with continual introduction of new devices and features.

The obvious question is, which platform do you target? Our answer is to start with Android; then, by leveraging Flash technology, you avoid being locked into any particular platform.

This book focuses on creating applications on devices running the Android operating system. The reason for this is that Android is quickly becoming the most popular mobile operating system in the world, with the best support for different hardware platforms and multiple form factors.

According to the Nielsen Company, Android was the top choice among people who bought a smartphone in the second half of 2010. BlackBerry RIM and Apple iOS were in a statistical dead heat for second place, as shown in Figure 1–1.

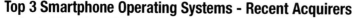

Top 3 Smartphone Operating Systems - Recent Acquirers
Acquired Smartphone within 6 months, Jan 2010 to Aug 2010, USA

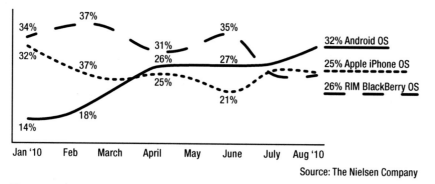

Source: The Nielsen Company

Figure 1–1. *Mobile OS traffic share in the United States[1]*

This could be due to many different factors, including the fact that the platform is open source, which attracts device manufacturers, the relative freedom provided by Android Market, Google's in-device application storefront, or the Google experience, which provides a seamless integration of Gmail, Google Maps, Gtalk, YouTube, and Google Search for end users. Regardless of the reason for Android's popularity, chances are that a large percentage of your customers already have Android devices, or are considering purchasing one in the near future.

At the same time, you are building on a platform with tremendous horizontal growth potential. Android is only the beginning for the Flash Platform, which benefits from an abstract virtual machine and APIs designed to work across multiple different operating systems and devices. You can take advantage of the same cross-platform transparency that Flash has brought to the desktop for all your mobile applications.

Flash on Other Platforms

Adobe started the Open Screen Project™,[2] which is an industry-wide initiative to bring the benefits of Flash-powered applications to all the screens of your life. Adobe has already announced plans to support iOS, BlackBerry, Windows 7, and webOS, freeing you from platform lock-in.

BlackBerry support is initially targeted at its Tablet OS, with the first available device being the BlackBerry PlayBook. Expect this support to be broadened in the future to include its other mobile devices.

---

[1] Source: The Nielsen Company, http://nielsen.com/, 2010

[2] Adobe, "Open Screen Project", http://www.openscreenproject.org/

Apple still has a restriction on running Flash in the browser, but it has opened up the App Store to allow third-party frameworks. This means that for iOS devices, you can deploy Flash as AIR applications on any iOS device, including the iPod touch, iPhone, and iPad.

You also have the ability to deploy Flash web applications on any devices that support Flash in the browser. This includes Google TV, webOS, and Windows 7. In the future, expect to see even more platforms supporting Flash technology.

Exploring Android

Android is a full mobile stack that includes an operating system, services and infrastructure, and a core set of applications. While you do not need to be an expert in Android to effectively write and deploy Flash applications to Android devices, it does help to be familiar with how Android works.

At its core, Android is based on the Linux operating system. It uses a modified version of the Linux kernel that has additional drivers and support for mobile hardware devices.

On top of this, there is a set of libraries and core services that make up the base Android functionality. You will rarely interact directly with these libraries, but whenever you play a media file, browse to a web page, or even draw on the screen, you are going through one of the core Android libraries.

Native Android applications are written using the Java programming language compiled down to Dalvik bytecodes. Dalvik is the name of Android's special virtual machine that abstracts the hardware and supports advanced features like garbage collection. All the Android applications that you run (including Adobe AIR applications) execute within the Dalvik virtual machine.

The full Android system architecture, broken down by the Linux Kernel, Libraries and Runtime, Application Framework, and Applications, is shown in Figure 1–2.

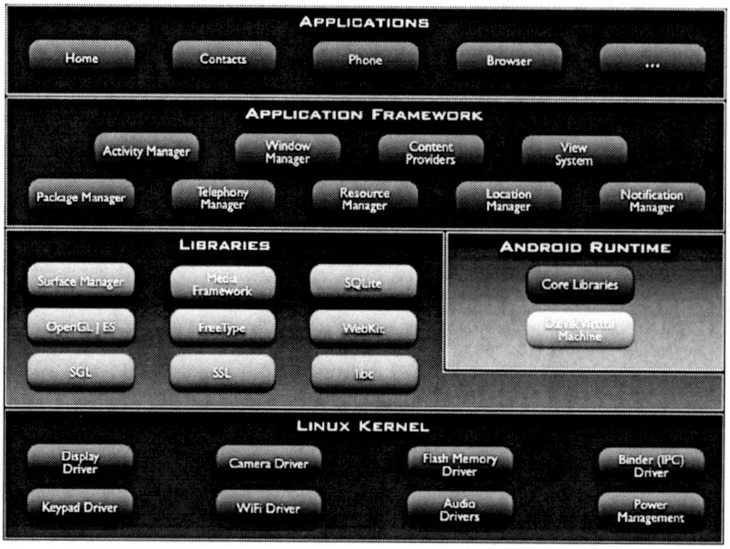

Figure 1–2. *Android system architecture*[3]

Besides having a very solid technology foundation, Android is continually evolving to embrace new hardware advances as they become available. Some of the current features of the Android platform include the following:

- *Mobile browser*: WebKit, a modern framework that supports all of the HTML5 proposed extensions and powers Android's built-in browser

- *Flash player*: Starting with Android 2.2, you can run Flash content from within a web browser as a standard feature.

- *Multitouch*: All Android phones support touchscreens, and most have at least two touch points, which you can use for gesture recognition.

- *Camera*: Android phones are required to have a rear-facing camera, and many now include a front-facing camera as well.

- *GPS, compass*: All Android phones are required to have a three-way GPS and compass, which can be used for navigation applications.

- *Multitasking*: Android was the first mobile OS to expose application switching and background operations to installed applications.

- *GSM telephony*: Android devices that operate as phones give you the full capabilities of GSM telephony.

---

[3] Reproduced from work created and shared by the Android Open Source Project and used according to terms described in the Creative Commons 2.5 Attribution License: Google, "What is Android?", `http://developer.android.com/guide/basics/what-is-android.html`, 2011

- *Bluetooth, Wi-Fi, and USB*: All Android devices come with Bluetooth and Wi-Fi for connectivity and a standard USB port for data transfer and debugging.

- *Audio and video support*: Android supports playback of most common audio and video formats that are in use on the Web, including MP3, Ogg, and H.264.

These capabilities make the Android platform an exceptionally strong foundation for building mobile applications. Furthermore, Adobe Flash and AIR build on these base capabilities, making Flash a great platform to develop Android applications.

The Flash Platform

The Adobe Flash Platform is a complete system of integrated tools, frameworks, servers, services, and clients that run across operating systems, browsers, and devices. Companies across many industries use the Flash Platform to eliminate device and platform fragmentation, and develop consistent and expressive interactive user experiences regardless of device. Let's take a look at the Flash Platform runtimes and tools.

The Flash Runtime

When creating a Flash application, you have the choice of two different deployment targets. The first is the Adobe Flash Player, which is an embedded browser plug-in, and the second is Adobe AIR, which is a stand-alone client runtime. Both of these options are available on desktop and mobile, and give you a lot of flexibility in tailoring your application deployment to the needs of your end users.

Adobe Flash Player

According to Adobe, Flash Player is installed on 98% of Internet-connected PCs and more than 450 million devices,[4] offering the widest possible reach for applications that run on the client. For 2011, Adobe projects that Flash Player will be supported on more than 132 million smartphones, and it already comes pre-installed on over 20 million smartphones. An additional 50 new tablet devices are expected to support Flash Player in 2011 as well.

Adobe Flash Player runs inside the browser in a secure container. This allows you to intermingle your Flash content with other web content written in HTML and JavaScript. You also get the benefit of installer-less operation.

---

[4] Source: Adobe, "Benefits of rich internet applications", www.adobe.com/resources/business/rich_internet_apps/benefits/#, 2009

Adobe AIR

Designers and developers that currently publish content for Flash Player can also repurpose that same content to make apps for the Adobe AIR runtime. At the time of writing, there are 84 million smartphones and tablets that can run Adobe AIR applications, and Adobe expects more than 200 million smartphones and tablets to support Adobe AIR applications by the end of 2011.

Adobe AIR extends Flash beyond the browser, allowing your content to be downloaded from Android Market and installed as a first-class application. In addition, Adobe AIR applications can request permission from the user to get access to restricted hardware such as the camera, microphone, and filesystem.

Table 1–1 summarizes the benefits of deploying within Flash Player or as an Adobe AIR mobile application. Since AIR is a proper superset of the Flash APIs, it is also possible to create a single application that is deployed under both.

Table 1–1. *Flash Player vs. AIR Deployment*

	Flash Player	Adobe AIR
Delivery	Web browser	Android Market
Installation	No installation required	Applications installed from Android Market
Updates	Updated via containing web site	AIR application update service
Background operation	Only executing when the browser window is visible	Can run in the background and provide notifications
Multitouch and gestures supported	Fully supported	Fully supported
Accessible hardware	Limited to browser sandbox	Display, keyboard, camera, microphone, GPS, accelerometer
Media playback	Yes	Yes
Data storage	Temporary browser storage only	Persistent/encrypted local storage plus full filesystem access

Adobe Flex

Flex is an open source software development kit that is tailored for building professional business applications on the Flash Platform. It includes some additional libraries for quickly and easily building user interfaces with layouts, controls, and charts. Also, most Flex UIs are written declaratively in an XML dialect called MXML, which makes it easier to build nested user interface layouts than straight ActionScript.

Adobe is very aggressively adding mobile features such as Views, touch support, and mobile-optimized skins to the Flex framework. Throughout this book, we will take advantage of Adobe Flex technology to demonstrate the mobile APIs. At the same time, we will demonstrate use of pure ActionScript APIs, which you can use if you are building an application that does not include the Flex SDK.

Flash Tooling

Since the Creative Suite 5.5 (CS5.5) release, all of the Adobe tools for doing Flash and Flex development also support mobile development.

Table 1–2 lists the tools provided by Adobe that you can use to develop mobile applications with Flash and Flex. They all interoperate very closely, making it easy to use each tool for its strengths. This extends to the Adobe design tools, such as InDesign, Photoshop, Illustrator, and Fireworks, which can be used to develop content for your application that will plug directly into your Flash and Flex applications.

Table 1–2. *Adobe Mobile Development Tools*

Tool Name	Description	Supports	Android Deployment
Adobe Flash Professional CS5.5	Visual design tool for building Flash applications with some ActionScript	ActionScript	USB deployment
Adobe Flash Builder 4.5	Professional Flex and ActionScript development environment	Flex, ActionScript	USB deployment
Device Central	Device library and runtime emulation environment	N/A	N/A
Flex 4.5 SDK	Stand-alone development toolkit	Flex, ActionScript	Build script
Adobe Flash Catalyst CS5.5	Rapid development platform for building Flex user interfaces	Flex, ActionScript	Via Flash Builder integration

Adobe Flash Professional

Adobe Flash Professional provides designers and developers with a set of drawing tools, a timeline, and the ability to add interactivity to create rich, interactive experiences for multiple platforms. It actually has its origins as an animation tool. This, of course, means that at its core it's great for working with animation and graphics. But, from its humble beginnings, it has grown up to be a full-fledged program, able to create rich, immersive experiences, complete with advanced interactivity written in ActionScript that can be published to multiple platforms.

If you are new to Flash development, Flash Professional is a great starting place. It offers a graphical movie and timeline editor that can be used to build content, and a very functional ActionScript editor with code templates, API help, and advanced features like code completion.

Adobe Flash Builder

Adobe Flash Builder software is designed to help developers rapidly develop cross-platform rich Internet applications and games for the Flash Platform. Users can create a game by writing ActionScript code just like you would with Flash Professional. With Flash Builder, you can also write applications using the Flex framework, which is a free, highly productive, open source framework for developing and deploying Rich Internet Applications (RIAs).

If you are developing a large application with a complex UI and complex algorithms or business logic, you will definitely want to add in Flash Builder 4.5. This is based on the full-featured Eclipse IDE and offers everything you would expect from a professional development environment, including code navigation, keyboard accelerators, and a complete GUI builder.

Device Central

Device Central is a complementary application that comes with Flash Professional and allows you to emulate different mobile devices on your desktop, including support for tilt, multitouch, and accelerometers. It also gives you access to a huge information repository that lists all the available mobile and embedded devices supported by the Flash Platform, including full specifications and custom emulators.

> **NOTE:** As of the time of writing, Device Central had not been updated to AIR 2.6 for Android device support.

Adobe Flash Catalyst

Flash Catalyst is Adobe's rapid application development platform. It allows you to take art assets made in Photoshop, Illustrator, or Flash, and turn them into first-class UI controls. The mobile workflow for Catalyst is to create or modify an FXP file that contains your components and assets, and then open it in Flash Builder to add business logic and run it on a mobile platform.

All of these applications are available with free trials; however, if you want to develop with a pure open source stack, you can do Flex and ActionScript development right from the command line using the Flex SDK. All the components that are the basis for Flash Builder and Catalyst are part of the Flex SDK and can be programmatically accessed. This is also what you would want to use if you were configuring an automated build to compile and test your Flex applications.

Workflow

Aside from the tooling already listed, Adobe has a powerful workflow, allowing designers to use programs like Adobe InDesign, Adobe Photoshop, Adobe Illustrator, and Adobe Fireworks to move graphics into Flash Professional or Flash Builder for further development, as shown in Figure 1–3. This means there are rarely conversion issues when dealing with graphics, nor is there a lengthy process to move graphics from design to development.

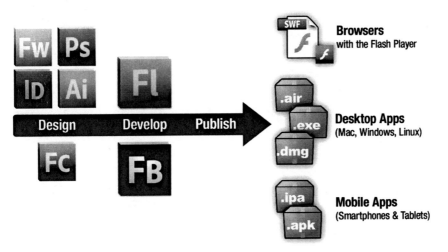

Figure 1–3. *The Flash workflow from design to development to publishing to multiple platforms/devices*

We talk about the designer/developer workflow in more detail in Chapter 9, giving real-world examples of how you can streamline your workflow between different tools.

Running Applications from Flash Professional

The easiest way to get started with writing Flash applications is to use Adobe Flash Professional. It provides a visual environment for building simple movies and also has good ActionScript editing capabilities for building more complex logic.

Creating a New Android Project

To create a new AIR for Android project, open the new project dialog from File ➤ New... and click the Templates tab. Here you can select an AIR for Android project and choose your device template, as shown in Figure 1–4.

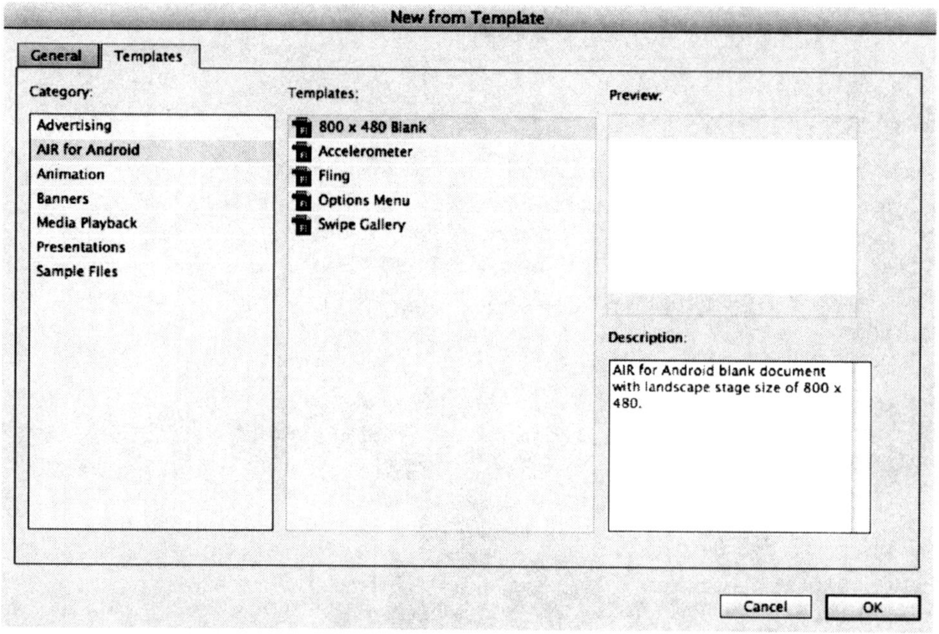

Figure 1–4. *Flash Professional new template dialog*

This will create a new project with the canvas perfectly sized for a mobile project in portrait mode, and it will allow you to test your application in Flash Professional or on a device via USB. For more information about device deployment, see Chapter 5, "Application Deployment and Publication".

Writing the Flash Capability Reporter

To demonstrate the device capabilities, we will create a simple application called the Flash Capability Reporter. It will have a simple scrolling list that enumerates all the capabilities of the emulator or device you are running on.

For the ActionScript code, we will use static constants from the `Capabilities` and `Multitouch` classes. Most of these return `true` or `false`, but some will return `string` or integer values. By using the string concatenation operator, we can easily format them for display, as shown in Listing 1–1.

Listing 1–1. *Flash Capability Checking Code*

```
import flash.system.Capabilities;
import flash.ui.Multitouch;

capabilityScroller.capabilities.text =
  "AV Hardware Disable: " + Capabilities.avHardwareDisable + "\n" +
  "Has Accessibility: " + Capabilities.hasAccessibility + "\n" +
  "Has Audio: " + Capabilities.hasAudio + "\n" +
  "Has Audio Encoder: " + Capabilities.hasAudioEncoder + "\n" +
  "Has Embedded Video: " + Capabilities.hasEmbeddedVideo + "\n" +
  "Has MP3: " + Capabilities.hasMP3 + "\n" +
  "Has Printing: " + Capabilities.hasPrinting + "\n" +
  "Has Screen Broadcast: " + Capabilities.hasScreenBroadcast + "\n" +
  "Has Screen Playback: " + Capabilities.hasScreenPlayback + "\n" +
  "Has Streaming Audio: " + Capabilities.hasStreamingAudio + "\n" +
  "Has Video Encoder: " + Capabilities.hasVideoEncoder + "\n" +
  "Is Debugger: " + Capabilities.isDebugger +  "\n" +
  "Language: " + Capabilities.language + "\n" +
  "Local File Read Disable: " + Capabilities.localFileReadDisable + "\n" +
  "Manufacturer: " + Capabilities.manufacturer + "\n" +
  "OS: " + Capabilities.os + "\n" +
  "Pixel Aspect Ratio: " + Capabilities.pixelAspectRatio + "\n" +
  "Player Type: " + Capabilities.playerType + "\n" +
  "Screen Color: " + Capabilities.screenColor + "\n" +
  "Screen DPI: " + Capabilities.screenDPI + "\n" +
  "Screen Resolution: " + Capabilities.screenResolutionX + "x"
  + Capabilities.screenResolutionY + "\n" +
  "Touch Screen Type: " + Capabilities.touchscreenType + "\n" +
  "Version: " + Capabilities.version + "\n" +
  "Supports Gesture Events: " + Multitouch.supportsGestureEvents + "\n" +
  "Supports Touch Events: " + Multitouch.supportsTouchEvents + "\n" +
  "Input Mode: " + Multitouch.inputMode + "\n" +
  "Max Touch Points: " + Multitouch.maxTouchPoints + "\n" +
  "Supported Gestures: " + Multitouch.supportedGestures;
```

The "\n" character at the end of each line adds line breaks for readability. The resultant string is then assigned to the Flash text field with ID capabilities defined in the capabilityScroller movie. The use of an embedded movie in Flash cleans up the main timeline by hiding the scrolling animation of the text.

While this would have been functionally complete, we added some extra graphic niceties to the completed book sample, including the following:

1. *A graphic clip layer*: In order to make the text appear from behind the graphics as it scrolls in and disappear as it scrolls out, we added an additional layer with a solid background and a section cut out where the text should be visible. This is in lieu of using a clip mask, so we could get the performance advantages of using device fonts.

2. *Blinking lights*: A simple animation was created on the left side by using the Flash Deco Tool with a Grid Fill using a Brick Pattern. Two different colors were chosen with the "Random order" option checked to create the visual appearance of blinking lights over a three-frame animation.

3. *Android logo and text*: No Android application is complete without a little bit of eye candy. With the full-color, high-resolution display available on Android, you can do a lot with the graphics look of your application. In this case, vector graphics were chosen for smooth scaling to any size of device.

To run the completed example, go to Control ➤ Test Movie ➤ in AIR Debug Launcher (Mobile). This will run the application within the AIR Debug Launcher (ADL) runtime, as shown in Figure 1–5.

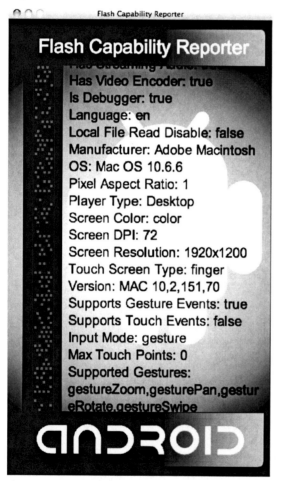

Figure 1–5. *Flash Capability Reporter application running in ADL on the desktop*

You can make use of this sample during your own development to compare device features across desktop and mobile. Feel free to add to the list of capabilities and experiment with running on different devices.

You will notice that even though we are running in ADL's mobile mode, the values returned are not consistent with what you would get when running on a device. We will show you how to run your application in the Android emulator or on a device via USB later in this chapter.

Running Applications from Flash Builder

The new version of Flash Builder has great support for building Flash and Flex applications for mobile devices and running and debugging them right from the IDE. In this section, we will show you how to create a new mobile project from scratch that demonstrates the basics of Flex mobile development, including views, controls, and multitouch gesture recognition.

The application we will be creating is called Gesture Check. It allows you to analyze your device to visually discover what gestures are supported as well as test that they are recognized successfully. In creating this example, you will get a full tour of the mobile capabilities of Flash Builder, including how to create a new Flex mobile project, debugging your application with the Flash Builder debugger, and running on a device via USB deployment.

Creating a New Flex Mobile Project

To create a new Flex mobile project, open the new project dialog from File ➤ New ➤ Flex Mobile Project. You will get a project creation wizard dialog that allows you to enter the project name, as shown in Figure 1–6.

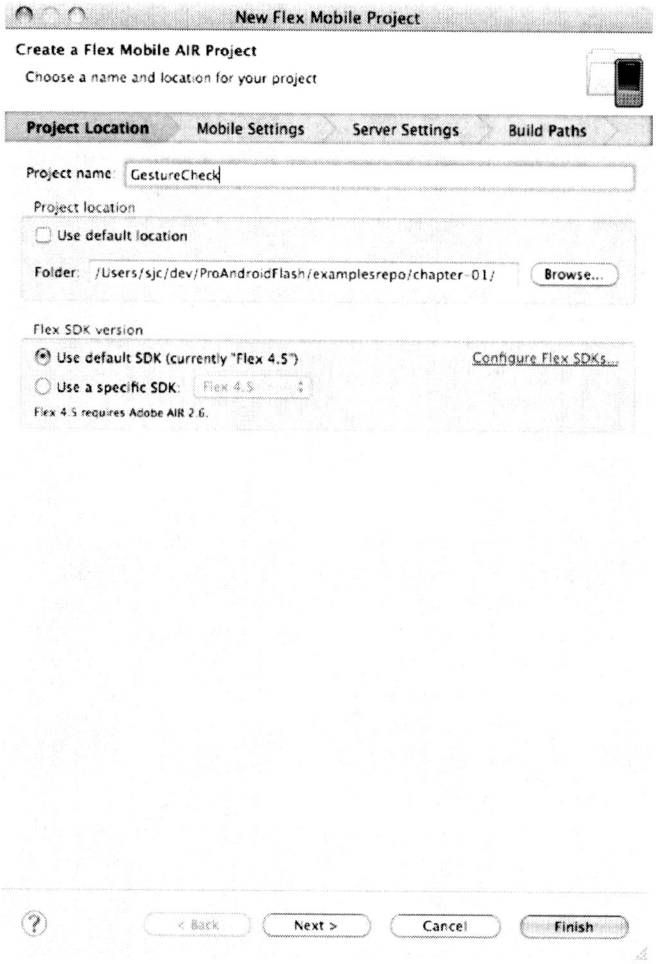

Figure 1–6. *Flex mobile project creation wizard*

Name your project GestureCheck, and choose a folder to store the project in.

> **TIP:** If you create a project name without spaces in it, Flex will create project files that match your chosen name. If your name has spaces, dashes, or other characters that are not valid in ActionScript identifiers, it will use a generic name of "Main" instead.

Once you are done with this, click Next to get to the Mobile Settings page of the wizard, as shown in Figure 1–7.

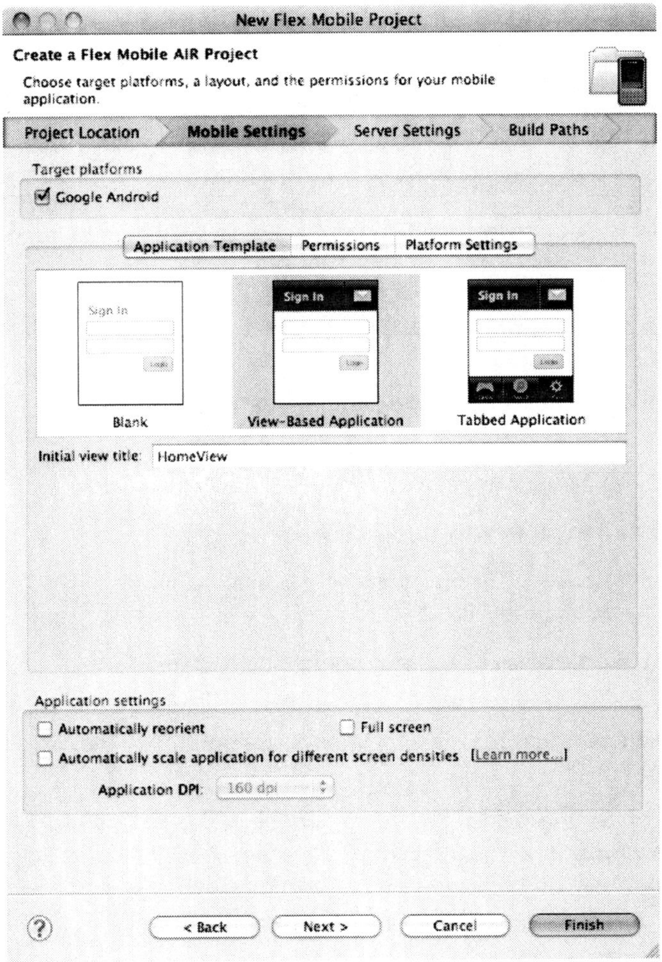

Figure 1-7. *Mobile Settings tab for selecting the application template and settings*

Flash Builder comes with several built-in templates for developing mobile projects that can be used to quickly bootstrap a new project. These include a simple Blank Application, a View-Based Application that starts on a home page, and a Tabbed Application that lets you switch between different named views. You can find more information about view and tab navigation in Chapter 3.

For this exercise, choose the basic View-Based Application template, which is the default. You are also presented with options for reorientation, full-screen mode, and density scaling. Make sure to disable automatic reorientation so that the application stays in portrait mode. We cover portrait/landscape switching in more depth in Chapter 2.

When you are finished on the Mobile Settings page, click Finish to create your mobile application.

To start with, the Flex template gives you the following project structure (files marked `internal` you should never modify directly):

- `.actionScriptProperties`: [internal] Flash Builder settings file containing libraries, platforms, and application settings

- `.flexProperties`: [internal] Flex server settings

- `.project`: [internal] Flex Builder project settings

- `.settings`: [internal] Eclipse settings folder

- `bin-debug`: This is the output folder where the XML and SWF files are stored during execution.

- `libs`: Library folder where you can add your own custom extensions later

- `src`: Source folder containing all your application code

  - `views`: Package created to store your application views

    - `[AppName]HomeView.mxml`: The main view of your application (as referenced by the main `Application`)

  - `[App-Name]-app.xml`: Application descriptor containing mobile settings

  - `[AppName].mxml`: Main `Application` class of your project and entry-point for execution

The files that we will be focusing on for the rest of the tutorial are all in the `src` directory. This includes your application descriptor and main `Application` class, both of which are in the root package, and your `HomeView`, which is created in a package called `views`.

Writing the Flex Mobile Configurator

The first thing we will do to create the application is to build a declarative XML layout for the UI. For this we are going to use some of the basic layout and UI classes of Flex, including the following:

- `H/VGroup`: The `HGroup` and `VGroup` classes let you arrange a set of components in a simple vertical or horizontal stacked layout. The components are laid out in order, with the distance between set by the gap property.

- `Label`: A simple component that displays an uneditable text string; this is commonly used as the label for another control in a form.

- `Image`: The `Image` class lets you display a graphic that can be loaded from a GIF, JPEG, PNG, SVG, or SWF file. In this example, we will be using transparent PNGs.

■   CheckBox: A form control that has a value of either selected or
unselected with a visual indicator; it also includes a text description as
part of the display.

Using these layouts and controls, we can put together a simple user interface that
displays the status of whether a particular multitouch gesture is enabled on the device
and whether the user has successfully tested the gesture. The code for the first gesture
of "Swipe" is displayed in Listing 1–2. This code should be updated in the view file,
which can be found in src/views/GestureCheckHomeView.mxml.

Listing 1–2. *UI Elements for the First Gesture Display*

```
<?xml version="1.0" encoding="utf-8"?>
<s:View xmlns:fx="http://ns.adobe.com/mxml/2009"
    xmlns:s="library://ns.adobe.com/flex/spark"
    title="Supported Gestures" initialize="init()">
  <s:VGroup paddingTop="15" paddingBottom="15"
                    paddingLeft="20" paddingRight="20" gap="10">
    <s:HGroup verticalAlign="middle" gap="20">
      <s:Label text="Swipe" fontSize="36" width="110"/>
      <s:Image source="@Embed('/gestures/swipe.png')" width="137"/>
      <s:VGroup gap="10">
        <s:CheckBox content="Enabled" mouseEnabled="false"/>
        <s:CheckBox content="Tested" mouseEnabled="false"/>
      </s:VGroup>
    </s:HGroup>
  </s:VGroup>
</s:View>
```

To run this application, go to **Run ➤ Run As ➤ Mobile Application**. This will bring up the Run
Configurations dialog, as shown in Figure 1–8.

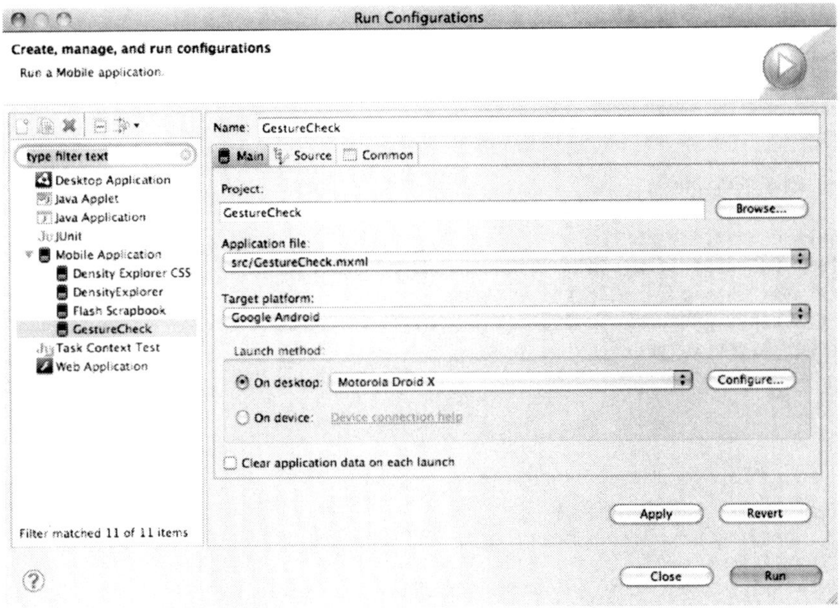

Figure 1–8. *Flash Mobile run configuration dialog*

To start with, we will run the application using the AIR Debug Launcher (ADL) on the desktop. To do this, select the desktop launch method, and choose an appropriate device to emulate (for this example, you will want to choose a device with a high-density display, such as the Droid X).

Clicking the Run button will execute the application within ADL, showing you the UI elements you added earlier, as depicted in Figure 1–9.

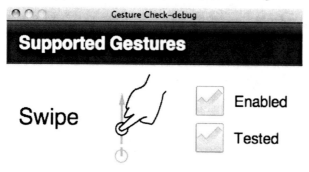

Figure 1–9. *Gesture Check user interface*

This builds out the basic UI pattern, but doesn't have any application logic hooked up to set the state of the CheckBoxes. In order to accomplish this, we are going to make use of an initialize function that iterates through all of the supportedGestures as reported by the Multitouch class. This is shown in Listing 1–3.

Listing 1–3. *Additional Code to Detect Gesture Support and Usage Highlighted in Bold*

```
<?xml version="1.0" encoding="utf-8"?>
<s:View xmlns:fx="http://ns.adobe.com/mxml/2009"
    xmlns:s="library://ns.adobe.com/flex/spark"
    title="Supported Gestures" initialize="init()">
  <fx:Script>
    <![CDATA[
      import flash.ui.Multitouch;

      private function init():void {
        for each(var gesture:String in Multitouch.supportedGestures) {
          this[gesture+"Enabled"].selected = true;
          addEventListener(gesture, function(e:GestureEvent):void {
            e.currentTarget[e.type+"Tested"].selected = true;
          });
        }
      }
    ]]>
  </fx:Script>
  <s:VGroup paddingTop="15" paddingBottom="15"
              paddingLeft="20" paddingRight="20" gap="10">
    <s:HGroup verticalAlign="middle" gap="20">
      <s:Label text="Swipe" fontSize="36" width="110"/>
      <s:Image source="@Embed('/gestures/swipe.png')" width="137"/>
      <s:VGroup gap="10">
```

```
            <s:CheckBox id="gestureSwipeEnabled" content="Enabled" mouseEnabled="false"/>
            <s:CheckBox id="gestureSwipeTested" content="Tested" mouseEnabled="false"/>
        </s:VGroup>
      </s:HGroup>
    </s:VGroup>
</s:View>
```

Notice that we have added a few IDs to the CheckBoxes in order to reference them from the initialize function. The naming convention is the gesture name appended with the words "Enabled" or "Tested". The same naming convention is used in the code that sets the selected state.

The init function gets called once when the view is created, and iterates through all the supportedGestures. It sets the state of the enabled CheckBox to true and adds an event listener that will set the state of the tested CheckBox to true when that gesture is used in the application. We cover gestures and the event listeners in more detail in Chapter 2, if you want to learn more about this functionality.

If you run the updated example, you will get the same UI, but also trigger an error. The ActionScript error dialog is shown in Figure 1–10, and while it may be obvious to you what the issue in the program is, we will use this opportunity to demonstrate how the Flash Builder debugger works.

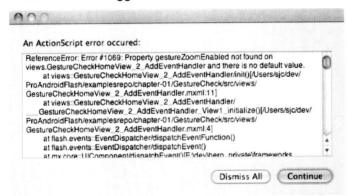

Figure 1–10. *ActionScript error on execution of the updated application*

> **NOTE:** You will get the foregoing error only if you are running on a computer with gesture support enabled, such as a Macintosh with a touchpad. You can instead run against a mobile device with a touchscreen to reproduce the same error.

Using the Flash Builder Debugger

In the last section, we got an error in running the application, but the error window wasn't particularly helpful in identifying what happened or letting us inspect the current state. In fact, if we had run the application on a mobile device, it would have continued execution without even letting us know that an error had occurred. While this behavior is ideal for production applications where you don't want minor bugs plaguing your end user if execution can safely continue, it makes debugging the application challenging.

Fortunately, Flash Builder comes with a built-in debugger that you can use to diagnose your application. To use the debugger, you have to start the application via the **Run ➤ Debug As ➤ Mobile Application** command.

When you do this, the only noticeable difference under a normal application run is that you will now get trace output and errors in the Console panel. This in itself is immensely useful when trying to diagnose application behavior; however, if you hit an error during execution, you will be asked if you want to switch to the Flash Debug perspective, which is shown in Figure 1–11.

Figure 1–11. *The Flash Debug perspective highlighting an error in the Gesture Check application*

The Flash Debug perspective gives you the ability to look inside your application as it is executing, which is extremely powerful. In the top left Debug pane, you have the ability to start and stop your application, as well as navigation stack frames, such as the error condition that we hit.

When you select a frame in the Debug panel, it shows the state of the execution context in the top-right Variable pane, as well as the associated source code in the center panel. This makes it very easy to identify that we failed on the call to set the enabled CheckBox to true, because there is no CheckBox with the id "gestureZoom". This is a result of having additional gestures that we did not yet add UI elements to handle.

Since we have identified the problem already, you can stop the application and switch back to the code perspective by using the perspective picker in the top-right corner of the Flash Builder window.

As you will learn in Chapter 2, there are five different gesture events that are supported in Flash on Android. These are as follows:

- *Pan*: Drag two fingers across the display.

- *Rotate*: Place two fingers on the display and rotate them clockwise or counterclockwise.

- *Zoom*: Use two fingers, and move them apart or together at the same time.

- *Swipe*: Press and flick a single finger across the display horizontally or vertically.

- *Two-Finger Tap*: Touch the display with two fingers simultaneously.

Listing 1–4 shows the completed application, which will let you try each of these gestures.

Listing 1–4. *Complete Code Listing for the Gesture Check Sample Application*

```
<?xml version="1.0" encoding="utf-8"?>
<s:View xmlns:fx="http://ns.adobe.com/mxml/2009"
    xmlns:s="library://ns.adobe.com/flex/spark"
    title="Supported Gestures" initialize="init()">
  <fx:Script>
    <![CDATA[
      import flash.ui.Multitouch;

      private function init():void {
        for each(var gesture:String in Multitouch.supportedGestures) {
          this[gesture+"Enabled"].selected = true;
          addEventListener(gesture, function(e:GestureEvent):void {
            e.currentTarget[e.type+"Tested"].selected = true;
          });
        }
      }
    ]]>
  </fx:Script>
  <s:VGroup paddingTop="15" paddingBottom="15"
                paddingLeft="20" paddingRight="20" gap="10">
```

```
        <s:HGroup verticalAlign="middle" gap="20">
          <s:Label text="Pan" fontSize="36" width="110"/>
          <s:Image source="@Embed('/gestures/pan.png')" width="137"/>
          <s:VGroup gap="10">
            <s:CheckBox id="gesturePanEnabled" content="Enabled" mouseEnabled="false"/>
            <s:CheckBox id="gesturePanTested" content="Tested" mouseEnabled="false"/>
          </s:VGroup>
        </s:HGroup>
        <s:HGroup verticalAlign="middle" gap="20">
          <s:Label text="Rotate" fontSize="36" width="110"/>
          <s:Image source="@Embed('/gestures/rotate.png')" width="137"/>
          <s:VGroup gap="10">
            <s:CheckBox id="gestureRotateEnabled" content="Enabled" mouseEnabled="false"/>
            <s:CheckBox id="gestureRotateTested" content="Tested" mouseEnabled="false"/>
          </s:VGroup>
        </s:HGroup>
        <s:HGroup verticalAlign="middle" gap="20">
          <s:Label text="Zoom" fontSize="36" width="110"/>
          <s:Image source="@Embed('/gestures/zoom.png')" width="137"/>
          <s:VGroup gap="10">
            <s:CheckBox id="gestureZoomEnabled" content="Enabled" mouseEnabled="false"/>
            <s:CheckBox id="gestureZoomTested" content="Tested" mouseEnabled="false"/>
          </s:VGroup>
        </s:HGroup>
        <s:HGroup verticalAlign="middle" gap="20">
          <s:Label text="Swipe" fontSize="36" width="110"/>
          <s:Image source="@Embed('/gestures/swipe.png')" width="137"/>
          <s:VGroup gap="10">
            <s:CheckBox id="gestureSwipeEnabled" content="Enabled" mouseEnabled="false"/>
            <s:CheckBox id="gestureSwipeTested" content="Tested" mouseEnabled="false"/>
          </s:VGroup>
        </s:HGroup>
        <s:HGroup verticalAlign="middle" gap="20">
          <s:Label text="Two-Finger Tap" fontSize="36" width="110"/>
          <s:Image source="@Embed('/gestures/twoFingerTap.png')" width="137"/>
          <s:VGroup gap="10">
            <s:CheckBox id="gestureTwoFingerTapEnabled"
                        content="Enabled" mouseEnabled="false"/>
            <s:CheckBox id="gestureTwoFingerTapTested"
                        content="Tested" mouseEnabled="false"/>
          </s:VGroup>
        </s:HGroup>
        <s:Label text="Graphics courtesy of GestureWorks.com" fontSize="12"/>
      </s:VGroup>
</s:View>
```

If you test this application from the ADL desktop emulator, you will get different results based on your desktop gesture support. For machines that have no multitouch support, none of the gestures will be enabled; however, if you are fortunate enough to have a desktop or laptop with a touchpad that supports multitouch, you may be able to do some limited testing of the application, as shown in Figure 1–12.

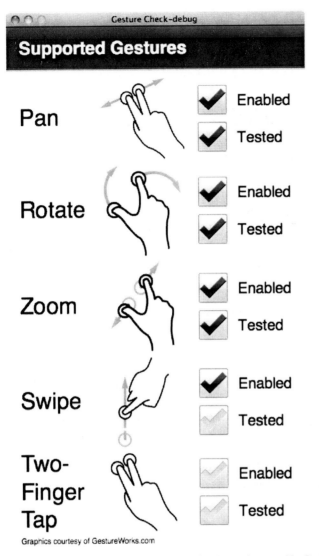

Graphics courtesy of GestureWorks.com

Figure 1–12. *Limited gesture support available running on a MacBook Pro with a trackpad*

While it reports four out of five of the gestures as enabled, it is physically possible to execute only Pan, Rotation, and Zoom on the computer we used to execute this example. As we will see in the next section, it is much more interesting to run it on a device that has full support for all the multitouch gestures.

Running Flash on Device

Flash Builder makes it very easy to execute your application on a mobile device. With a single click, it will deploy the application, launch it on the device, and even hook up a remote debugger.

To run your application on a physical device, you will need to make sure that it is set up properly for USB debugging. On most devices, you can enable USB debugging by going into **Settings ➤ Applications ➤ Development**, where you will find the options shown in Figure 1–13.

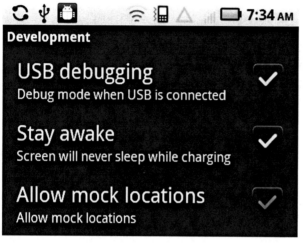

Figure 1–13. *Android development settings screen*

Make sure USB debugging is enabled on this page. You may also want to enable support for staying awake at the same time, so you don't have to continually log back into the phone each time it goes to sleep.

Once USB debugging is enabled and you have hooked your phone up to your computer via a USB cable, your device should be visible to Flash Builder. To switch to running on the device, go to **Run ➤ Run Configurations…**, and referring back to Figure 1–8, you can choose the option for launching on the device. Once selected, each time you run your application, it will launch on your attached Android device, as shown in Figure 1–14.

As you can see, on a real device, it is possible to exercise all the gesture events. This application should come in handy when testing different devices to see what gestures they support and how they respond to them.

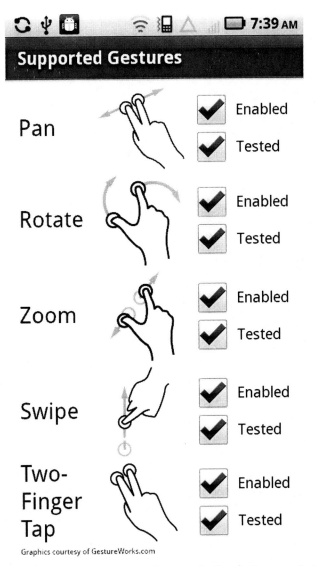

Figure 1–14. *Finished Gesture Check application running on an Android mobile device*

In case you are having trouble getting your Android phone to connect with your computer, here are some troubleshooting steps you can follow:

- Make sure that your device has a USB connection to the computer. The notification area on your Android device will say that it is connected via USB when this is successful.

- You also need to ensure that device debugging is enabled via the foregoing steps. Again, this will be listed in the notification area when it is working correctly.

- If you are not getting a USB connection, it could be an issue with drivers. Macintosh computers do not require drivers; however, on Windows you may need to install a special USB driver for your phone.

- It could also be an issue with the connection to your computer. Try using a different cable or a different USB port.

- If you have a USB connection, but device debugging is not working, you may need to change your USB connection mode on the Android device. Look for an option that says "Charge Mode" or "Disable Mass Storage."

If you are still having problems, you should verify that your phone is in the list of supported devices for the release of Flash Builder you are using, and check with your manufacturer to make sure you have the correct drivers and settings.

Running Applications from the Command Line

In addition to running from within Flash Professional and Flash Builder, you can also launch your application from the command line using the AIR Debug Launcher (ADL). This is also how you would test your application if you were using Flex directly without tooling support.

To use ADL, you will have to download the Flex 4.5 SDK, which is a free download, or navigate to the sdks/4.5.0 folder of your Flash Builder installation. Make sure that the bin folder of the Flex SDK is in your path so you can invoke the ADL command line tool.

The syntax for the ADL tool is as follows:

```
adl ( -runtime <runtime-dir> )? ( -pubid <pubid> )? -nodebug? ( -profile PROFILE )? ( -
extdir <extensions-dir> )? ( -screensize SCREEN_SIZE )? <app-desc> <root-dir>? ( -- ...
)?
```

ADL supports a number of optional arguments, most of which are optional. Here is a brief description of all the arguments, with the ones that are important for mobile development highlighted in bold:

- runtime: Optional parameter to specify an alternate AIR runtime; by default the runtime that is contained within the SDK will be used.

- pubid: Deprecated parameter for specifying the application ID; you should use the ID tag in the application descriptor instead.

- nodebug: Disables debugging support, yielding a slight performance gain and application behavior that is closer to production

- **profile**: The type of application you are debugging; for mobile development, we will be using the mobileDevice profile. Here is the full list of values:

  - mobileDevice, extendedMobileDevice, desktop, extendedDesktop, tv, extendedTV

- `extdir`: Optional directory for ActionScript extensions

- `screensize`: The size of the application window, which can be one of the keywords listed in Table 1–3 or a string of this format:

  - `<width>x<height>:<fullscreen width>x<fullscreen height>`

- `app-desc`: This is the only required parameter for the ADL runtime, and should refer to the application descriptor of the AIR program you want to execute.

- `root-dir`: By default ADL will make the root application directory the folder the application descriptor is stored in, but you can override it by setting this to another path.

- `(-- …)`: Finally, you can pass in parameters to your application by adding them after two dashes.

Table 1–3. *Valid Screen Size Settings for ADL*

Screen Size Keyword	Normal Size	Full-Screen Size
iPhone	320x460	320x480
iPhoneRetina	640x920	640x960
iPod	320x460	320x480
iPodRetina	640x920	640x960
iPad	768x1004	768x1024
Droid	480x816	480x854
NexusOne	480x762	480x800
SamsungGalaxyS	480x762	480x800
SamsungGalaxyTab	600x986	600x1024
QVGA	240x320	240x320
WQVGA	240x400	240x400
FWQVGA	240x432	240x432
HVGA	320x480	320x480
WVGA	480x800	480x800

Screen Size Keyword	Normal Size	Full-Screen Size
FWVGA	480x854	480x854
1080	1080x1920	1080x1920
720	720x1080	720x1080
480	480x720	480x720

To run the Gesture Check application you developed earlier, navigate to the root project folder and execute the following command:

```
adl -profile mobileDevice -screensize Droid bin-debug/GestureCheck-app.xml
```

This will execute the Gesture Check application in the AIR Debug Launcher using a mobile profile and a screen size of the Motorola Droid. Since the Gesture Check application does not have full-screen set to true in its application descriptor, the window size used by ADL will be 480x816.

Upon execution, you should get results identical to those shown in Figure 1–12, matching the earlier run you executed in Flash Builder.

Summary

It is an exciting time to get started with mobile development. The adoption of smartphones, and in particular Android-based devices, is exponentially rising, and you can finally use modern development frameworks with full authoring tool support, such as Flash and Flex.

In the short span of this first chapter, you have already learned how to do the following:

- Create mobile applications using both Flash Professional and Flex Builder
- Run applications in the AIR Debug Launcher
- Deploy and test on Android devices via a USB connection
- Use the Flash Builder debugger to diagnose your application
- Test your application with different screen sizes from the command line

This is just the tip of the iceberg for Flash Android mobile development. In the upcoming chapters, we show you how to build engaging, immersive Flash applications that take full advantage of all the mobile features. Then we demonstrate how to deploy and publish your application to Android Market. Finally, we cover advanced topics such as native Android integration, performance tuning, and extending your application to tablets, TV, and beyond.

Chapter 2

Targeting Applications for the Mobile Profile

Mobile devices are significantly resource-constrained when compared to their desktop brethren. Mobile processors are quickly catching up to the speed of yesterday's desktops, but RAM and storage are still at a premium. At the same time, users expect mobile applications to start up instantaneously and be entirely fault-tolerant to hard or soft crashes at any time.

For example, to conserve memory resources, the Android OS can choose to kill a background application at any time. When the user accesses the application, it depends upon the last known Activity state to start it up. If the application takes longer than one second to relaunch, the delay will be noticeable to the user, who believes the application is still running in the background.

While a lot of the same concepts apply as in desktop application development, such as the tools and programming languages used, server communication protocols available, and controls and skins available for UI development, there are unique characteristics of mobile devices that affect the UI and application design, such as screen size, input methods, and deployment.

Many of the same constraints on space, footprint, and startup time have existed on the Web for quite a while. Flash browser applications are often expected to fit within a confined web page, download quickly, share limited computing resources, and start instantaneously. As a result, your existing Flash and Flex applications may be good candidates for porting to mobile. In this chapter, we will show you how to build applications that take full advantage of the Android mobile platform.

Screen Size

Android is an operating system and software stack, not a hardware platform. Google provides an open source platform that includes a modified Linux kernel and Java-based applications that can run on a variety of hardware platforms. However, they don't control the exact characteristics of the final devices on which Android runs. This means that the exact configuration of the devices varies greatly, and screen size is one area where there are a lot of variations in terms of resolution, physical size, and pixel density. Table 2–1 shows the screen characteristics of a variety of common Android devices that end users may run your applications on.

Table 2–1. *Android Devices and Screen Characteristics*

Device Name	Manufacturer	Resolution	Size	Density	Type
HTC Dream/T-Mobile G1	HTC	320x480	3.2"	180ppi	HVGA
HTC Hero	HTC	320x480	3.2"	180ppi	HVGA
Motorola Droid	Motorola	480x854	3.7"	265ppi	FWVGA
Google Nexus One	HTC	480x800	3.7"	252ppi	WVGA
Xperia X10 mini	Sony Ericsson	240x320	2.55"	157ppi	QVGA
Xperia X10	Sony Ericsson	480x854	4"	245ppi	FWVGA
HTC Evo 4G	HTC	480x800	4.3"	217ppi	WVGA
Droid X	Motorola	480x854	4.3"	228ppi	FWVGA
Motorola ATRIX	Motorola	540x960	4"	275ppi	qHD

In Table 2–1, resolution is the number of physical pixels in the horizontal and vertical directions, size is the diagonal dimension of the screen, and density is the number of pixels per inch (ppi). Type gives you the common name for the screen resolution, which is one of the following:

- *QVGA (Quarter Video Graphics Array)*: 240x320 pixels or one quarter of the resolution of a VGA display (480x640)

- *HVGA (Half Video Graphics Array)*: 320x480 or half the resolution of a VGA display

- *WVGA (Wide Video Graphics Array)*: 480x800 with the same height as VGA, but 800 width (when viewed in landscape)

- *FWVGA (Full Wide Video Graphics Array)*: 480x854 with the same height as VGA, but a 16:9 ratio for displaying uncropped HD video

- *qHD (Quarter High Definition)*: 540x960 or one quarter of a 1080p display with a 16:9 ratio for displaying uncropped HD video

The usable area of your application will also be reduced by the height of the Android status bar. The height of the bar is 25 pixels on a medium-density display (such as the HTC Hero), 38 pixels on a high-density display (such as the Nexus One), or 50 pixels on an ultra-high-density display. This also changes when the display is switched from portrait to landscape mode. For example, the usable area of a Nexus One in portrait mode is 480x762, while in landscape mode it changes to 442x800.

You will likely have only one or two of these devices to test against, but this doesn't mean that your application can't support them all. Flash can automatically scale your application to fit the screen size, and it is very easy to get the screen resolution to modify your interface programmatically. Listing 2–1 shows how you can retrieve the screen resolution and density from ActionScript code.

Listing 2–1. *Programmatic Screen Resolution and Density Capture*

```
var resY = Capabilities.screenResolutionX;
var resX = Capabilities.screenResolutionY;
var dpi = Capabilities.screenDPI;
trace("Screen Resolution is " + resX + "x" + resY + " at " + dpi + "ppi");
```

Note: The terms dots per inch (dpi) and pixels per inch (ppi) are equivalent measures. These are used interchangeably throughout the ActionScript APIs.

Screen Resolution vs. Density

While application developers are more likely to focus on differences in screen resolution, screen density is equally important. Your application needs to be able to scale to larger or smaller devices so that text is still readable and targets are large enough to be manipulated. Figure 2–1 compares the physical size as well as the screen resolution of several handsets with different characteristics.

While the screen resolution of the Xperia X10 mini is minuscule compared to the Nexus One, the physical size of the screen is only 30% smaller. This means that all the graphics in your user interface need to be scaled down significantly to fit on the screen. On the other hand, when building for the Xperia X10 mini, even small targets can easily be manipulated by the user since the pixels are so large. For a Nexus One, you need to make the targets much larger.

In a study done in 2006, researchers at the University of Oulu and in Maryland found that the minimum target size for manipulating a touchscreen using your thumb ranged from 9.2mm to 9.6mm.[1] This is very helpful in determining how large to make hit targets in an Android user interface.

---

[1]Pekka Parhi, Amy K. Karlson, and Benjamin B. Bederson, "Target size study for one-handed thumb use on small touchscreen devices", http://portal.acm.org/citation.cfm?id=1152260, 2006

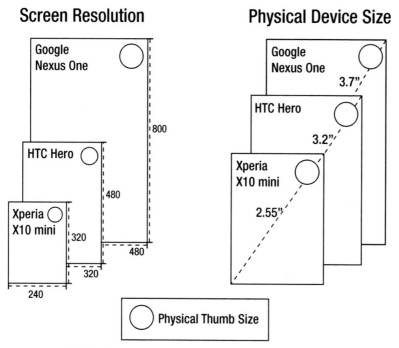

Figure 2–1. *Physical size and resolution of several Android devices*

For example, to allow for touch interaction, you would need to size your targets at 57 pixels wide on the Xperia X10 mini, or a whopping 92 pixels on the Nexus One. By sizing your UI to take density into account, you can ensure the UI is still usable while maximizing the screen real estate of the active device.

Simulating Device-Independent Pixels in Flash

Android has a concept of device-independent pixels, which can be used to do layouts that will appear similar even if the physical size of the display is different. It is based on the reference platform of a 160 dpi screen, which translates to approximately one 13x13 pixel square per inch. If you specify an Android layout with device-independent pixels, the platform will automatically adjust based on the device your app is running on.

Flash does not have a concept of device-independent pixels, but it is very easy to simulate in code. The basic formula is dips = pixels * (160 / density). Listing 2–2 demonstrates how you can calculate this in ActionScript.

Listing 2–2. *ActionScript Function to Calculate Device-Independent Pixels (dips)*

```
function pixelsToDips(pixels:int) {
    return pixels * (160 / Capabilities.screenDPI);
}
trace("100 pixels = " + pixelsToDips(100) + " dips");
```

Using simulated device-independent pixels, you can reproduce similar layout behavior in your Flash application to that of a native Android application.

If you plan on scaling your application graphics based on the current device density, make sure that your application is not set to auto-resize to fill the screen or center content on rotation. More information about how to do this can be found in the section entitled "Automatic Orientation Flipping in Flash" found later in this chapter.

Density in Flex Applications

Flex has built-in support to scale the user interface of your application, including graphics, fonts, and controls. Rather than doing arbitrary scaling, it supports three discrete scale factors for common display densities. Table 2–2 lists all of the different display densities along with the mapped DPI range that is used to select a density for the current device.

Table 2–2. *Flex Display Densities*

Density	DPI	Mapped DPI Range	Example Devices
Medium Density (mdpi)	160	Below 200	T-Mobile G1, Xperia X10 mini, HTC Hero
High Density (hdpi)	240	200 to 280	Motorola Droid, Google Nexus One, HTC Evo 4G
Extra High Density (xhdpi)	320	Above 280	N/A

To take advantage of the Flex density support, set the `applicationDPI` property on your `Application` object to the scale the application was originally designed for. At runtime your application will be automatically scaled based on the density of the device screen. An example of what your application descriptor should look like for a 240 dpi is included in Listing 2–3.

Listing 2–3. *Application Descriptor to Set the* `applicationDPI`

```
<s:ViewNavigatorApplication xmlns:fx="http://ns.adobe.com/mxml/2009"
    xmlns:s="library://ns.adobe.com/flex/spark" firstView="views.MainHomeView"
    applicationDPI="240">
</s:ViewNavigatorApplication>
```

The only valid values for `applicationDPI` are the text strings of "160", "240", and "320", corresponding to the three supported densities. The `applicationDPI` property can be set only via MXML.

Based on the ratio of the author density to the device density, the portions of your application built using vector graphics and text are smoothly scaled up or down as needed. In the case of fonts, the font size is adjusted, ensuring that text is easily readable on any display.

Bitmap graphics will also be scaled, but may look blurry when scaled up or lose detail when scaled down. To ensure that your bitmaps are sized optimally for different densities, you can provide alternative images that will automatically be swapped in based on the display density by using the `MultiDPIBitmapSource` class.

Density Explorer Application

To better understand how density affects your Flex applications, we will guide you through the creation of the Density Explorer application. This application lets you input the application `dpi` and device `dpi` as parameters, and calculate the Flex-adjusted device density and scale factor that will be used on different devices.

To start, create a new Flex mobile project with the name "Density Explorer", using the Mobile Application template. This will automatically generate a standard project template that includes an Adobe AIR application descriptor (`DensityExplorer-app.xml`), a ViewNavigatorApplication (`DensityExplorer.mxml`), and an initial View (`DensityExplorerHomeView.mxml`).

The first step is to open `DensityExplorerHomeView.mxml` and add in some controls that let you set the Author Density and the Device DPI. We will cover Flex controls in more detail in Chapter 5, but for this application a few labels, radio buttons, and a horizontal slider should be good enough.

Listing 2–4 shows the basic code to allow input of author density and device dpi using the RadioButton and HSlider classes.

Listing 2–4. *Density Explorer Controls for* `applicationDPI` *and* `deviceDPI` *Entry*

```
<fx:Script>
  <![CDATA[
    [Bindable]
    protected var applicationDPI:Number;
    [Bindable]
    public var deviceDPI:Number;
  ]]>
</fx:Script>
<s:VGroup paddingTop="20" paddingLeft="15" paddingRight="15" paddingBottom="15"
        gap="20" width="100%" height="100%">
  <s:Label text="Application DPI:"/>
  <s:HGroup gap="30">
    <s:RadioButton id="ad160" content="160" click="applicationDPI = 160"/>
    <s:RadioButton id="ad240" content="240" click="applicationDPI = 240"/>
    <s:RadioButton id="ad320" content="320" click="applicationDPI = 320"/>
  </s:HGroup>
  <s:Label text="Device DPI: {deviceDPI}"/>
  <s:HSlider id="dpiSlider" minimum="130" maximum="320" value="@{deviceDPI}"
          width="100%"/>
</s:VGroup>
```

First, a few bindable script variables are introduced to hold the `applicationDPI` and `deviceDPI`. These are not required to display the basic UI, but they will make hooking up the output portion much easier later on. The main controls are organized vertically in a VGroup, while the RadioButtons are organized horizontally using an HGroup.

The RadioButtons are wired up to applicationDPI using a simple click handler. A bi-directional data binding expression (prefixed by the @ operator) is used to update the value of dpi when the slider changes. To complete this portion of the UI, the Device DPI text contains a bound reference to dpi so you can see the value of the slider as it changes.

Running this will give you a simple Flex application, as shown in Figure 2–2. You can validate the functionality by moving the slider, which will update the deviceDPI setting.

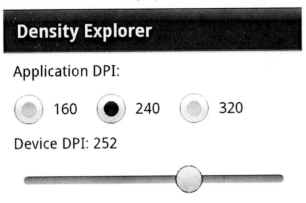

Figure 2–2. *Density Explorer part 1: basic controls*

The goal of this application is to calculate the adjusted device density and scale factor that Flex will use. Fortunately, there is a new Flex 4.5 API that exposes this information via ActionScript. The class that we need to invoke is called DensityUtil and can be found in the mx.utils package. DensityUtil has two static methods with the following signatures:

- getRuntimeDPI():Number: This function returns the applicationDPI if set, otherwise the current runtime DPI classification of the application; it will always return one of the following values: 160, 240, or 320.

- getDPIScale(sourceDPI:Number, targetDPI:Number):Number: This function calculates the scale that will be used by Flex given an application DPI (source) and a device DPI (target).

In addition to these functions, we also need to know the current applicationDPI and device dpi values so we can populate the initial values of the UI controls. These can be queried via the following APIs:

- Application.applicationDPI: Member variable on the Application object that can be queried to get the initial applicationDPI value

- Capabilities.screenDPI: Static method on the Capabilities object that returns the numeric dpi value of the screen

Making use of these APIs, we can augment the previous code to add in initialization logic and a readout of density and scale. Listing 2–5 shows the updated code with new additions in bold.

Listing 2–5. *Updated Density Explorer Code with Initialization and Output*

```
<?xml version="1.0" encoding="utf-8"?>
<s:View xmlns:fx="http://ns.adobe.com/mxml/2009"
    xmlns:mx="library://ns.adobe.com/flex/mx"
    xmlns:s="library://ns.adobe.com/flex/spark"
    title="Density Explorer" initialize="init()">
  <fx:Script>
    <![CDATA[
      import mx.binding.utils.BindingUtils;
      import mx.utils.DensityUtil;
      [Bindable]
      protected var applicationDPI:Number;
      [Bindable]
      public var deviceDPI:Number;
      [Bindable]
      protected var dpiClassification:Number;
      protected function updateDensity(dpi:Number):void {
        dpiClassification = dpi < 200 ? 160 : dpi >= 280 ? 320 : 240;
      }
      protected function init():void {
        applicationDPI = parentApplication.applicationDPI;
        if (applicationDPI != null) {
          this["ad" + applicationDPI].selected = true;
        }
        BindingUtils.bindSetter(updateDensity, this, "deviceDPI");
        deviceDPI = Capabilities.screenDPI;
      }
    ]]>
  </fx:Script>
  <s:VGroup paddingTop="20" paddingLeft="15" paddingRight="15" paddingBottom="15"
                   gap="20" width="100%" height="100%">
    <s:Label text="Application DPI:"/>
    <s:HGroup gap="30">
      <s:RadioButton id="ad160" content="160" click="applicationDPI = 160"/>
      <s:RadioButton id="ad240" content="240" click="applicationDPI = 240"/>
      <s:RadioButton id="ad320" content="320" click="applicationDPI = 320"/>
    </s:HGroup>
    <s:Label text="Device DPI: {dpi}"/>
    <s:HSlider id="dpiSlider" minimum="130" maximum="320" value="@{deviceDPI}"
             width="100%"/>
    <s:Group width="100%" height="100%">
      <s:BorderContainer bottom="0" minHeight="0" width="100%" borderStyle="inset"
               backgroundColor="#d0d0d0" borderColor="#888888" backgroundAlpha=".6">
        <s:layout>
          <s:VerticalLayout gap="10" paddingLeft="10" paddingRight="10"
                  paddingTop="10" paddingBottom="10"/>
        </s:layout>
        <s:Label text="Adjusted Device Density: {dpiClassification}"/>
        <s:Label text="Scale Factor: {DensityUtil.getDPIScale(applicationDPI,
                                            dpiClassification)}"/>
      </s:BorderContainer>
```

```
    </s:Group>
  </s:VGroup>
</s:View>
```

Initialization is performed inside a method called by `View.initialize` to ensure that all values are available. The `applicationDPI` is updated first from the `parentApplication` object, and the correct `RadioButton` is selected by performing an ID lookup on the returned string. Next the `dpi` is set from the `Capabilities` object. To ensure that all updates to `dpi` from both the initial value assignment and subsequent updates to the slider will recalculate the `deviceDensity`, a bind setter is configured to fire on all updates to `dpi`.

In order to display the current values of `deviceDensity` and the calculated scale, a `BorderContainer` with a few `Label`s is added to the end of the `View`. By using a `BorderContainer` as the surrounding group, it is easy to change the style to make the outputs visually distinct from the inputs.

The final touch is to add an extra group that will fade in device pictures as the `dpi` setting is updated. To ensure that the images are optimally scaled for different density displays, we make use of a `MultiDPIBimapSource` that refers to different pre-scaled artifacts. This code is shown in Listing 2–6.

Listing 2–6. *MXML Code for Displaying Representative Device Images Using a* `MultiDPIBitmapSource`

```
<s:Group id="phones" width="100%" height="100%">
  <s:Image alpha="{1-Math.abs(deviceDPI-157)/20}" horizontalCenter="0">
    <s:source>
      <s:MultiDPIBitmapSource
        source160dpi="@Embed('assets/xperia-x10-mini160.jpg')"
        source240dpi="@Embed('assets/xperia-x10-mini240.jpg')"
        source320dpi="@Embed('assets/xperia-x10-mini320.jpg')" />
    </s:source>
  </s:Image>
  <s:Image alpha="{1-Math.abs(deviceDPI-180)/20}" horizontalCenter="0">
    <s:source>
      <s:MultiDPIBitmapSource
        source160dpi="@Embed('assets/htc-hero160.jpg')"
        source240dpi="@Embed('assets/htc-hero240.jpg')"
        source320dpi="@Embed('assets/htc-hero320.jpg')" />
    </s:source>
  </s:Image>
  <s:Image alpha="{1-Math.abs(deviceDPI-217)/20}" horizontalCenter="0">
    <s:source>
      <s:MultiDPIBitmapSource
        source160dpi="@Embed('assets/htc-evo-4g160.jpg')"
        source240dpi="@Embed('assets/htc-evo-4g240.jpg')"
        source320dpi="@Embed('assets/htc-evo-4g320.jpg')" />
    </s:source>
  </s:Image>
  <s:Image alpha="{1-Math.abs(deviceDPI-252)/20}" horizontalCenter="0">
    <s:source>
      <s:MultiDPIBitmapSource
        source160dpi="@Embed('assets/nexus-one160.jpg')"
        source240dpi="@Embed('assets/nexus-one240.jpg')"
        source320dpi="@Embed('assets/nexus-one320.jpg')" />
    </s:source>
```

```
    </s:Image>
    <s:Image alpha="{1-Math.abs(deviceDPI-275)/20}" horizontalCenter="0">
      <s:source>
        <s:MultiDPIBitmapSource
          source160dpi="@Embed('assets/atrix160.jpg')"
          source240dpi="@Embed('assets/atrix240.jpg')"
          source320dpi="@Embed('assets/atrix320.jpg')" />
      </s:source>
    </s:Image>
  </s:Group>
```

All of the pictures chosen are scaled versions of standard press images for the phones. In order to fade the devices in slowly as the dpi value is approached, a simple mathematical formula is applied to alpha:

```
1-Math.abs(deviceDPI-{physicalDPI})/{threshold}
```

For each of the phones, the actual dpi is substituted for the physicalDPI for that device, and the threshold is set to a value low enough that there will not be two phones overlapping for the target dpi value. For the devices selected, a threshold of 20 is lower than the difference between any of the phone dpi values.

The finished Density Explorer application is shown in Figure 2–3. This is a good opportunity to experiment with different values for application dpi and device dpi to see the effect they will have on your deployed application.

Figure 2–3. *Completed Density Explorer application*

For a side-by-side comparison, Figure 2–4 demonstrates screenshots of the Density Explorer running at 160, 240, and 320 dpi on a physical device. Notice that even though the physical dimensions of the screens are vastly different, the layout of the application and quality of the graphs are preserved. By setting the author density to 240, you are guaranteed that your application will have the same look and feel on a device of any density with no code modifications.

Figure 2–4. *Side-by-side comparison of the Density Explorer when run on a device classified as 160 dpi (left), 240 dpi (center), and 320 dpi (right)*

Density Support in CSS

While the applicationDPI setting in Flex gives you a simple mechanism to write your application for one density and let Flex take care of the resizing, it doesn't give you fine-grained control over the precise layout and style of your application when viewed on different devices. Setting applicationDPI to a constant works fine for simple applications, but as the complexity of the UI increases this is often not good enough. This is where CSS media queries come in.

Flex media queries let you exercise fine-grained control over the styles on different devices from within your CSS. They are based on the W3C CSS Media Query Candidate Recommendation,[2] but contain only a subset of the functionality that is most relevant to Flex and mobile applications.

There are two types of selectors supported in Flex. The first type lets you choose the style based on the device type. The code in Listing 2–7 demonstrates how you can change the font color based on the type of device you are running on.

---

[2] www.w3.org/TR/css3-mediaqueries/

Listing 2–7. *Code Sample Demonstrating a Media Selector for Devices*

```
@namespace s "library://ns.adobe.com/flex/spark";

@media (os-platform: "IOS") {
  s|Label
  {
    color: red;
  }
}

@media (os-platform: "Android") {
  s|Label {
    color: blue;
  }
}
```

Adding this style sheet to your application will turn the color of all Labels to blue or red, depending on the mobile platform you are running on. However, when running as a desktop application, this will have no effect.

The second type of selector lets you change the style based on the application dpi. The valid values to match against are the standard Flex densities of 160, 240, and 320. Using a dpi selector lets you fine-tune the layout and fonts, or even substitute images for different density displays.

> **IMPORTANT:** In order to use CSS media selectors, you need to ensure that you have not set the applicationDPI property on your mobile application class.

To demonstrate the use of a dpi selector, we will update the Density Explorer example to make use of a style sheet to substitute the images rather than embedding it in the code with the MultiDPIBitmapSource. The simplified application code for the application images is shown in Listing 2–8.

Listing 2–8. *Updated DensityExplorer Code for Integration CSS Media Queries*

```
<s:Group id="phones" width="100%" height="100%">
  <s:Image alpha="{1-Math.abs(deviceDPI-157)/20}" horizontalCenter="0"
      source="{phones.getStyle('xperiaX10Mini')}"/>
  <s:Image alpha="{1-Math.abs(deviceDPI-180)/20}" horizontalCenter="0"
      source="{phones.getStyle('htcHero')}"/>
  <s:Image alpha="{1-Math.abs(deviceDPI-217)/20}" horizontalCenter="0"
      source="{phones.getStyle('htcEvo4g')}"/>
  <s:Image alpha="{1-Math.abs(deviceDPI-252)/20}" horizontalCenter="0"
      source="{phones.getStyle('nexusOne')}"/>
  <s:Image alpha="{1-Math.abs(deviceDPI-275)/20}" horizontalCenter="0"
      source="{phones.getStyle('atrix')}"/>
</s:Group>
```

Notice that we are making use of the getStyle method on the parent object to assign the image sources. This would normally not be required if you were working with a style such as icons or button states, but the source on the image class is a plain property.

Using this technique to bind to a named style makes the Image source accessible via CSS.

To complete the example, we also need to create a style sheet that makes use of the dpi media selector to substitute an appropriately scaled image. This is similar to the device selector and is shown in Listing 2–9.

Listing 2–9. *CSS for Switching Images Based on the Application dpi*

```
@media (application-dpi: 160) {
  #phones {
    xperiaX10Mini: Embed("/assets/xperia-x10-mini160.jpg");
    htcHero: Embed("/assets/htc-hero160.jpg");
    htcEvo4g: Embed("/assets/htc-evo-4g160.jpg");
    nexusOne: Embed("/assets/nexus-one160.jpg");
    atrix: Embed("/assets/atrix160.jpg");
  }
}

@media (application-dpi: 240) {
  #phones {
    xperiaX10Mini: Embed("/assets/xperia-x10-mini240.jpg");
    htcHero: Embed("/assets/htc-hero240.jpg");
    htcEvo4g: Embed("/assets/htc-evo-4g240.jpg");
    nexusOne: Embed("/assets/nexus-one240.jpg");
    atrix: Embed("/assets/atrix240.jpg");
  }
}

@media (application-dpi: 320) {
  #phones {
    xperiaX10Mini: Embed("/assets/xperia-x10-mini320.jpg");
    htcHero: Embed("/assets/htc-hero320.jpg");
    htcEvo4g: Embed("/assets/htc-evo-4g320.jpg");
    nexusOne: Embed("/assets/nexus-one320.jpg");
    atrix: Embed("/assets/atrix320.jpg");
  }
}
```

The final step is to make sure we have referenced the style sheet in our ViewNavigatorApplication. You will also need to remove the applicationDPI setting, otherwise the style sheet selector will always report the dpi as a constant value, as shown in Listing 2–10.

Listing 2–10. *Completed DensityExplorer Application Class for Integrating Media Query Support*

```
<?xml version="1.0" encoding="utf-8"?>
<s:ViewNavigatorApplication xmlns:fx="http://ns.adobe.com/mxml/2009"
            xmlns:s="library://ns.adobe.com/flex/spark"
            splashScreenImage="@Embed('ProAndroidFlash400.png')"
            firstView="views.DensityExplorerHomeView">
  <fx:Style source="DensityExplorer.css"/>
</s:ViewNavigatorApplication>
```

The output of running this program on different devices is nearly identical to the earlier results in Figure 2–4, with some slight differences in spacing. The reason for this is that the Flex control team has also put dpi hints in their controls so that they automatically resize based on the target device, even without having applicationDPI fixed to a constant value.

Now that you have learned about CSS media selectors, you have a powerful tool to extract the styles out of your code, even for density-aware applications.

Screen Orientation

One of the unique aspects of mobile devices is the ability to rotate them in your hand. The equivalent to this in the desktop world would be to flip your monitor on its side. While there are some creative uses for rotating desktop monitors, as demonstrated in Figure 2–5, this is certainly not a common use case.

Figure 2–5. *Unique use of monitor rotation to create a light arc*[3]

In mobile devices, rotation is an important UI paradigm that lets you take full advantage of the limited screen real estate. A well-behaved mobile application should resize the UI on rotation simply to let the user stay in his or her preferred orientation, often displaying an entirely different view that is custom-built for that orientation.

---

[3] Creative Commons licensed photograph taken by Tim Pritlove: www.flickr.com/photos/timpritlove/123865627/.

Portrait/Landscape Switching in Flex

To turn on automatic orientation in a Flex project, there are two methods. The most convenient one is to simply check the "Automatically reorient" check box when creating a new Flex mobile application from the standard template. Figure 2–6 has a screenshot of the project creation wizard with the "Automatically reorient" option checked.

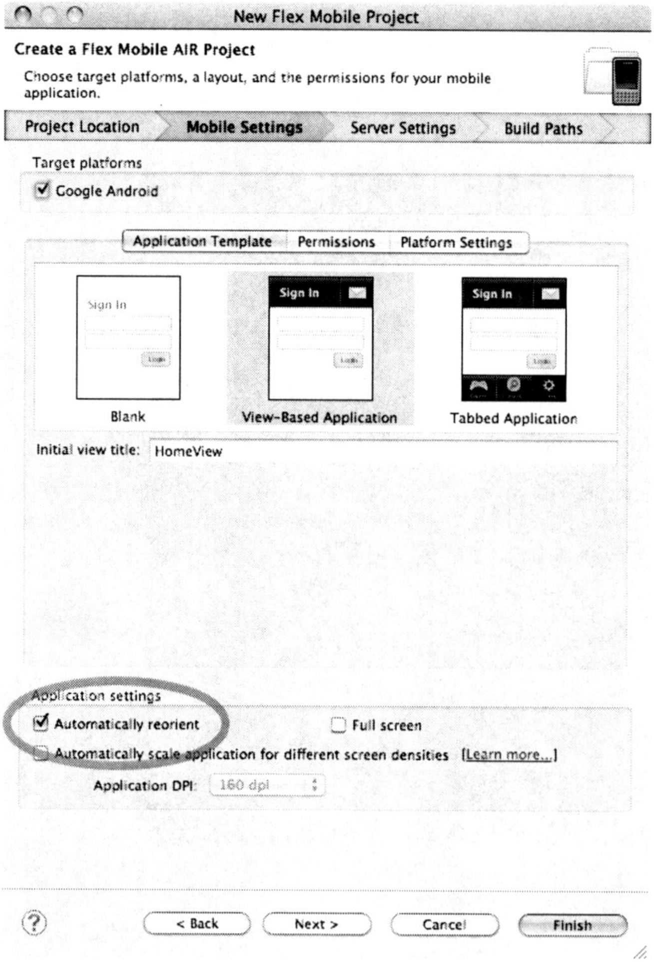

Figure 2–6. *Flex builder project wizard with the "Automatically reorient" option checked*

If you have an existing project or want to change auto-orientation manually, you need to set the autoOrients property in your application descriptor. The application descriptor is located in a file called *-app.xml in your root project directory, within which the autoOrients property should be created as a child of the initialWindow element and set to true, as shown in Listing 2–11.

Listing 2–11. *Application Descriptor Changes to Allow Automatic Orientation of the Stage*

```
<initialWindow>
  <content>[This value will be overwritten by Flash Builder in the output
app.xml]</content>
  <autoOrients>true</autoOrients>
</initialWindow>
```

This both rotates and resizes the stage, and also causes events to be fired that you can listen to in order to change your application layout.

However, simply turning on automatic orientation will often produce less than desirable results. For example, if you enable automatic orientation on the Density Explorer application, the bottom of the UI gets cropped off, as shown in Figure 2–7.

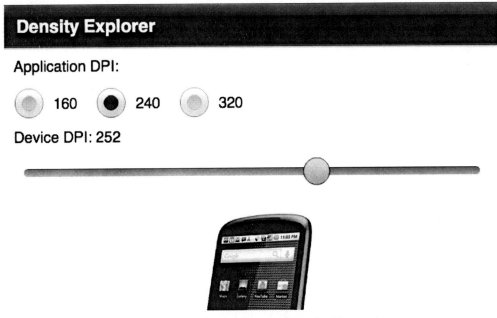

Figure 2–7. *Density Explorer application in landscape mode with noticeable cropping*

For a landscape orientation of the Density Explorer application, the ideal layout would be to have the phone picture to the left of the controls. There are two ways you can accomplish this in a Flex application. The first is to add an event handler for rotation events that changes the layout dynamically. Since this is a pure ActionScript approach, it also works equally well from Flash Professional. The second is to take advantage of the new portrait and landscape states, which are accessible only from MXML. In the following sections, we will demonstrate both of these approaches.

Portrait/Landscape Switching with Events

Each time a Flash mobile device is rotated, orientation events are fired to notify any listeners. Orientation event handlers are added via the standard addEventListener method on the Stage object. The event class for orientation events is StageOrientationEvent, with an event type of StageOrientationEvent.ORIENTATION_CHANGE.

> **CAUTION:** There is also an ORIENTATION_CHANGING event type on the StageOrientationEvent class, but this is not applicable for Android devices.

The StageOrientationEvent has two variables on it that are particularly useful for handling orientation changes:

- beforeOrientation: The handset orientation prior to the current rotation event being fired

- afterOrientation: The current handset orientation

Putting all of this together, you can modify the Density Explorer to change the layout based on the orientation of the phone.

The first step is to update the declarative MXML UI to include an additional HBox that will be used for the landscape orientation, to name the outer HBox and inner VBox with unique IDs, and to hook up an addedToStage event listener. The code to accomplish this is shown in Listing 2–12.

Listing 2–12. *MXML Additions to Supported Stage Layout Changes*

```
<s:HGroup id="outer" width="100%" height="100%" addedToStage="stageInit()">
  <s:VGroup paddingTop="20" paddingLeft="15" paddingRight="15"
                  paddingBottom="15" gap="20" width="100%" height="100%">
    ...
    <s:Group id="inner" width="100%" height="100%">
      <s:Group id="phones" width="100%" height="100%">
      ...
  </s:VGroup>
</s:HGroup>
```

The next step is to implement the stageInit function to hook up an orientation change event listener. In addition to hooking up the listener, it is often helpful to fire an initial event with the current orientation. This will ensure that even if your application starts in landscape mode, it will follow the same code path as if it opened in portrait and then was rotated by the user. The ActionScript for this is shown in Listing 2–13.

Listing 2–13. *Implementation of the* stageInit *and* orientationChange *Functions*

```
protected function orientationChange(e:StageOrientationEvent):void {
  switch (e.afterOrientation) {
    case StageOrientation.DEFAULT:
    case StageOrientation.UPSIDE_DOWN:
```

```
      inner.addElementAt(phones, 0);
      break;
    case StageOrientation.ROTATED_RIGHT:
    case StageOrientation.ROTATED_LEFT:
      outer.addElementAt(phones, 0);
      break;
  }
}
protected function stageInit():void {
  stage.addEventListener(StageOrientationEvent.ORIENTATION_CHANGE, orientationChange);
  orientationChange(new StageOrientationEvent(
                          StageOrientationEvent.ORIENTATION_CHANGE, false, false,
                          null, stage.orientation));
}
```

In this case, the behavior for right and left rotation is identical, although if you wanted to get creative you could put the device display on a different side of the screen based on which way the phone is rotated.

The result of running the modified Density Explorer application is shown in Figure 2–8. As you can see, the device display is shown at a usable size and the rest of the controls are no longer stretched across a very wide display. The most impressive part is that the layout will dynamically update to optimize for portrait and landscape as you rotate the phone.

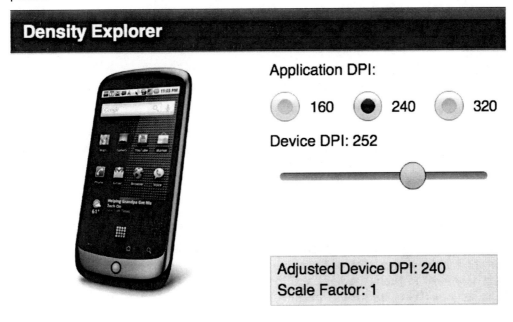

Figure 2–8. *Density Explorer application with an improved landscape layout*

Portrait/Landscape Switching with States

A second technique you can use in Flex for portrait/landscape switching is to make use of two built-in states that are triggered on device rotation called portrait and landscape. While this is accessible only from MXML and does not provide as much information as the event API about the orientation of the device, the code to implement this is much simpler and more declarative in nature, making it easier to read and maintain.

To expose the new portrait and landscape states, you need to add a states declaration to your view code that defines a portrait and landscape state, as shown in Listing 2–14.

Listing 2–14. *State Declaration for portrait and landscape Modes*

```
<s:states>
  <s:State name="portrait"/>
  <s:State name="landscape"/>
</s:states>
```

These states will automatically get triggered whenever the device changes orientation. To modify the layout, you can then take advantage of the includedIn property and Reparent tag in order to move the phone image position. The code changes you will need to make to accomplish this are shown in Listing 2–15.

Listing 2–15. *UI Changes to Reparent the Phone Image When the State Changes*

```
<s:HGroup width="100%" height="100%">
  <fx:Reparent target="phones" includeIn="landscape"/>
  ...
    <s:Group width="100%" height="100%">
      <s:Group id="phones" width="100%" height="100%" includeIn="portrait">
      ...
  </s:VGroup>
</s:HGroup>
```

The end result is that with 8 lines of MXML code you can do what took 21 lines using the event approach. The results of running this application are identical to those obtained in Figure 2–8.

Automatic Orientation Flipping in Flash

Flash applications can also be configured to automatically flip the orientation of the stage when the device is rotated. To enable automatic orientation switching in a Flash project, you need to check the box for automatic orientation in the AIR for the Android publish settings dialog, as shown in Figure 2–9.

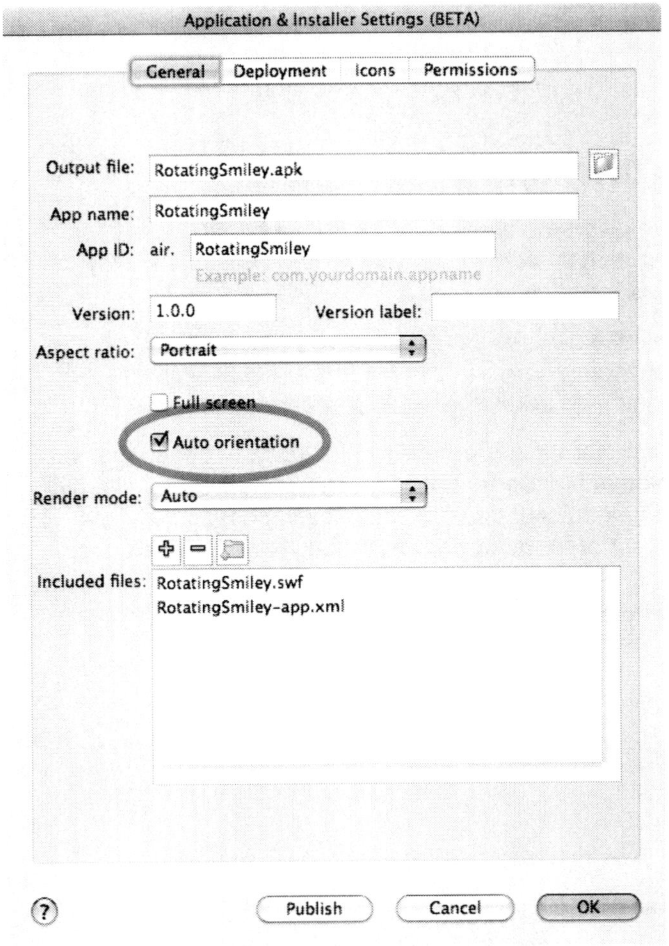

Figure 2–9. *Auto-orientation setting for Flash CS5.5 circled*

Setting this option will cause the aspect ratio of the application to automatically flip from landscape to portrait as the user rotates the device. Upon orientation change, the stage will be rotated so it is oriented vertically, resized to fill the new dimensions after rotation, and then centered within the display.

If you want to change the layout of your content to fill the screen and have full control over resizing the stage, you will need to disable the automatic scale and positioning. This can be accomplished in ActionScript by changing the scaleMode and align properties of the Stage object, as shown in Listing 2–16.

Listing 2–16. *Disabling Stage Scaling and Alignment from ActionScript*

```
stage.scaleMode = StageScaleMode.NO_SCALE;  // turn off scaling
stage.align = StageAlign.TOP_LEFT;  // align content to the top-left of the stage
```

This can be added to any key frame in your application that executes on startup, and will keep the stage top-left aligned with no resizing of the content. You can then add event listeners on orientation changes in order to modify your application to fit the screen size.

Rotating Smiley Flash Orientation Example

To demonstrate how you can quickly create content in Flash CS5.5 that adjusts for orientation, you will create a small sample application that morphs a happy smiley picture to a devilish one upon an orientation change.

To start with, you will need to create a new AIR for Android project with a size of 480x480 pixels. The reason for choosing a square canvas that is equal in size to the smaller device dimension is to ensure no additional scaling will take place upon rotation.

Figure 2–10 shows the starting state for the happy smiley picture, with boxes drawn denoting the extents of the landscape and portrait modes. The intersection of the two boxes is the 480x480 canvas, with additional graphics overflowing horizontally and vertically. These will get cropped out of frame upon orientation change, leaving the smiley face nicely centered.

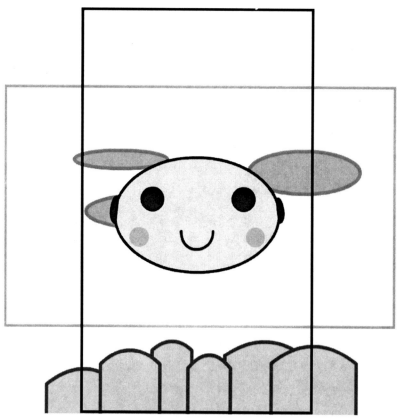

Figure 2–10. *Happy smiley picture starting state, with boxes showing the landscape and portrait extents*

Feel free to get creative with your own graphics, but keep elements in separate layers to make it easier to animate and morph them later.

The next step is to create the devilish smiley keyframe at around one second. This should include motion or shape tweens for a smooth transition from the happy smiley face. Figure 2–11 shows a few time-lapsed frames that animate the smiley face as well as some of the background scene elements.

Figure 2–11. *Animation of the smiley face from happy to devilish*

At the same time, also create the reverse animation to get back to the happy smiley face at around two seconds. While there are some ActionScript techniques to reverse an animation in Flash, they are non-intuitive and generally carry a performance penalty.

Now that you have completed the graphics, you need to add in ActionScript code to animate the smiley face upon device rotation. This should be added to the first keyframe in the timeline, and should include both stopping the animation from automatically playing and attaching an orientation event listener to the scene, as shown in Listing 2–17.

Listing 2–17. *ActionScript Code to Respond to Orientation Change Events*

```
import flash.events.StageOrientationEvent;

stop();

stage.addEventListener(StageOrientationEvent.ORIENTATION_CHANGE, onChanged);

function onChanged(event:StageOrientationEvent):void {
  play();
}
```

Notice that the onChanged event handler simply has to play the movie on each orientation change event. All the heavy lifting for the animation is already taken care of by the timeline.

The final bit of required code is to add a stop() call on the devilish smiley frame so that it will stop there after a rotation event.

As a bonus, you can add in a warning to the user if orientation events are not supported on his or her device, such as if the user is running on desktop or TV. The simplest way to give feedback is to create a hidden layer that you make visible based upon checking the orientation support, as shown in Listing 2–18.

Listing 2–18. *Orientation Check Code to Hide/Show Error Page*

```
if (Stage.supportsOrientationChange) {
  orientationNotSupported.visible = false;
}
```

The completed rotating smiley face application running on the device is shown in Figure 2–12. While this example is fairly simple, it demonstrates how easy it is to add orientation support to your applications.

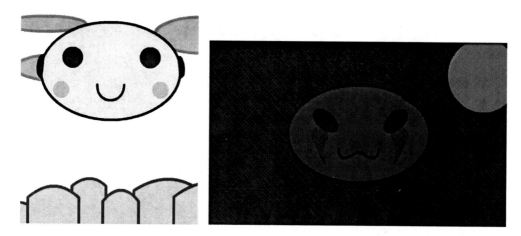

Figure 2–12. *Completed rotating smiley face example in portrait (left) and landscape (right) orientations*

Multitouch and Gestures

User interfaces have long been limited by the constraints of the desktop mouse. The first mouse was invented by Douglas Engelbart in 1963. It had two perpendicular wheels for tracking motion and a long cord that resembled the tail of a rodent or mouse. After this, mice with internal balls, optical tracking, and multiple buttons appeared, such as the Dépraz mouse produced in the early 80s. Both of these early devices are shown in Figure 2–13.

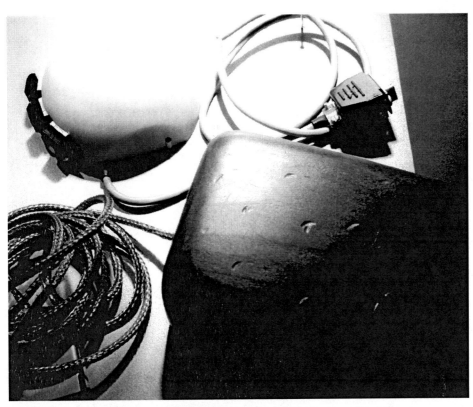

Figure 2–13. *Photo of the Engelbart mouse (bottom-right) and Dépraz mouse (top-left)*

Modern mice include features such as scroll wheels, laser tracking, and cordless operation. However, all mice share a common limitation, which is that they can support only a single cursor on the screen at a time.

Mobile interfaces originally started with the same limitation of pointer-driven, single touch interaction. However, they have evolved to take advantage of the human physique. We have two hands with ten fingers total, each capable of individually interacting with and manipulating a touch point on the device.

Most Android devices support at least two simultaneous touch points, which is the minimum required to handle all the mobile gestures. This is also the most common usage scenario where the mobile device is supported by the fingers and operated with both thumbs. However, new devices are being introduced that support a virtually unlimited number of touch points.

You can retrieve the number of touch points your device supports by querying the `Multitouch` object, as shown in Listing 2–19.

Listing 2–19. *Retrieving the Number of Touch Points via ActionScript*

```
trace("Max Touch Points: " + Multitouch.maxTouchPoints);
```

In this section, you will learn how to take advantage of multitouch and user gestures, improving the user experience and usability of your Flash applications.

Mobile Gestures

The easiest way to work with multitouch is to take advantage of the predefined gestures that Flash supports. For any Android device with at least two touch points, you will be able to use the gestures in Table 2–3.

Table 2–3. *Mobile Gestures Supported by Flash Android*[4]

Gesture	Name	Event	Description
	Pan	gesturePan	Place two fingers on the screen, and drag left or right; commonly used for scrolling the contents of the whole screen
	Rotate	gestureRotate	Touch the screen with two fingers, and move them in an arc. This is an interactive gesture that will often be used to perform arbitrary rotation of objects.
	Zoom	gestureZoom	Place two fingers on the screen, and move them apart or together along a single line. Moving the fingers apart indicates zooming in, and moving the fingers together indicates zooming out.

---

[4] Creative Commons licensed illustrations provided by Gestureworks (www.gestureworks.com)

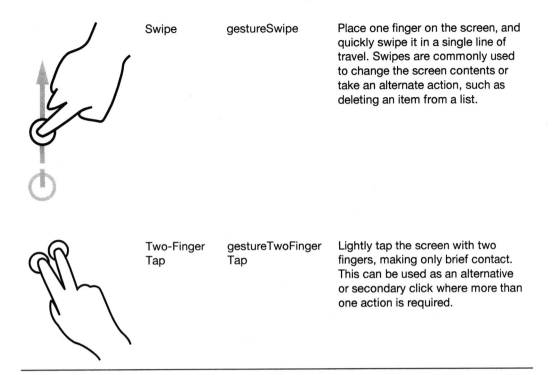

| | Swipe | gestureSwipe | Place one finger on the screen, and quickly swipe it in a single line of travel. Swipes are commonly used to change the screen contents or take an alternate action, such as deleting an item from a list. |
| | Two-Finger Tap | gestureTwoFinger Tap | Lightly tap the screen with two fingers, making only brief contact. This can be used as an alternative or secondary click where more than one action is required. |

It is usually a good idea to provide some other mechanism to accomplish the same behavior in your application in case gestures are not supported; however, mobile users have come to expect the convenience and speed that gestures offer, so mapping them appropriately in your application design is important.

To discover if the device your application is running on supports gestures and to query the gesture capabilities dynamically, you can call the following static methods on the Multitouch class:

- Multitouch.supportsGestureEvents: Whether the device you are running on supports emitting gesture events

- Multitouch.supportedGestures: A list of strings, one for each of the supported multitouch events

Before using gesture events, you need to set the touchMode to gesture input mode, as shown in Listing 2–20.

Listing 2–20. *ActionScript Code to Enable Gesture Recognition Support*

```
Multitouch.inputMode = MultitouchInputMode.GESTURE;
```

This should be called within your program before you expect to receive gesture events.

Flash Scrapbook Example

To demonstrate how to handle gesture events, we will go through a sample program to build a picture scrapbook that responds to multitouch events. For simplicity, we will load the images as resources (see Chapter 7 for more information about retrieving images from the camera roll).

Here are some of the multitouch events that we will support:

- *Zoom*: Increase or decrease the size of the pictures

- *Rotate*: Rotate the images to arbitrary angles

- *Pan*: Move the entire page of images as a unit

- *Swipe*: Swipe the header to switch between pages of images

- *Two-Finger Tap*: Tap an image with two fingers to open it in its own view

Also, while it is not a multitouch gesture, we will hook in drag listeners so you can position the images by dragging them with a single finger.

There are two different ways to hook up multitouch listeners in a Flash application. The first is via pure ActionScript and will work equally well from a Flash- or Flex-based application. The second is by using the event hooks on the `InteractiveObject` class, which is the most convenient option if you are working with Flex components. We will show examples of both in this section.

Zoom and Rotate Gesture Handling

The core of the Flash Scrapbook example will be a `MultitouchImage` component that extends the spark `Image` class to add in resizing and rotation. For this class, we will use the `addEventListener` mechanism of hooking up multitouch listeners for the zoom and rotate gestures. The code for this is shown in Listing 2–21.

Listing 2–21. *MultitouchImage Class to Add Rotation and Resizing Support*

```
package com.proandroidflash {
  import flash.events.TransformGestureEvent;
  import flash.geom.Point;
  import flash.ui.Multitouch;
  import flash.ui.MultitouchInputMode;
  import mx.events.ResizeEvent;
  import spark.components.Image;

  public class MultitouchImage extends Image {
    public function MultitouchImage() {
      addEventListener(ResizeEvent.RESIZE, resizeListener);
      addEventListener(TransformGestureEvent.GESTURE_ROTATE, rotateListener);
      addEventListener(TransformGestureEvent.GESTURE_ZOOM, zoomListener);
      Multitouch.inputMode = MultitouchInputMode.GESTURE;
    }
```

```
    protected function resizeListener(e:ResizeEvent):void {
      transformX = width/2;
      transformY = height/2;
    }

    protected function rotateListener(e:TransformGestureEvent):void {
      rotation += e.rotation;
    }

    protected function zoomListener(e:TransformGestureEvent):void {
      scaleX *= e.scaleX;
      scaleY *= e.scaleY;
    }
  }
}
```

In the constructor, we add listeners for both rotation and zooming by calling the addEventListener method and passing in the GESTURE_ROTATE and GESTURE_ZOOM constants. The rotation callback simply takes the rotation parameter of the TransformGestureEvent and adds it to the current rotation of the node, saving the value back. In both cases, the rotation is expressed in degrees as a numeric value. The zoom listener similarly takes the scaleX and scaleY parameters of the TransformGestureEvent and multiplies them by the scaleX and scaleY of the node to get the new values. In both cases, the gesture event gives you the delta since the last time the listener was called, so you can simply incrementally adjust the node values.

To ensure that the rotation and zoom occur at the center of the Image node, we set transformX and transformY to be at the midpoint of the node in the resizeListener. This is also hooked up via the addEventListener in the constructor so it will fire each time the node size changes.

The last thing we do is to set the inputMode to MultitouchInputMode.GESTURE so that the event listeners will fire. It is safe to set this value as frequently as we want, so we take the liberty of doing this on each constructor call.

For the rest of the gesture events, we will take advantage of the InteractiveObject event hooks for easy wiring via MXML; however, you can also hook up all the other gestures using the addEventListener mechanism by following the class and constant information in Table 2–4.

Table 2–4. *Gesture Names, Classes, and Constants for Use in the* addEventListener *Method*

Gesture Name	Class	Constant
Pan	TransformGestureEvent	GESTURE_PAN
Rotate	TransformGestureEvent	GESTURE_ROTATE
Zoom	TransformGestureEvent	GESTURE_ZOOM
Swipe	TransformGestureEvent	GESTURE_SWIPE
Two-Finger Tap	PressAndTapGestureEvent	GESTURE_PRESS_AND_TAP

Press and Drag Mouse Events

Another helper class we will be using is the DraggableGroup class. This implements a standard point and drag metaphor as an extension of a spark Group, as shown in Listing 2–22. Besides being good for encapsulation, extracting the mouse events from the gesture events allows you to handle multiple events simultaneously.

Listing 2–22. *DraggableGroup Class That Implements Point and Drag Mechanics*

```
package com.proandroidflash {
  import flash.events.MouseEvent;
  import mx.core.UIComponent;
  import spark.components.Form;
  import spark.components.Group;

  public class DraggableGroup extends Group {
    public function DraggableGroup() {
      mouseEnabledWhereTransparent = false;
      addEventListener(MouseEvent.MOUSE_DOWN, mouseDownListener);
      addEventListener(MouseEvent.MOUSE_UP, mouseUpListener);
    }

    protected function mouseDownListener(e:MouseEvent):void {
      (parent as Group).setElementIndex(this, parent.numChildren-1);
      startDrag();
    }

    protected function mouseUpListener(e:MouseEvent):void {
      stopDrag();
      // fix for bug in Flex where child elements don't get invalidated
      for (var i:int=0; i<numElements; i++) {
        (getElementAt(i) as UIComponent).invalidateProperties();
      }
    }
  }
}
```

The code for the DraggableGroup is a fairly straightforward Flex component implementation, and uses the same addEventListener/callback paradigm as the gesture code did. While you could implement the same code using touch events, the advantage of sticking to mouse-up and mouse-down events is that this portion of the UI will work even where there is no touch support.

A few subtleties in the code are worth pointing out.

- By default the Group class fires events for any clicks in their bounding area. By setting mouseEnabledWhereTransparent to false, you avoid misfires outside the bounds of the children.

- To raise this object when clicked, you need to change the order in the parent container. This implementation assumes the parent is a Group and uses the setElementIndex function to push this node to the front.

> There is a bug in Flex where child elements won't have their layout properties invalidated after the drag. Manually calling `invalidateProperties` on all of the children works around this problem. For example, without this fix you would notice that the center of rotation/zoom does not translate with the drag.

Swipe Gesture Handling

To display the images, we will be using a simple view that delegates rendering of individual image pages to an `ItemRenderer`. First we will take a look at the `View` class that makes up the main screen of the Scrapbook example. The full code is shown in Listing 2–23.

Listing 2–23. *Flash Scrapbook Main View Code with the Swipe Event Handler Highlighted in Bold*

```
<?xml version="1.0" encoding="utf-8"?>
<s:View xmlns:fx="http://ns.adobe.com/mxml/2009"
    xmlns:s="library://ns.adobe.com/flex/spark"
    xmlns:mx="library://ns.adobe.com/flex/mx"
    xmlns:proandroidflash="com.proandroidflash.*"
    title="Home" backgroundColor="#333333" destructionPolicy="never">
  <fx:Script>
    <![CDATA[
      import mx.core.IVisualElement;
      [Bindable]
      protected var page:int = 0;
      protected function swipe(e:TransformGestureEvent):void {
        page = (page + e.offsetX + pages.numElements) % pages.numElements;
        updateVisibility();
      }
      protected function updateVisibility():void {
        for (var i:int=0; i<pages.numElements; i++) {
          var element:IVisualElement = pages.getElementAt(i);
          if (element != null) {
            element.visible = i == page;
          }
        }
      }
    ]]>
  </fx:Script>
  <s:layout>
    <s:VerticalLayout horizontalAlign="center" paddingTop="10" paddingLeft="10"
                      paddingRight="10" paddingBottom="10"/>
  </s:layout>
  <fx:Declarations>
    <s:ArrayList id="images">
      <fx:Object image1="@Embed(source='images/cassandra1.jpg')"
                 image2="@Embed(source='images/cassandra2.jpg')"
                 image3="@Embed(source='images/cassandra3.jpg')"/>
      <fx:Object image1="@Embed(source='images/cassandra4.jpg')"
                 image2="@Embed(source='images/cassandra5.jpg')"
                 image3="@Embed(source='images/cassandra6.jpg')"/>
      <fx:Object image1="@Embed(source='images/cassandra7.jpg')"
                 image2="@Embed(source='images/cassandra8.jpg')"
                 image3="@Embed(source='images/cassandra9.jpg')"/>
```

```
          <fx:Object image1="@Embed(source='images/cassandra10.jpg')"/>
        </s:ArrayList>
      </fx:Declarations>
      <s:VGroup gestureSwipe="swipe(event)">
        <s:Label text="Flash Scrapbook" fontSize="32" color="white"/>
        <s:Label text="Drag, Rotate, and Zoom with your fingers." fontSize="14"
              color="#aaaaaa"/>
      </s:VGroup>
      <s:DataGroup id="pages" itemRenderer="com.proandroidflash.ScrapbookPage"
                dataProvider="{images}" width="100%" height="100%"
                added="updateVisibility()"/>
    </s:View>
```

While there is a fair amount of code to create the view, the actual view definition itself consists of only five lines to create a VGroup for the title and a DataGroup to display the images. The remainder is primarily a large chunk of code to simply load the embedded images into an ArrayList, and a few helper functions embedded in a Script tag.

The code needed to hook up the swipe event handler is highlighted in bold. By taking advantage of the gesture* event properties on InteractiveObject, you can rapidly hook up event listeners like this to your application. Each time the user swipes the title VGroup, the protected swipe method will get called with information about the direction of the swipe. Unlike rotate and zoom events that get continual calls for the duration of the gesture, swipe gets called exactly once at the end of the gesture. You can decipher the direction of the swipe by inspecting the offsetX and offsetY properties.

- offsetX=0, offsetY=-1: Swipe Up

- offsetX=0, offsetY=1: Swipe Down

- offsetX=-1, offsetY=0: Swipe Left

- offsetX=1, offsetY=0: Swipe Right

It is worth noting that the swipes will always be in the horizontal or vertical direction. Diagonal swipes are not supported and will not be recognized as a gesture. Also, you need to ensure that the component you hook the swipe listener up to is wide or tall enough to provide enough travel for the gesture to be recognized. Once the user's finger leaves the component, the gesture recognition will end.

Adding Pan and Two-Finger-Tap Event Listeners

Now that we have a main page with a DataGroup, we need to implement the referenced ItemRenderer that will build the scrapbook page. This will also be the link between the MultitouchImage, DraggableGroup, and main view that we defined earlier.

Start by creating a new MXML file that has an outer ItemRenderer element with the page content declared inside. In this class, we will hook up two new gesture event listeners. On the outer BorderContainer, we will hook up a pan event listener so that the user can drag the entire page and all the images on it in one gesture. Also, on each of the MultitouchImages, we will add a two-finger-tap event listener for switching to a full-screen view.

The complete code for the ScrapbookPage implementation is shown in Listing 2–24.

Listing 2–24. *Flash* ScrapbookPage *Item Renderer Code with the Pan and Two-Finger-Tap Event Handlers Highlighted in Bold*

```xml
<?xml version="1.0" encoding="utf-8"?>
<s:ItemRenderer xmlns:fx="http://ns.adobe.com/mxml/2009"
        xmlns:s="library://ns.adobe.com/flex/spark"
        xmlns:proandroidflash="com.proandroidflash.*"
        autoDrawBackground="false" width="100%" height="100%">
  <s:BorderContainer backgroundColor="#cccccc" borderColor="#555555"
                     gesturePan="pan(event)" rotation="5" x="50" width="100%"
                     height="100%">
    <fx:Script>
      <![CDATA[
        import spark.components.View;
        import views.ImageView;
        protected function pan(e:TransformGestureEvent):void {
          e.target.x += e.offsetX;
          e.target.y += e.offsetY;
        }
        protected function expand(source:Object):void {
          (parentDocument as View).navigator.pushView(ImageView, source);
        }
      ]]>
    </fx:Script>
    <proandroidflash:DraggableGroup>
      <proandroidflash:MultitouchImage source="{data.image1}" y="-70" x="10" width="350"
                           rotation="-3" gestureTwoFingerTap="expand(data.image1)"/>
    </proandroidflash:DraggableGroup>
    <proandroidflash:DraggableGroup>
      <proandroidflash:MultitouchImage source="{data.image2}" y="100" x="40" width="350"
                           rotation="13" gestureTwoFingerTap="expand(data.image2)"/>
    </proandroidflash:DraggableGroup>
    <proandroidflash:DraggableGroup>
      <proandroidflash:MultitouchImage source="{data.image3}" y="300" x="5" width="350"
                           rotation="-8" gestureTwoFingerTap="expand(data.image3)"/>
    </proandroidflash:DraggableGroup>
  </s:BorderContainer>
</s:ItemRenderer>
```

Both the pan and two-finger-tap event listeners are hooked up similarly to how we hooked up the swipe event listener earlier. The pan gesture happens to use the same offsetX and offsetY variables as the swipe gesture, but with a very different meaning. The pan event gets called continually for the duration of the user gesture with the delta in pixels passed in for offsetX and offsetY.

For the two-finger-tap gesture, we chose to not pass in the event, and instead to substitute a context-dependent variable that contains the image to display. This is then passed in as the data parameter of the ViewNavigator's pushView method.

Flash Scrapbook Image View

The final step is to implement the `ImageView` class referenced in the `pushView` method call. Since Flex takes care of all the view navigation logic for us, the implementation is extremely straightforward. The only extra feature we add in is another two-finger-tap gesture so you can navigate back to the main view without clicking the Android back button.

The code for the `ImageView` class is shown in Listing 2–25.

Listing 2–25. *ImageView Code with the Two-Finger-Tap Event Handler Highlighted in Bold*

```
<?xml version="1.0" encoding="utf-8"?>
<s:View xmlns:fx="http://ns.adobe.com/mxml/2009"
    xmlns:s="library://ns.adobe.com/flex/spark"
    title="Image Viewer" backgroundColor="#333333">
  <s:Image source="{data}" width="100%" height="100%"
          gestureTwoFingerTap="navigator.popView()"/>
</s:View>
```

Simple expressions can be inlined in the event handler as we have done here. This avoids the need to create a `Script` tag, making the code listing extremely concise.

This also completes the last file of the Flash Scrapbook application, so you can now give it a test drive. Upon launching the application, you should see a screen similar to that shown in Figure 2–14.

On this page of the application, try doing the following:

- Drag an image around the canvas by using one finger to press and drag—this exercises the `DraggableGroup`.

- Zoom in on an image by using two fingers to press and drag in opposite directions—this exercises the zoom listener on the `MultitouchImage`.

- Rotate an image by using two fingers to press and drag in a circle—this exercises the rotate listener on the `MultitouchImage`.

- Swipe one finger horizontally across the words "Flash Scrapbook" to change the page—this exercises the swipe listener on the main view.

- Drag the images out of the way so you can see the background and use two fingers to drag across the background, panning the scene—this exercises the pan listener on the `ScrapbookPage`.

- Use two fingers to tap one of the images and switch to the `ImageView`—this exercises the two-finger-tap listener wired up to each `MultitouchImage`.

Figure 2–14. *Completed Flash Scrapbook application on the home view page*

Once you finish the last step, you will be on the ImageView page of the application, as shown in Figure 2–15. To get back to the main view, you can either two-finger-tap on the image again, or use the Android back button.

Figure 2–15. *Completed Flash Scrapbook example on the Image Viewer page*

By completing this simple example, you have successfully explored all of the available gesture events that are available on Flash Android. Try using these gestures in your own application in new and innovative ways!

Touch Point API

The other way to process multitouch input is to use the touch point API to get direct access to the events being generated on the device. This allows you to do custom multitouch processing that is tailored to your application needs. To determine if your device supports touch event processing, you can query the Multitouch object as shown in Listing 2–26.

Listing 2–26. *Code Snippet That Prints Out Whether Touch Events Are Supported*

```
trace("Supports touch events: " + Multitouch.supportsTouchEvents);
```

Since processing touch events directly conflicts with gesture recognition, you need to change the input mode of your application to start receiving touch point events. This can be accomplished by setting the `Multitouch.inputMode` variable to `TOUCH_POINT`, as shown in Listing 2–27.

Listing 2–27. *Code Snippet to Enable Touch Point Events*

```
Multitouch.inputMode = MultitouchInputMode.TOUCH_POINT;
```

> **NOTE:** Setting the `inputMode` to `TOUCH_POINT` will disable recognition of any gestures, such as zoom, rotate, and pan.

The touch point API is fairly low-level in the number and type of events that get dispatched. You can register and listen for any of the events listed in Table 2–5, as long as the target object extends `InteractiveObject`.

Table 2–5. *Touch Point API Events Dispatched to* `InteractiveObjects`

Touch Constant	Event Name	Description
TOUCH_BEGIN	touchBegin	Event dispatched when the user initially touches the object (finger down)
TOUCH_END	touchEnd	Event dispatched when the user removes contact with the object (finger up)
TOUCH_MOVE	touchMove	Event dispatched when the user drags across the object (finger slide)
TOUCH_OVER	touchOver	Event dispatched when the user drags into the object or any of its children; this event may get fired multiple times and is equivalent to a MOUSE_OVER event.
TOUCH_OUT	touchOut	Event dispatched when the user drags out of the object or any of its children; this event may get fired multiple times and is equivalent to a MOUSE_OUT event.
TOUCH_ROLL_OVER	touchRollOver	Event dispatched when the user drags into the combined bounds of the object and all its children; this event does not propagate upward and is equivalent to a mouse ROLL_OVER event.
TOUCH_ROLL_OUT	touchRollOut	Event dispatched when the user drags out of the combined bounds of the object and all its children; this event does not propagate upward and is equivalent to a mouse ROLL_OUT event.
TOUCH_TAP	touchTap	Event dispatched after the user finishes a gesture that involves touching and removing contact with the object; a high tolerance of movement in the middle is allowed as long as it is within the bounds of the object.

Most of the touch events are fairly self-explanatory, but the touchOver, touchOut, touchRollOver, and touchRollOut can be a little confusing. As an example, take three nested rectangles labeled A (outer), B (middle), and C (inner). As the finger rolls from A to C, you would receive the following roll events:

`touchRollOver(A)` -> `touchRollOver(B)` -> `touchRollOver(C)`

At the same time, you would also receive the following over/out events:

`touchOver(A)` -> `touchOut(A)` / `touchOver(B)` -> `touchOut(B)` / `touchOver(C)`

The events that rectangle A would directly receive are highlighted in bold. The roll events don't propagate, so you receive only one touchRollOver event. However, the touchOver/Out events do propagate to parents, so you receive three touchOver events besides the two additional touchOut events.

The easiest way to remember how these work is to relate the roll events to the implementation of a rollover effect. For a rollover effect, you typically want to display the effect if the node or any of its children are being touched, which is the semantic for touchRollOver.

Caterpillar Generator Example

As a simple example of the touch point API, we will guide you through how to create a multitouch-enabled Flash application that generates caterpillars as you drag your fingers around the screen.

To start with, we will create a few art assets that can be used to construct the example:

- *Background*: Create a layer called Background that will be the backdrop for the application. We chose to use the pattern paint brush to draw a virtual garden for the caterpillars to crawl in, but be as creative as you can.

- *Green Ball*: Create a simple movie clip called GreenBall that will make up the body of the caterpillars. For this we did a simple radial gradient on an oval primitive.

- *Blue Ball*: Create a simple movie clip called BlueBall that will make up the alternate body of the caterpillars. For this we did another radial gradient on an oval.

- *Red Ball*: Create a movie clip called RedBall with a sequence of faces that will be displayed on the caterpillars. Make sure to code a `stop()` on each frame so we can step through them one at a time.

The mechanics of the application logic are extremely simple. As the user drags his or her finger around the screen, we will continually create new ball objects for the body of the caterpillar at the current touch location or locations. Once the user's finger leaves the screen, we will draw the head of the caterpillar. In addition, if the user taps one of the caterpillar heads, we will play the movie to change the face that is shown.

In order to accomplish this, we need to introduce the TouchEvent class, which is returned by each of the touch event callbacks. The variables on TouchEvent that are relevant to this example include the following:

- stageX/stageY: The location that the touch event occurred at specified in global coordinates; to get the location relative to the current Sprite, use localX/localY instead.

- pressure: The amount of pressure used on the display screen (typically related to the size); this is device-dependent, so you can't rely on it being available on all devices.

- target: The object that is being interacted with

- isPrimaryTouchPoint: Whether this is the first touch point registered or an additional touch point that was added later; we will use this to color the caterpillars differently.

The full code listing for the Caterpillar Generator application is shown in Listing 2–28. You will probably want to put this on the first frame of a separate layer called Actions to distinguish it from the graphical elements in the program.

Listing 2–28. *Code Listing for the Caterpillar Generator Application*

```
import flash.ui.Multitouch;
import flash.ui.MultitouchInputMode;
import flash.events.TouchEvent;
import flash.events.KeyboardEvent;
import flash.ui.Keyboard;

Multitouch.inputMode = MultitouchInputMode.TOUCH_POINT;
stage.addEventListener(TouchEvent.TOUCH_BEGIN, beginListener);
stage.addEventListener(TouchEvent.TOUCH_MOVE, moveListener);
stage.addEventListener(TouchEvent.TOUCH_END, endListener);
stage.addEventListener(KeyboardEvent.KEY_DOWN, keyListener);

var lastScale:Number;
var startX:Number;
var startY:Number;

function beginListener(event:TouchEvent):void {
  lastScale = 0;
}

function moveListener(event:TouchEvent):void {
  var ball;
  if (event.isPrimaryTouchPoint) {
    ball = new GreenBall();
  } else {
    ball = new BlueBall();
  }
  ball.x = event.stageX;
  ball.y = event.stageY;
  lastScale = Math.max(lastScale, event.pressure*7);
  ball.scaleX = lastScale;
  ball.scaleY = lastScale;
```

```
    addChild(ball);
}

function endListener(event:TouchEvent):void {
  var ball = new RedBall();
  ball.x = event.stageX;
  ball.y = event.stageY;
  ball.scaleX = lastScale;
  ball.scaleY = lastScale;
  ball.addEventListener(TouchEvent.TOUCH_MOVE, ballMoveListener);
  ball.addEventListener(TouchEvent.TOUCH_TAP, changeFace);
  addChild(ball);
}

function ballMoveListener(event:TouchEvent):void {
  event.stopImmediatePropagation();
}

function changeFace(event:TouchEvent):void {
  event.target.play();
}

function keyListener(event:KeyboardEvent):void {
  if (event.keyCode = Keyboard.MENU) {
    clearAll();
  }
}

function clearAll():void {
  for (var i:int=numChildren-1; i>=0; i--) {
    if (getChildAt(i).name != "background") {
      removeChildAt(i);
    }
  }
}
```

Notice that we add the event listeners to the Stage rather than the background. The reason for this is that as additional nodes are added under the finger to make up the caterpillar body, they will block the background, preventing additional move events from getting fired. However, the stage receives all events regardless of what object they occurred within.

Adding event listeners to the Stage is a dual-edged sword, because it also means that it is extremely hard to receive any tap events. To prevent the move events on a caterpillar's face from trickling up to the stage, we call event.stopImmediatePropogation(). This allows the tap gesture to be processed without interference from the stage event listeners.

One other technique we use is to ensure that each subsequent ball added is larger than the previous by using the Math.max function. This ensures that the caterpillar perspective is maintained even as the pressure decreases while the user removes his or her finger from the screen.

The final application should look similar to Figure 2–16 when run on a device.

Figure 2–16. *Caterpillar Generator application showing a few caterpillars in the weeds*

This application also serves as a crude performance test since it continually generates and adds Sprites to the stage. You can clear the scene and reset the application at any time by pressing the menu button on your phone, which has been wired up to the clearAll function.

Try experimenting with different multipliers for the pressure to tweak the application for optimal performance on your device.

Summary

In this chapter, you learned how to design and build applications that take full advantage of the mobile platform. Some of the takeaways that you will be able to apply to your future mobile projects include the following:

- The importance of not just designing for screen resolution, but also taking density into account
- How to calculate device-independent pixels and take advantage of `applicationDPI`
- Tailoring your application layout for portrait and landscape modes
- Improving the usability of your application with multitouch gestures
- How to consume and process raw touch events within your application

We will continue to use these concepts throughout the book to build more intricate and powerful applications, but you should already have a good start to designing your own mobile user interfaces.

Chapter 3

Building Flash and Flex Applications for Android

Chapters 1 and 2 have served as an introduction to using Flash and Flex as a platform for creating mobile applications. By now you know the reasons for choosing the Flash platform and some of the considerations involved in writing applications for devices with a wide variety of screens that use touch gestures as their main form of user input. The next step is to get down to the business of writing your own applications. By the end of this chapter, you will know how to decide between the various types of Flex applications, how to write your own Views, and how to provide rich content to those Views using the mobile-ready controls in the Flex SDK.

In short, it's time to show you everything you need to know to start turning your application ideas into reality!

Constructing Mobile UIs with Flex

Because of its convenience and developer productivity features, MXML is the preferred way to define the main user interfaces of a Flex mobile application. The convenience of MXML does come with a performance cost, however. For that reason, there are some tasks, such as List item renderers, that are best done in pure ActionScript. We will cover that particular topic in more depth in Chapter 10.

Due to the small size of the screen, most mobile applications are broken down into multiple Views. It is unsurprising, then, that most AIR for Android applications are built with either a ViewNavigatorApplication or TabbedViewNavigatorApplication. These application containers take care of initializing and wiring together all of the application's View-related goodness. This includes one or more the following components:

■ ViewNavigator: This class handles linking a set of Views together, passing data back and forth, and transitioning between the Views. The ViewNavigator also owns the application's ActionBar, which displays the title of the current View, optional action controls—usually buttons—and optional navigation controls—typically a Home or Back button.

■ View: These Flex components provide most of the actual interface of the application. Each View has a reference to its ViewNavigator and the ActionBar. Each View can populate the ActionBar with its own content or even hide it completely. Views use the ViewNavigator to trigger the display of other Views based on user interaction.

Figure 3–1 shows the basic anatomy of a mobile ViewNavigatorApplication in both portrait and landscape orientations. The source code can be found in the ViewAppAnatomy sample project located in the chapter-03 directory of this book's sample code.

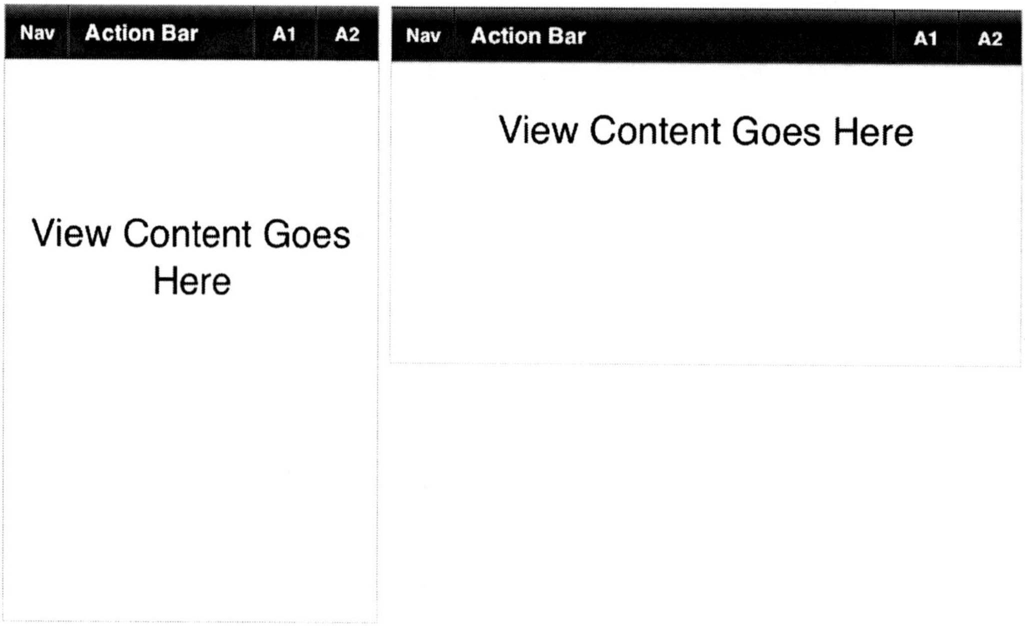

Figure 3–1. *The basic anatomy of a Flex mobile* ViewNavigatorApplication

The application's ActionBar stretches itself across the top of the screen in Figure 3–1. ActionBars are made up of three areas: the navigation area, the title area, and the actions area. The ActionBar in Figure 3–1 contains one button, labeled Nav, in the ActionBar's navigation area, while the title area is displaying the "ActionBar" string. The ActionBar's action area contains two buttons labeled A1 and A2. The View's content area is comprised of the rest of the screen below the ActionBar. Remember that, although the View uses the ActionBar to display its title and controls, the two are siblings in the component hierarchy. The View's width and height do not include the area occupied by the `ActionBar` unless `ViewNavigator`'s `overlayControls` property is set to true. If `overlayControls` is set to true, the `ActionBar`, as well as the tab bar of a `TabbedViewNavigatorApplication`, will be partially transparent so that any `View` content under them will be visible.

As an alternative to this `View`-based application structure, you are also free to create a completely custom interface by starting with a normal `Application` MXML file just as you would for a web-based or desktop-based application.

If you are using Flash Builder 4.5, you can click the application's **File** menu and select **New ➤ Flex Mobile Project**. After you name your new project and click the Next button, you will be given the choice to start with a plain old `Application`, a `ViewNavigatorApplication`, or a `TabbedViewNavigatorApplication`. We will examine the differences between these three choices in the following sections.

ViewNavigatorApplication

The `ViewNavigatorApplication` creates a single `ViewNavigator` that manages the transitions between `Views` for the entire mobile application. The application container also has a `firstView` property that determines which `View` component will be displayed when the application starts. Listing 3–1 shows the code for a very basic `ViewNavigatorApplication`. This code comes from the HelloView sample project in the `examples/chapter-03` directory of the book's sample code.

Listing 3–1. *A Simple Start: Your First Flex Mobile* `ViewNavigatorApplication`

```
<!-- HelloView.mxml - the application container -->
<?xml version="1.0" encoding="utf-8"?>
<s:ViewNavigatorApplication xmlns:fx="http://ns.adobe.com/mxml/2009"
                            xmlns:s="library://ns.adobe.com/flex/spark"
                            splashScreenImage="@Embed('assets/splash.png')"
                            firstView="views.FirstView">
</s:ViewNavigatorApplication>

<!-- FirstView.mxml - one of the application container's View components -->
<?xml version="1.0" encoding="utf-8"?>
<s:View xmlns:fx="http://ns.adobe.com/mxml/2009"
        xmlns:s="library://ns.adobe.com/flex/spark"
        title="Hello World">

  <s:VGroup width="100%" horizontalAlign="center" gap="20" top="20" left="10"
            right="10">
    <s:Label text="This is a ViewNavigatorApplication." width="100%"
             textAlign="center"/>
    <s:Button label="Next View" click="navigator.pushView(SecondView)"/>
  </s:VGroup>
</s:View>

<!-- SecondView.mxml - the application's other View component -->
<?xml version="1.0" encoding="utf-8"?>
<s:View xmlns:fx="http://ns.adobe.com/mxml/2009"
        xmlns:s="library://ns.adobe.com/flex/spark"
        title="Hello Again">
```

```
    <s:Label text="Press the back button to return to the first view." top="20"
             left="10" right="10"/>
</s:View>
```

Amazing! In about 20 lines of code, we have a fully functional mobile application complete with multiple `Views` and animated transitions between them. This is why Flex is a compelling choice for mobile development. The team at Adobe has made it very easy for you to get off the ground quickly and on your way to developing Android mobile applications.

The `ViewNavigatorApplication` container's `firstView` property is set to `views.FirstView` using an XML attribute. Flash Builder creates a *views* package under the application's default package when the project is created. So `views.FirstView` is the fully qualified path name of the `FirstView.mxml` file. Additionally, we have specified a `splashScreenImage` property on our `ViewNavigatorApplication`. This is usually a good idea since mobile applications can sometimes take a little while to start. The `@Embed` directive causes this image to be embedded in the application so it can be displayed on startup.

The source code for `FirstView` is shown immediately below the application container in Listing 3–1. The root component in the file is a Spark `View` component. The `title` attribute of the `<s:View>` tag specifies the string that will be displayed in the `ActionBar` when the `View` is activated. Like any MXML file, the child elements of the `View` tag specify various Spark components that make up the user interface of the `View`. In this case, we have a Spark `Label` and `Button` laid out inside a vertical group, or `VGroup`.

Note that the `Button`'s `click` event handler makes a call to the `pushView` function of the `navigator` object, which is the `View`'s reference to the application's `ViewNavigator` instance. The first parameter of this method is the class name of the `View` that should be displayed. In this case, we tell the `navigator` to display `SecondView` next. `SecondView`, on the other hand, simply instructs the user to use Android's built-in "back" button to return to the `FirstView`. There is no explicit call made to the `navigator` object anywhere in `SecondView`'s code. This is possible because the `ViewNavigator` automatically adds a listener to Android's back button. Since the `ViewNavigator` also maintains a stack of the `Views` that have been displayed, it can pop the most recent `View` off of its stack and return to the previous `View` in response to a "back" button press without any extra code being written by the application developer. This first Hello World application is shown running in Figure 3–2.

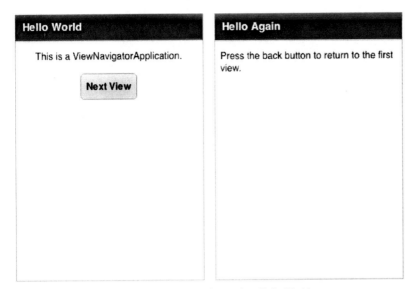

Figure 3–2. *A simple* ViewNavigatorApplication *Hello World program*

Important Events in the Life of a View

Events are the lifeblood of any Flex and Flash application. Not only do they allow you to react to what is going on in your application, but also it is important to know the order in which events arrive so that you can select the appropriate handlers in which to place your program logic. Figure 3–3 shows the order in which some of the more important events are received during three application stages: startup, shutdown, and transitioning from one View to another. The boxes in the figure that represent events received by the application container are dark, while the events received by Views are light-colored.

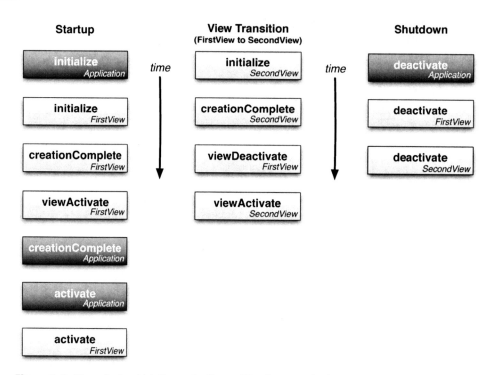

Figure 3–3. *The order in which the application and its* Views *receive important events*

The application receives the initialize event before the first View is created. Therefore, we know that the initialize handler is a good place to set the ViewNavigatorApplication's firstView and firstViewData properties if you need to do so programmatically rather than as a simple string in an XML attribute. One example where this comes in handy is when you persist data during shutdown and you want to read it back in and restore the application's View state the next time it starts up.

After the application receives the initialize event, the first View will receive its initialize, creationComplete, and viewActivate events. It's important to keep this sequence in mind when setting up your Views. If you need to programmatically set some initial state on your controls, it is better to do it in the initialize handler if possible. If you wait until the creationComplete handler is called, then the control is effectively initialized twice. It probably won't create a noticeable lag, but it always pays to be conscious of performance considerations when developing for a mobile platform. Likewise, the viewActivate event will be your last chance to have your say during the View startup sequence.

Once the first View completes its initial startup sequence, the application will receive its creationComplete and activate events. Then the first View will receive one last activate event as well. Only the application's first View will receive the activate event. That event handler is the right place for code that you want to run only when the View is the first to be created when the application is run.

During a `View` transition sequence, the new `View` will receive its `initialize` and `creationComplete` event before the old `View` receives its `viewDeactivate` event. Although the old `View` will still be valid, you should avoid interdependencies between the Views. Any data that needs to be passed from one `View` to the next can be passed using the new View's data parameter. We will show you how that is done later in this chapter. The final step in the `View` transition sequence is when the new `View` receives its `viewActivate` event. The important thing to keep in mind about this sequence is that the `initialize` and `creationComplete` events will be received by the new `View` before the `ViewNavigator` plays the animated transition to the new `View`. The `viewActivate` event will be received after the transition plays. If you want the new View's controls to be in a certain state as the transition plays—and they become visible to the user—you need to use either the `initialize` or `creationComplete` events. And again, `initialize` is preferred so that controls are not initialized twice. On the other hand, doing a lot of processing before the transition plays will cause a noticeable lag between the user's input and the time at which the `View` transitions start, which will cause your interface to feel sluggish. So it is a good idea to delay processing to the `viewActivate` event where possible.

When the application shuts down, the application container will receive the `deactivate` event, followed by each `View` in the `View` stack. If a `View` was instantiated more than once, it will receive multiple `deactivate` events, one in each instance. In a mobile environment, shutting down doesn't always mean that the application is removed from memory. In Android, for example, pushing the "home" button while an application is running will cause the application to receive its `deactivate` events. But the application hasn't exited; it is just running in the background. If you really want your application to exit when deactivated, you can call the exit function in the `NativeApplication` class from the application container's `deactivate` handler, as shown in Listing 3–2.

Listing 3–2. *Causing a Mobile Application to Exit Fully When Deactivated*

```
<?xml version="1.0" encoding="utf-8"?>
<s:ViewNavigatorApplication xmlns:fx="http://ns.adobe.com/mxml/2009"
                            xmlns:s="library://ns.adobe.com/flex/spark"
                            deactivate="onDeactivate()"
                            firstView="views.FirstView">

   <fx:Script>
     <![CDATA[
       private function onDeactivate():void {
         NativeApplication.nativeApplication.exit();
       }
     ]]>
   </fx:Script>
</s:ViewNavigatorApplication>
```

TabbedViewNavigatorApplication

A `TabbedViewNavigatorApplication` allows you to partition your application such that each group of Views relating to a particular application function gets its own tab. For example, a stock portfolio application may have one tab that allows you to view your portfolio, with one `View` that shows lists all of the stocks you own and another detailed

View that lets you examine one particular stock in detail. Another tab might show market news with a View that lists stories and another that lets you view an individual story. And finally you might have an account tab that lets you manage your account settings.

In this scenario, each tab has its own ViewNavigator that is responsible for managing the Views associated with that tab. You define these ViewNavigators in the application container's MXML file, as shown in Listing 3–3.

Listing 3–3. *Declaring a TabbedViewNavigatorApplication*

```
<?xml version="1.0" encoding="utf-8"?>
<s:TabbedViewNavigatorApplication xmlns:fx="http://ns.adobe.com/mxml/2009"
                                  xmlns:s="library://ns.adobe.com/flex/spark">

  <s:ViewNavigator label="Hello" width="100%" height="100%"
                    icon="@Embed('assets/smiley.png')"
                    firstView="views.HelloView"/>

  <s:ViewNavigator label="World" width="100%" height="100%"
                    icon="@Embed('assets/globe.png')"
                    firstView="views.WorldView"/>

</s:TabbedViewNavigatorApplication>
```

You can enclose your ViewNavigator declarations inside a <s:navigators> tag, but it is unnecessary since the navigators property is the TabbedViewNavigatorApplication's default property. This allows us to declare our ViewNavigators as direct child elements of the TabbedViewNavigatorApplication. The width and height of the ViewNavigators are set to 100%. This is needed if you want the Views to be sized correctly. Otherwise they will be only as large as it takes to hold their content. And an ActionBar that extends only part way across the top of the screen looks a little weird! The size of the icon is also critical. The tab components do not attempt to resize the image. If it is too large, your tab could take up the whole screen. Although we haven't done so in this simple example, in a real application you would want to make use of a MultiDPIBitmapSource to define your tab icons so they look good across a whole range of device screens.

Another difference from a regular ViewNavigatorApplication is that the firstView property is defined on the ViewNavigators rather than in the TabbedViewNavigatorApplication. This makes sense since each ViewNavigator manages its own set of Views. The first ViewNavigator declared in the MXML file is the one that will be active by default when the application starts. Listing 3–4 shows the MXML for the two Views that make up the Hello tab of this application, the HelloView and the LanguageView.

Listing 3–4. *The two Views of the Hello tab in our TabbedViewNavigatorApplication*

```
<!-- HelloView.mxml -->
<?xml version="1.0" encoding="utf-8"?>
<s:View xmlns:fx="http://ns.adobe.com/mxml/2009"
        xmlns:s="library://ns.adobe.com/flex/spark"
        initialize="onInitialize()"
        title="Hello" >

  <fx:Script>
```

```
    <![CDATA[
      import spark.events.IndexChangeEvent;

      private function onChange(event:IndexChangeEvent):void {
        data.selectedIndex = event.newIndex;
        navigator.pushView(LanguageView, listData.getItemAt(event.newIndex));
      }

      /**
       * Initializes the data object if it does not exist. If it does,
       * then restore the selected list index that was persisted.
*/
      private function onInitialize():void {
        if (data == null) {
          data = {selectedIndex: -1};
        }

        helloList.selectedIndex = data.selectedIndex;
      }
    ]]>
  </fx:Script>

  <s:List id="helloList" width="100%" height="100%" labelField="hello"
          change="onChange(event)">
    <s:ArrayCollection id="listData">
      <fx:Object hello="Hello" lang="English"/>
      <fx:Object hello="Hola" lang="Spanish"/>
      <fx:Object hello="nuqneH" lang="Klingon"/>
      <!-- and a bunch of others… -->
    </s:ArrayCollection>
  </s:List>
</s:View>

<!-- LanguageView.mxml -->
<?xml version="1.0" encoding="utf-8"?>
<s:View xmlns:fx="http://ns.adobe.com/mxml/2009"
        xmlns:s="library://ns.adobe.com/flex/spark"
        initialize="onInitialize()"
        title="Language">

<fx:Script>
    <![CDATA[
      private function onInitialize():void {
        hello.text = data.hello;
        lang.text = "("+data.lang+")";
      }
    ]]>
  </fx:Script>

  <s:VGroup horizontalAlign="center" width="100%" paddingTop="20">
    <s:Label id="hello" fontSize="36"/>
    <s:Label id="lang" fontSize="36"/>
  </s:VGroup>
</s:View>
```

The HelloView defines a static ArrayCollection of objects with two properties: a hello property that contains the word "Hello" written in some particular language, and the lang property that specifies what that language is. This ArrayCollection is then used as the dataProvider for a Spark List that is displayed in the View. The first thing to note about this View is that it uses its data property to persist data for itself while other Views are displayed. This is done in the onInitialize function. If the View's data object is null, in other words, if this is the first time the View has been initialized, then a new data object is created using ActionScript's object literal notation. Otherwise the existing data object—which is persisted while other Views are displayed—is used to retrieve the index of the item that was previously selected in the List and re-select it when the View is reactivated.

The HelloView source code also demonstrates how to pass data to another View as is done in the List's onChange handler. When the user selects an item in HelloView's List, the onChange handler will first save the newIndex property of the IndexChangeEvent in its own data object so the List selection can be restored the next time the View is activated. The handler function then uses that same newIndex property to get a reference to the selected object from the ArrayCollection. It passes the object to the LanguageView's data property by passing it as the second parameter of the ViewNavigator's pushView function. At the bottom of Listing 3–4, you can see that the code for the LanguageView displays the data object's hello and lang properties to the user with two Label components, whose text properties are bound to the properties of the data object.

Figure 3–4 shows these two Views of the Hello tab running in the HelloTabbedView sample application. The source code for this project can be found in the examples/chapter-03 directory of this book's sample code.

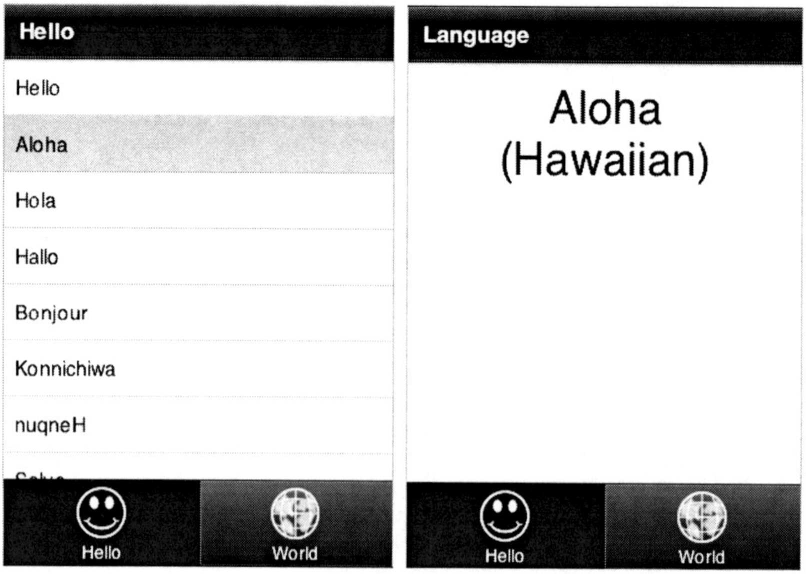

Figure 3–4. *The Views under the Hello tab of the Hello World* TabbedViewNavigatorApplication

What about the World tab? The World tab contains one `View`, named, creatively enough, the `WorldView`. Unintuitively, it does not contain a picture of the earth. Instead it demonstrates another staple of GUI-based Hello World programs: the greeting message. Figure 3–5 shows this `View` in action.

Figure 3–5. *The* `View` *under the World tab of the Hello World* `TabbedViewNavigatorApplication`

The unique thing about this particular implementation is that it demonstrates that `ActionBars` can contain just about any kind of Spark control, not just buttons. Listing 3–5 demonstrates how this is accomplished.

Listing 3–5. *A Simple Implementation of a Greeting Message*

```
<?xml version="1.0" encoding="utf-8"?>
<s:View xmlns:fx="http://ns.adobe.com/mxml/2009"
        xmlns:s="library://ns.adobe.com/flex/spark">

  <fx:Script>
    <![CDATA[
      import spark.events.TextOperationEvent;

      private function onChange(event:TextOperationEvent):void {
        viewLabel.text = "Hello, "+textInput.text;
      }
    ]]>
  </fx:Script>

  <s:titleContent>
    <s:TextInput id="textInput" prompt="Enter your name..." width="100%"
                 change="onChange(event)"/>
  </s:titleContent>

  <s:VGroup horizontalAlign="center" width="100%" paddingTop="20">
    <s:Label id="viewLabel" text="Hello, World" fontSize="44"/>
```

```
    </s:VGroup>
</s:View>
```

The View's `titleContent`, which usually displays the View's title string, has been replaced by a Spark `TextInput` control. The `TextInput`'s change handler simply copies the characters that have been entered to the `Label`'s `text` property. This is a good example of the kind of flexibility you have to customize the `ActionBar` of your Views.

Just an Application

The third option when creating a new Flex mobile project is to start with a blank application. You might select this option if you are working on a unique mobile application that does not use the typical pattern of multiple "views" for its interface. You also might take advantage of this option if you are working on an application that has only one `View` and you therefore don't need the `ViewNavigator` and all that it brings along with it. When you opt to start with a blank application, you will get just that, as shown in Listing 3–6.

Listing 3–6. *A Blank Mobile Application*

```
<?xml version="1.0" encoding="utf-8"?>
<s:Application xmlns:fx="http://ns.adobe.com/mxml/2009"
               xmlns:s="library://ns.adobe.com/flex/spark">
  <fx:Declarations>
    <!-- Place non-visual elements (e.g., services, value objects) here -->
  </fx:Declarations>
</s:Application>
```

However, the fact that you start with a blank application doesn't mean that you can't make use of the mobile-specific controls included with Flex 4.5. Take the example where you are working on an application with just one screen. Setting up an entire View-based system for a single screen is not worth it. But that doesn't mean that you cannot still use an `ActionBar` to make your application look more like a traditional mobile application! Listing 3–7 shows an application that started life as a blank application and now looks like any other Flex mobile app.

Listing 3–7. *A Flex Mobile Application Without the* `ViewNavigator`

```
<?xml version="1.0" encoding="utf-8"?>
<s:Application xmlns:fx="http://ns.adobe.com/mxml/2009"
               xmlns:s="library://ns.adobe.com/flex/spark">

  <fx:Declarations>
    <s:SkinnablePopUpContainer id="myAlert" x="{(width-myAlert.width)/2}"
                               y="{(height-myAlert.height)/2}">
      <s:Panel title="Nice Button Click!">
        <s:VGroup horizontalAlign="center" paddingTop="20" paddingBottom="20"
                  paddingLeft="20" paddingRight="20" gap="20" width="100%">
          <s:Label text="You clicked on an ActionBar button."/>
          <s:Button label="OK" click="myAlert.close()"/>
        </s:VGroup>
      </s:Panel>
    </s:SkinnablePopUpContainer>
  </fx:Declarations>
```

```
  <s:ActionBar id="ab" left="0" right="0" top="0" title="Just an App"
               titleAlign="center">
    <s:navigationContent>
      <s:Button label="Nav" click="myAlert.open(this, true)"/>
    </s:navigationContent>
    <s:actionContent>
      <s:Button label="Act" click="myAlert.open(this, true)"/>
    </s:actionContent>
  </s:ActionBar>

  <s:VGroup top="100" horizontalCenter="0" horizontalAlign="contentJustify">
    <s:Label text="ActionBars are just another component.
They can even be placed on the:"
             width="400" fontSize="32" textAlign="center"/>
    <s:Button label="Top" click="ab.top=0;ab.bottom=null;ab.left=0;ab.right=0"/>
    <s:Label text="or" fontSize="32" textAlign="center"/>
    <s:Button label="Bottom" click="ab.top=null;ab.bottom=0;ab.left=0;ab.right=0"/>
  </s:VGroup>

</s:Application>
```

This application declares its own ActionBar just as it would any other component. In fact, the application allows you to place the ActionBar at the top or bottom of the screen. The ActionBar defined in this listing also contains buttons in its navigationContent and its actionContent that display a pop-up container. The SkinnablePopupContainer is one of the new Spark controls that can be used in mobile applications. One common design pattern for Android interfaces is that a long tap on a component can display a pop-up container that allows the user to select more options. The SkinnablePopupContainer is how you would implement such a pattern in a Flex mobile application. We will go into more detail about Android design patterns and the Flex mobile components later in this chapter. Figure 3–6 shows this application running with the ActionBar on the bottom and the pop-up container visible.

Just to be clear, though, ActionBars belong at the top of the screen; don't try this at home—we are professionals! We have now touched upon the ViewNavigators, Views, and the ActionBar several times in previous examples. In the next section, we will dive deeper into these staples of mobile Flex applications.

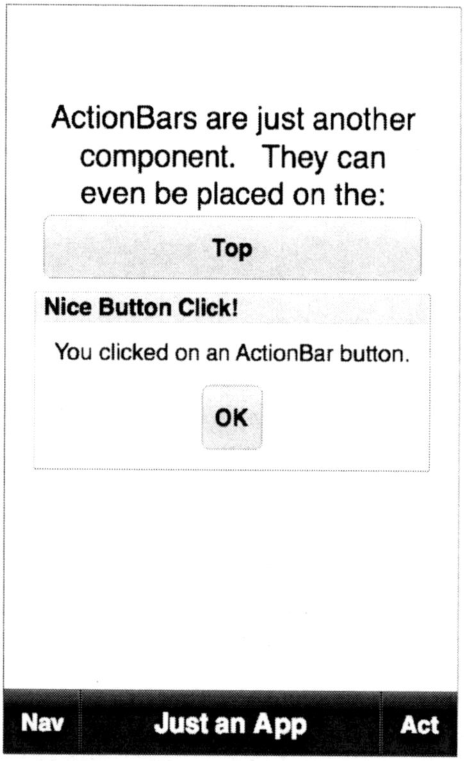

Figure 3–6. *An application with an* ActionBar *component and a pop-up container visible*

ViewNavigator and Views

The ViewNavigator is a skinnable container that holds a stack of View objects where only the topmost View in the stack is visible and active at any given time. Pushing a new View onto the stack automatically causes an animated transition to be played and the new View to be displayed. To return to the previous View, the application simply pops the top View off the stack.

The ViewNavigator also displays an ActionBar that shows contextual information defined by the active View. The ViewNavigator automatically updates the ActionBar whenever a new View is shown. The methods of main interest in the ViewNavigator class are as follows:

  ▪ pushView: Pushes a new View onto the stack, automatically making it visible on the screen; the first parameter to this function is the class of the View to display. The method has three more optional parameters: a data object that will be passed to the new View, a context object that is stored by the ViewNavigator and is also readable by the new View, and a transition to play between the Views. We will go into more detail about these three optional parameters later in the chapter.

- popView: Removes the current View from the stack and displays the previous View; the function has one optional parameter: the transition to play between the Views.

- popToFirstView: Removes all Views from the stack except for the very first one, which then becomes the visible View; this function also accepts a transition parameter.

- popAll: Removes all Views from the stack and displays a blank screen; the transition parameter is once again optional.

- hideActionBar/showActionBar: Hides or shows the ActionBar; some mobile applications have the option to go full screen by tapping on a control in the ActionBar. In full-screen mode, tapping on the screen will cause the ActionBar to be shown again. These methods can be used to implement such a system in your Flex application. The hiding and showing of the ActionBar will be animated by default, but you can pass a Boolean parameter to these functions to turn that off.

The ViewNavigator will automatically handle presses of Android's back button and call popView on behalf of the application. The ActionBar, View, and ViewNavigator classes all collaborate to provide many such features to the mobile developer. The rest of this section will explore several facets of how these classes work together to provide you with a productive, flexible, and robust framework for developing your mobile applications.

The ActionBar

In mobile applications, the ActionBar is the conventional place for View titles and controls. The ActionBar has three distinct areas: a navigation area, a title area, and an actions area. Refer back to Figure 3–1 for an example that shows these areas. All three areas can contain arbitrary controls, but the title area will display a title string by default. And although the title area can also display arbitrary controls, it will not display the title string if it has been given alternative content to display.

Each ViewNavigator has one ActionBar control that is shared among the Views instantiated by the navigator. Therefore, a ViewNavigatorApplication will have only one ActionBar for the entire application, while a TabbedViewNavigatorApplication will have one separate ActionBar for each ViewNavigator in the application. The ActionBar has seven properties that determine its content and layout.

- actionContent: An array of controls that determine what is displayed in the ActionBar's action area (to the right of the title)

- actionLayout: A Spark layout that allows a custom layout of the controls specified by the actionContent array

- navigationContent: An array of controls that determine what is displayed in the ActionBar's navigation area (to the left of the title)

▦   navigationLayout: A Spark layout that allows a custom layout of the controls specified by the navigationContent array

▦   title: A string that will be displayed in the title area if titleContent is null

▦   titleContent: An array of controls that determine what is displayed in the ActionBar's title area (the center of the ActionBar)

▦   titleLayout: A Spark layout that allows a custom layout of the controls specified by the actionContent array

These seven properties are replicated in the ViewNavigatorApplication, ViewNavigator, and View classes. If you assign values to these properties in ViewNavigatorApplication, you are, in essence, defining the default appearance of the ActionBar for the whole application. Defining these properties in the ViewNavigator works as a default for all Views that will be displayed by that ViewNavigator. In TabbedViewNavigatorApplications, this is the only way to specify default ActionBar settings—once for each ViewNavigator. When a new View is displayed, its ViewNavigator will update the ActionBar with that View's ActionBar-related properties, thus overriding any default values specified by the application or the navigator. In addition, Views have one extra property, actionBarVisible, which determines whether the ActionBar should be shown at all when the View is shown.

We have already shown sample applications that display controls in the navigation and action area, as well as one that replaced the title content with a TextField, so we won't rehash those examples in this section. One additional piece of information you might find useful is the use of two special styles that affect the appearance of the ActionBar. The titleAlign style allows you to set the alignment of the title string to left, right, or center. The defaultButtonAppearance style can be set to either normal or beveled. On Android these default to a left-aligned title and normal button appearances. You can change them as needed for your application, or you may also need to change them if you plan to port your application to the iOS platform. In that case, ActionBars on iOS normally have beveled buttons and centered titles. Figure 3–7 shows how this would look.

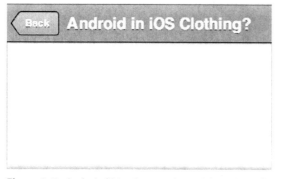

Figure 3–7. *An Android* ActionBar *dressed for a date with an iPhone*

Applying the beveled style to defaultButtonAppearance even adds the traditional iOS arrow shape to buttons placed in the navigation content. It's the little touches that make all the difference. Listing 3–8 shows the code that created the ActionBar appearance of Figure 3–7.

Listing 3–8. *An iOS-Style* ActionBar, *with Style!*

```
<?xml version="1.0" encoding="utf-8"?>
<s:ViewNavigatorApplication xmlns:fx="http://ns.adobe.com/mxml/2009"
                            xmlns:s="library://ns.adobe.com/flex/spark"
                            firstView="views.MainHomeView">
  <fx:Style>
    @namespace s "library://ns.adobe.com/flex/spark";
    s|ActionBar {
      titleAlign: "center";
      defaultButtonAppearance: "beveled";
      chromeColor: "0x7893AB"
    }
  </fx:Style>

  <s:navigationContent>
    <s:Button label="Back"/>
  </s:navigationContent>
</s:ViewNavigatorApplication>
```

We have taken advantage of the ability to define navigationContent directly in the MXML file for a ViewNavigatorApplication. Due to this placement, the Back button would appear on every View in the entire application. In addition to the titleAlign and defaultButtonAppearance styles, we also defined a custom color for the ActionBar. The ActionBar will use the chromeColor style as the basis for the gradient that it generates to fill the ActionBar's background. Defining a custom chromeColor for the ActionBar is a common way to customize a mobile application for branding or uniqueness.

Animated View Transitions

View transitions control the animation that is played when one View replaces another. The default transition when pushing a new View is a SlideViewTransition to the left, while popping a View causes a SlideViewTransition to the right. Both of these default transitions use their push mode. You can customize the View transition animations in a myriad of different ways, however. Table 3–1 shows the transitions, their modes, and their directions.

Table 3–1. *The* View *Transition Classes, Their Modes, and Their Directions*

Transition	Modes	Directions
SlideViewTransition	push, cover, uncover	up, down, left, right
FlipViewTransition	card, cube	up, down, left, right
ZoomViewTransition	in, out	N/A
CrossFadeViewTransition	N/A	N/A

When you add different easers to the mix, you really have a large number of combinations to play with. For example, a SlideViewTransition in uncover mode and the down direction will look like the current View is sliding downward off the screen to reveal the new View that was sitting underneath it. Throw in a Bounce easer, and the top View will slide down and bounce when it hits the bottom of the screen. You can even write your own custom transitions by extending the ViewTransitionBase class and your own easers by implementing the IEaser interface. You really are limited only by your imagination!

You can specify the transition that the ViewNavigator will use by passing your transition as the fourth parameter to the pushView or replaceView functions. ViewNavigator's popView, popAll, and popToFirstView also take a single optional parameter that specifies which transition to play while changing Views. Ah, but what if the user pushes Android's back button? We don't get to call a pop function explicitly in this case, so instead you must set the ViewNavigator's defaultPopTransition property to the transition you would like it to play by default. If you do not specify a transition parameter to a pop function or set the defaultPopTransition property, the ViewNavigator will play its default slide transition when it pops the View. Even if you used a custom transition to push a View, the ViewNavigator will make no attempt to play the push transition in reverse when the View is popped. It should also be noted that ViewNavigator has a corresponding defaultPushTransition. You can use these two properties to set the default values for all of the transitions played by a particular ViewNavigator.

The only logical, and fun, thing to do now is to write an application to try out some of these transition combinations, right? Right! Listing 3–9 shows the code for the TransitionListView of the ViewTransitions sample program. This View displays a List of all the built-in View transitions, each showing a few different combinations of modes, directions, and easers. The ViewTransitions project can be found with the rest of the example projects for Chapter 3 in the sample code for this book.

Listing 3–9. *Demonstrating Several Different Varieties of Each* View *Transition*

```
<?xml version="1.0" encoding="utf-8"?>
<s:View xmlns:fx="http://ns.adobe.com/mxml/2009"
        xmlns:s="library://ns.adobe.com/flex/spark"
        title="Home">

  <fx:Declarations>
    <s:Bounce id="bounce"/>
    <s:SlideViewTransition id="slide"/>
    <s:SlideViewTransition id="slideBounce" easer="{bounce}" duration="1000"/>
    <s:SlideViewTransition id="slideCover" mode="cover"/>
    <s:SlideViewTransition id="slideUncover" mode="uncover"/>
    <s:SlideViewTransition id="uncoverBounce" mode="uncover" easer="{bounce}"
                           direction="down" duration="1000"/>
    <s:FlipViewTransition id="flip"/>
    <s:FlipViewTransition id="flipBounce" easer="{bounce}" duration="1000"/>
    <s:FlipViewTransition id="flipCube" mode="cube"/>
    <s:CrossFadeViewTransition id="fade"/>
    <s:ZoomViewTransition id="zoom"/>
    <s:ZoomViewTransition id="zoomBounce" easer="{bounce}" duration="1000"/>
    <s:ZoomViewTransition id="zoomIn" mode="in"/>
```

```
            <s:ZoomViewTransition id="zoomInBounce" mode="in" easer="{bounce}"
                                  duration="1000"/>
        </fx:Declarations>

        <fx:Script>
          <![CDATA[
            import spark.events.IndexChangeEvent;
            import spark.transitions.ViewTransitionBase;

            private function onChange(event:IndexChangeEvent):void {
              var selectedItem:Object = transitionList.selectedItem;
              var transition:ViewTransitionBase = selectedItem.transition;
              var data:Object = {name: selectedItem.name};

              navigator.defaultPopTransition = transition;
              navigator.pushView(TransitionedView, data, null, transition);
            }

          ]]>
        </fx:Script>

        <s:navigationContent/>

        <s:List id="transitionList" width="100%" height="100%" labelField="name"
                change="onChange(event)">
          <s:ArrayCollection>
            <fx:Object name="Default - Push Slide" transition="{slide}"/>
            <fx:Object name="Push Slide with Bounce" transition="{slideBounce}"/>
            <fx:Object name="Cover Slide" transition="{slideCover}"/>
            <fx:Object name="Uncover Slide" transition="{slideUncover}"/>
            <fx:Object name="Uncover Slide with Bounce" transition="{uncoverBounce}"/>
            <fx:Object name="Flip" transition="{flip}"/>
            <fx:Object name="Flip with Bounce" transition="{flipBounce}"/>
            <fx:Object name="Cube Flip" transition="{flipCube}"/>
            <fx:Object name="Fade" transition="{fade}"/>
            <fx:Object name="Zoom Out" transition="{zoom}"/>
            <fx:Object name="Zoom Out with Bounce" transition="{zoomBounce}"/>
            <fx:Object name="Zoom In" transition="{zoomIn}"/>
            <fx:Object name="Zoom In with Bounce" transition="{zoomInBounce}"/>
          </s:ArrayCollection>
        </s:List>
      </s:View>
```

The <fx:Declarations> section is used to declare a Bounce easer and variety of different transitions. Some transitions use their default settings, while others specify special modes or directions. Several of the transitions also use the duration property to specify the total number of milliseconds the transition should take. The default durations for the built-in transitions range from 300 to 400 milliseconds. This is a little too fast for an effective bounce animation, so those transitions that use the Bounce easer have longer durations.

When a transition is selected from the List, the onChange handler function retrieves the selected object and passes the transition's name to the next View in its data.name property. The objects contained in the List also keep a reference to the desired transition. So this transition property is passed as the fourth parameter to the navigator's pushView method. But note that the transition is also used to set the navigator's defaultPopTransition property just before the call to pushView. This will ensure that if a FlipViewTransition was played during the push, that same transition will be played when returning to the TransitionListView. This is cheating a little bit, because while you would normally want to play the same type of transition on the push and pop of a particular pair of Views, you would normally reverse the direction of the pop transition. This is easily accomplished in a regular application, but in this case it was not worth the extra clutter in the example code to define an opposite-direction transition for each of the current transition objects. Figure 3–8 shows the ViewTransitions sample program caught during a FlipViewTransition in cube mode.

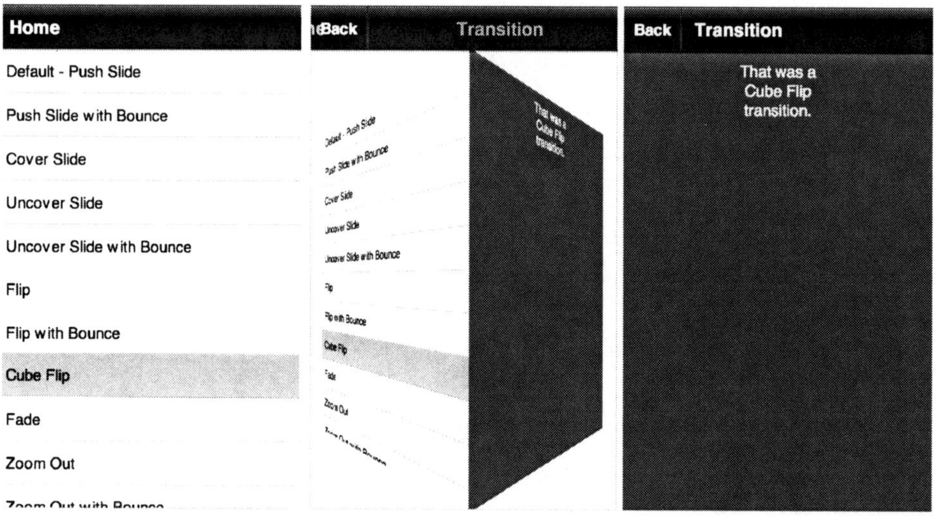

Figure 3–8. *Using a cube flip transition to go from one View to the next*

If you look closely at the ActionBar while the ViewTransitions sample program runs, or if you examine the center image in Figure 3–8, you will notice that the ActionBar does not transition with the View. This is because the ActionBar is considered to belong to the entire application—or the entire tab—rather than just one View. But there are times when the transition would look better if the ActionBar took part. You can set the transitionControlsWithContent property of the View transition class to true in those cases. So if we change the cube flip declaration in the sample application as follows, we can then achieve the effect shown in Figure 3–9.

```
<s:FlipViewTransition id="flipCube" mode="cube"
        transitionControlsWithContent="true"/>
```

Figure 3–9. *Transitioning the* ActionBar *with the* View *on a cube flip transition*

View Menus

All Android devices have a built-in menu button that displays an onscreen menu. AIR supports this functionality with the ViewMenu and ViewMenuItem classes. ViewMenu acts as a container for a single level of ViewMenuItems; sub-menus are not supported. Each View in your application can define its own ViewMenu. Listing 3–10 shows how a ViewMenu is declared for a View.

Listing 3–10. *Declaring a* ViewMenu

```
<?xml version="1.0" encoding="utf-8"?>
<s:View xmlns:fx="http://ns.adobe.com/mxml/2009"
        xmlns:s="library://ns.adobe.com/flex/spark"
        title="MenuItem Example">
```

```
<fx:Script>
  <![CDATA[
    private function onClick(event:MouseEvent):void {
      message.text = "You selected " + (event.target as ViewMenuItem).label
    }
  ]]>
</fx:Script>

<s:viewMenuItems>
  <s:ViewMenuItem label="Pro" click="onClick(event)"
                  icon="@Embed('assets/ProAndroidFlashIcon36.png')"/>
  <s:ViewMenuItem label="Android" click="onClick(event)"
                  icon="@Embed('assets/android.png')" />
  <s:ViewMenuItem label="Flash" click="onClick(event)"
                  icon="@Embed('assets/flash.png')" />
  <s:ViewMenuItem label="Book" click="onClick(event)"
                  icon="@Embed('assets/book.png')" />
</s:viewMenuItems>

<s:Label id="message" width="100%" top="20" textAlign="center"/>
</s:View>
```

A ViewMenuItem is really just another kind of button. It even extends the Spark
ButtonBase class. Therefore, just like any other button, you can define label and icon
properties as well as a click event handler. In this example, each ViewMenuItem is given
the same onClick handler, which uses the ViewMenuItem's label to display the selection
to the user. What makes the ViewMenu container and ViewMenuItem buttons different from
their normal Spark counterparts is that their layouts are designed to mimic the native
Android menus.

> **TIP:** Remember that Ctrl+N on Windows and Cmd+N on a Mac will show the **View** menu in the
> desktop emulator.

Figure 3–10 shows what the resulting ViewMenu looks like when run on an Android
device.

Figure 3–10. *A* `ViewMenu` *with icons*

Passing Data Between Views

The `ViewNavigator` will ensure that only one `View` is in memory at any given time in order to conserve resources. When a `View` is pushed on top of the stack, the old `View`'s data object is automatically persisted, and a new `data` object is passed to the new `View` if one was provided as the second parameter of the `pushView` function. If no data object is provided, then the new `View`'s data property will be null. Since a `View`'s data object is persisted when a new `View` is pushed onto the stack, that `data` object will be restored when the `View` is reactivated as a result of other `Views` being popped off the stack.

It would seem, then, that communication via data object is one-way: a `View` can pass a data object to the `View` that it is pushing onto the stack, but that `View` has no way to return data back to the original `View` when it is popped off the stack. So how would the new `View` return data to the original `View` if it needed to? The answer is that the new `View` would simply override `View`'s `createReturnObject` function. This function returns an object that is saved into `ViewNavigator`'s `poppedViewReturnedObject` property, which is of type `ViewReturnObject`. So in order to access the object returned by the new `View`, the original `View` would access `navigator.poppedViewReturnedObject.object`.

You can also pass data to a new `View` by using the `context` object. You can pass a `context` object as the third parameter of the `ViewNavigator`'s `pushView` function. The `context` behaves much like the `data` object; it is accessible to the new `View` at any time by accessing the `navigator.context` property. The previous `View`'s `context` is also restored when the top `View` is popped from the `ViewNavigator` `View` stack. The popped `View`'s `context` object is also present in the `poppedViewReturnedObject.context` property of the `navigator`.

The use of the `data` and `context` objects are somewhat interchangeable, and in those cases where either would do the job, you should prefer to use the `data` object. The `context` object is useful for those cases where you have a `View` that should display itself slightly differently depending on how the user has navigated to the `View`. For example, you may have a details `View` that displays a person's contact information. Sometimes, depending on how the user navigates to the `View`—whether it's by tapping a "view" button versus an "edit" button—the `View` should adjust its display accordingly. This is a good place to use the `context` object to differentiate whether the contact information contained in the `data` object should be simply presented to the user or should be made editable.

Persisting View and Session Data

We have already seen in Listing 3–4, and briefly discussed in the previous section, that a `View`'s `data` object is restored to it when the `View` is reactivated by one of the `ViewNavigator` pop functions. Therefore, one persistence strategy for `View` data is to store values in its `data` object either before calling `pushView` or in the handler for the `viewDeactivate` event. If that new `View` calls one of the pop functions, then the data previously stored by the original `View` will be accessible via its `data` object again. This strategy will work only for persisting data between `Views` in a running application. If the application is shut down by the user triggering an action that calls the `NativeApplication`'s exit function or by the Android OS, then all `View` data objects are lost.

The `PersistenceManager` class is used to persist data between runs of your application. The `ViewNavigatorApplication` and the `TabbedViewNavigatorApplication` containers have a reference to a `persistenceManager` instance that can be used to save and load persisted data when the application starts or shuts down. Listing 3–11 shows a simple example of using the `persistenceManager` to save the number of times an application has been launched. This code is part of the Chapter 3 sample project named SimplePersistence.

Listing 3–11. *Persisting Data Between Application Runs*

```
<?xml version="1.0" encoding="utf-8"?>
<s:ViewNavigatorApplication xmlns:fx="http://ns.adobe.com/mxml/2009"
                            xmlns:s="library://ns.adobe.com/flex/spark"
                            splashScreenImage="@Embed('assets/splash.png')"
                            initialize="onInitialize()"
                            deactivate="onDeactivate()"
                            applicationDPI="160">
```

```
<fx:Script>
  <![CDATA[
    import views.PersistenceCountView;
    private static const RUN_COUNT:String = "runCount";

    private function onInitialize():void {
      var rc:Number = Number(persistenceManager.getProperty(RUN_COUNT));
      navigator.pushView(views.PersistenceCountView, rc);
    }

    private function onDeactivate():void {
      var rc:Number = Number(persistenceManager.getProperty(RUN_COUNT));
      persistenceManager.setProperty(RUN_COUNT, ++rc);

      NativeApplication.nativeApplication.exit(0);
    }
  ]]>
</fx:Script>
</s:ViewNavigatorApplication>
```

The application's onDeactivate handler is called when the application is being put in the background or closed by the Android OS. So in this handler we increment the run count and call the persistenceManager's setProperty function to persist it. Then we make a call to the NativeApplication's exit function just to make sure the application is being closed between runs. This ensures that our data really is being persisted and restored.

The application's run count is then retrieved from the persistenceManager using the getProperty function when the application's onInitialize handler is triggered. The getProperty function takes one parameter that is the key String of the property to retrieve. This run count is cast to a Number and passed to the application's first View, where it is displayed as shown in Figure 3–11.

Figure 3–11. *Displaying the application's persisted run count*

The View navigator-based applications also have a property called persistNavigatorState that, when set to true, will automatically persist the ViewNavigator's state and View stack. The persisted data is automatically loaded back in the next time the program is run. In addition to the ViewNavigator data, the application's version and the time that the data is persisted is also saved. These two pieces of data are accessible using the PersistenceManager's getProperty function with the "applicationVersion" and "timestamp" keys.

Now that we have explored the mobile application containers, it is time to focus on the controls (pun intended) that are available to mobile Flex applications.

Visual Controls

At the core of any Flex application is a rich set of UI controls that let you express common elements within your UI. We have already been using many of these in the code and applications found earlier in this book; however, in this section, we will focus specifically on the different types of controls available for mobile Flex applications.

For mobile applications, both performance and skinning are extremely important to ensure that the user interface is usable. For this reason, it is highly recommended to stay away from the older MX packages in Flex, and to focus on Spark controls that have mobile skins.

A full list of the Spark controls is shown in Table 3–2, along with their suitability for mobile applications.

Table 3–2. *Flex 4.5 Controls*

Control	Mobile Skin	Recommended Usage
BorderContainer	No	This component lacks a mobile skin and is not recommended for mobile use.
BusyIndicator	Yes	Recommended for mobile use
Button	Yes	Recommended for mobile use
ButtonBar	Yes	Recommended for mobile use
CheckBox	Yes	Recommended for mobile use
ComboBox	No	This component lacks a mobile skin and is not recommended for mobile use.
DataGrid	No	This component lacks a mobile skin and is not recommended for mobile use. For most mobile applications, a List is more suitable.
DropDownList	No	This component lacks a mobile skin and is not recommended for mobile use.
Form	No	This component lacks a mobile skin and is not recommended for mobile use.
HSlider	Yes	Recommended for mobile use
Image	Yes	For performance reasons, use a Bitmap unless you need specific features of the Image class, such as skinning.
Label	Yes	Recommended for mobile use
List	Yes	Recommended for mobile use
NumericStepper	No	This component lacks a mobile skin and is not recommended for mobile use.
Panel	No	This component lacks a mobile skin and is not recommended for mobile use.

Control	Mobile Skin	Recommended Usage
RadioButton	Yes	Recommended for mobile use
RichEditableText	Yes	Not recommended for mobile use due to performance reasons
RichText	Yes	Not recommended for mobile use due to performance reasons
Scroller	N/A	Recommended for mobile use
Spinner	No	This component lacks a mobile skin and is not recommended for mobile use.
TabBar	Yes	Recommended for mobile use
TextArea	Yes	Recommended for mobile use
TextInput	Yes	Recommended for mobile use
ToggleButton	No	This component lacks a mobile skin and is not recommended for mobile use.
VSlider	No	This component lacks a mobile skin and is not recommended for mobile use.

A number of the controls do not currently have mobile optimized skins, and therefore should not be used on mobile devices at this time. For example, the ComboBox, NumericStepper, and DropDownList won't have a consistent look and interaction if used on mobile with their desktop skins. If you need a control with the functionality of one of these, you can create your own custom skin that matches the style of your mobile application.

Some of the available components are also not optimized for performance on mobile devices. We cover this topic in more detail in Chapter 10, but if you follow the foregoing guidelines and use TextArea and TextInput instead of RichText and RichEditableText, you should be fine. The same is true for the Image class, which can be heavyweight when used repeatedly, such as in ListItemRenderers.

This list is current as of Flex 4.5, but Adobe is working on adding additional mobile skins for the remaining controls, so please refer to the API documentation for the very latest information about mobile control compatibility.

In the rest of this chapter, we go into detail on how to use the full capabilities of each mobile-enabled control.

Text Controls

The three controls that are optimized for mobile and will give you the best performing application are `Label`, `TextArea`, and `TextInput`. Each of these controls is highly customizable via CSS styles.

`Label` gives you the ability to display single or multiline text with uniform formatting. It uses the Flash Text Engine (FTE) behind the scenes, which makes it fast and lightweight, but not as flexible as the `RichText` control that uses the full Text Layout Framework (TLF). `Label`s should be used anywhere where you have short snippets of unmodifiable text that you want to display onscreen, such as labels for controls or section headings.

`TextInput` and `TextArea` provide text input for single-line and multiline use, respectively. When used on a mobile device, they use the `StyleableTextField` class behind the scenes, making them extremely performant, but with a limited set of functionality. On desktop these controls are backed by the TLF, giving you international language support, improved typography, and embedded CFF fonts. If you need these features on mobile, you will have to use the `RichEditableText` control, which comes with a significant performance penalty.

The mobile styles of the three recommended text components are shown in Table 3–3. While there are additional style attributes available when running on the desktop profile, such as `kerning`, `lineBreak`, and `renderingMode`, these are not supported on mobile due to the lighterweight text engine used in the mobile themes.

Table 3–3. *Text Styles Recommended for Mobile Use*

Style	Label	TextInput	TextArea	Description
backgroundAlpha	Y	Y	Y	The alpha value (opacity) of the background color used
backgroundColor	Y	Y	Y	The color that the component's background will be painted with
borderVisible	N	Y	Y	Whether the border is visible (true by default)
color	Y	Y	Y	Color that will be used for displaying text
contentBackgroundAlpha	N	Y	Y	The alpha value (opacity) of the content area within the text field
contentBackgroundColor	N	Y	Y	The color that the component's content area will be painted with

Style	Label	TextInput	TextArea	Description
focusAlpha	N	Y	Y	The alpha value (opacity) for the focus ring
focusColor	N	Y	Y	The color used to paint the component's focus ring
fontFamily	Y	Y	Y	The name of the font to be used for text rendering (can be a comma-separated list of fonts in order of preference)
fontSize	Y	Y	Y	The size of the font used for rendering in pixel units
fontStyle	Y	Y	Y	The font style, which can be italic or normal (default is normal)
fontWeight	Y	Y	Y	The font weight, which can be bold or normal (default is normal)
leading	Y	Y	Y	Vertical space between lines of text
letterSpacing	Y	Y	Y	Space between letters in pixel units
locale	Y	Y	Y	Text locale used for internationalization
textAlign	Y	Y	Y	Alignment of text within the container, which can be left, right, or center (default is left)
textDecoration	Y	Y	Y	The text decoration, which can be underline or none
textIndent	N	Y	Y	The indentation of the first line of text (must be greater than or equal to 0)

As you can see, the set of styles supported by these text components is almost identical, with the addition of some styles for the content area, border, and focus for TextInput and TextArea.

The biggest difference in the use of the different text components comes in the use of different properties for text editing. Many of these properties are available on TextInput and TextArea, but not needed for Label since it is intended for text rendering only. Table 3–4 lists all the available properties of the three text components.

Table 3–4. *Public Properties Available on* Label, TextInput, *and* TextArea

Property	Label	TextInput	TextArea	Description
displayAsPassword	N	Y	Y	Renders the text as a series of dots, hiding the text as it is typed
editable	N	Y	Y	Whether the text component is editable (default is true)
isTruncated	Y	N	N	Read-only property that tells you if the text was too long and got truncated
maxChars	N	Y	Y	The alpha value (opacity) of the content area within the text field
maxDisplayedLines	Y	N	N	Maximum number of lines to display before truncation occurs with an ellipse (default is 0 – no truncation)
prompt	N	Y	Y	Text that will be displayed prior to the user typing in a value of his or her own
restrict	N	Y	Y	The set of permitted characters allowed, specified with regexp-like ranges
selectable	N	Y	Y	Whether the text can be selected (true by default)
selectionActivePosition	N	Y	Y	Read-only position of the selection end
selectionAnchorPosition	N	Y	Y	Read-only position of the selection start
showTruncationTip	Y	N	N	Boolean property for whether a tool-tip will be shown when the text is truncated (default is false)
text	Y	Y	Y	The text that will be displayed by the component
typicalText	N	Y	Y	Text that will be used to set the initial size of the control

To demonstrate the different styles and capabilities of the text components, we put together a small sample application that renders the first few paragraphs of the US Declaration of Independence along with an editable list of the signatories. The code for this application is shown in Listing 3–12.

Listing 3–12. Text Component Sample Code to Display the Declaration of Independence

```
<?xml version="1.0" encoding="utf-8"?>
<s:View xmlns:fx="http://ns.adobe.com/mxml/2009"
    xmlns:s="library://ns.adobe.com/flex/spark" title="Text">
  <fx:Style>
    @namespace s "library://ns.adobe.com/flex/spark";
    .title {
      fontFamily: Times;
      fontSize: 30;
      fontWeight: bold;
    }
    .body {
      color: #222222;
      fontFamily: Times;
      fontSize: 12;
      fontStyle: italic;
      textAlign: justify;
    }
    .main-signature {
      fontFamily: Helvetica;
      fontSize: 18;
    }
    .state-signatures {
      fontFamily: Helvetica;
      fontSize: 12;
    }
  </fx:Style>
  <s:VGroup left="15" top="15" right="15" width="100%" gap="12">
    <s:Label styleName="title" text="Declaration of Independence"/>
    <s:Label styleName="body" width="100%"
        text="When in the Course of human events, it becomes necessary for one people
to …"
        />
    <s:Label styleName="body" width="100%" maxDisplayedLines="12"
        text="We hold these truths to be self-evident, that all men are created equal,
that they are …"
        />
    <s:HGroup verticalAlign="baseline" width="100%">
      <s:Label styleName="main-signature" text="President of Congress:"/>
      <s:TextInput styleName="main-signature" text="John Hancock" editable="false"
width="100%"/>
    </s:HGroup>
    <s:Label styleName="main-signature" text="State Representatives:"/>
    <s:TextArea styleName="state-signatures" width="100%"
        text="Josiah Bartlett, William Whipple, Matthew Thornton, Samuel Adams, John
Adams, …"
        />
  </s:VGroup>
</s:View>
```

Note the use of inline CSS to abstract the styles out from the code. It is also possible to directly declare the styles on the text components as XML attributes, although for modularity you would probably prefer to go the opposite direction and extract the CSS to a separate file altogether.

Running this example would give you the output shown in Figure 3–12.

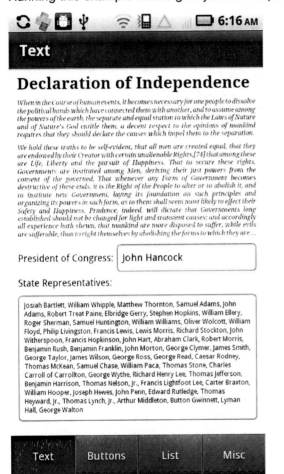

Figure 3–12. *Declaration of Independence test sample*

As an exercise to test out the text components, try making the following changes to the application:

- Use password protection on the TextArea component.

- Change the sizing of the TextInput to exactly match the initial text size.

- Change the TextInput default text to be a prompt that disappears when the user starts typing.

- Change the styling and interactivity of the TextInput to match that of a Label.

> **TIP:** Using a TextInput with editability disabled and similar styling to a Label is higher performance than using a Label component directly, due to the use of the StyleableTextField implementation behind the scenes.

Soft Keyboard Support

When using the text components, the Android soft keyboard will automatically trigger upon focus as you would expect. However, sometimes you need finer-grained control over when the soft keyboard gets triggered and what happens when it gets activated.

The soft keyboard in Flex is controlled by the application focus. When a component that has the needsSoftKeyboard property set to true is given the focus, the soft keyboard will come to the front and the stage will scroll so that the selected component is visible. When that component loses focus, the soft keyboard will disappear and the stage will return to its normal position.

With the understanding of the focus, you can control the soft keyboard by doing the following:

- *To show the soft keyboard declaratively*: Set needsSoftKeyboard to true for your component.

- *To show the soft keyboard programmatically*: Call requestSoftKeyboard() on a component that already has needsSoftKeyboard set.

- *To hide the soft keyboard*: Call setFocus() on a component that does not have needsSoftKeyboard set.

This works fine for components that do not normally trigger the soft keyboard; however, for components that automatically raise the keyboard, setting needsSoftKeyboard to false has no effect. A workaround to prevent the keyboard from popping up on these components is to listen for the activating event and suppress it with code like the following:

```
<fx:Script>
  <![CDATA[
    private function preventActivate(event:SoftKeyboardEvent):void {
      event.preventDefault();
    }
  ]]>
</fx:Script>
<s:TextArea text="I am a text component, but have no keyboard?"
  softKeyboardActivating="preventActivate(event)"/>
```

This code catches the softKeyboardActivating event on the TextArea component and suppresses the default action of raising the soft keyboard.

In addition to getting events on activation, you can also catch `softKeyboardActivate` and `softKeyboardDeactivate` events in order to perform actions based on the soft keyboard status.

Listing 3–13 shows a soft keyboard sample application that demonstrates all these techniques used together to take complete control over the soft keyboard.

Listing 3–13. *Soft Keyboard Interaction Example Code*

```
<?xml version="1.0" encoding="utf-8"?>
<s:Application xmlns:fx="http://ns.adobe.com/mxml/2009"
        xmlns:s="library://ns.adobe.com/flex/spark"
        splashScreenImage="@Embed('ProAndroidFlash400.png')">
  <fx:Script>
    <![CDATA[
      [Bindable]
      private var state:String;

      [Bindable]
      private var type:String;

      private function handleActivating(event:SoftKeyboardEvent):void {
        state = "Activating...";
        type = event.triggerType;
      }

      private function handleActivate(event:SoftKeyboardEvent):void {
        state = "Active";
        type = event.triggerType;
      }

      private function handleDeactivate(event:SoftKeyboardEvent):void {
        state = "Deactive";
        type = event.triggerType;
      }

      private function preventActivate(event:SoftKeyboardEvent):void {
        event.preventDefault();
      }
    ]]>
  </fx:Script>
  <s:VGroup left="20" top="20" right="20" gap="15"
      softKeyboardActivating="handleActivating(event)"
      softKeyboardActivate="handleActivate(event)"
      softKeyboardDeactivate="handleDeactivate(event)">
    <s:HGroup>
      <s:Label text="Keyboard State: " fontWeight="bold"/>
      <s:Label text="{state}"/>
    </s:HGroup>
    <s:HGroup>
      <s:Label text="Trigger Type: " fontWeight="bold"/>
      <s:Label text="{type}"/>
    </s:HGroup>
    <s:Button id="needy" label="I Need the Keyboard" needsSoftKeyboard="true"
emphasized="true"/>
    <s:TextArea text="I am a text component, but have no keyboard?"
        softKeyboardActivating="preventActivate(event)"/>
```

```
    <s:HGroup width="100%" gap="15">
      <s:Button label="Hide Keyboard" click="{setFocus()}" width="50%"/>
      <s:Button label="Show Keyboard" click="{needy.requestSoftKeyboard()}"
width="50%"/>
    </s:HGroup>
  </s:VGroup>
</s:Application>
```

This code creates several controls and attaches actions to them so that you can hide and show the soft keyboard at will, as well as see the current soft keyboard state as reported by the events that trickle up. Upon running the application, you will see a UI like that shown in Figure 3–13.

Figure 3–13. *Sample application that demonstrates how to control the soft keyboard*

Notice that the TextArea control, which normally triggers the soft keyboard, no longer brings it up, while the highlighted button immediately raises the soft keyboard whenever it gets focus. The two buttons at the bottom to show and hide the keyboard merely play focus tricks to get Flash to show and hide the keyboard at will.

You can use the same techniques in your application to take full control over the soft keyboard.

Button Controls

Perhaps one of the most basic elements of any UI is the button. It has existed since the very first graphical user interface on the Xerox Alto in 1973. Figure 3–14 shows a picture of the desk-sized Alto along with the button style used in its file manager. We have come a long way since then, but the basic concepts have not changed much.

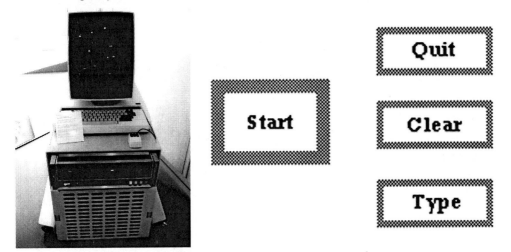

Figure 3–14. *Image of a Xerox Alto (left) and a reproduction of the button style used in its GUI (right)*

Flex has several built-in button controls with mobile-optimized styles for rendering them on device at a usable size. These include the following button types:

- Button
- CheckBox
- RadioButton
- ButtonBar

The standard Button control is highly customizable, including the ability to include an embedded image icon. The CheckBox control provides a custom button with a label and a visual toggle that can be enabled or disabled by clicking. The RadioButton is similar to a CheckBox, but uses a circular indicator and works together with a group of related RadioButtons, only one of which can be selected at once. Finally, the ButtonBar merges together a set of toggle buttons in a row, only one of which can be selected at a given time, similar to a RadioButton group.

All of these controls have similar styles that can be used to customize them. Due to the difference in mobile skins, not all of the desktop styles are available, such as cffHinting, direction, and renderingMode. Table 3–5 lists the mobile-enabled styles on the button classes.

Table 3–5. *Button Styles Recommended for Mobile Use*

Style	Button	Check Box	Radio Button	Button Bar Button	Description
accentColor	Y	N	N	N	Color used when the button emphasis is set to true
color	Y	Y	Y	Y	Color used for the text of the button
focusAlpha	Y	Y	Y	Y	The alpha value (opacity) for the focus ring
focusColor	Y	Y	Y	Y	The color used to paint the component's focus ring
fontFamily	Y	Y	Y	Y	The name of the font to be used for text rendering (can be a comma-separated list of fonts in order of preference)
fontSize	Y	Y	Y	Y	The size of the font used for rendering in pixel units
fontStyle	Y	Y	Y	Y	The font style, which can be italic or normal (default is normal)
fontWeight	Y	Y	Y	Y	The font weight, which can be bold or normal (default is normal)
icon	Y	N	N	Y	An image that will be rendered next to the button text; can be a Bitmap, BitmapData, DisplayObject, or image file name
iconPlacement	Y	Y	Y	Y	Placement of the icon, which can be top, right, bottom, or left (the default)
leading	Y	Y	Y	Y	Vertical space between lines of text

Style	Button	Check Box	Radio Button	Button Bar Button	Description
letterSpacing	Y	Y	Y	Y	Space between letters in pixel units
locale	Y	Y	Y	Y	Text locale used for internationalization
repeatDelay	Y	Y	Y	Y	Delay before starting to repeat buttonDown events (default is 500 milliseconds)
repeatInterval	Y	Y	Y	Y	Delay between the buttonDown event repeats (default is 35 milliseconds)
symbolColor	N	Y	Y	N	Color of the check mark or radial button symbol
textAlign	Y	N	N	Y	Alignment of text within the container, which can be left, right, or center (default is left)
textAlpha	Y	Y	Y	Y	The alpha value (opacity) for the text displayed in the button
textDecoration	Y	Y	Y	Y	The text decoration, which can be underline or none
textShadowAlpha	Y	N	N	Y	The alpha value (opacity) for the text shadow
textShadowColor	Y	N	N	Y	The color of the text shadow
touchDelay	Y	Y	Y	Y	The delay before a touch action is registered; this is set to 100ms when in a Scroller component to prevent flicker.

Most of these styles are supported across all the button types, including buttons embedded in a ButtonBar of type ButtonBarButton. There are a few exceptions where styles have been explicitly excluded from subclasses, such as textAlign and icon, which are not supported in either CheckBoxes or Radiobuttons. For setting the style on ButtonBarButtons, it is usually sufficient to set the style on the ButtonBar and let CSS inheritance take care of applying it to the child buttons that get created.

Due to the difference in functionality, the available properties for manipulating the buttons differ slightly as well. Table 3–6 lists the available public properties, including which button class they apply to.

Table 3–6. *Public Button Properties Recommended for Mobile Use*

Property	Button	Check Box	Radio Button	Button Bar Button	Description
autoRepeat	Y	Y	Y	Y	Whether the button dispatches repeated buttonDown events when the mouse is held down
content	Y	Y	Y	Y	Arbitrary object to be displayed by a custom button skin
emphasized	Y	N	N	N	Whether this button is the default and should be displayed with the accentColor
label	Y	Y	Y	Y	The text that will be displayed on the button
selected	N	Y	Y	Y	Whether this button is in a selected state (true) or deselected state (false)
stickyHighlighting	Y	Y	Y	Y	By default buttons display their down skin only when the mouse is hovering; set this to true to keep the down skin until the user releases the mouse.

In addition to these properties, there are a few events and methods on the button classes that help with interactivity. The most important of these is the clickHandler function that gets called whenever the user presses and releases the mouse over a button. In addition you can listen for a buttonDown event and override the buttonReleased and mouseEventHandler functions to do more advanced interactions. An additional event available on the toggleable button subclasses (CheckBox, RadioButton, and ButtonBarButton) is the change event, which gets triggered whenever the selected property changes.

To demonstrate the use of different button controls, we put together a small button sample that parodies the complicated set of controls on a modern microwave. The code for this example is shown in Listing 3–14.

Listing 3–14. *Code for the Modern Microwave Example*

```
<?xml version="1.0" encoding="utf-8"?>
<s:View xmlns:fx="http://ns.adobe.com/mxml/2009"
```

```
      xmlns:s="library://ns.adobe.com/flex/spark" title="Buttons">
  <fx:Style>
    @namespace s "library://ns.adobe.com/flex/spark";
    .number {
      touchDelay: 500;
    }
    .header {
      color: #660000;
    }
  </fx:Style>
  <s:VGroup left="60" right="60" top="20" width="100%">
    <s:ButtonBar styleName="header" requireSelection="true" width="100%">
      <s:dataProvider>
        <s:ArrayCollection source="['Defrost', 'Cook', 'Irradiate']" />
      </s:dataProvider>
    </s:ButtonBar>
    <s:RadioButton label="Meat" color="#404040" symbolColor="green"/>
    <s:RadioButton label="Poultry" color="#404040" symbolColor="yellow"/>
    <s:RadioButton label="Alien Fish" color="#d02525" symbolColor="#d02525"/>
    <s:CheckBox label="Trigger Meltdown" symbolColor="red"/>
    <s:HGroup width="100%">
      <s:Button styleName="number" label="9" width="100%"/>
      <s:Button styleName="number" label="8" width="100%"/>
      <s:Button styleName="number" label="7" width="100%"/>
    </s:HGroup>
    <s:HGroup width="100%">
      <s:Button styleName="number" label="6" width="100%"/>
      <s:Button styleName="number" label="5" width="100%"/>
      <s:Button styleName="number" label="4" width="100%"/>
    </s:HGroup>
    <s:HGroup width="100%">
      <s:Button styleName="number" label="3" width="100%"/>
      <s:Button styleName="number" label="2" width="100%"/>
      <s:Button styleName="number" label="1" width="100%"/>
    </s:HGroup>
    <s:HGroup width="100%">
      <s:Button styleName="number" label="π" width="100%"/>
      <s:Button styleName="number" label="0" width="100%"/>
      <s:Button styleName="number" icon="@Embed('alien.gif')" width="100%"/>
    </s:HGroup>
    <s:HGroup width="100%">
      <s:Button label="End" width="100%"/>
      <s:Button label="Start" width="100%" emphasized="true"/>
    </s:HGroup>
  </s:VGroup>
</s:View>
```

When run on a mobile device, the application will look similar to that shown in Figure 3–15.

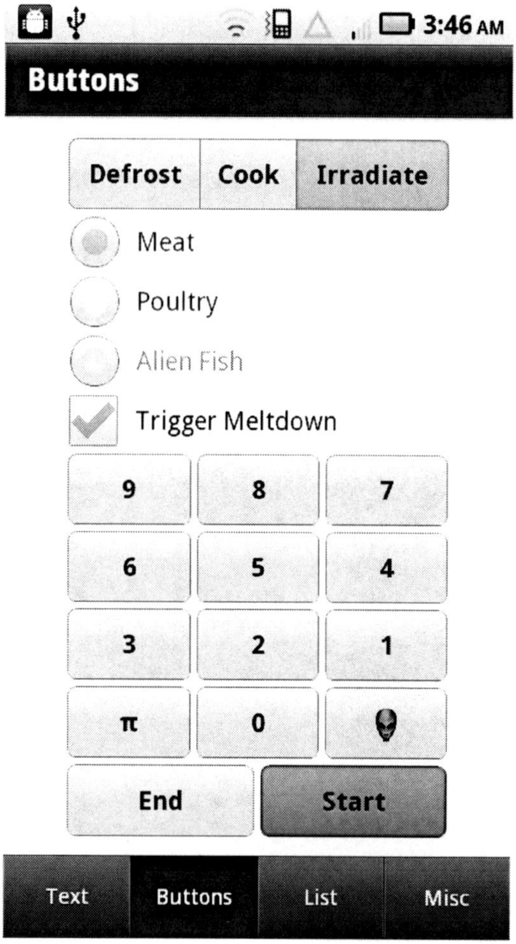

Figure 3–15. *Output of running the modern microwave example*

To practice with some of the new styles and properties you have learned, try the following:

- Change the size and color of the label font in the number buttons.
- Add a clickHandler that will play a sound when the microwave is started.
- Add a Label that repeatedly appends the number on the button to the text.

Flex Lists

Lists are probably one of the most important controls for mobile applications. Due to the limited screen real estate, they take the place of data grids, and are often used for drill-down navigation through menus or hierarchical structures.

The Flex `List` control has been completely revamped for mobile use, and behaves similarly to what you would expect from a mobile device. This includes large graphics with icons and decorators, and a scroll "bounce" as you pass the beginning or end of a `List`.

At its simplest, you can create and display a Flex `List` by simply giving it a collection of objects to render, as shown in Listing 3–15.

Listing 3–15. *Code to Create a* `List` *from an* `ArrayCollection`

```
<s:List width="100%" height="100%">
  <s:ArrayCollection source="['Alabama', 'Alaska', 'Arizona']" />
</s:List>
```

The foregoing code sets the default `dataProvider` property to an `ArrayCollection` of strings. By default it will use the `LabelItemRenderer`, which simply displays each entry of the `List` in a `StyleableTextField`. Executing this program will produce a basic `List` as shown in Figure 3–16.

Figure 3–16. *Basic* `List` *example using the* `LabelItemRenderer`

To create a more complicated `List`, you can change the `itemRenderer` to use a more complicated renderer. Flex 4.5 comes with a second built-in renderer called the `IconItemRenderer`, which has additional capabilities to display the following item components:

- Icon: A graphic icon displayed to the left of the text, selected by setting `iconField` or assigning `iconFunction`

- Label: A single line of text displayed in a large font, selected by setting `labelField` or assigning `labelFunction`

- Message: A multiline description displayed in a smaller typeface, selected by setting `messageField` or assigning `messageFunction`

- Decorator: An icon displayed on the right side of the image, set on the `decorator` property

To demonstrate the use of `IconItemRenderers`, we put together a sample that lets you browse the list of mottos and commemorative coins for all 50 states. The code for this sample is shown in Listing 3–16.

Listing 3–16. `IconItemRenderer` *Sample Application Code*

```
<?xml version="1.0" encoding="utf-8"?>
<s:View xmlns:fx="http://ns.adobe.com/mxml/2009"
    xmlns:s="library://ns.adobe.com/flex/spark" title="List">
  <fx:Declarations>
    <s:ArrayCollection id="stateInfo">
      <fx:Object state='Alabama' coin="@Embed('coins/Alabama.jpg')"
        motto="Audemus jura nostra defendere -- We dare defend our rights"/>
      <fx:Object state='Alaska' coin="@Embed('coins/Alaska.jpg')"
        motto="Futurum aquilonem -- North to the future"/>
      <fx:Object state='Arizona' coin="@Embed('coins/Arizona.jpg')"
        motto="Ditat Deus -- God enriches"/>
      <fx:Object state='Arkansas' coin="@Embed('coins/Arkansas.jpg')"
        motto="Regnat populus -- The people rule"/>
      <fx:Object state='California' coin="@Embed('coins/California.jpg')"
        motto="Eureka (      ) -- I have found it"/>
      ...
    </s:ArrayCollection>
  </fx:Declarations>
  <s:Group width="100%" height="100%">
    <s:List dataProvider="{stateInfo}" width="100%" height="100%">
      <s:itemRenderer>
        <fx:Component>
          <s:IconItemRenderer labelField="state" messageField="motto" iconField="coin"
              decorator="@Embed('usflag.png')"/>
        </fx:Component>
      </s:itemRenderer>
    </s:List>
    <s:Label text="United States Mint images." fontSize="10" left="2" bottom="2"/>
  </s:Group>
</s:View>
```

Notice that instead of having a nested `dataProvider`, we abstracted it out to a declaration and referenced it by `id`. Typically your data would be provided by a web service or database lookup, in which case you would simply substitute your `dataProvider` for the one used in the sample code.

For the `IconItemRenderer`, we created an inline instance using the `Component` tag and assigned it directly to the `itemRenderer` property. Also notice that we chose to use the `*Field` version to select the label, message, and icon. This is preferable for performance reasons, because it means that the `IconItemRenderer` knows the value is static and can do more caching to improve performance.

Figure 3–17 shows the state information example running on a mobile device.

Figure 3–17. *State information application showing commemorative coins and mottos*

You can further customize the list by taking advantage of the styling properties on the IconItemRenderer class. Here are some suggestions on changes you can try experimenting with:

- Change the font family, size, and color to further distinguish the motto from the state name.

> **TIP:** Styles set on the IconItemRenderer will be inherited by the label, while the messageStyleName class can be used to change the style of the message.

- Increase the size of the coin graphic by changing its width and scale mode programmatically.

    ▨   Enable multi-select on the List component using the `allowMultipleSelection` property.

Slider, Scroller, and BusyIndicator Controls

There are several other controls that you will find useful in the creation of mobile applications. These include the `HSlider`, `Scroller`, and `BusyIndicator` controls.

HSlider

The `HSlider` is a standard horizontal slider control that lets you specify a range of values over which the user can select. Some of the features of the `HSlider` include the following:

    ▨   A mobile-sized slider bar

    ▨   A data tip that shows the precise value

    ▨   Support for configurable value ranges and stepping

The style of the scroller itself is limited to a few simple properties, including `focusAlpha`, `focusColor`, `liveDragging`, and `slideDuration`. The first two styles are the same as their counterparts on other controls. In addition you can disable `liveDragging` by setting it to `false`, which will force the value to get updated only when the user lets go of the mouse button. The `slideDuration` style controls how long it takes for the thumb to move when the background of the slider is pressed, which defaults to 300 milliseconds.

In addition to this, you can control the display of the data tip with several properties, including a `dataTipFormatFunction` that turns the `Numeric` value into a string, `dataTipPrecision` to choose the number of decimal places, and `showDataTip`, which lets you disable data tips altogether. The data tip text uses the same text style properties as the button components mentioned in the previous section. For mobile use, the following text styles are supported: `fontFamily`, `fontStyle`, `leading`, `letterSpacing`, `locale`, and `textDecoration`.

To control the range of the slider, you have several properties available, including `minimum`, `maximum`, `stepSize`, and `snapInterval`. These are all `Numeric` values and let you control the extents of the slider as well as the stepping and snapping behavior. You can set the initial value of the slider by using the `value` property. This property is also updated dynamically as the user interacts with the slider.

Finally, there are several events you can track to do interactive behavior when the slider is in use. This includes events on `change`, `changing`, `thumbDrag`, `thumbPress`, and `thumbRelease`.

Scroller

The Scroller is a mobile-enabled control that lets the user page around a body of content that is larger than the viewable area. The mobile skin is a complete redesign that uses touch events to pan around the viewport rather than static scrollbars. This makes it much easier to manipulate on a touchscreen display, while providing equivalent functionality.

The child of the Scroller must implement the IViewport interface, which includes the Group, DataGroup, and RicheditableText components in the Spark library. The following example code shows how you can create a new Scroller instance to navigate around a static image:

```
<s:Scroller width="100%" height="100%">
  <s:VGroup>
    <s:BitmapImage source="@Embed('/ProAndroidFlash.png')"/>
  </s:VGroup>
</s:Scroller>
```

In this example, the default property of viewport is set to a VGroup, which contains a large BitmapImage. The Group is simply there to wrap the BitmapImage, ensuring the outer component is of type IViewport, but otherwise is invisible to the user. Upon running this example, the user would be able to drag across the screen to navigate around the image.

Beyond this there is really nothing to customize due to the simplified mobile user interface. None of the text or scrollbar styles apply, including fonts, colors, and hiding or showing the scrollbars.

BusyIndicator

This final component displays a simple busy indicator widget with a circular set of rotating blades. It will continually animate the graphics while displayed on screen, indicating that activity, such as loading, is going on in the background.

The diameter of the BusyIndicator is calculated as the minimum of the height and width, rounded down to a multiple of two. The only other two dials specific to the BusyIndicator component are a rotationInterval to control the speed of the animation, specified in milliseconds, and a symbolColor that lets you change the color used in the waiting graphic.

Combined Sample

To demonstrate the use of these three controls, we put together a quick demonstration that uses all the controls together to provide zooming and panning around an image. The HSlider control is used to change the zoom level of the image, the Scroller component provides panning while the image is zoomed in, and the BusyIndicator shows activity when either of these actions is taking place.

The full code for this sample is shown in Listing 3–17.

Listing 3–17. *Example Code Demonstrating Use of the* HSlider, Scroller, *and* BusyIndicator *Controls*

```
<?xml version="1.0" encoding="utf-8"?>
<s:View xmlns:fx="http://ns.adobe.com/mxml/2009"
    xmlns:s="library://ns.adobe.com/flex/spark" title="Misc">
  <fx:Script>
    <![CDATA[
      [Bindable]
      private var scale:Number = .5;
      [Bindable]
      private var busy:Boolean = false;
    ]]>
  </fx:Script>
  <s:VGroup top="15" left="15" right="15" bottom="15" gap="10" width="100%"
height="100%">
    <s:HGroup width="100%" verticalAlign="middle">
      <s:Label text="Scale:"/>
      <s:HSlider width="100%" value="@{scale}" minimum=".01" maximum="1" stepSize="0"
          changeStart="{busy=true}" changeEnd="{busy=false}"/>
      <s:BusyIndicator visible="{busy}"/>
    </s:HGroup>
    <s:Scroller width="100%" height="100%"
        mouseDown="{busy=true}" mouseUp="{busy=false}" mouseOut="{busy=false}">
      <s:VGroup>
        <s:BitmapImage source="@Embed('/ProAndroidFlash.png')"
            scaleX="{scale}" scaleY="{scale}"/>
      </s:VGroup>
    </s:Scroller>
  </s:VGroup>
</s:View>
```

Upon running this example, you will see output similar to Figure 3–18, which is captured mid-stream during a Scroller drag operation.

Figure 3–18. *Scroller example captured during a pan operation*

Try manipulating the controls to zoom and pan the image, and feel free to replace the image in this example with one of your choosing.

After reading the past few sections on all the available controls and experimenting with the samples, you now have a very good understanding of the UI capabilities of the Flex toolkit.

Summary

This chapter was a detailed examination of the anatomy of mobile Flex applications. Armed with this knowledge, you should now be able to begin writing your own mobile applications. The following topics are now part of your development arsenal:

- The TabbedViewNavigatorApplication and ViewNavigatorApplication application containers and when to use one or the other

- The relationship between the ViewNavigator and Views

- How to specify the animated transitions between Views

- How to pass data back and forth between Views

- The proper methods to use when persisting application state between runs

- Which controls are optimized for mobile applications

- How to use text controls to display output and collection input from the user

- How to control Android's soft keyboard

- Some tricks and tips for using and styling mobile Button controls

- How to use IconItemRenderers to display rich content in your List controls

- How to use sliders to enter values within a range

- The use of Scrollers to pan around in content that is larger than the constrained screen of mobile devices

- How to use a BusyIndicator to inform the user of an operation in progress

You now know how to create mobile applications. In the next chapter, we'll show you how to add some pizzazz with graphics, animation, and charts!

Chapter 4

Graphics and Animation

Graphics are a fun "crowd pleaser" for people of all ages. If you enjoy graphics as much as we do, you'll be glad to discover that the Flex-based graphics code samples that work on a desktop browser will also work on a mobile device. In addition, you can take advantage of touch-related events and gestures (which were discussed in Chapter 2) when you create graphics-based applications for mobile devices.

The first part of this chapter shows you how to render various two-dimensional shapes, such as rectangles, ellipses, Bezier curves, and paths. The second part of this chapter contains a code sample of rendering geometric objects with linear gradients and radial gradients. The third part of this chapter provides a code sample that illustrates how to use filter effects, including `Blur`, `DropShadow`, and `Glow`.

You will also see mobile code samples that illustrate how to perform transformations (translating, scaling, rotating, and shearing) on graphics shapes that are discussed in the first part of this chapter. Next you'll learn how to render charts and graphs (which use MX components), followed by the final example in this chapter, which shows you how to create a sketching program that ties together various graphics-related notions introduced earlier in the chapter. This sketching program also includes touch events, the ability to sketch on top of a JPG file, and a save option that enables you to save your sketches as a JPG on a mobile device.

After you have read this chapter, you'll have a good sense of the graphics-related capabilities for mobile devices, and perhaps some of the code samples in this chapter will inspire you to write your own esthetically pleasing graphics code!

Using Spark Primitives for 2D Shapes

The mobile code samples in this section illustrate how to render various 2D shapes, such as rectangles, ellipses, Bezier curves, polygons, and paths. In addition, some of the code samples contain multiple graphics images with various shading techniques, which will enable you to make a side-by-side comparison of the code for the graphics images.

Drawing Rectangles and Ellipses

Let's start with rendering two rectangles and an ellipse, which are two 2D shapes that are familiar to everyone. Create a new Flex mobile project called RectEllipse1, using the Mobile Application template, and add the code shown in Listing 4–1.

Listing 4–1. *Rendering Two Rectangles and an Ellipse*

```
<?xml version="1.0" encoding="utf-8"?>
<s:View xmlns:fx="http://ns.adobe.com/mxml/2009"
        xmlns:s="library://ns.adobe.com/flex/spark"
        title="Rectangle and Ellipse">
    <s:Rect id="rect1" x="10" y="10" width="250" height="200">
        <s:fill>
            <s:SolidColor color="0xFF0000"/>
        </s:fill>
        <s:stroke>
            <s:SolidColorStroke color="0xFFFF00" weight="4"/>
        </s:stroke>
    </s:Rect>

    <s:Ellipse id="ellipse1" x="10" y="220" width="250" height="200">
        <s:fill>
            <s:SolidColor color="0x0000FF"/>
        </s:fill>
        <s:stroke>
            <s:SolidColorStroke color="0xFF0000" weight="4"/>
        </s:stroke>
    </s:Ellipse>

  <s:Rect id="rect2" x="10" y="460" width="250" height="100">
    <s:fill>
      <s:SolidColor color="0xFFFF00"/>
    </s:fill>
    <s:stroke>
      <s:SolidColorStroke color="0x0000FF" weight="8"/>
    </s:stroke>
  </s:Rect>

    <fx:Declarations>
        <!-- Place non-visual elements (e.g., services, value objects) here -->
    </fx:Declarations>
</s:View>
```

Listing 4-1 starts with an XML Rect element that specifies values for the attributes id, x, y, width, and height. Note that the XML Rect element contains an XML fill element and an XML stroke element instead of a fill attribute and a stroke attribute, which differs from SVG, where you specify the fill and stroke values via attributes. However, the XML stroke element contains an XML SolidColorStroke child element that specifies the color and weight as attributes instead of values of XML elements. Note that SVG uses a stroke and a stroke-width attribute instead of a color attribute and a weight attribute.

Listing 4–1 also contains an XML `Ellipse` element that defines an ellipse, with almost identical attributes and values for attributes as the XML `Rect` element, but the generated output is an ellipse instead of a rectangle.

The second XML `Rect` element is similar to the first `Rect` element, but with different colors and a different position on the screen.

Figure 4–1 displays the two rectangles and the ellipse.

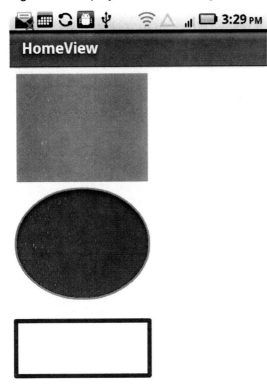

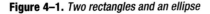

Figure 4–1. *Two rectangles and an ellipse*

Using Linear and Radial Gradients

Flex mobile applications support linear gradients as well as radial gradients. As the name implies, a linear gradient calculates intermediate colors in a linear fashion between the start color and the end color. For instance, if a linear gradient varies from black to red, then the initial color is black and the final color is red, with a linear "transition" of the shades of the colors "between" black and red.

A radial gradient differs from a linear gradient in that the transition occurs in a radial fashion. Think of a pebble dropped in a pond, and watch the ripple-like effect of the circles of increasing radius, and that gives you a sense of how radial gradients are rendered.

As an illustration, the following mobile code renders a rectangle with a linear gradient and an ellipse with a radial gradient. Create a new Flex mobile project called LinearRadial1, using the Mobile Application template, and add the code shown in Listing 4-2.

Listing 4-2. *Using Linear Gradients and Radial Gradients*

```
<?xml version="1.0" encoding="utf-8"?>
<s:View xmlns:fx="http://ns.adobe.com/mxml/2009"
        xmlns:s="library://ns.adobe.com/flex/spark"
        xmlns:mx="library://ns.adobe.com/flex/mx"
        title="Linear and Radial Gradients">

  <s:Panel title="Linear and Radial Gradients">
    <s:Group>
      <s:Rect id="rect1" x="10" y="10"
            height="250" width="300">
        <s:fill>
          <s:LinearGradient>
            <s:GradientEntry color="0xFF0000"
                             ratio="0"   alpha=".5"/>
            <s:GradientEntry color="0xFFFF00"
                             ratio=".33" alpha=".5"/>
            <s:GradientEntry color="0x0000FF"
                             ratio=".66" alpha=".5"/>
          </s:LinearGradient>
        </s:fill>

        <s:stroke>
          <s:SolidColorStroke color="0x000000" weight="2"/>
        </s:stroke>
      </s:Rect>

      <s:Ellipse id="ellipse1" x="10" y="270"
                   height="300" width="250">
        <s:fill>
          <s:RadialGradient>
            <s:GradientEntry color="0xFF0000"
                             ratio="0"   alpha="1"/>
            <s:GradientEntry color="0xFFFF00"
                             ratio=".9" alpha="1"/>
          </s:RadialGradient>
        </s:fill>

        <s:stroke>
          <s:SolidColorStroke color="0x000000" weight="2"/>
        </s:stroke>
      </s:Ellipse>
    </s:Group>
```

```
    </s:Panel>

    <fx:Declarations>
      <!-- Place non-visual elements (e.g., services, value objects) here -->
    </fx:Declarations>
</s:View>
```

Listing 4–2 contains one XML Panel element that contains one XML Group element whose attributes specify the layout of the panel. The XML Group element contains two XML child elements: an XML Rect element and an XML Ellipse element. The XML Rect element defines a rectangle with a linear gradient, as shown here:

```
        <s:Rect id="rect1" x="10" y="10"
                      height="100" width="200">
            <s:fill>
                <s:LinearGradient>
                    <s:GradientEntry color="0xFF0000"
                                     ratio="0"   alpha=".5"/>
                    <s:GradientEntry color="0xFFFF00"
                                     ratio=".33" alpha=".5"/>
                    <s:GradientEntry color="0x0000FF"
                                     ratio=".66" alpha=".5"/>
                </s:LinearGradient>
            </s:fill>

            <s:stroke>
                <s:SolidColorStroke color="0x000000" weight="2"/>
            </s:stroke>
        </s:Rect>
```

The preceding XML Rect element specifies values for the attributes id, x, y, width, and height. Next, the XML Rect element contains an XML fill element (as you saw in the previous example) that in turn contains an XML LinearGradient element that specifies three XML GradientEntry elements, each of which specifies a decimal value (between 0 and 1) for the ratio and alpha attributes. The last section of the XML Rect element contains an XML stroke element, which contains an XML SolidColorStroke element that specifies values for the attributes color and weight.

Listing 4–2 also contains an XML Ellipse element that defines an ellipse with a radial gradient. This code contains almost the same attributes and values as the XML Rect element, except that it represents an ellipse instead of a rectangle.

Figure 4–2 displays a rectangle with a linear gradient and an ellipse with a radial gradient.

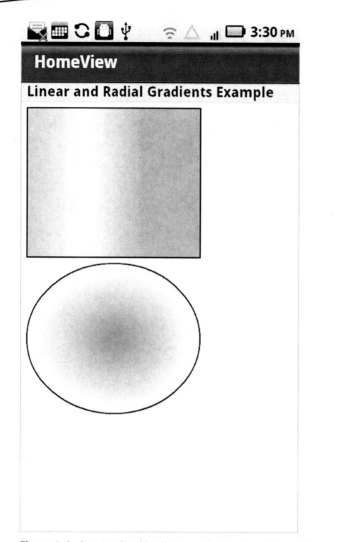

Figure 4–2. *A rectangle with a linear gradient and an ellipse with a radial gradient*

Rendering Cubic Bezier Curves

Flex supports cubic Bezier curves (which have two endpoints and two control points) and quadratic Bezier curves (which have two endpoints and only one control point). You can easily identify a cubic Bezier curve because it starts with the letter "C" (or "c"), and a quadratic Bezier curve starts with the letter "Q" (or "q"). The uppercase letters "C" and "Q" specify an "absolute" location, whereas the lowercase letters "c" and "q" specify a position that is relative to the preceding point in the XML Path element.

The first point listed in the points for a cubic or quadratic Bezier curve is the first control point, followed by another control point in the case of cubic Bezier curves, and then the second endpoint. The first endpoint in quadratic and cubic Bezier curves is the preceding point that is specified in the XML Path element; if no point is specified, then the origin (0,0) is used as the first endpoint.

You can also specify a sequence of Bezier curves using the letter "S" (for a cubic Bezier curve) or the letter "T" (for a quadratic Bezier curve).

Create a new Flex mobile project called BezierCurves1, using the Mobile Application template, and add the code shown in Listing 4–3, which displays the code for four Bezier curves: one cubic Bezier curve, one quadratic Bezier curve, two combined cubic Bezier curves, and a combined cubic and quadratic Bezier curve.

Listing 4–3. *Rendering Cubic and Quadratic Bezier Curves*

```xml
<?xml version="1.0" encoding="utf-8"?>
<s:View xmlns:fx="http://ns.adobe.com/mxml/2009"
        xmlns:s="library://ns.adobe.com/flex/spark"
        title="Cubic and Quadratic Bezier Curves">

    <s:Panel width="500" height="500"
                    title="Cubic and Quadratic Bezier Curves">
        <!-- cubic Bezier curve -->
        <s:Path data="C 100 150 200 20 300 100">
            <s:fill>
            <s:LinearGradient rotation="90">
              <s:GradientEntry color="#FFFFFF" alpha="0.5"/>
              <s:GradientEntry color="#FF0000" alpha="0.5"/>
            </s:LinearGradient>
            </s:fill>
            <s:stroke>
              <s:SolidColorStroke color="0x0000FF" weight="4"/>
            </s:stroke>
        </s:Path>

        <!-- quadratic Bezier curve -->
        <s:Path data="Q 250 200 100 300">
          <s:fill>
            <s:RadialGradient rotation="90">
              <s:GradientEntry color="#000000" alpha="0.8"/>
              <s:GradientEntry color="#0000FF" alpha="0.8"/>
            </s:RadialGradient>
          </s:fill>

          <s:stroke>
            <s:SolidColorStroke color="0xFF0000" weight="8"/>
          </s:stroke>
        </s:Path>

        <!-- two combined cubic Bezier curves -->
        <s:Path data="C 100 300 200 20 300 100 S 250 200 300 250">
          <s:fill>
            <s:LinearGradient rotation="90">
              <s:GradientEntry color="#FF0000" alpha="0.5"/>
              <s:GradientEntry color="#FFFF00" alpha="0.5"/>
            </s:LinearGradient>
          </s:fill>

          <s:stroke>
```

```
        <s:SolidColorStroke color="0x00FF00" weight="2"/>
      </s:stroke>
    </s:Path>

    <!-- two combined cubic and quadratic Bezier curves -->
    <s:Path data="C 250 400 200 150 350 100 T 250 250 400 280">
      <s:fill>
        <s:LinearGradient rotation="90">
          <s:GradientEntry color="#FFFF00" alpha="0.5"/>
          <s:GradientEntry color="#FF0000" alpha="0.5"/>
        </s:LinearGradient>
      </s:fill>

      <s:stroke>
        <s:SolidColorStroke color="0x000000" weight="4"/>
      </s:stroke>
    </s:Path>
  </s:Panel>
</s:View>
```

Listing 4–3 contains an XML Panel element, which in turn contains four XML Path elements that specify Bezier curves with various types of shading. The first XML Path element specifies a cubic Bezier curve, as shown here:

```
<s:Path data="C 100 300 200 20 300 100 S 250 200 300 250">
[other elements omitted]
</s:Path>
```

The first endpoint for this cubic Bezier curve is (0,0) because no point is specified; the control points are (100,300) and (200,20); and the destination endpoint is (300,100).

This XML Path element contains an XML LinearGradient element that varies from white to red, with an opacity of 0.5, followed by a blue stroke of width 4, as shown here:

```
<s:LinearGradient rotation="90">
  <s:GradientEntry color="#FFFFFF" alpha="0.5"/>
  <s:GradientEntry color="#FF0000" alpha="0.5"/>
</s:LinearGradient>
</s:fill>
<s:stroke>
  <s:SolidColorStroke color="0x0000FF" weight="4"/>
</s:stroke>
```

The second XML Path element specifies a quadratic Bezier curve, whose first endpoint for this cubic Bezier curve is (0,0) because no point is specified; the single control point for this quadratic Bezier curve is (250,200); and the destination endpoint is (100,300). This XML Path element contains an XML LinearGradient element that varies from black to blue, with an opacity of 0.8.

The third XML Path element specifies a cubic Bezier curve that is "concatenated" with a second cubic Bezier curve, as shown here:

```
<s:Path data="C 100 300 200 20 300 100 S 250 200 300 250">
[other elements omitted]
</s:Path>
```

The two control points for this cubic Bezier curve are (100,300) and (20,300), and the destination endpoint is (300,100). The second part of this XML Path element specifies a quadratic Bezier curve whose control point is (250,200) and whose target endpoint is (300,250).

This XML Path element contains an XML LinearGradient element that specifies a linear gradient that varies from yellow to red, followed by an XML stroke element that specifies the color black and a line width of 4 units.

The final XML Path element specifies a cubic Bezier curve, followed by a second cubic Bezier curve, as shown here:

```
<s:Path data="C 250 300 200 150 350 100 T 250 250 400 280">
  [other elements omitted]
</s:Path>
```

The control points for this cubic Bezier curve are (250,300) and (200,150), and the destination endpoint is (350,100). The second part of this XML Path element specifies a quadratic Bezier curve whose control point is (250,250) and whose target endpoint is (400,280).

This XML Path element contains an XML LinearGradient element that specifies a linear gradient that varies from yellow to red, with an opacity of 0.5, followed by an XML stroke element that specifies the color black and a line width of 4 units.

Figure 4–3 displays the cubic, quadratic, and combined Bezier curves.

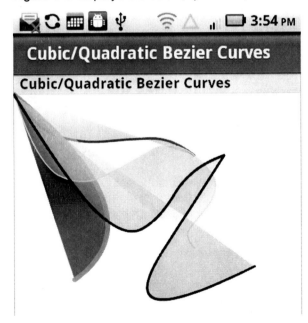

Figure 4–3. *Cubic, quadratic, and combined Bezier curves*

Another Path Element Example

In the previous example, you saw how to use the Path element in order to render a set of Bezier curves. The Path element enables you to combine other 2D shapes as well, such as line segments and Bezier curves with linear gradients and radial gradients. Create a new Flex mobile project called Path1, using the Mobile Application template, and add the code shown in Listing 4–4.

Listing 4–4. *Combining Line Segments and Bezier Curves*

```
<?xml version="1.0" encoding="utf-8"?>
<s:View xmlns:fx="http://ns.adobe.com/mxml/2009"
        xmlns:s="library://ns.adobe.com/flex/spark"
        title="Path-based Lines and Bezier Curves">

   <s:Panel width="500" height="500"
                  title="Path-based Lines and Bezier Curves">
      <s:Path data="M 50 50 L150 50 350 150 50 150z
             C 250 300 200 150 350 100 T 250 250 400 500">
         <s:fill>
           <s:LinearGradient rotation="90">
             <s:GradientEntry color="#FF0000" alpha="1"/>
             <s:GradientEntry color="#0000FF" alpha="1"/>
           </s:LinearGradient>
         </s:fill>

         <s:stroke>
           <s:SolidColorStroke color="0x000000" weight="8"/>
         </s:stroke>
      </s:Path>
   </s:Panel>
</s:View>
```

The XML Panel element in Listing 4–4 contains one XML Path element that uses line segments to render a trapezoid, followed by a pair of cubic Bezier curves. The data attribute of the XML Path element is shown here:

```
<s:Path data="M 50 50 L150 50 350 150 50 150z
       C 250 300 200 150 350 100 T 250 250 400 280">
```

The first portion of the data attribute (which starts with the letter M) specifies a trapezoid; the second portion of the data attribute (which starts with the letter C) renders a cubic Bezier curve; the third portion of the data attribute (which starts with the letter T) specifies another cubic Bezier curve.

Figure 4–4 displays a trapezoid and two cubic Bezier curves.

Figure 4–4. *A path-based trapezoid and Bezier curves*

Using Spark Filters

Flex filter effects are useful for creating rich visual effects in Flex-based applications, and these effects can really enhance the appeal of your applications. Spark primitives support a variety of filters, including Blur filter, a DropShadow filter, and a Glow filter, all of which belong to the spark.filters package.

Create a new Flex mobile project called RectLGradFilters3, using the Mobile Application template, and add the code shown in Listing 4–5.

Listing 4–5. *Drawing Rectangles with Spark Filters*

```xml
<?xml version="1.0" encoding="utf-8"?>
<s:View xmlns:fx="http://ns.adobe.com/mxml/2009"
        xmlns:s="library://ns.adobe.com/flex/spark"
        title="Rectangle: Gradient and Filters">

  <s:Rect id="rect1" x="50" y="50" height="300" width="250">
    <s:fill>
      <s:LinearGradient>
        <s:GradientEntry color="0xFF0000"
                         ratio="0"   alpha=".5"/>
          <s:GradientEntry color="0xFFFF00"
                           ratio=".33" alpha=".5"/>
          <s:GradientEntry color="0x0000FF"
                           ratio=".66" alpha=".5"/>
      </s:LinearGradient>
    </s:fill>
    <s:stroke>
      <s:SolidColorStroke color="0xFF0000" weight="2"/>
    </s:stroke>
    <s:filters>
      <s:DropShadowFilter distance="80" color="#0000FF"/>
      <s:BlurFilter/>
      <s:GlowFilter/>
    </s:filters>
  </s:Rect>
</s:View>
```

Listing 4–5 contains an XML Rect element that defines a rectangle that is rendered with a linear gradient. The ratio attribute is a decimal number between 0 and 1 that specifies the fraction of the distance from the start point to the destination point for the color transition. In Listing 4–5, the first GradientEntry element has a ratio attribute whose value is 0, which means that the rectangle is rendered with the color 0xFF0000 (hexadecimal value for red). The second GradientEntry element has a ratio attribute whose value is 0.33, which means that the rectangle is rendered with the color 0xFFFF00 (hexadecimal value for yellow) from the location that is 33% of the way from the initial location to the destination. The third GradientEntry element has a ratio attribute whose value is 0.66, and therefore the rectangle is rendered with the color 0x0000FF (hexadecimal value for blue) from the location that is 66% of the way from the initial location to the destination.

The alpha attribute is the opacity, which is a decimal number between 0 (invisible) and 1 (fully visible). The three GradientEntry elements in Listing 4–5 have an alpha attribute of 0.5, so the rectangle is partially visible. Experiment with different values for the ratio attribute and the alpha attribute so that you can find the combinations that create pleasing visual effects.

The last portion of the XML Rect element contains an XML stroke element that specifies the color red and a stroke width of 2, followed by three Spark filters, as shown here:

```xml
    <s:filters>
      <s:DropShadowFilter distance="80" color="#0000FF"/>
      <s:BlurFilter/>
      <s:GlowFilter/>
```

```
    </s:filters>
```

The three Spark filters in this example have intuitive names that suggest the effects that you can create when you include them in your code. The first Spark filter is a DropShadowFilter that adds a "drop shadow" to the XML Rect element. The second Spark filter is a BlurFilter, which adds a blurring effect. The third and final Spark filter is a GlowFilter, which creates a glow filter effect.

Figure 4–5 displays a rectangle with a linear gradient and three Spark filters.

Figure 4–5. *A rectangle with a linear gradient and three Spark filters*

Applying Transformations to Geometric Shapes

This section of the chapter shows how to apply transformations to geometric objects, including those that were discussed in the previous part of this chapter. The Spark primitives support the following effects and transformations:

- Animate
- AnimateColor
- AnimateFilter
- AnimateShaderTransition
- AnimateTransform

- Fade
- Move
- Resize
- Rotate
- Scale
- Wipe
- CrossFade

These Spark primitives are in the `spark.effects` package, and they can be applied to Spark components as well as MX components; the `mx.effects` package (which is included in the Flex 4 SDK) contains the corresponding functionality that can be applied to MX components.

The following sub-section contains a Flex code sample that illustrates how to create a scaling effect in Flex.

Creating Scaled Effects

Scaled effects (i.e., expanding or contracting a shape) can be useful for game-oriented applications, and they are very easy to create in Flex-based applications. Create a new Flex mobile project called ScaleEffect1, using the Mobile Application template, and add the code shown in Listing 4–6.

Listing 4–6. *Creating Scaled Effects with Linear Gradients*

```
<?xml version="1.0" encoding="utf-8"?>
<s:View xmlns:fx="http://ns.adobe.com/mxml/2009"
        xmlns:s="library://ns.adobe.com/flex/spark"
        title="Scale Effect">

   <fx:Library>
     <fx:Definition name="MyRect1">
       <s:Rect x="50" y="50" height="40" width="20">
         <s:fill>
           <s:LinearGradient>
             <s:GradientEntry color="0xFF0000"
                              ratio="0"   alpha=".5"/>
             <s:GradientEntry color="0xFFFF00"
                              ratio=".33" alpha=".5"/>
             <s:GradientEntry color="0x0000FF"
                              ratio=".66" alpha=".5"/>
           </s:LinearGradient>
         </s:fill>
         <s:stroke>
           <s:SolidColorStroke color="0xFF0000" weight="1"/>
         </s:stroke>
         <s:filters>
           <s:BlurFilter/>
           <s:GlowFilter/>
         </s:filters>
```

```
        </s:Rect>
      </fx:Definition>

      <fx:Definition name="MyEllipse1">
        <s:Ellipse x="200" y="200" height="40" width="80">
          <s:fill>
            <s:LinearGradient>
              <s:GradientEntry color="0xFF0000"
                               ratio="0"    alpha=".5"/>
              <s:GradientEntry color="0xFFFF00"
                               ratio=".33" alpha=".5"/>
              <s:GradientEntry color="0x0000FF"
                               ratio=".66" alpha=".5"/>
            </s:LinearGradient>
          </s:fill>
          <s:stroke>
            <s:SolidColorStroke color="0xFF0000" weight="1"/>
          </s:stroke>
          <s:filters>
            <s:DropShadowFilter distance="20" color="#FF0000"/>
          </s:filters>
        </s:Ellipse>
      </fx:Definition>
    </fx:Library>

  <s:Group>
    <fx:MyRect1    scaleX="6" scaleY="4"/>
    <fx:MyEllipse1 scaleX="3" scaleY="8"/>
    <fx:MyRect1    scaleX="2" scaleY="2"/>
    <fx:MyEllipse1 scaleX="2" scaleY="2"/>
  </s:Group>
</s:View>
```

Listing 4–6 contains an XML `Definition` element that specifies an XML `Rect` element with the definition for a rectangle, and another XML `Definition` element that specifies an XML `Ellipse` element with the definition of an ellipse. The XML `Group` element contains two references to the rectangle and two references to the ellipse, as shown here:

```
  <s:Group>
    <fx:MyRect1    scaleX="6" scaleY="4"/>
    <fx:MyEllipse1 scaleX="3" scaleY="8"/>
    <fx:MyRect1    scaleX="2" scaleY="2"/>
    <fx:MyEllipse1 scaleX="2" scaleY="2"/>
  </s:Group>
```

The first XML element scales the previously defined rectangle by specifying values of 6 and 3 for the attributes `scaleX` and `scaleY`. The second XML element scales the previously defined rectangle by specifying values of 3 and 8 for the attributes `scaleX` and `scaleY`.

Figure 4–6 displays two scaled rectangles and two scaled ellipses.

Figure 4–6. *Two scaled rectangles and ellipses*

Creating Animation Effects in Spark

This section contains mobile code that shows how to apply animation effects on geometric objects, including those that were discussed in the previous part of this chapter. The Spark primitives for animation effects are here:

- Animate
- AnimateColor
- AnimateFilter
- AnimateShaderTransition
- AnimateTransform
- CrossFade
- Fade

- Move

- Resize

- Rotate

- Scale

- Wipe

The following sections provide mobile code samples that illustrate how to use the XML Animate element and how to define animation effects in parallel and in sequence.

Using the Animate Element

Animation effects are obviously very popular for game-oriented applications, and they can also be used effectively in other types of applications. At the same time, keep in mind that it's probably a good idea to use animation effects sparingly in business-focused applications.

Create a new Flex mobile project called AnimPropertyWidth, using the Mobile Application template, and add the code shown in Listing 4–7.

Listing 4–7. *Animating the Width of a Rectangle*

```
<?xml version="1.0" encoding="utf-8"?>
<s:View xmlns:fx="http://ns.adobe.com/mxml/2009"
        xmlns:s="library://ns.adobe.com/flex/spark"
        title="Animate Rectangle Width">

   <fx:Declarations>
      <s:Animate id="MyAnimate1">
         <s:motionPaths>
            <s:MotionPath property="width">
               <s:keyframes>
                  <s:Keyframe time="0"    value="200"/>
                  <s:Keyframe time="2000" value="400"/>
               </s:keyframes>
            </s:MotionPath>
         </s:motionPaths>
      </s:Animate>
   </fx:Declarations>

   <s:VGroup>
      <s:Rect id="rect1" x="10" y="50" height="300" width="200">
         <s:fill>
            <s:LinearGradient>
               <s:GradientEntry color="0xFF0000"
                                ratio="0"    alpha=".5"/>
               <s:GradientEntry color="0xFFFF00"
                                ratio=".33" alpha=".5"/>
               <s:GradientEntry color="0x0000FF"
                                ratio=".66" alpha=".5"/>
            </s:LinearGradient>
         </s:fill>
         <s:stroke>
```

```
                <s:SolidColorStroke color="0xFF0000" weight="2"/>
            </s:stroke>
        </s:Rect>

        <s:Button id="MyButton1" label="Animate Width"
                click="MyAnimate1.play([rect1])"
                bottom="150" right="50">
        </s:Button>
    </s:VGroup>
</s:View>
```

Listing 4–7 contains an XML Declarations element that in turn contains an XML Animate element that defines the animation-specific details. The XML Animate element has an id attribute whose value is MyAnimate1, which is referenced in the click-handling event that is described later in this section.

Listing 4–7 contains an XML VGroup element that in turn contains an XML Rect element whose contents are similar to examples that you have already seen in this chapter. Listing 4–7 contains an XML Button element that enables you to start the animation effect. Whenever users click or tap this button, the code will execute the event handler whose id attribute is MyAnimate1, which is defined earlier in the code sample. The animation effect is simple: the rectangle width increases from 200 units to 400 units during a period of two seconds (2000 milliseconds).

Figure 4–7 and Figure 4–8 display two snapshots of a rectangle that moves horizontally across the screen when users click the button.

Figure 4–7. *A rectangle with animation (initial position)*

Figure 4–8. *A rectangle with animation (final position)*

Animation: Parallel and Sequence

Flex supports two categories of animation effects. Parallel animation effects involve two or more animation effects that occur at the same time. On the other hand, sequential animation effects involve two or more animation effects that occur in sequence, which means that only one animation effect takes place at any given time. With this in mind, create a new Flex mobile project called SequentialAnimation1, using the Mobile Application template, and add the code shown in Listing 4–8.

Listing 4–8. *Creating Sequential Animation Effects*

```
<?xml version="1.0" encoding="utf-8"?>
<s:View xmlns:fx="http://ns.adobe.com/mxml/2009"
        xmlns:s="library://ns.adobe.com/flex/spark"
        title="Sequential Animation">

  <fx:Declarations>
    <s:Sequence id="transformer1" target="{button1}">
      <s:Move xFrom="50" xTo="150"
              autoCenterTransform="true"/>
      <s:Rotate angleFrom="0" angleTo="360"
              autoCenterTransform="true"/>
      <s:Scale scaleXFrom="1" scaleXTo="2"
              autoCenterTransform="true"/>
    </s:Sequence>

    <s:Sequence id="transformer2" target="{button2}">
      <s:Move xFrom="50" xTo="150"
```

```
                    autoCenterTransform="true"/>
        <s:Scale scaleXFrom="1" scaleXTo="2"
                    autoCenterTransform="true"/>
        <s:Rotate angleFrom="0" angleTo="720"
                    autoCenterTransform="true"/>
      </s:Sequence>
    </fx:Declarations>

    <s:Rect id="rect1" x="10" y="10" width="400" height="400">
      <s:fill>
        <s:SolidColor color="0xFF0000"/>
      </s:fill>
      <s:stroke>
        <s:SolidColorStroke color="0x0000FF" weight="4"/>
      </s:stroke>
    </s:Rect>

    <s:Button id="button1" x="50" y="100" label="Transform Me"
                click="transformer1.play()"/>

    <s:Button id="button2" x="50" y="200" label="Transform Me Too"
                click="transformer2.play()"/>
</s:View>
```

Listing 4–8 contains an XML Declarations element, which in turn contains two XML Sequence elements that specify three transformation effects. The animation effect starts with the XML Move element (which provides a translation effect), followed by the XML Rotate element (which provides a rotation effect), and finally the XML Scale element (which provides a scaling effect). When users tap the first XML Button element, this will invoke the animation effects that are defined in the XML Sequence element whose id attribute has the value transformer1.

Similar comments apply to the second XML Sequence element and the second button, except that the animation effect involves two full rotations instead of one rotation.

Note that you can easily change the animation effect from sequential to parallel by replacing the XML Sequence element with an XML Parallel element, as shown here:

```
    <s:Parallel id="transformer" target="{button}">
      <s:Move xFrom="50" xTo="150"
            autoCenterTransform="true"/>
      <s:Rotate angleFrom="0" angleTo="360"
            autoCenterTransform="true"/>
      <s:Scale scaleXFrom="1" scaleXTo="2"
            autoCenterTransform="true"/>
    </s:Parallel>
```

Figure 4–9 and Figure 4–10 display two buttons that undergo animation effects in a sequential fashion. Since the screenshots capture only the initial and final animation effects, launch this mobile application on a mobile device so that you can also see the sliding effect and the rotation effect.

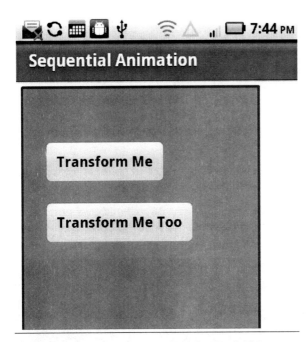

Figure 4–9. *A button with sequential animation (initial)*

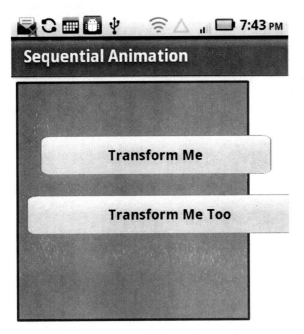

Figure 4–10. *A button with sequential animation (later)*

Creating 3D Effects

Flex supports several 3D effects, including moving, rotating, and scaling a JPG file. The 3D "move" effect involves moving a JPG image as well as decreasing the size of the image, whereas a 3D scaling effect involves increasing (or decreasing) the width and height of a JPG image from a start value (typically 1) to a final value (which can be bigger or smaller than 1). A 3D "rotate" effect involves rotating a JPG image so that it appears to be rotating in three dimensions.

The following code sample in Listing 4.9 shows you how to create 3D effects for moving, rotating, and scaling a JPG file in a mobile-based application.

Figure 4–11 displays the JPG image Cassandra4.jpg of Cassandra Chin (Stephen Chin's daughter), which is used in the code samples that illustrate these three 3D animation effects.

Figure 4–11. *A JPG for 3D effects*

Listing 4–9. *Creating 3D Animation Effects*

```
<?xml version="1.0" encoding="utf-8"?>
<s:View xmlns:fx="http://ns.adobe.com/mxml/2009"
        xmlns:s="library://ns.adobe.com/flex/spark"
        title="Creating 3D Effects">

  <fx:Declarations>
    <s:Move3D id="moveEffect" target="{targetImg}" xBy="100" zBy="100"
```

```
                  repeatCount="2" repeatBehavior="reverse"
                  effectStart="playMoveButton.enabled=false"
                  effectEnd="playMoveButton.enabled=true;"/>

    <s:Rotate3D id="rotateEffect" target="{targetImg}"
                angleYFrom="0" angleYTo="360"
                repeatCount="4" repeatBehavior="reverse"
                effectStart="playRotateButton.enabled=false;"
                effectEnd="playRotateButton.enabled=true;"/>

    <s:Scale3D id="atScale" target="{targetImg}"
               scaleXBy="-.45" repeatCount="2"
               repeatBehavior="reverse"
               effectStart="playScaleButton.enabled=false"
               effectEnd="playScaleButton.enabled=true;"/>
  </fx:Declarations>

  <s:VGroup width="100%" height="100%" >
    <s:Image id="targetImg"
             horizontalCenter="0"
             verticalCenter="0"
             source="@Embed(source='images/Cassandra4.jpg')"/>

    <s:HGroup>
      <s:Button id="playMoveButton"
                left="10" bottom="25"
                label="Move"
                click="moveEffect.play();"/>

      <s:Button id="playRotateButton"
                left="110" bottom="25"
                label="Rotate"
                click="rotateEffect.play();"/>

      <s:Button id="playScaleButton"
                left="222" bottom="25"
                label="Scale" click="atScale.play();"/>
    </s:HGroup>
  </s:VGroup>

</s:View>
```

Listing 4–9 contains an XML Declarations element that contains three elements for 3D effects, along with three XML Button elements that users click in order to create a 3D effect. The XML Move3D element specifies the target location via the attributes xBy and zBy, along with a repeatCount of 2 (which performs the animation effect twice), and a repeatBehavior whose value is reverse (which returns to the original position every time). The corresponding XML Button element contains a label attribute whose value is Move, and a click attribute whose value is moveEffect.play(), which invokes the move animation effect that is specified in the XML MoveEffect element that is defined in the XML Declarations element.

The rotation effect is handled via the XML Rotate3D element, whose attributes angleYFrom and angleYTo specify the start and end angles of 0 and 360, respectively (i.e., a complete rotation). This rotation effect occurs four times. The XML Button element contains a label attribute whose value is Rotate, and a click attribute whose value is rotateEffect.play(), which invokes the scaling animation effect that is specified in the XML Rotate3D element that is defined in the XML Declarations element.

The scale effect (which is the third and final effect) is handled via the XML Scale3D element, which contains several attributes whose values specify the details of the animation behavior of the same JPG image. The id attribute has a value of atScale, which serves to reference this element elsewhere in the code. The target attribute references the XML element whose id has the value targetImg, which references the JPG image. The scaleXBy attribute has the value -0.25, which shrinks the JPG image by a factor of 25%. The repeatCount attribute has the value 4, and the repeatBehavior attribute has the value reverse, which means that the animation effect occurs four times, alternating back and forth from left to right. The other two attributes are effectStart and effectEnd, which specify the behavior at the beginning and the end of the animation, which in this case is to disable and then enable the playButton.

Note that the XML Image element specifies the location of Cassandra4.jpg, which is in the images subfolder of the top-level directory for this mobile project. For layout purposes, the XML Image element is specified inside an XML VGroup element, which also contains an XML HGroup element that contains the three XML Button elements.

Figure 4–12 displays a JPG after having undergone a 3D "move" effect.

Figure 4–12. *A JPG after a 3D move effect*

Figure 4–13 displays a JPG after having undergone a 3D "rotate" effect.

Figure 4–13. *A JPG after a 3D rotate effect*

Figure 4–14 displays a JPG after having undergone a 3D "scale" effect.

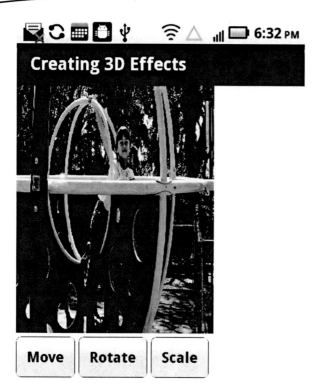

Figure 4–14. *A JPG after a 3D scale effect*

Creating Spark Skins

Custom skins are useful whenever you want to create richer visual effects in certain aspects of your mobile applications. For example, you can create multiple custom skins that apply graphics effects (including those that you learned earlier in this chapter) to a button. The code sample that we will discuss clearly demonstrates the process for creating Spark custom skinning effects.

Listings 4–10 through 4–12 display the contents of the code in CustomSkinHomeView.mxml, ButtonSkin1.mxml, and ButtonSkin2.mxml, respectively.

Before discussing the MXML files in this section, let's look at the following list of steps for adding the file ButtonSkin1.mxml (in the skins package) to your project.

1. Add the new folder skins to your project.

2. Right-click your project, and navigate to New->MXML Skin.

3. Specify skins for the package name of the new skin.

4. Specify ButtonSkin1 for the name of the skin.

5. Specify spark.components.Button as the name of the component.

6. Deselect the check box to the left of the label "Create as a copy of:".

Repeat the preceding set of steps for the custom skin ButtonSkin2.mxml, and also for any additional custom skins that you want to add to this project. Now let's look at the contents of CustomSkin.mxml, which are displayed in Listing 4–10

Listing 4–10. *Creating Custom Spark Skins*

```
<?xml version="1.0" encoding="utf-8"?>
<s:View xmlns:fx="http://ns.adobe.com/mxml/2009"
        xmlns:s="library://ns.adobe.com/flex/spark"
        title="Custom Skins">
<s:VGroup>
    <s:Label text="This is a Normal Button:" x="10" y="0"/>
    <s:Button label="Button1" x="10" y="25"/>

    <s:Label text="First Skinned Button:"   x="10" y="60"/>
    <s:Button skinClass="skins.ButtonSkin1" x="10" y="85"/>

    <s:Label text="Second Skinned Button:"  x="10" y="100"/>
    <s:Button skinClass="skins.ButtonSkin2" x="10" y="125"/>

    <s:Label text="Third Skinned Button:"   x="10" y="140"/>
    <s:Button skinClass="skins.ButtonSkin1" x="10" y="165"/>

    <s:Label text="Fourth Skinned Button:"  x="10" y="180"/>
    <s:Button skinClass="skins.ButtonSkin2" x="10" y="205"/>
</s:VGroup>
</s:View>
```

Listing 4–10 contains an XML VGroup element containing ten "paired" XML elements for rendering a standard XML Label element and a standard XML Button element, the first of which is a normal button, as shown here:

```
<s:Label text="This is a Normal Button:" x="10" y="0"/>
<s:Button label="Button1" x="10" y="25"/>
```

The preceding XML elements are straightforward: the first is a label ("This is a Normal Button"), and the second renders a button.

The first pair of XML elements involving skinned buttons displays the label "First Skinned Button:", and the second element in this pair renders an XML Button element based on the contents of the Flex skin ButtonSkin1 in the package skins. Similarly, the next pair of XML elements involving skinned buttons displays the label "Second Skinned Button:", and the second element in this pair renders an XML Button element based on the contents of the Flex skin ButtonSkin2 in the package skins. Similar comments apply to the other two custom buttons.

Now let's look at the contents of ButtonSkin1.mxml, which contains the data for rendering the second button (which is the first skinned button), in Listing 4–11.

Listing 4–11. *Creating a Button Skin with Graphics*

```
<s:Skin xmlns:fx="http://ns.adobe.com/mxml/2009"
        xmlns:s="library://ns.adobe.com/flex/spark" >

    <fx:Metadata>
      [HostComponent("spark.components.Button")]
    </fx:Metadata>

    <s:states>
      <s:State name="disabled" />
      <s:State name="down" />
      <s:State name="over" />
      <s:State name="up" />
    </s:states>

    <s:Rect id="rect1" x="0" y="0" height="40" width="100">
      <s:fill>
        <s:LinearGradient>
          <s:GradientEntry color="0xFF0000"
                           ratio="0"   alpha=".5"/>
          <s:GradientEntry color="0xFFFF00"
                           ratio=".33" alpha=".5"/>
          <s:GradientEntry color="0x0000FF"
                           ratio=".66" alpha=".5"/>
        </s:LinearGradient>
      </s:fill>

      <s:stroke>
        <s:SolidColorStroke color="0x000000" weight="2"/>
      </s:stroke>
    </s:Rect>
</s:Skin>
```

Listing 4–11 contains an XML Skin root node with three XML child elements that define
the behavior of the custom skin. The first child element is the XML Metadata element, as
shown here:

```
<fx:Metadata>
  [HostComponent("spark.components.Button")]
</fx:Metadata>
```

The preceding XML element specifies the package name for the Button class, which is
also what you specified when you added the custom skin ButtonSkin1.mxml to your
project.

The second child element is the XML states element, as shown here:

```
<s:states>
  <s:State name="disabled" />
  <s:State name="down" />
  <s:State name="over" />
  <s:State name="up" />
</s:states>
```

The preceding XML states element contains four child elements that correspond to a
button state and three mouse-related events, and you can include additional code if you

want to handle these states. The third child element is the XML `Rect` element that specifies a linear gradient for the shading effect and a black border.

Listing 4–12. *Creating a Second Button Skin*

```
<s:Skin xmlns:fx="http://ns.adobe.com/mxml/2009"
        xmlns:s="library://ns.adobe.com/flex/spark" >

    <fx:Metadata>
      [HostComponent("spark.components.Button")]
    </fx:Metadata>
    <s:states>
      <s:State name="disabled" />
      <s:State name="down" />
      <s:State name="over" />
      <s:State name="up" />
    </s:states>

    <s:Path data="M 0 0 L 100 0 L 100 40 L 0 40 Z ">
      <s:fill>
        <s:SolidColor color="#FF0000" alpha="1"/>
      </s:fill>
      <s:stroke>
        <s:SolidColorStroke color="#0000FF" weight="4"/>
      </s:stroke>
    </s:Path>
</s:Skin>
```

Note that the only difference between Listing 4–12 and Listing 4–11 is the XML `Path` element instead of an XML `Rect` element.

The XML `Path` element is straightforward: it contains a data attribute whose value is a set of line segments that specify a rectangle, whose color is #FF0000 (red) and whose border is #0000FF (blue) with a width of 4.

As you can see, Flex makes it very easy to define custom skins. However, the more complex (and more interesting) custom skins often specify the behavior of mouse events (such as mouse-down, mouse-up, and so forth) and the corresponding touch events in terms of state changes. You can "bind" ActionScript functions (written by you) that are executed during those events in order to change the visual display of various aspects of your application.

Figure 4–15 displays a standard Flex button and four buttons that use custom skins.

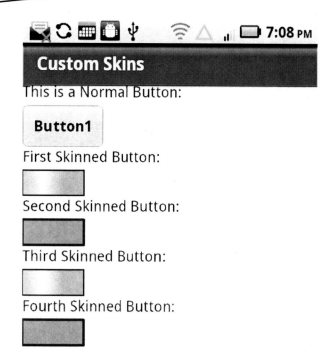

Figure 4–15. *A standard button and four buttons with custom Spark skins*

Generating 2D Charts and Graphs in Spark

Flex 4 provides nice support for the following 2D charts and graphs:

- Area graphs
- Column charts
- Bar charts
- Line graphs
- Pie charts
- Scatter charts

In the following examples, you will learn how to write mobile code samples for rendering 2D bar charts and 2D pie charts, and you will also see code samples that have animation effects and can handle mouse events and touch events. Note that Flex uses the term "bar chart" for a horizontal bar chart (i.e., each bar element is rendered horizontally from left to right), and the term "column chart" refers to a vertical bar chart.

Creating 2D Bar Charts

Bar charts are very popular, especially in business-oriented applications, because they enable you to easily see trends in data that might otherwise be difficult to discern from a tabular display of data. In the upcoming example, you will learn how to create a mobile application that reads XML-based data from an XML document and then renders that data in a 2D bar chart. This data is for the purposes of illustration, and obviously you would use your own real data rather than the "fictitious" data that is contained in Listing 4–12. Also keep in mind that the full source for the examples in this book is available online from the book's web page.

Now create a new Flex mobile project called BarChart1, using the Mobile Application template, add a new top-level folder called `chartdata`, and then add a new XML document in this folder called `ChartData.xml` that contains the data shown in Listing 4–13.

Listing 4–13. *Defining XML-Based Chart Data*

```
<?xml version="1.0"?>
<chartdata>
  <data>
    <month>January</month>
    <revenue>1500</revenue>
  </data>
  <data>
    <month>February</month>
    <revenue>1400</revenue>
</data>
[data omitted for brevity]
  <data>
    <month>November</month>
    <revenue>1900</revenue>
  </data>
  <data>
    <month>December</month>
    <revenue>1800</revenue>
  </data>
</chartdata>
```

Listing 4–13 contains an XML chartdata element that contains twelve XML data elements, each of which holds chart-related data for a single month of the year. Each XML data element in Listing 4–13 contains an XML month element and an XML revenue element. For example, the first XML data element specifies a revenue element with the value 1500 and a month element whose value is January (no currency units are specified).

Now let's look at Listing 4–14, which contains the code for rendering the bar chart using the XML-based data in Listing 4–13.

Listing 4–14. *Creating a Bar Chart*

```
<?xml version="1.0" encoding="utf-8"?>
<s:View xmlns:fx="http://ns.adobe.com/mxml/2009"
        xmlns:mx="library://ns.adobe.com/flex/mx"
        xmlns:s="library://ns.adobe.com/flex/spark"
```

```
                title="Bar Chart">

    <!-- XML-based chart data -->
    <fx:Declarations>
      <fx:Model id="chartModel" source="chartdata/ChartData.xml"/>
      <s:ArrayCollection id="chartData" source="{chartModel.data}"/>
      <mx:NumberFormatter id="nf" precision="1" rounding="nearest"/>
    </fx:Declarations>

    <fx:Style>
      @namespace s  "library://ns.adobe.com/flex/spark";
      @namespace mx "library://ns.adobe.com/flex/mx";
      mx|ColumnChart
      {
        font-size:12;
        font-weight:bold;
      }
    </fx:Style>

    <!-- specify a column chart with appropriate attributes -->
    <mx:ColumnChart dataProvider="{chartData}"
                    height="70%" width="100%">
        <mx:horizontalAxis>
        <mx:CategoryAxis dataProvider="{chartData}"
                         categoryField="month"/>
      </mx:horizontalAxis>
      <mx:series>
        <mx:ColumnSeries xField="month" yField="revenue"/>
      </mx:series>
    </mx:ColumnChart>
</s:View>
```

Listing 4–14 defines the location of the XML document ChartData.xml in the XML Model element, along with an ArrayCollection consisting of the XML-based data, and a simple data formatter. Listing 4–14 contains an XML Style element that specifies values for two CSS attributes—font-size and font-weight—with values of 12 and bold, respectively, which are used for rendering the text in the pie chart.

The XML ColumnChart element specifies a column chart, along with appropriate values for the attributes dataProvider, height, and weight, whose values are chartData, 75%, and 80%, respectively. Notice that chartData is an ArrayCollection variable that is defined in the XML Declarations element, and that chartData is populated with the data values that are specified in the XML document ChartData.xml.

The values of the height and weight attributes are specified as a percentage of the dimensions of the screen on which the pie chart is rendered; adjust the values of these attributes according to the percentage of the screen that you want to occupy with the bar chart (50% for half width or height, 25% for one-quarter width or height, and so forth).

The XML ColumnChart element contains two important elements. First there is an XML horizontalAxis element that specifies the month values (which are specified in ChartData.xml) for the horizontal axis. Second, there is an XML series element that references the month values for the horizontal axis and the revenue values for the vertical axis for the bar chart.

Figure 4–16 displays a bar chart that is based on the data in the XML file ChartData.xml, which is displayed in Listing 4–13.

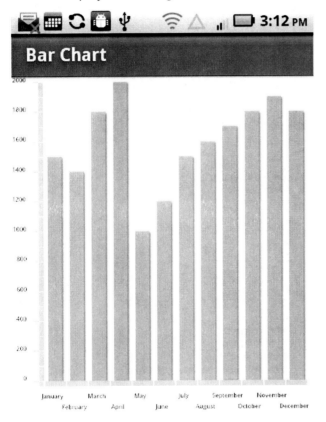

Figure 4–16. *A 2D bar chart*

Keep in mind that Figure 4–16 lacks some useful information, such as the currency for the revenue, the current year, the name and location of the company, and the region (or country) for the revenue data. If you add such extra information, make the appropriate changes to the code in Listing 4–14 in order to ensure that the modified code specifies the correct path to access the revenue-related data.

Creating 2D Pie Charts

Pie charts are also very popular for displaying data in a manner that makes it simpler to understand the relationship among the data elements. We are going to create a pie chart that uses the data in the XML document ChartData.xml in Listing 4–13, which is the same data that was used in the previous example in order to render a bar chart. Create a new Flex mobile project called PieChart1, using the Mobile Application template, and add the code shown in Listing 4–15.

Listing 4–15. *Creating a Pie Chart*

```
<?xml version="1.0" encoding="utf-8"?>
<s:View xmlns:fx="http://ns.adobe.com/mxml/2009"
        xmlns:mx="library://ns.adobe.com/flex/mx"
        xmlns:s="library://ns.adobe.com/flex/spark"
        title="Pie Chart">

    <!-- XML-based chart data -->
    <fx:Declarations>
        <fx:Model id="chartModel" source="chartdata/ChartData.xml"/>
        <s:ArrayCollection id="chartData" source="{chartModel.data}"/>
        <mx:NumberFormatter id="nf" precision="1" rounding="nearest"/>
    </fx:Declarations>

    <fx:Style>
        @namespace s  "library://ns.adobe.com/flex/spark";
        @namespace mx "library://ns.adobe.com/flex/mx";
        mx|PieChart
        {
            font-size:12;
            font-weight:bold;
        }
    </fx:Style>

    <!-- wedge information is a name:value pair -->
    <fx:Script>
        <![CDATA[
            private function getWedgeLabel (item:Object,
                                            field:String,
                                            index:Number,
                                            percentValue:Number):String
            {
                return item.month+": "+item.revenue;
            }
        ]]>
    </fx:Script>

    <!-- specify a pie chart with appropriate attributes -->
    <mx:PieChart dataProvider="{chartData}"
                 height="50%" width="80%"
                 horizontalCenter="0" verticalCenter="0">
        <mx:series>
            <mx:PieSeries field="revenue"
                          labelFunction="getWedgeLabel"
                          labelPosition="callout"
                          explodeRadius="0.05"/>
        </mx:series>
    </mx:PieChart>
</s:View>
```

Listing 4–15 contains an XML Declarations element and an XML Style element that are the same as Listing 4–14. The XML Script element that defines a private function getWedgeLabel returns a string consisting of a name:value pair for each pie wedge, as shown here:

```
<fx:Script>
    <![CDATA[
        private function getWedgeLabel (item:Object,
                                        field:String,
                                        index:Number,
                                        percentValue:Number):String
        {
            return item.month+": "+item.revenue;
        }
    ]]>
</fx:Script>
```

The XML PieChart element specifies a pie chart, along with attributes whose values specify how the pie chart will be rendered. For example, the height and the width attributes both have the value 80%, which means that the chart is rendered with a height and width that is 80% of the screen dimensions. Adjust the values of these attributes according to the percentage of the screen that you want to occupy with the pie chart (just as you did with the bar chart).

The XML PieChart element also contains an XML PieSeries element that in turn contains four attributes that enable you to specify how to render the pie chart data and the pie chart wedges. The field attribute has the value revenue, which means that the data values of the XML revenue element are rendered in the pie chart.

The labelFunction attribute has the value getWedgeLabel, which is an ActionScript function (defined earlier in the fx:Script element) that specifies the label for each pie "wedge" in the pie chart.

The labelPosition attribute has the value callout, which means that the label for each pie wedge is rendered outside the pie wedge, with a "broken" line segment from the pie wedge to its label. Note that the labelPosition attribute can have three other values: inside, outside, or insideWithCallout. Experiment with these values to see how they change the rendering of the pie chart.

Finally, the explodeRadius attribute has the value 0.05, which renders the pie chart with space between adjacent pie wedges, creating an "exploded" effect.

Figure 4–17 displays a 2D pie chart.

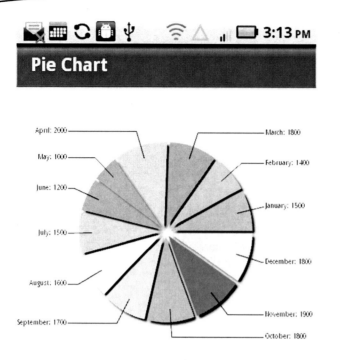

Figure 4–17. *A 2D pie chart*

Using FXG with Spark

Chapter 3 contains a very brief introduction to FXG, and this section contains a code sample that demonstrates how to convert Listing 4–1 (which contains code for rendering a rectangle and an ellipse) into a Flex project that uses FXG.

Create a new Flex mobile project called FXG1, using the Mobile Application template, create a top-level folder called `components`, and then create a file inside this folder called `RectEllipse1.fxg` with the contents that are shown in Listing 4–16.

Listing 4–16. *Using FXG to Define Graphics Elements*

```
<?xml version="1.0" encoding="utf-8"?>
<Graphic xmlns="http://ns.adobe.com/fxg/2008" version="2">
  <Rect id="rect1" x="10" y="10" width="250" height="200">
    <fill>
      <SolidColor color="#FF0000"/>
    </fill>
    <stroke>
      <SolidColorStroke color="#FFFF00" weight="4"/>
    </stroke>
  </Rect>

  <Ellipse id="ellipse1" x="10" y="220" width="250" height="200">
    <fill>
      <SolidColor color="#0000FF"/>
    </fill>
```

```
        <stroke>
          <SolidColorStroke color="#FF0000" weight="4"/>
        </stroke>
      </Ellipse>

      <Rect id="rect2" x="10" y="460" width="250" height="100">
        <fill>
          <SolidColor color="#FFFF00"/>
        </fill>
        <stroke>
          <SolidColorStroke color="#0000FF" weight="8"/>
        </stroke>
      </Rect>

</Graphic>
```

The XML Graphic element contains two XML elements whose data values are the same as the XML Rect element and the XML Ellipse element in Listing 4–1, along with the following differences:

  ▪ The elements do not contain a namespace prefix.

  ▪ The elements belong to the default namespace.

  ▪ The color attribute uses a "#" symbol instead of a "0x" prefix.

Listing 4–17 shows you how to reference an element that is defined in Listing 4–16.

Listing 4–17. *Referencing FXG Components*

```
<?xml version="1.0" encoding="utf-8"?>
<s:View xmlns:fx="http://ns.adobe.com/mxml/2009"
        xmlns:mx="library://ns.adobe.com/flex/mx"
        xmlns:s="library://ns.adobe.com/flex/spark"
        xmlns:comps="components.*">

  <s:VGroup>
      <comps:RectEllipse1 id="rect1"/>
  </s:VGroup>
</s:View>
```

Listing 4–17 contains a namespace that references the FXG file RectEllipse1.fxg, which is in the components subdirectory. The XML VGroup element contains an XML RectEllipse1 element in the comps namespace that references an XML element whose id attribute has the value rect1, which is defined in the FXG file RectEllipse1.fxg shown in Listing 4–16.

Figure 4–18 displays an ellipse and two rectangles, which are the same as those in Figure 4–1.

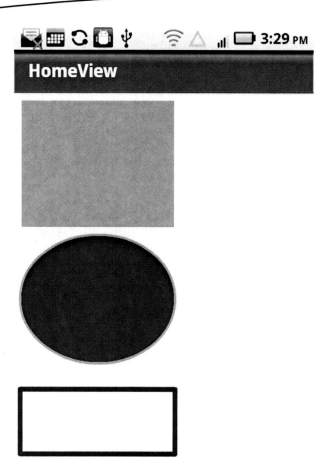

Figure 4–18. *A rectangle and an ellipse*

As you can surmise from this example, FXG enables you to modularize the code in your Flex projects. Moreover, the following Adobe products enable you to export projects as FXG files that you can then import into Flex projects:

- Adobe Photoshop
- Adobe Illustrator
- Adobe Fireworks

You can see more sophisticated examples of FXG files in Chapter 9.

A Sketching Program

The mobile code that you will see in this section shows you how to create a sketching program that ties together various graphics-related notions introduced earlier in the chapter, along with touch events, sketching on top of a JPG file, and the ability to save the sketch as a JPG on a mobile device.

Create a new Flex mobile project called Sketch1, using the Mobile Flex Application template, and add the code that is displayed in Listing 4–18. For the purposes of discussion, the code is presented in smaller blocks of code, and remember that the complete code is available for download from the web site for the book.

Listing 4–18. *Rendering and Saving Sketches*

```
<?xml version="1.0" encoding="utf-8"?>
<s:View xmlns:fx="http://ns.adobe.com/mxml/2009"
        xmlns:s="library://ns.adobe.com/flex/spark" title="HomeView">
   <fx:Script>
     <![CDATA[
        import flash.ui.Multitouch;
        import flash.ui.MultitouchInputMode;
        import flash.events.TouchEvent;

        import mx.graphics.ImageSnapshot;
        import mx.graphics.SolidColor;
        import mx.graphics.codec.JPEGEncoder;

        private var colors:Array = [0xFF0000, 0x00FF00, 0xFFfF00, 0x0000FF];
        private var singleTapCount:int = 0;
        private var touchMoveCount:int = 0;
        private var widthFactor:int = 0;
        private var heightFactor:int = 0;
        private var currentColor:int = 0;
        private var rectWidth:int = 20;
        private var rectHeight:int = 20;

        Multitouch.inputMode = MultitouchInputMode.TOUCH_POINT;

        function touchMove(event:TouchEvent):void {
           //event.stopImmediatePropagation();
           ++touchMoveCount;

           if (event.isPrimaryTouchPoint) {
             currentColor = colors[touchMoveCount%colors.length];
           } else {
             currentColor = colors[(touchMoveCount+2)%colors.length];
           }

           var myRect:Rect = new Rect();
           myRect.x = event.localX;
           myRect.y = event.localY;
           myRect.width  = rectWidth;
           myRect.height = rectHeight;
           myRect.fill = new SolidColor(currentColor);

           var myGroup1:Group = event.target as Group;
           myGroup1.addElement(myRect);
        }
```

Listing 4–18 starts with an XML Script element that contains various import statements and definitions of aptly named variables (e.g., for tracking touch events) that are used in some of the ActionScript 3 methods.

MultiTouch.inputMode is set for multitouch mode, and so more than one rectangle is rendered when you drag multiple fingers across the screen. In case you need to refresh your memory regarding multitouch, you can read the appropriate section in Chapter 2.

The function touchMove contains code for handling move events. This function first increments the variable touchMoveCount and then uses this variable as an index into the array colors, thereby rendering a set of rectangles whose colors iterate through this array. The rest of the code in this function creates a small rectangle at the location of the touch event. This is actually the "heart" of the graphics rendering code, but the other functions handle other events.

The next block of code contains the code for the function touchEnd(), which is actually optional, but it shows you an example of what you can do in this event handler.

```
function touchEnd(event:TouchEvent):void {
    ++touchMoveCount;

    if (event.isPrimaryTouchPoint) {
      currentColor = colors[touchMoveCount%colors.length];
    } else {
      currentColor = colors[0];
    }

    widthFactor = (touchMoveCount%3)+1;
    heightFactor = (touchMoveCount%3)+2;

    var myRect:Rect = new Rect();
    myRect.x = event.localX;
    myRect.y = event.localY;
    myRect.width  = rectWidth*widthFactor;
    myRect.height = rectHeight*heightFactor;
    myRect.fill = new SolidColor(currentColor);

    var myGroup1:Group = event.target as Group;
    myGroup1.addElement(myRect);
}
```

The code for handling "touch up" events in the function touchEnd increments the variable touchMoveCount and then uses this variable as an index into the array colors, but in this case some simple arithmetic is performed to render a rectangle with different dimensions.

```
function touchSingleTap(event:TouchEvent):void {
    var myRect:Rect = new Rect();
    myRect.x = event.localX;
    myRect.y = event.localY;

    ++singleTapCount;
    if (event.isPrimaryTouchPoint) {
      currentColor = colors[singleTapCount%colors.length];
      myRect.width  = rectWidth*3;
      myRect.height = rectHeight*2;
    } else {
      currentColor = colors[(singleTapCount+1)%colors.length];
      myRect.width  = rectWidth*2;
      myRect.height = rectHeight*3;
```

```
    }

        myRect.fill = new SolidColor(currentColor);

        var myGroup1:Group = event.target as Group;
        myGroup1.addElement(myRect);
    }
```

The logic for handling single-tap events is in the function touchSingleTap. This function increments the variable touchSingleTapCount and then applies some simple logic to determine the dimensions of the rectangle that is rendered at the location of the single-tap event.

```
    function touchMoveHandlerImage(event:TouchEvent):void {
        touchMove(event);
    }

    function touchTapHandlerImage(event:TouchEvent):void {
        touchSingleTap(event);
    }

    private function saveImageToFileSystem():void {
        var jPEGEncoder:JPEGEncoder = new JPEGEncoder(500);
        var imageSnapshot:ImageSnapshot = ImageSnapshot.captureImage(imgPanel, 0,
                                                        jPEGEncoder);

        var fileReference:FileReference = new FileReference();
        fileReference.save(imageSnapshot.data, "fingersketch.jpg");
    }
  ]]>
</fx:Script>
```

The two functions touchMoveHandlerImage and touchTapHandlerImage (as suggested by their names) handle move events and single-tap events for the JPG file fingersketch.jpg, which is stored in the images subdirectory of this Flex application. These two functions contain one line of code that invokes the corresponding functions touchMove and touchTapHandler, which were discussed earlier in this section.

The function saveImageToFileSystem is invoked whenever you click the Save Sketch button, and it contains the code for saving the current sketch to the filesystem of the mobile device. A pop-up dialog box will appear that contains the default location and name of the JPG file, both of which you can change before saving the current sketch.

```
    <s:Panel id="imgPanel" title="Finger Sketching For Fun!" width="100%" height="100%" >
        <s:Button id="saveImage"
                    left="150" bottom="5"
                    label="Save Sketch"
                    click="saveImageToFileSystem();"/>

        <s:Group name="myGroup1" width="500" height="500"
                    touchMove="touchMove(event)"
                    touchEnd="touchEnd(event)"
                    touchTap="touchSingleTap(event)">
            <s:Ellipse id="ellipse1" x="10" y="10" width="100" height="50">
                <s:fill> <s:SolidColor color="0xFFFF00"/> </s:fill>
                <s:stroke> <s:SolidColorStroke color="red" weight="5"/> </s:stroke>
```

```
                    </s:Ellipse>
                    <s:Rect id="rect1" x="110" y="10" width="100" height="50">
                        <s:fill> <s:SolidColor color="0xFF0000"/> </s:fill>
                            <s:stroke> <s:SolidColorStroke color="blue" weight="5"/> </s:stroke>
                    </s:Rect>
                    <s:Ellipse id="ellipse2" x="210" y="10" width="100" height="50">
                        <s:fill> <s:SolidColor color="0xFFFF00"/> </s:fill>
                        <s:stroke> <s:SolidColorStroke color="red" weight="5"/> </s:stroke>
                    </s:Ellipse>
                    <s:Rect id="rect2" x="310" y="10" width="100" height="50">
                        <s:fill> <s:SolidColor color="0xFF0000"/> </s:fill>
                            <s:stroke> <s:SolidColorStroke color="blue" weight="5"/> </s:stroke>
                    </s:Rect>

                    <s:Path data="C100 300 200 20 300 100 S 250 200 300 250">
                        <s:fill>
                            <s:LinearGradient rotation="90">
                                <s:GradientEntry color="#FF0000" alpha="0.8"/>
                                <s:GradientEntry color="#0000FF" alpha="0.8"/>
                            </s:LinearGradient>
                        </s:fill>

                        <s:stroke>
                            <s:SolidColorStroke color="0x00FF00" weight="2"/>
                        </s:stroke>
                    </s:Path>

                    <s:Path data="C 350 300 200 150 350 100 T 250 250 400 280">
                        <s:fill>
                            <s:LinearGradient rotation="90">
                                <s:GradientEntry color="#FFFF00" alpha="0.5"/>
                                <s:GradientEntry color="#FF0000" alpha="0.5"/>
                            </s:LinearGradient>
                        </s:fill>

                        <s:stroke>
                            <s:SolidColorStroke color="0x000000" weight="4"/>
                        </s:stroke>
                    </s:Path>
                </s:Group>

            <s:Image id="img" width="480" height="320" source="images/fingersketch.jpg"
                    touchMove="touchMoveHandlerImage(event)"
                    touchTap="touchTapHandlerImage(event)"
                    horizontalCenter="-10" verticalCenter="60"/>
        </s:Panel>
</s:View>
```

The next major section of code consists of an XML Panel element that contains an XML Button element for saving the current sketch, followed by an XML Group element that specifies the touch-related event handlers touchMove, touchEnd, and touchTap, which were discussed earlier in this example.

The XML Group element also contains definitions for various graphics objects, including ellipses, rectangles, and Bezier curves, which you learned about earlier in this chapter.

These graphics objects are clearly optional, and they are simply meant to give you an idea of how to make a sketch program that is attractive and visually appealing to users.

The XML Image element specifies the JPG file `fingersketch.jpg`, which is in the `images` subdirectory of this Flex application. The XML Image element specifies the function `touchMoveHandlerImage` for touch motion events and the function `touchTapHandlerImage` for tap-related events. Experiment with different values for the attributes `horizontalCenter` and `verticalCenter`, which alter the horizontal and vertical layout positions for this JPG image.

Figure 4–19 displays a sample sketch after launching the sketch program in a mobile device.

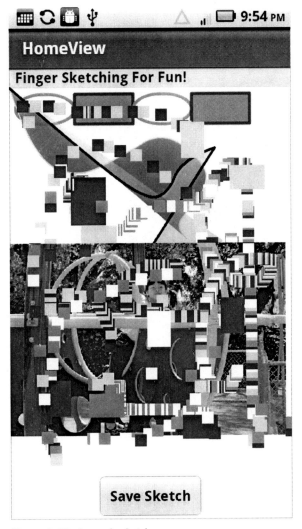

Figure 4–19. *A sample sketch*

Summary

In this chapter, you learned how to use Spark components to render a variety of 2D graphics shapes in graphics-oriented applications for mobile devices. If you are already familiar with rendering Flex-based graphics, then you can leverage your existing knowledge quickly and easily in order to create mobile applications that use graphics.

The graphics images and graphics effects that you use depend on your application-specific requirements, and some of the effects that you can use in your own mobile projects include the following:

- Rendering basic shapes such as rectangles, ellipses, and line segments

- Rendering quadratic and cubic Bezier curves for mobile applications that require more "artistic" non-linear visual effects

- Applying linear gradients, radial gradients, and filter effects to produce richer and more compelling visual effects

- Applying transformations (translating, scaling, rotating, and shearing)

- Creating custom skins to replace "standard" buttons

- Using parallel or sequential animation effects in conjunction with touch events

Performing effective data visualization with bar charts and pie charts

Chapter 5

Application Deployment and Publication

Up to this point, we have shown you how to build engaging applications on the Flash platform that take advantage of mobile features in both Flash Professional and Flash Builder. However, in order to showcase your newly developed applications, you need to know how to prepare your applications for deployment, install them on development devices, and deploy your applications to Android Market, where end users can download them.

In this chapter, we will start off by showing you how to install and configure the Android SDK and run in the Android Emulator. This is a great way to experiment with your application on an array of different device types and OS combinations that would normally require a dedicated device testing lab.

Next we show you how to deploy your applications from both Flash Professional and Flash Builder, using some of the applications that you developed in earlier chapters as examples. This is in addition to demonstrating advanced topics such as certificate creation, command line deployment, and packaging for the Android Emulator.

Finally, we show you how to publish your application to both Android Market and the Amazon Appstore. Once you have successfully published an application, it will appear like any other native application in the store, the fact that it was built on the Flash platform being completely transparent to your end users.

Setting Up an Android Emulator

If you do not have ready access to an Android device, or are looking for a way to deploy and test your code on new or different hardware, the Android Emulator is an excellent option. The Android Emulator that ships with the SDK is as close as you can get to running the real thing, including running a full Android OS stack and supporting similar developer interaction with a USB attached device.

Table 5–1 compares the experience of running on device, in the emulator, and in the AIR Debug Launcher (ADL).

Table 5–1. *Comparison of Running on Device, in the Emulator, and in ADL*

	On Device	**In Emulator**	**In ADL**
Operating system	Android Linux	Android Linux (emulated)	Host OS (no emulation)
Multitouch	Device supported (usually 2-touch points + all gestures)	None	Limited (only on Mac OS X)
Rotation	Supported via physical rotation	Rotation via keyboard (Ctrl+F11, Ctrl+F12)	Rotation via menu options
Deployment	APK files via Android Debug Bridge (ADB)	APK files via ADB	None
File storage	Built-in or SD card	Built-in or SD card (emulated)	Host filesystem (no emulation)
Android Market	Built-in app, supports installation	Built-in app, supports installation	None

As you can see, ADL is a convenient way to test Flash applications during development, but it is not a full Android environment. In contrast, the Android Emulator runs a full version of the Android OS on a virtual device, so you can test how your application would behave on different OS version and screen combinations.

There are some constraints when running in an emulator on the desktop. The most notable one is that you have no multitouch support. Also, some of the Android buttons and features are available only via command line options or key bindings, as detailed in the upcoming section entitled "Emulator Key Bindings."

Despite these limitations, the Android Emulator is a very cost-effective way to test your application on multiple different devices and versions of the Android OS, and it is a tool you won't want to be without.

Installing the Android SDK

A prerequisite to installing and running Flash on devices is to have the Android SDK installed. You need to download and install both the Java SDK and Android SDK in order to run the emulator. You can download the latest version of Java for your platform here:

http://java.sun.com/javase/downloads

NOTE: Java is pre-installed on Mac OS X.

The Android SDK is free for personal and commercial use and can be downloaded from Google at the following URL:

`http://developer.android.com/sdk`

The initial download is relatively small, and can be extracted to a directory of your choice. To complete the installation, you have to run the SDK Setup application in the main directory. This will prompt you with a package installation dialog, as shown in Figure 5–1.

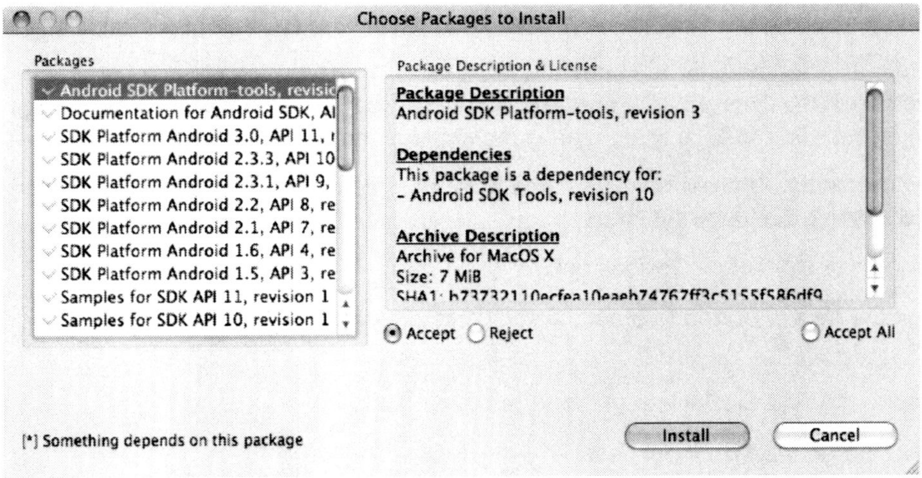

Figure 5–1. *AIR for Android package installation dialog*

You can choose which packages you want by selecting them individually and clicking the Accept button, or by simply clicking Accept All. Once you click the Install button, your accepted packages will be downloaded and installed.

NOTE: Windows users must install an additional package for USB connectivity to use a phone with a USB cable. If you are using a Google Android Developer Phone, you can find the drivers here: `http://developer.android.com/sdk/win-usb.html`.

An optional step is to install Eclipse and the Android Development Tools (ADT) plug-in for Eclipse. This is helpful if you want to do any native Android development, as discussed in the next chapter. The ADT Eclipse plug-in can be downloaded from the following URL:

`http://developer.android.com/sdk/eclipse-adt.html`

It is also possible to use your IDE of choice to develop native Android applications. You will simply have to use the command line tools that come with the Android SDK to do compilation and packaging of your project.

Creating an Android Virtual Device

The core of the Android Emulator is Android Virtual Devices (AVDs). Each AVD specifies settings unique to that device, including API version, screen size, and hardware properties. Using AVDs you can have your own private, virtual device lab with a different configuration for each of the target devices that you want to test your application on.

To start with, you need to create your first AVD for running Flash platform applications. This is done in the Android SDK and AVD Manager, which you ran upon first installing the SDK.

You can relaunch the Android SDK and AVD Manager from the command line by navigating to the sdk/tools directory and launching the android executable.

After a few moments, Android will launch the SDK Manager. Here you can create a new AVD by performing the following steps.

1. Navigate to the Virtual Devices pane.

2. Click the New... button to open the AVD creation dialog shown in Figure 5–2.

3. Specify "MyAndroidDevice" in the Name input field.

4. Enter "50" in the Size input field.

5. Select "Android 2.3.3 - API Level 10" (or later) from the Target drop-down list.

6. Select the built-in skin called "WVGA854".

7. Click the Create AVD button.

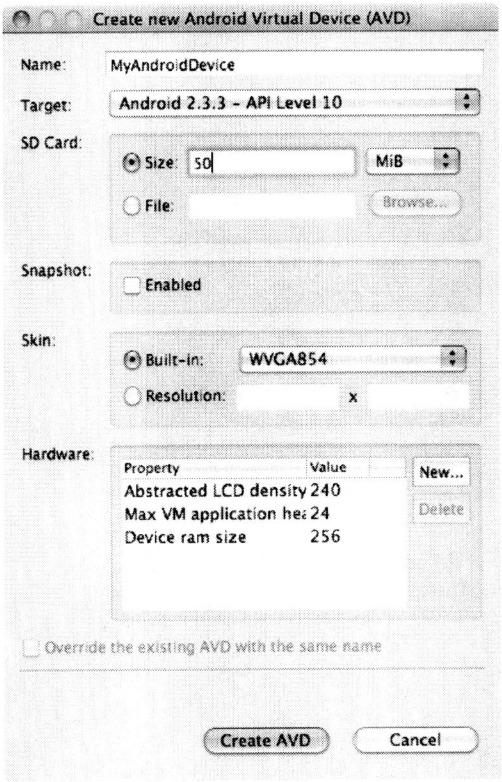

Figure 5–2. *Dialog to create new Android Virtual Devices (AVDs)*

The name of the AVD in step 3 is simply a suggestion, so you can replace this string with another name.

To launch your newly created AVD, select it in the list and click the Start... button. It will show you the standard Android boot screen followed by a lock screen. Upon unlocking the emulator by dragging the lock symbol across, you will be greeted by the familiar home screen shown in Figure 5–3.

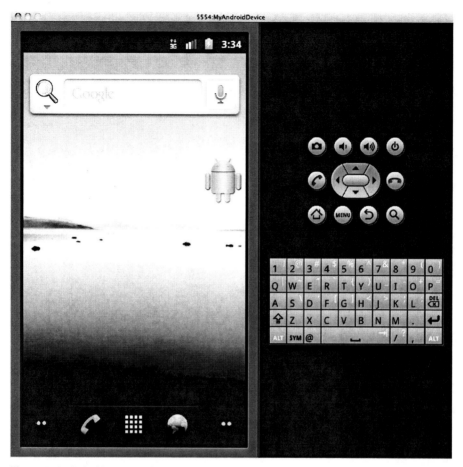

Figure 5–3. *Android 2.3.3 running in the emulator on desktop*

The Android standard skin for the emulator shows your device screen on the left and the full complement of Android buttons and keys on the right. Some of the keys, such as the dial and hang-up buttons, may not be found on every Android device, but the emulator still lets you test how your application behaves when these keys are pressed.

Almost everything you can do on a normal Android device is enabled in the emulator, so before continuing on to installing your own applications, familiarize yourself with the user interface. You can launch pre-installed applications, such as the Browser, Contacts, or E-mail, or new applications from Android Market. By default the emulator image comes with all the development options enabled, such as USB debugging, "stay awake," and mock locations, but it is also worthwhile to familiarize yourself with the Settings application.

Installing AIR Within the Emulator

When you run on a physical device via USB Debugging, Flash Builder will automatically prompt you to upgrade your installed version of AIR if your AIR SDK contains a newer version. You also have the option of downloading and installing released versions of AIR directly from Android Market, which is exactly what happens when you run a Flash Android application without AIR installed.

However, in the case of the emulator, you can't use the versions of AIR directly out of Android Market, because they are not compatible. Also, since Flash Builder does not directly integrate with the Android Emulator, you can't use the auto-update mechanism to install AIR either.

The solution to this is to manually install the AIR runtime from the SDK. The AIR SDK can be found in the `sdks/<version>` folder of the Flash Builder installation (as of the time of writing, the latest version was 4.5.0). Within the AIR SDK folder, you can find the emulator runtime at the following location:

```
runtimes/air/android/emulator/Runtime.apk
```

> **NOTE:** There are separate AIR runtimes for devices and emulators, so make sure to choose the emulator runtime for this purpose.

This file can be installed by using the Android Debug Bridge (ADB) program from the command line. ADB is one of the tools that comes with the Android SDK and can be found in the `platform-tools` folder. Listing 5–1 shows an example of what the command to install the emulator APK should look like for the default install location on Mac OS X.

Listing 5–1. Installation Command for the AIR Emulator Runtime

```
adb install "/Applications/Adobe Flash Builder
4.5/sdks/4.5.0/runtimes/air/android/emulator/Runtime.apk"
```

On Windows the command is very similar, except for the path location of the Flash Builder installation.

> **TIP:** You can also use the AIR Debug Tool (ADT) to install the AIR runtime. Configuring ADT is described later in this chapter in the section entitled "Setting Up ADT". The command to install the AIR runtime using ADT is as follows:
>
> ```
> adt -installRuntime -platform android
> ```

Emulator Key Bindings

When running in the Android Emulator, you have the option of using your normal desktop keyboard as input. This works fairly well, except that there are several special keys on Android devices that do not have normal mappings to a desktop keyboard. Examples of this are the power button, audio volume, and camera button.

To make it easy to press these buttons on an Android device, the default device skins include these buttons on the physical emulator panel so you can click them with the mouse. However, there is no guarantee that future Android skins or custom skins that you install yourself will have the full complement of buttons. One such skin, shown in Figure 5–4, gives you a near photograph-quality Nexus S device appearance,[1] but lacks some buttons.

Figure 5–4. *Nexus S Android Emulator skin*

---

[1] Nexus S Skin by Heiko Behrens: http://heikobehrens.net/2011/03/15/android-skins/

To overcome this limitation, the Android Emulator has a full complement of keybindings. Table 5–2 lists the mapping from common Android keys to the desktop keyboard modifier equivalent that you can type when using any emulator skin.

Table 5–2. *Mapping of Android Device Keys to Desktop Modifiers*

Android Key	Emulator Keybinding
Back	ESC
Menu	F2 or
	Page-up
Search	F5
Home	HOME
Call/Dial	Dial: F3
	Hang-up: F4
Power	F7
Camera	Ctrl-F3 or
	Ctrl-Numpad-5
Raise Audio Volume	Ctrl-F5 or
	Numpad-Plus
Lower Audio Volume	Ctrl-F6 or
	Numpad-Minus
DPad	Up: Numpad-8
	Down: Numpad-2
	Left: Numpad-4
	Right: Numpad-6
	Center: Numpad-5

In addition to remapping the Android buttons, there are also some hidden features of the emulator that are accessible only via keybindings. Table 5–3 shows some of the special key bindings that you will find useful when testing applications in the emulator.

Table 5–3. *Special Key Bindings for Android Emulator Features*

Feature	Keybinding	Description
Previous Layout	`Ctrl-F11` or `Numpad 7`	Simulates physical rotation of the device, switching from Portrait to Landscape mode (or vice versa)
Next Layout	`Ctrl-F12` or `Numpad-9`	Simulates physical rotation of the device, switching from Portrait to Landscape mode (or vice versa)
Full Screen Mode	`Alt-Enter`	Toggles full-screen mode on or off for the emulator; in full-screen mode, the display is proportionally scaled to fill the screen with a black matte.
Trackball Mode	`F6` or hold `Delete`	Trackball mode allows you to simulate a physical trackball with your mouse. F6 allows you to toggle this mode on or off, and Delete temporarily enables it.
Cell Networking	`F8`	Toggles the virtual cellular network on or off, which can be useful for testing applications in the absence of a network
Code Profiling	`F9`	Toggles code profiling on or off; to use this feature, you have to launch the emulator with the `-trace` startup option.
Onion Alpha	Increase: `Numpad-Multiply` Decrease: `Numpad-Divide`	Allows you to change the transparency of the onion overlay; to use this feature, you have to specify an onion overlay graphic with the `-onion` startup option.

To take full advantage of the foregoing key bindings, you will need to know how to launch the emulator from the command line and pass in arguments. Launching an Android Emulator from the command line is a straightforward call to the `emulator` executable, which can be found in the `sdk/tools` directory:

```
emulator -avd <Virtual Device Name>
```

The virtual device names you substitute are exactly the same as those defined in the Android tool, as shown in the previous section. You can then append any additional options you want to use, such as `-trace` or `-onion`.

Deploying AIR Applications

If you have been using a device to test your applications via USB, you have already been doing a limited form of deployment during your development process. However, you were likely using a debug version and did not have to worry about a lot of things that are important for your end users when they get a fully packaged application, such as permissions, proper certificates, and icons.

In this section, we will delve into the application descriptor in much more detail, demonstrating how to fine-tune your application deployment to improve the user experience and brand it for your company image.

Setting Up ADT

While it is possible to do the entire publication workflow through Flash Professional and Flash Builder, for automation and scripting purposes it is very useful to be able to do the same activities from the command line. The Adobe AIR SDK provides a command line called the AIR Developer Tool (ADT) that let you do everything from a script or build file.

To use ADT from the command line, you must set up the following in advance:

- Install the AIR SDK for your platform (this is automatically installed with Flash Builder).
- Install a valid Java Runtime Environment (JRE).
- Add the Java runtime to your PATH environment variable.
  - For Windows this would be %JRE_HOME%\bin.
  - For Mac OS X this would be $JRE_HOME/bin.
  - Where JRE_HOME is the fully qualified path to the JRE install location
- Add the AIR SDK to your PATH environment variable.
  - For Windows this would be %AIR_SDK%\bin.
  - For Mac OS X this would be $AIR_SDK/bin.
  - Where AIR_SDK is the fully qualified path to the AIR SDK install location

Once set up, you can use ADT to accomplish many different packaging and deployment activities from the command line. These include the following:

- *Creating signing certificates*: ADT lets you create code signing certificates from the command line that can be used when packaging your application.

- *Packaging applications*: By passing in a list of project files and a valid certificate, you can package up an APK file for deployment to an Android device. This supports creating an APK file with or without debugging symbols and also allows you to target the Android Emulator.

- *Installing applications*: The APK file created by the packaging step can be installed on device. This requires a path to the Android SDK.

- *Launching applications*: ADT can also be used to launch your application on device. This also requires a path to the Android SDK.

Throughout this chapter, we will make use of ADT to demonstrate the automation potential of the Flash workflow.

Application Permissions

The first impression that the user will have of your application will be a list of different permissions that it is requesting upon installation. Therefore, it behooves you to make sure that the permissions you are requesting make sense for your application, and are the minimal set that you can deliver the functionality with.

Requesting permissions that are too broad may give users pause in installing your application. For instance, there is no reason a Twitter client needs to write to external storage, so asking for that permission might prevent savvy users from installing your application over security concerns.

> **TIP:** One of the permissions that you probably have enabled by default is the INTERNET permission. This permission is required for USB debugging of your application, so it is an important permission to have enabled during development. Most applications will also need to access the Internet runtime, so it is likely that you will also need this permission for your published application version; but if not, remember to disable this.

Changing Permissions in Flash Professional

Flash Professional has a dedicated user interface to manage all the deployment options, including permissions. To open the settings panel, choose **Air for Android Settings...** from the **File** menu. Then click the Permissions tab, and you will get a dialog with check boxes for each of the permissions, as shown in Figure 5–5.

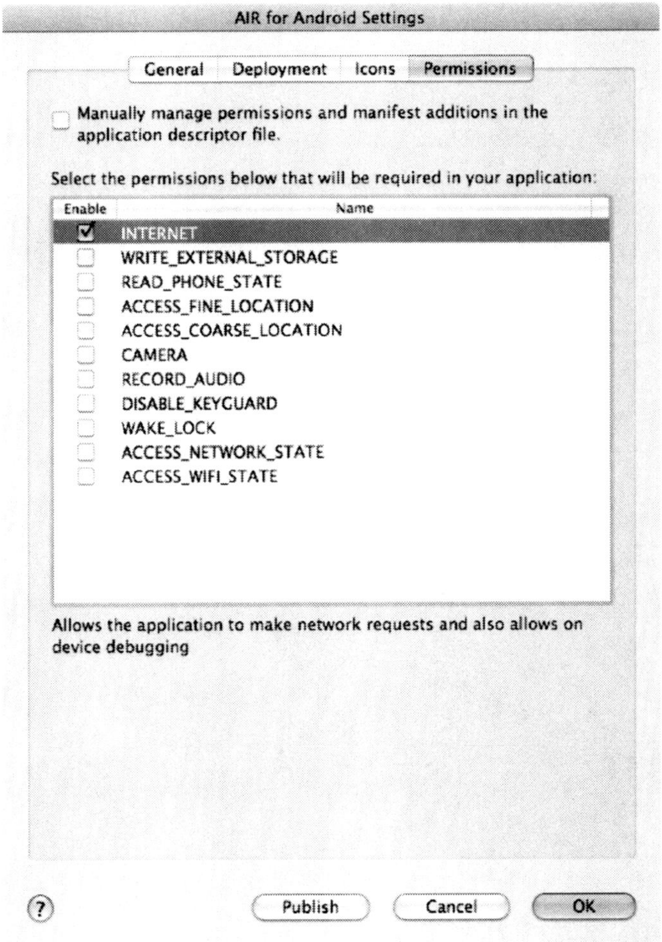

Figure 5–5. *Flash Professional Permissions tab in the AIR for Android Settings dialog*

You also have the option of manually setting the permissions in your application descriptor file by selecting the top check box. If you would like to do this, see the section "Manually Changing Permissions in the Application Descriptor".

Setting Initial Permissions in Flash Builder

Flash Builder lets you set permissions when you first create a project. To do this, click the Permissions tab in the second page of the new mobile project wizard, as shown in Figure 5–6.

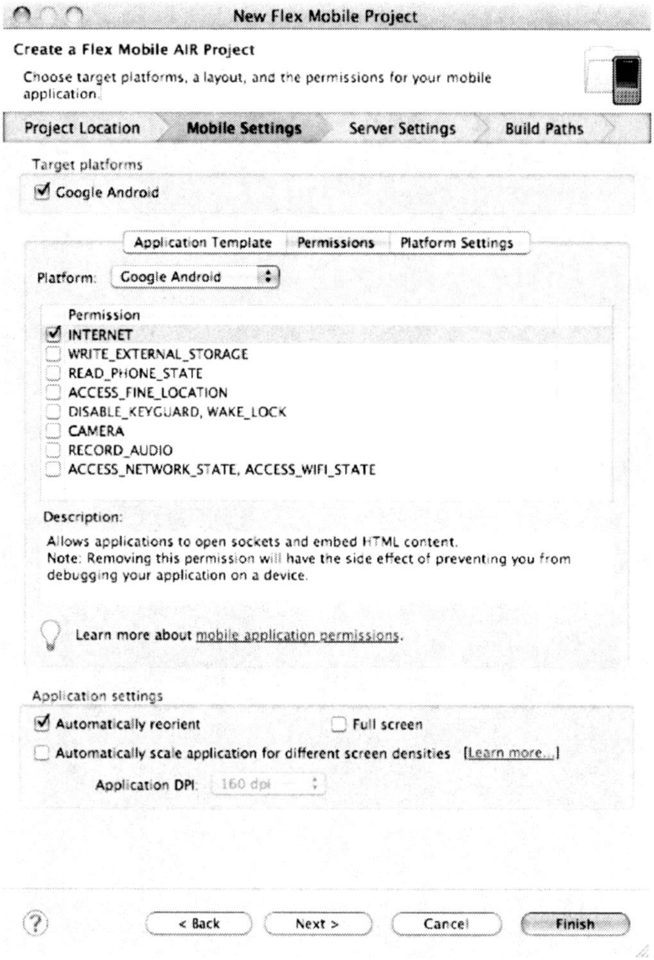

Figure 5-6. *Flash Builder Permissions tab in the new project wizard*

Notice that the INTERNET permission is preselected when you enter the dialog. This is required for USB device debugging to work. If you require any additional permissions, you can set them now before starting on your project.

Once the project has been created, it is no longer possible to change permissions via the project settings dialog. Instead, you can directly edit the application descriptor file that was created for you per the instructions in the next section.

Manually Changing Permissions in the Application Descriptor

If you have chosen to manage permissions manually (in the case of Flash Professional) or are modifying your permissions after project creation (in the case of Flash Builder), then you need to know how to modify the application descriptor file to change permissions.

The application descriptor file is typically in the source root of the project and is named with the convention `<project-name>-app.xml`. It is formatted as XML tagged markup with sections for all the different application settings that you can declaratively control. The permissions settings can be found toward the bottom of the file under the android tag, as shown in Listing 5–2.

Listing 5–2. *Example Permissions Section of an AIR Application Descriptor*

```
<android>
  <manifestAdditions>
    <manifest android:installLocation="auto">
      <![CDATA[
        <uses-permission android:name="android.permission.PERMISSION_NAME" />
      ]]>
    </manifest>
  </manifestAdditions>
</android>
```

For each permission you want to enable, you would copy the `uses-permission` tag and replace the `PERMISSION_NAME` placeholder with the appropriate permission name. Listing 5–3 shows an example of all the available Android permissions in the appropriate format for directly including in an application descriptor.

Listing 5–3. *Full Set of Available Android Permissions*

```
<uses-permission android:name="android.permission.INTERNET" />
<uses-permission android:name="android.permission.WRITE_EXTERNAL_STORAGE" />
<uses-permission android:name="android.permission.READ_PHONE_STATE" />
<uses-permission android:name="android.permission.ACCESS_FINE_LOCATION" />
<uses-permission android:name="android.permission.DISABLE_KEYGUARD" />
<uses-permission android:name="android.permission.WAKE_LOCK" />
<uses-permission android:name="android.permission.CAMERA" />
<uses-permission android:name="android.permission.RECORD_AUDIO" />
<uses-permission android:name="android.permission.ACCESS_NETWORK_STATE"/>
<uses-permission android:name="android.permission.ACCESS_WIFI_STATE"/>
```

Of these permissions, there are a few that make sense to enable and disable as a group—for example:

- AIR's `SystemIdleMode` APIs require both `DISABLE_KEYGUARD` and `WAKE_LOCK` permissions.

- AIR's `NetworkInfo` APIs require both `ACCESS_NETWORK_STATE` and `ACCESS_WIFI_STATE`

So if you are planning to use either of these APIs, make sure to enable both permissions at the same time.

Icons and Resources

Each time users open your application, they will see the Android launcher icon that you have selected, so it is important that this is professional and representative of your application.

Starting with Android 2.0, they standardized on a forward-facing icon design with the recommendation to select one aspect of your application and emphasize that with a full-size depiction. Figure 5–7 highlights some launcher icons that are model examples of the recommended Android look and feel.

Figure 5–7. *Sample Android launcher icons for applications*[2]

To make it easier to build application icons that meet these standards, the Android team provides a bundle that contains sample materials and templates for different size icons. You can download the Android Icon Templates pack at the following URL:

`http://developer.android.com/guide/practices/ui_guidelines/icon_design.html#tem`
`platespack`

This package includes Photoshop templates that you can use to precisely line up your graphics within the bounding rectangle and filters configured to apply the appropriate effects, such as the icon drop shadow.

Figure 5–8 shows the Photoshop file for the Pro Android Flash icon used in the examples throughout this book. It takes the "cyber fruit" graphic that is the center of the cover art and uses that single element as a representative icon for the book.

---

[2] Reproduced from work created and shared by the Android Open Source Project and used according to terms described in the Creative Commons 2.5 Attribution License: `http://developer.android.com/guide/practices/ui_guidelines/icon_design_launcher` `.html`

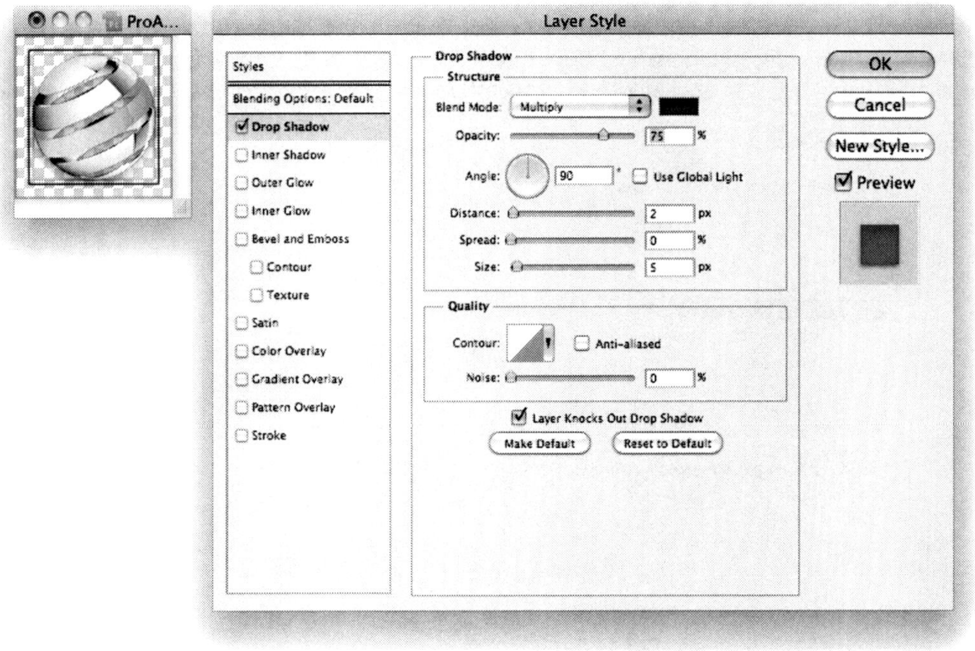

Figure 5–8. *Android icon template in Adobe Photoshop*

Since the shape we are using is circular, it is allowed to touch the outer blue boundary border (1/6th standoff). Square-shaped icons should not extend beyond the orange boundary line (2/9ths standoff). We are also using the recommended high-density drop shadow settings of 2 pixel distance, 5 pixel size, and a 90-degree angle. Table 5–4 lists the icon dimensions, border sizes, and drop shadow settings for different density icons.

Table 5–4. *Dimension, Border, and Drop Shadow Settings for Different Density Icons*

Density	Dimensions	Border (circular/square)	Drop Shadow (distance/size/angle)
Low density (ldpi)	36x36 pixels	6px/8px	1px/2px/90deg
Medium density (mdpi)	48x48 pixels	8px/10px	1px/3px/90deg
High density (hdpi)	72x72 pixels	12px/16px	2px/5px/90deg

To complete preparation of your icons, hide any guide layers you may have used for creating your icon and save it as a transparent portable network graphics (PNG) file. If you are using Photoshop, the best way to accomplish this is by using the **Save for Web and Devices…** command in the **File** menu. This ensures that your image files are the smallest possible size, removing any unnecessary header information.

Once you have created your graphics, you can include them in your application descriptor so they will be bundled with your application and displayed in the launcher and menu for your deployed application. Flash Professional has a configuration page that lets you select icons and link them against your application, as shown in Figure 5–9.

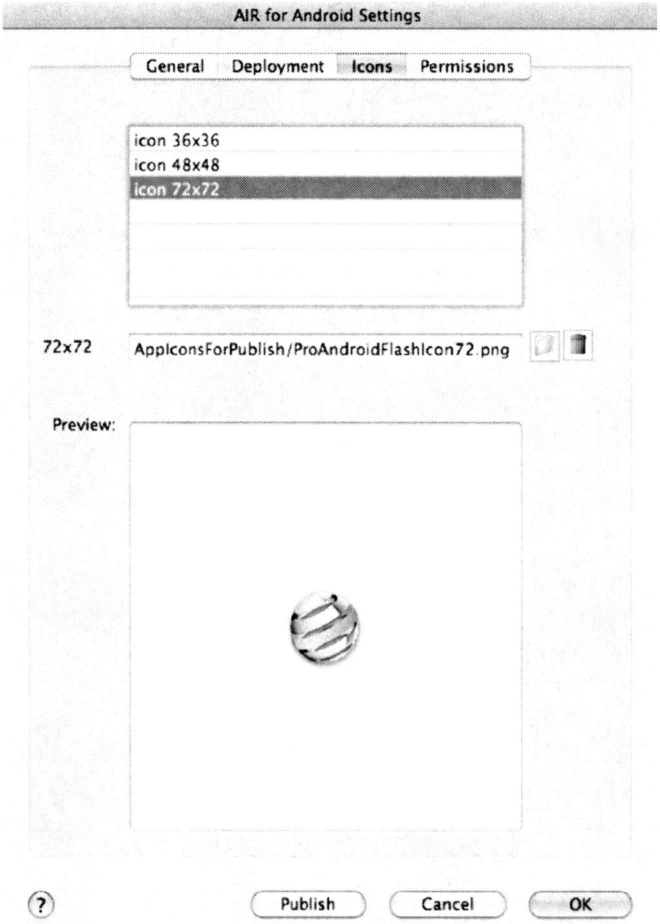

Figure 5–9. *Icon selection tab of the Flash Professional settings dialog*

Each graphic file that you select will be moved to a folder called AppIconsForPublish, which is rooted in your project file location. Upon deployment these icons will be copied to the generated .apk file, and linked as the corresponding density asset.

If you are using Flash Builder or manually managing your application descriptor, you will have to edit the XML manually. After opening up the application descriptor in a text editor, add in an icon section that lists an absolute or relative path to the different density icons your application supports. Listing 5–4 shows a sample of what the icon portion of your application descriptor should look like.

Listing 5–4. *Example* `icon` *Section of an AIR Application Descriptor*

```
<icon>
  <image36x36>ProAndroidFlashIcon36.png</image36x36>
  <image48x48>ProAndroidFlashIcon48.png</image48x48>
  <image72x72>ProAndroidFlashIcon72.png</image72x72>
</icon>
```

The `icon` tag should be directly underneath the outer `application` tag of the file. In this example, all the icon resources are in the same folder as the application descriptor file, so the path is a simple file name. You can name your files anything you want as long as they match what is written in the descriptor file.

Code Signing Certificates

Android requires that all deployed applications are signed. For deploying applications to Android Market, you do not have to purchase an expensive code signing certificate from a certificate authority. A simple self-signed certificate is all that is required, because Google takes care of checking the identity of parties that sell applications in their market.

Both Flash Professional and Flash Builder provide user interfaces to quickly and easily create certificates. You can also use the AIR Developer Tool (ADT) to create certificates from the command line. The certificates created by all of these mechanisms are identical and can be used interchangeably between tools.

To create a certificate in Flash Professional, open **Air for Android Settings…** from the **File** menu. On the Deployment tab of this dialog, you can click the Create… button to generate a new certificate via the pop-up shown in Figure 5–10.

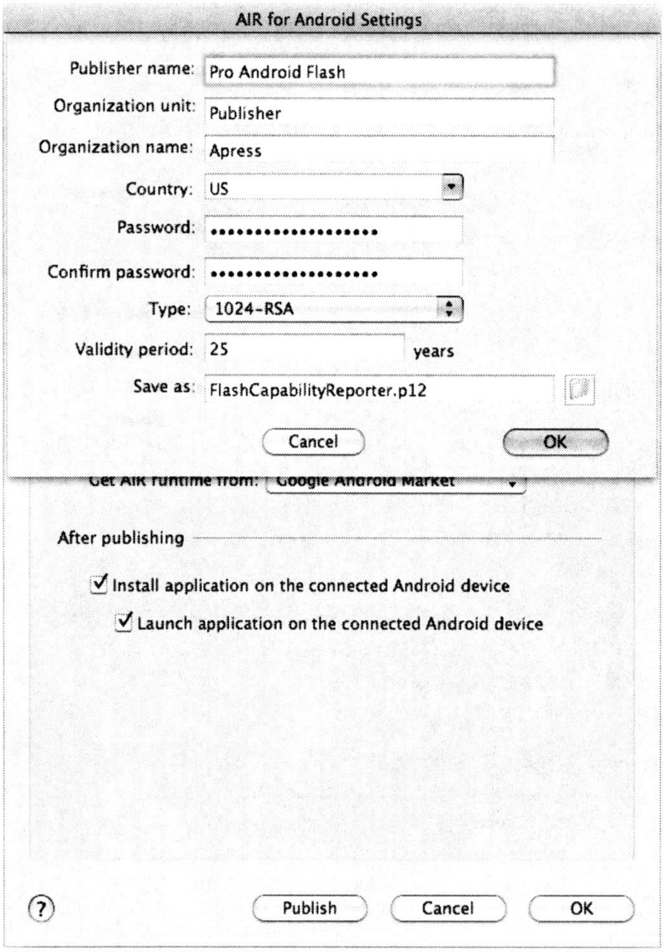

Figure 5–10. *Flash Professional certificate creation dialog*

We talk about the fields for creating a certificate in more detail ahead, but if you are creating a certificate for development purposes you can put in anything you want. Flash Professional requires that you fill in all the fields before continuing.

Flash Builder has an identical form that can be accessed from the Project Properties dialog in the **Google Android ➤ Digital Signature** section. Again, click the Create... button to open a certificate creation dialog, as shown in Figure 5–11.

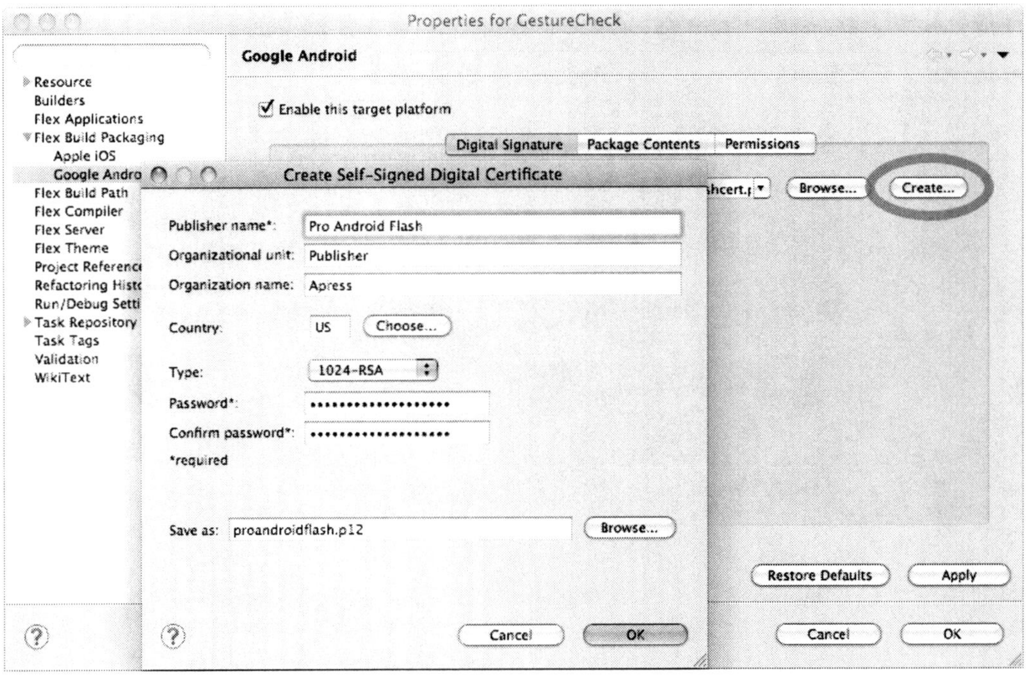

Figure 5–11. *Flash Builder certificate creation dialog*

The Flash Builder dialog is almost identical to the Flash Professional one, with the omission of the validity period. This will be defaulted to 25 years automatically for you.

Creating Certificates Using ADT

To create certificates from the command line, you can use the AIR Developer Tool (ADT). For more information about setting up ADT, please refer to the section entitled "Setting Up ADT" earlier in this chapter.

To create a code signing certificate via the command line, the command you would type is the following:

```
adt -certificate -cn <name> ( -ou <org-unit> )? ( -o <org-name> )? ( -c <country> )? ( -
validityPeriod <years> )? <key-type> <pfx-file> <password>
```

The arguments surrounded in parentheses are optional, and may be omitted. Values that you can choose yourself are surrounded in angle brackets. The description and valid values for all the arguments are listed in Table 5–5.

Table 5–5. *ADT Code Signing Arguments*

Argument	Name	Required	Description
-cn	Common Name	Yes	Name associated with the certificate
-ou	Organizational Unit	No	Subgroup within a company or organization; can be a department, division, geographical region, etc.
-o	Organization Name	No	Organization or company name of the signing entity
-c	Country	No	Country that the signing entity exists within
-validityPeriod	Validity Period	No	Number of years that the generated certificate will be valid for
key-type	Key Type	Yes	Type and strength of cryptographic algorithm used by this key; valid values are 1024-RSA and 2048-RSA.
pfx-file	Signature File	Yes	File path where the signature file will be written to; it can be a file name, relative path, or absolute path.
password	Password	Yes	Password for the signature file required each time it is used for signing

NOTE: Android Market requires that certificates must be valid past October 22, 2033. Therefore, a validity period of at least 25 years is recommended.

For example, the following command would create a valid Android code signing certificate:

```
adt -certificate -cn ProAndroidFlash -validityPeriod 25 1024-RSA proandroidflash.p12
superSecretPassword
```

You can then validate that the certificate works by running the checkstore command:

```
adt -checkstore -storetype pkcs12 -keystore proandroidflash.p12 -storepass
superSecretPassword
```

If the certificate has been created successfully, this command will return "valid password".

Publishing from Flash Professional

Once you have set up the appropriate permissions, icons, and certificates, publishing applications from Flash Professional is as easy as pressing a button. In fact, you have your choice of several buttons or menu items:

- The Publish button found in the AIR for Android Settings dialog

- The Publish button found on the Publish Settings dialog

- The **Publish** menu item found in the **File** menu

These three locations are depicted in Figure 5–12. They all work identically, except that in the case of misentered or incomplete information (such as a missing password for the certificate), you will be redirected to the AIR for Android Settings dialog.

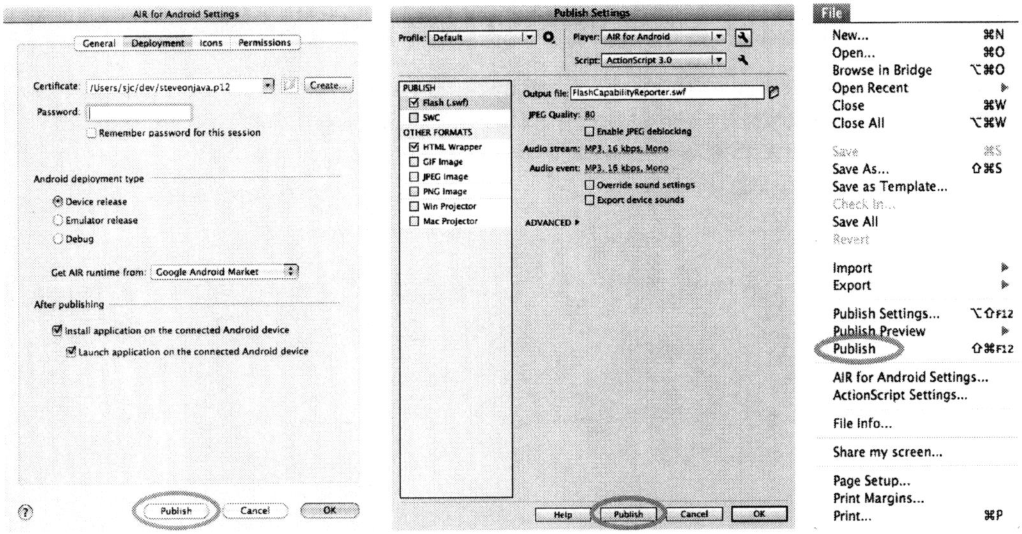

Figure 5–12. *AIR for Android deployment settings dialog*

There are a few deployment options found on the Deployment tab of the AIR for Android Settings dialog that we have not talked about yet, but they are important when publishing. The first is the choice of a Device, Emulator, or Debug release. If you are creating an Android package for end-user use, make sure to select a Device release.

The Emulator release is required if you are planning to test your application within the Android Emulator, so if this is how you plan to test your application, make sure to select this option. However, remember to switch back to a Device release for distribution to end users.

A Debug release is the type of project that normally gets built when you test your application via USB debugging. This has slower performance and slightly different behavior in error conditions than a Device release, so it is not recommended for distribution purposes.

You also have the option of choosing where you want your application to download the AIR runtime from. The two app stores that are supported today are Google Android Market and the Amazon Appstore. If you plan to deploy your application to both app stores, you should create a separate version for each with different AIR runtime settings.

The last set of options will automatically install and launch your application package onto the first connected USB device. These can be very handy to test your newly built application in its published form. If you have an emulator running, Flash Professional will see this as a connected device and can also deploy to it automatically.

Upon clicking Publish, an Android Package File (APK) will be created for your application. The APK file is a self-contained installation package that you can deploy to devices or publish via application storefronts. The location and name of the APK file are set in the Output File field of the Publish Settings dialog.

Exporting Release Builds from Flash Builder

Flash Builder also provides the ability to package up APK files for your application. The export process is started by selecting **Export Release Build…** from the **Project** menu, after which you will be presented with a wizard dialog as shown in Figure 5–13.

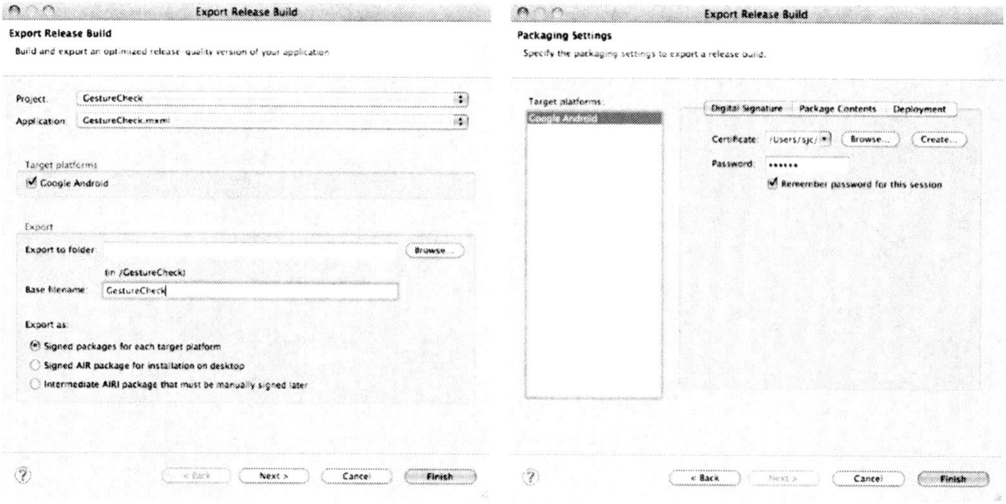

Figure 5–13. *Flash Builder export release build wizard*

The first page of the wizard lets you select the platform, file name, and signing options. For mobile applications, you will usually want to select the first option to sign packages for each target platform, which will be only one in our case. To proceed to the second page, click the Next button.

The second page contains a few tabs with options for the Digital Signature, Package Contents, and Deployment. If you have set up your signature as discussed earlier in this chapter, you won't have to make any changes on the first tab other than possibly entering a password. The Package Contents tab displays a list of all the resources that will be included in the APK file. Unless you want to specifically exclude any files, such as unused graphics, you don't need to make any changes here. Finally, the last tab has an option to automatically deploy and run on an attached mobile device if available, which is selected by default.

Once you click the Finish button, Flash Builder will package up an APK file for publication purposes, and possibly deploy and launch it on an installed device.

Running Flex Applications in the Android Emulator

Compared to the Flash Professional publication process, you may notice that there is no mention of the Android Emulator in the Flash Builder dialogs. Also, if you try to install the APK file created by Flash Builder on an Android Emulator, it will fail with an error upon installation.

However, you can manually create an emulator-friendly version of the same application by using the AIR Developer Tool (ADT) from the command line. For more information about setting up ADT, please refer to the section entitled "Setting Up ADT" earlier in this chapter.

As an example, Listing 5–5 shows you how to build an emulator-friendly APK for the GestureCheck project that was built in the first chapter. Make sure to execute this command from the bin-debug folder after Flash Builder has already built the SWF file.

Listing 5-5. Command to Build an APK File for the GestureCheck Project

```
adt -package -target apk-emulator -storetype pkcs12 -keystore <certificate file>
GestureCheck.apk GestureCheck-app.xml GestureCheck.swf ProAndroidFlashIcon*.png
```

This builds an APK file that is compatible with the Android Emulator. While the emulator is running, you can use the ADT tool to install it by executing the following command:

```
adt -installApp -platform android -package GestureCheck.apk
```

> **TIP:** You can also install APK files using the Android Debug Bridge (ADB) as follows:
>
> ```
> adb install GestureCheck.apk
> ```

Your application will now show up in the application menu on the emulator. You can manually launch your application via the menu, or programmatically launch it by using the following command:

```
adt -launchApp -platform android -appid com.proandroidflash.GestureCheck.debug
```

Notice that the appid is the same as the id used in your application descriptor, with the addition of ".debug" appended to the end.

> **TIP:** You can also launch AIR applications using ADB as follows:
>
> ```
> adb shell am start -a android.intent.action.MAIN -n
> air.com.proandroidflash.GestureCheck.debug/.AppEntry
> ```

Figure 5–14 shows a real example of the Gesture Check application running on a stock Android Emulator.

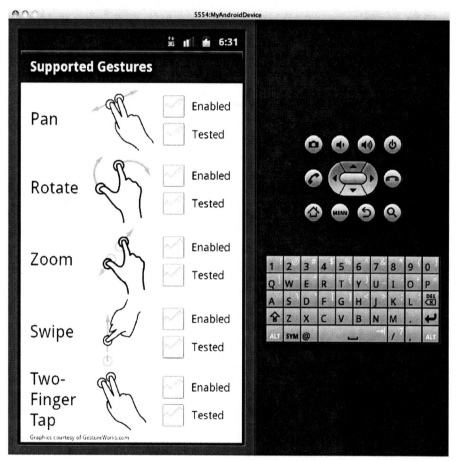

Figure 5–14. *Android 2.3.3 running in the emulator on desktop*

As mentioned previously, the Android Emulator doesn't support multitouch events, which is apparent by looking at the output of the Gesture Check application when running in the emulator.

Deploying from the Command Line

While Flash Professional and Flash Builder make deploying your application from within the tooling very convenient, it is often useful to be able to do the same deployments from the command line. This allows you to create a repeatable, automatable process that is tailored to the exact needs of your development workflow.

The command line tool we will be using is called the AIR Developer Tool (ADT) and automates several different tasks, from certificate creation to application packaging to device deployment. For more information about setting up ADT, see the foregoing section "Setting Up ADT".

The primary flag used in ADT for packaging AIR applications is -package. This indicates that you are going to package up an AIR application for desktop, mobile, or other deployment. Here is the full set of arguments for packaging Android applications with ADT:

```
adt -package -target ( apk | apk-debug | apk-emulator ) ( -connect <host> | -listen
<port>? )? ( -airDownloadURL <url> )? SIGNING_OPTIONS <output-package> ( <app-desc>
PLATFORM-SDK-OPTION? FILE-OPTIONS | <input-package> PLATFORM-SDK-OPTION? )
```

Table 5–6 talks about each of these arguments and what the valid values are.

Table 5–6. *Available Arguments for ADT Packaging*

Argument	Required	Description
-target	Yes	Type of package to build; it must be one of apk, apk-debug, or apk-emulator.
-connect/listen	No	Enables remote debugging via two possible methods:
		-connect <host>: Enables remote TCP/IP debugging by connecting to the specified host upon startup
		-listen <port>?: Enables remote USB debugging by waiting for a connection on the given port (default is 7936 if unspecified)
-airDownloadURL	No	Lets you choose which app store the AIR SDK is downloaded from; the default is Android Market. Use the following URL to switch to the Amazon Appstore:
		http://www.amazon.com/gp/mas/dl/android?p=com.adobe.air
SIGNING_OPTIONS	Yes	Code signing certificate store options; the most important ones are as follows:
		-storetype: The type of the keystore (usually

Argument	Required	Description
		pkcs12)
		`-keystore`: The location of the keystore
`<output-package>`	Yes	The name of the package file to be created; for Android this should have an extension of `.apk`.
`<input-package>`	No	Input AIR Intermediate (AIRI) file to sign; either this or `app-desc` must be specified.
`<app-desc>`	No	Application descriptor file in XML format; either this or `input-package` must be specified.
`PLATFORM-SDK-OPTION`	No	Optional path to a different AIR SDK than the default one for ADT; it should have the following syntax: `-platformsdk <platform-sdk-home-dir>`
`FILE-OPTIONS`	No	A sequence of file paths separated by spaces; it may refer to a whole directory and use the `*` wildcard character.

While the array of packaging options may seem daunting, you can do most tasks with only the required parameters. For example, the following would package a simple application using the information in its app descriptor:

```
adt -package -target apk -storetype pkcs12 -keystore cert.p12 Sample-app.xml Sample.swf
```

This has the minimal set of arguments for packaging an application from a descriptor and SWF file. To build a debugging version instead, you would do the following:

```
adt -package -target apk-debug -listen -storetype pkcs12 -keystore cert.p12 Sample-app.xml Sample.swf
```

This would listen on port 7936 for a USB debugging interface on startup.

AIR Intermediate (AIRI) files are very handy if you know you will be creating multiple deployments for the same project. You can either export an AIRI file from Flash Builder or create one on the command line using the `prepare` command with the following syntax:

```
adt -prepare Sample.airi Sample-app.xml Sample.swf
```

Then you can deploy to multiple different targets using the `input-package` variant of the package command:

```
adt -package -target apk -storetype pkcs12 -keystore cert.p12 Sample-android.apk Sample.airi
adt -package -target apk -airDownloadURL http://www.amazon.com/gp/mas/dl/android?p=com.adobe.air  -storetype pkcs12 -keystore cert.p12 Sample-amazon.apk Sample.airi
```

This would create two different APK files, one ready for deployment to Android Market, and the other with a different AIR download URL that will fetch the runtime from the Amazon Appstore.

COMMAND LINE DEPLOYMENT EXERCISE

The exercise will walk you step-by-step through the procedure to package, sign, install, and launch the Flash Capability Reporter example.

Here are the exercise prerequisites:

1. AIR SDK installed and in the PATH

2. Java Runtime Environment (JRE) installed and in the PATH

3. Android SDK installed

Start by opening a command prompt or terminal. You should be able to type in the command `adt` with no options and get back help with the command arguments. If it cannot find the `adt` command or complains about `java` not being in the path, verify that you have updated your PATH environment variable correctly.

Creating a Code Signing Certificate

To create a code signing certificate, you can issue the following command, where the values in angle brackets should be replaced with your name and password:

```
adt -certificate -cn <YourName> -validityPeriod 25 1024-RSA exercise.p12 <YourPassword>
```

If the command completes successfully, it will return with an exit code of 0.

Packaging the Application

To package up the application, make sure that you have run the application once in Flash Professional so the movie (`*.swf`) and application descriptor (`*-app.xml`) files can be created. Then package it into an APK file using the following command:

```
adt -package -target apk -storetype pkcs12 -keystore exercise.p12
FlashCapabilityReporter.apk FlashCapabilityReporter-app.xml FlashCapabilityReporter.swf
AppIconsForPublish/
```

This will create an APK file containing a deployable version of your application.

Installing and Launching the Application

As an additional bonus, you can install and launch your application to a device connected via USB using the following commands:

```
adt -installApp -platform android -package FlashCapabilityReporter.apk
adt -launchApp -platform android -appid com.proandroidflash.FlashCapabilityReporter
```

If this is successful, the Flash Capability Reporter application will be both installed and running on your Android phone.

Publishing AIR Apps to Android Market

Android Market is an application store for Android devices created and run by Google. Compared to other application stores, such as the Apple App Store or Amazon Appstore, Android Market is very open. It does not have a restrictive screening process, and it lets end users try an app for one day with the option for a full refund if they don't like it.

Google charges a 25 USD fee to developers in order to create an account that can be used to submit an unlimited number of applications. According to Google, this fee is designed to raise the quality of the market by preventing application spam.

This section provides an outline of the three-step process for publishing Adobe AIR applications to the Android marketplace.

Step 1: Create an Android Market Developer Account

To create an Android Market developer account, navigate to the following web site:

`http://market.android.com/publish/Home`

You will be asked to log in to the Google Account that you would like to link to your Android Market developer account. If you already have a Google Account you can use that, otherwise it is free to create a new account. However, keep in mind that once you have linked your Google Account, there is no way to change it in the future without creating a new Android Market developer account.

Next, provide the information that is required, such as your full name, a web site URL, and a phone number, and follow the prompts until you arrive at the Google Checkout site in order to submit your registration fee. To complete the process, follow the link back to the registration pages after checkout and agree to the Android Market license.

Step 2: Package Your Application

For upload to the Android store, you will need a signed application that is packaged as an APK file. You can do this either from Flash Professional, Flash Builder, or the command line, as detailed in the previous chapters.

Here are some points that you will want to keep in mind when submitting your application:

- Make sure that you are submitting a release version of your application (and not a debug or emulator version).

- If you do not need the `INTERNET` permission, which is required for debugging, remember to disable it.

- Make sure to include custom icons for your application in all the standard Android sizes (36x36, 48x48, and 72x72).

■ Make sure that you have the AIR runtime URL set to Android Market (which is the default).

Once you have built the APK file, you are ready to proceed to publishing your application to Android Market.

Step 3: Upload Your Adobe AIR Application

The Android Market application submission process is fully automated and includes detailed instructions of each step. Figure 5–15 shows an example of what the submission process would look like if you used the Gesture Check example application from Chapter 1.

Figure 5–15. *Android Market submission process*

The majority of the application submission process is taken care of simply by uploading your APK file. This includes choosing an icon, setting permissions, and choosing supported platforms.

In addition to the APK file, you are also required to submit at least two screenshots of your application as well as a large format icon (512 pixels square). To take screenshots of your application, you can either run it in an emulator on the desktop and crop the pictures to size, or use a screen capture utility to take photos right off your Android device.

After filling in the required fields, you can submit your application and it will be made available in Android Market immediately. Figure 5–16 shows the success result of a successful application deployment to Android Market.

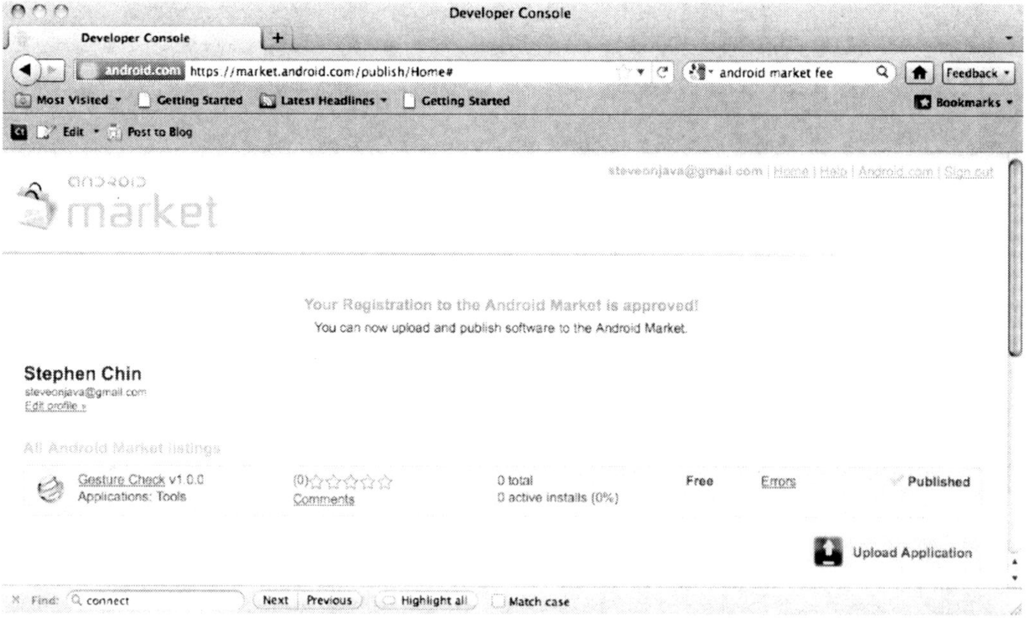

Figure 5–16. *Successfully deployed Android Market application*

Publishing AIR Apps to the Amazon Appstore

The Amazon Appstore is the second market for purchasing applications to be released for Android devices. It has very tight integration with Amazon's storefront, allowing you to purchase Android applications as well as books, CDs, and other products all from a single interface. Also, it uses Amazon's patented one-click purchase system to streamline the process of buying applications on mobile devices.

The fee for publishing applications via the Amazon Appstore is significantly higher, with a yearly subscription costing 99 USD. Fortunately, Amazon has waived the fee for the first year for developers who sign up for the Amazon developer program at the same time.

The requirements and process for publishing to the Amazon Appstore are very similar to Android Market. The same three steps for setting up your account, packaging your application, and uploading it to the store still apply.

When submitting to the Amazon Appstore, be sure to set the AIR runtime URL to point to the Amazon Appstore for download. This can be done via the deployment setting in the Flash Professional UI, or via the command line by setting the `-airDownloadURL` property of ADT to the following:

```
http://www.amazon.com/gp/mas/dl/android?p=com.adobe.air
```

Figure 5–17 shows an example of what the Amazon Appstore application submission looks like.

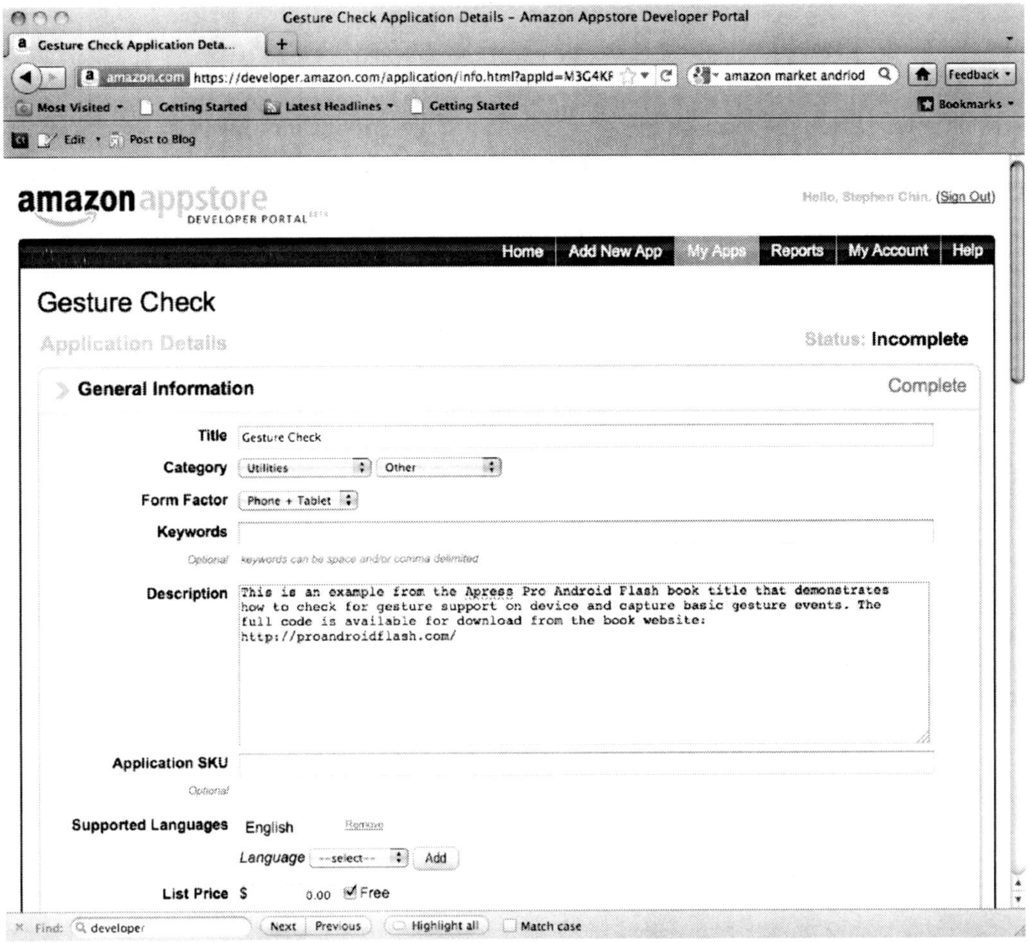

Figure 5–17. *Amazon Appstore submission proces*

Some of the main differences you will notice as a developer when submitting applications to the Amazon Appstore include the following:

▧ You are required to submit three screenshots of your application, and they must be exactly sized to 854x480 or 480x854.

- In addition to the 512x512 icon, the Amazon Appstore also requires a 114x114 icon.

- Rather than immediately seeing your application appear in the Amazon Appstore, you will have to wait for it to go through the review process.

Despite these differences, the majority of the application submission process is very similar, which makes it very easy to deploy your AIR Android applications to both app stores.

Summary

This chapter closes the loop on the end-to-end mobile application development story for the Flash platform. You now know how to take applications from inception through to fully published Android applications that end users can download from the market.

In this chapter, you learned how to do the following:

- Set up an Android Emulator and configure Android Virtual Devices

- Configure permissions that your application requests on installation

- Specify launcher icons and other resources as a part of your application

- Release AIR packages from Flash Professional, Flash Builder, and the command line

- Test your application package on devices or in the Android Emulator

- Publish your application to Android Market and the Amazon Appstore

We will take this even further in the next few chapters, as we delve into more detail on native integration with Android, performance tuning for mobile devices, and working together with designers.

Chapter 6

Adobe AIR and Native Android Apps

You have already learned how to create interesting Flex-based mobile applications, and in this chapter you will learn about other useful features that are available in Adobe AIR, and also how to merge Android-specific functionality into an Adobe AIR mobile application.

First you will learn how to do two things that are available in Adobe AIR: how to launch a native browser in an AIR application, and how to store application-specific data in a SQLite database. The next part of the chapter delves into Android fundamentals that you need to understand for the code samples that are discussed later in the chapter. This section shows you how to create a simple native Android application, along with a discussion of the main files in Android applications. You will also learn about important Android-specific concepts, such as Activities, Intents, and Services.

The third part of this chapter contains an example of an Adobe AIR mobile application that invokes an external API to provide status information about web sites that users have registered with an external service. Our Adobe AIR application stores the status of each web site in a SQLite database and then displays the status details in a datagrid. This mobile application also enables users to click a button that sends an update to native Android code, which in turn displays the update in the Android notification bar. The final part of this chapter contains the steps that are required to integrate an Adobe AIR mobile application with native Android code.

There are a few points to keep in mind regarding the material in this chapter. First, the Android content is intended to help you understand how to integrate native Android functionality into Adobe AIR applications. Consequently, only a subset of Android topics is covered, which is not enough to become a proficient Android application developer. Second, Adobe AIR is an evolving product, so it's possible that some of the Android features that are currently unavailable from Adobe AIR might become available in a future release. Third, the integration of Adobe AIR applications with native Android functionality is not officially supported by Adobe; as a result, if you experience difficulties with the integration process, there is no formal support mechanism available for you to resolve those difficulties.

Another point to consider pertains to the Android versions that are supported in the target devices for your Adobe AIR mobile application. For example, the number of mobile devices that support Android 2.2 is currently much greater than those that support Android 2.3.x or Android 3.0, both of which are currently limited to only a few tablets (such as the Samsung Galaxy Tab 10.1 and Motorola Xoom) and one smart phone (Samsung Galaxy S II).

On the other hand, if Adobe AIR supports all the functionality and features that you require for creating mobile applications, then you do not need any of the code samples in this chapter that illustrate how to merge an Adobe AIR application with an Android application. If this is the case, you can skip that material without loss of continuity.

Invoking URI Handlers in Adobe AIR

Currently there are five URI-related handlers available in Adobe AIR that enable you to perform the following actions in an Adobe AIR mobile application:

- tel (make telephone calls)

- sms (send text messages)

- mailto (send email)

- market (perform a market search)

- http and https (launch a web browser)

The code is very straightforward for each of these handlers, which makes it very simple to embed these handlers in your Adobe AIR mobile applications. One thing to keep in mind is that Adobe AIR does not provide support for the "geo" URI, but you can still navigate to maps.google.com, and users will be prompted about opening the URL in the browser session versions of the Maps application. This "workaround" gives you the ability to support maps-related functionality in Adobe AIR mobile applications.

Create a new Flex mobile project called URIHandlers, using the Mobile Application template, and add the code shown in Listing 6–1.

Listing 6–1. *Invoking URI Handlers*

```
<?xml version="1.0" encoding="utf-8"?>
<s:View xmlns:fx="http://ns.adobe.com/mxml/2009"
        xmlns:s="library://ns.adobe.com/flex/spark" title="Home">

  <fx:Script>
    <![CDATA[
      import flash.sensors.Geolocation;

      [Bindable]
      public var tel:String;
      [Bindable]
      public var sms:String;
```

```
        [Bindable]
        public var mailto:String;
        [Bindable]
        public var search:String;
        [Bindable]
        public var http:String;
        [Bindable]
        public var geo1:String;

        private var geo:Geolocation;

        private function onTel():void {
            navigateToURL(new URLRequest("tel:"+tel));
        }

        private function onSMS():void {
            navigateToURL(new URLRequest("sms:"+sms));
        }

        private function onMailto():void {
            navigateToURL(new URLRequest("mailto:"+mailto+"?subject=Hello%20AIR"));
        }

        private function onSearch():void {
            navigateToURL(new URLRequest("market://search?q=iReverse"));
        }

        private function onHTTP():void {
            navigateToURL(new URLRequest(http));
        }

        private function onGeo():void {
            this.geo = new Geolocation();
            this.geo.addEventListener(GeolocationEvent.UPDATE, onLocationUpdate);
        }

        private function onLocationUpdate(e:GeolocationEvent):void  {
            this.geo.removeEventListener(GeolocationEvent.UPDATE,onLocationUpdate);
            var long:Number = e.longitude;
            var lat:Number = e.latitude;
            navigateToURL(new URLRequest("http://maps.google.com/"));
        }
    ]]>
</fx:Script>

<s:VGroup>
  <s:Form backgroundColor="0xFFFFFF" width="300">
   <s:FormItem>
     <s:HGroup left="0">
     <s:TextInput width="180" height="50" text="{tel}"/>
     <s:Button id="telID" width="250" height="50" label="(Call)" click="onTel();"/>
     </s:HGroup>
   </s:FormItem>

   <s:FormItem>
     <s:HGroup left="0">        <s:TextInput width="180" height="50" text="{sms}"/>
     <s:Button id="smsID" width="250" height="50" label="(Text)" click="onSMS();"/>
```

```
          </s:HGroup>
        </s:FormItem>

        <s:FormItem>
          <s:HGroup left="0">
          <s:TextInput width="180" height="50" text="{mailto}"/>
          <s:Button id="mailtoID" width="250" height="50" label="(EMail)"
                  click="onMailto();"/>
          </s:HGroup>
        </s:FormItem>

        <s:FormItem>
          <s:HGroup left="0">
          <s:TextInput width="180" height="50" text="{search}"/>
          <s:Button id="searchID" width="250" height="50" label="(Search Market)"
                  click="onTel();"/>
          </s:HGroup>
        </s:FormItem>

        <s:FormItem>
          <s:HGroup left="0">
          <s:TextInput width="180" height="50" text="{http}"/>
          <s:Button id="httpID" width="250" height="50" label="(Go)" click="onHTTP();"/>
          </s:HGroup>
        </s:FormItem>

        <s:FormItem>
          <s:HGroup left="0">
          <s:TextInput width="180" height="50" text="{geo1}"/>
          <s:Button id="geoID" width="250" height="50" label="(Geo)" click="onGeo();"/>
          </s:HGroup>
        </s:FormItem>
      </s:Form>
    </s:VGroup>
</s:View>
```

Listing 6–1 contains a form with various input fields, each of which has an associated event handler that invokes the built-in method navigateToURL() with a different argument. For example, when users enter a URL and then click the associated button, the method onHTTP() launches a URL with the following line of code:

```
navigateToURL(new URLRequest(http));
```

Figure 6–1 displays a form with various input fields that illustrate how to use the URI-related functionality in AIR mobile applications.

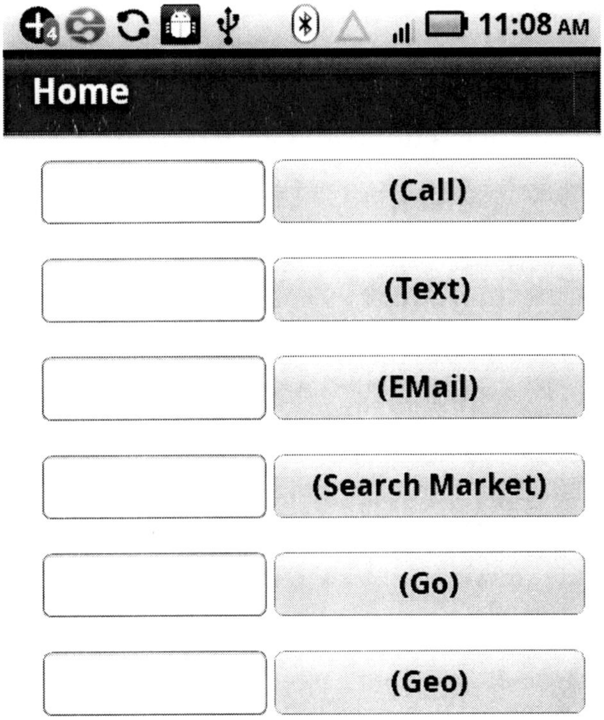

Figure 6–1. *Using URI-related functionality*

Launching Custom HTML Pages in Adobe AIR

Adobe AIR enables you to launch custom HTML pages (shown ahead) and also to navigate to arbitrary HTML pages (shown in Listing 6–2).

Create a new Flex mobile project called StageWebViewHTML1, using the ActionScript Mobile Application template, and add the code shown in Listing 6–2.

Listing 6–2. *Launching a Hard-Coded HTML Page*

```
package {
  import flash.display.Sprite;
  import flash.display.StageAlign;
  import flash.display.StageScaleMode;
  import flash.geom.Rectangle;
  import flash.media.StageWebView;

  public class StageWebViewHTML1 extends Sprite {
    public function StageWebViewHTML1() {
      super();

      // support autoOrients
      stage.align = StageAlign.TOP_LEFT;
      stage.scaleMode = StageScaleMode.NO_SCALE;
```

```
                var webView:StageWebView = new StageWebView();
                webView.stage = this.stage;
                webView.viewPort = new Rectangle( 0, 0,
                                                 stage.stageWidth,
                                                 stage.stageHeight );

            // create an HTML page
            var htmlStr:String = "<!DOCTYPE HTML>" +
              "<html>" +
              "<body>" +
                "<h3>An HTML Page in Adobe AIR</h3>" +
                "<p><strong>Hello from the Author Team:</strong></p>" +
                "<hr/>"+
                "<p>Stephen Chin</p>" +
                "<p>Dean Iverson</p>" +
                "<p>Oswald Campesato</p>" +
                "<p>Paul Trani</p>" +
                "<hr/>"+
                "<br/>"+
                "<p><i>This is the key line of code:</i></p>"+
                "<p>webView.loadString( htmlStr, 'text/html'; );</p>"+
                "<p>'htmlStr' contains the HTML contents</p>";
              "</body>" +
              "</html>";

            // launch the HTML page
            webView.loadString( htmlStr, "text/html" );
        }
      }
    }
```

Listing 6–2 contains several `import` statements and auto-generated code, and the variable `htmlStr` is a string with the contents of an HTML page that is launched with one line of code:

```
            webView.loadString( htmlStr, "text/html" );
```

If you plan to invoke hard-coded HTML pages in mobile applications, experiment with different HTML5 tags to create the stylistic effects that you need for your HTML page.

Figure 6–2 displays the output from Listing 6–2, which renders an HTML page with the hard-coded contents.

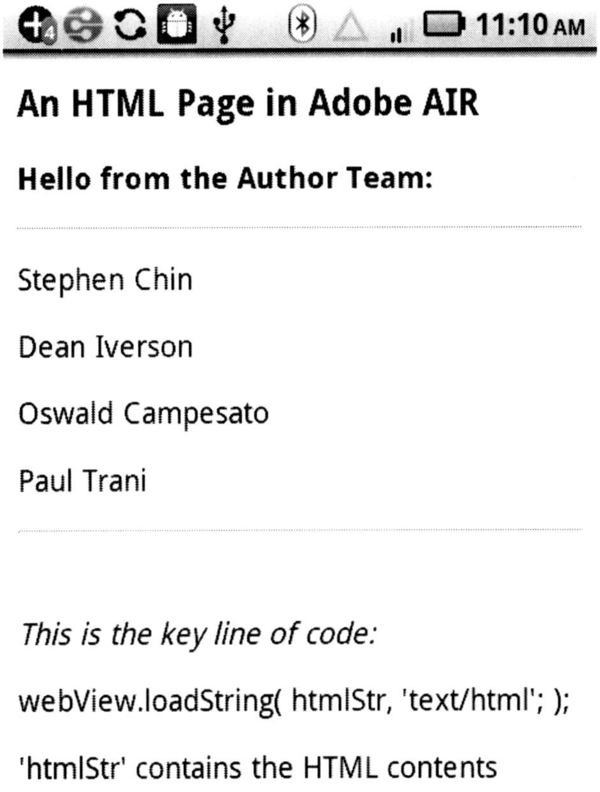

An HTML Page in Adobe AIR

Hello from the Author Team:

Stephen Chin

Dean Iverson

Oswald Campesato

Paul Trani

This is the key line of code:

webView.loadString(htmlStr, 'text/html';);

'htmlStr' contains the HTML contents

Figure 6–2. *Launching a hard-coded HTML page*

Navigating to HTML Pages in Adobe AIR

In the previous example, you learned how to launch a hard-coded HTML page, and in this section you will learn how to navigate to any HTML page and then launch that HTML page in an Adobe AIR mobile application.

Create a new Flex mobile project called StageWebViewLaunch2, using the ActionScript Mobile Application template, and add the code shown in Listing 6–3.

Listing 6–3. *Launching a User-Specified URL*

```
<?xml version="1.0" encoding="utf-8"?>
<s:View xmlns:fx="http://ns.adobe.com/mxml/2009"
        xmlns:s="library://ns.adobe.com/flex/spark"
        xmlns:mx="library://ns.adobe.com/flex/mx"
        title="HomeView" >

  <fx:Script source="StageWebViewLaunch.as"/>

  <s:Label x="10" y="50" width="150" height="50" text="Enter a URL: "/>
  <s:TextInput x="180" y="50" width="290" height="50" text="{url}"/>
```

```
    <s:Button x="10" y="120" width="300" height="50"
              label="Launch the URL" click="StageWebViewExample()" />
</s:View>
```

Listing 6–3 contains an input field that enables users to enter a URL, and also a button for launching the specified URL via the method `StageWebViewExample()` that is defined in the ActionScript3 file StageWebViewLaunch.as.

Now create the file StageWebViewLaunch.as and insert the code shown in Listing 6–4.

Listing 6–4. *The ActionScript3 Code for Launching a URL*

```
import flash.media.StageWebView;
import flash.geom.Rectangle;

import flash.events.ErrorEvent;
import flash.events.Event;
import flash.events.LocationChangeEvent;

[Bindable]
public var url:String = "http://www.google.com";

private var webView:StageWebView = new StageWebView();

public function StageWebViewExample() {
  webView.stage = this.stage;
  webView.viewPort = new Rectangle( 0, 0,
                                    stage.stageWidth,
                                    stage.stageHeight );

  webView.addEventListener(Event.COMPLETE, completeHandler);
  webView.addEventListener(ErrorEvent.ERROR, errorHandler);
  webView.addEventListener(LocationChangeEvent.LOCATION_CHANGING,
                           locationChangingHandler);
  webView.addEventListener(LocationChangeEvent.LOCATION_CHANGE,
                           locationChangeHandler);

  // launch the user-specified URL
  webView.loadURL( url );
}

// Dispatched after the page or web content has been fully loaded
protected function completeHandler(event:Event):void {
  dispatchEvent(event);
}

// Dispatched when the location is about to change
protected function locationChangingHandler(event:Event):void {
  dispatchEvent(event);
}

// Dispatched after the location has changed
protected function locationChangeHandler(event:Event):void {
  dispatchEvent(event);
}

// Dispatched when an error occurs
protected function errorHandler(event:ErrorEvent):void {
```

```
  dispatchEvent(event);
}
```

Listing 6–4 defines the `Bindable` variable `url` that references the user-specified URL, followed by the variable `webView` that contains URL-specific functionality. The method `StageWebViewExample()` defines various event handlers, all of which invoke the built-in method `dispatchEvent()`, and then the user-specified URL is launched with this line of code:

```
  webView.loadURL( url );
```

Figure 6–3 displays the Google home page, which is the default URL in Listing 6–4.

Figure 6–3. *Launching a user-specified URL*

Accessing SQLite in Adobe AIR

Adobe AIR provides support for accessing data in a SQLite database that is stored on a mobile device. You can also access a SQLite database directly from native Android code, but Adobe AIR provides a higher level of abstraction (and the code is simpler).

Create a new Flex mobile project called SQLite1, using the Mobile Application template, and add the code shown in Listing 6–5.

Listing 6–5. *Viewing Data in a SQLite Database*

```
<?xml version="1.0" encoding="utf-8"?>
<s:View xmlns:fx="http://ns.adobe.com/mxml/2009"
        xmlns:s="library://ns.adobe.com/flex/spark"
        title="HomeView" creationComplete="start()">

  <fx:Script source="SQLiteAccess.as"/>

  <s:Label x="10" y="10" width="400" height="50"
           text="Create New Person and Click 'Add'"/>
  <s:Label x="10" y="50" width="150" height="50" text="First name:"/>
  <s:TextInput x="250" y="50" width="200" height="50" id="first_name"/>

  <s:Label x="10" y="100" width="150" height="50" text="Last name:"/>
  <s:TextInput x="250" y="100" width="200" height="50" id="last_name"/>

  <s:Button x="10" y="160" width="200" height="50"
            label="Add" click="addItem()"/>

  <s:Button label="Remove Selected Person" height="50" x="10" y="230"
            click="remove()" enabled="{dg.selectedIndex != -1}"/>

  <s:DataGrid id="dg" left="10" right="10" top="300" bottom="80"
              dataProvider="{dp}">
    <s:columns>
      <s:ArrayList>
        <s:GridColumn headerText="Index"
                      dataField="id"
                      width="100" />
        <s:GridColumn headerText="First name"
                      dataField="first_name"
                      width="150" />
        <s:GridColumn headerText="Last name"
                      dataField="last_name"
                      width="150" />
      </s:ArrayList>
    </s:columns>
  </s:DataGrid>
</s:View>
```

Listing 6–5 contains a XML Script element that references an ActionScript3 file containing methods that access a SQLite database, and its contents will be shown in Listing 6–6. The labels and text input fields enable users to enter a first name and a last name for each new person that will be added to our database.

There is one XML Button element for adding a new person via the addPerson() method, and also one XML Button for deleting an existing person from our database via the removePerson() method. Both methods are defined in SQLiteAccess.as. The variable dp is a Bindable variable that contains the data that is displayed in the datagrid, and since users can add as well as delete rows of data, dp is a Bindable variable.

Since we are accessing data that is stored in a SQLite database, we need to define several methods in ActionScript3 for managing the creating, accessing, and updating of the contents of the database. Create a new ActionScript3 file called SQLiteAccess.as in the same directory as the file SQLite1HomeView.mxml, and add the code shown in Listing 6–6.

Listing 6–6. *Defining Database Access Methods in ActionScript3*

```
import flash.data.SQLStatement;
import flash.errors.SQLError;
import flash.events.Event;
import flash.events.SQLErrorEvent;
import flash.events.SQLEvent;
import flash.events.TimerEvent;
import flash.filesystem.File;
import flash.utils.Timer;

import mx.collections.ArrayCollection;
import mx.utils.ObjectUtil;

import org.osmf.events.TimeEvent;
```

Listing 6–6 contains various SQL-related import statements and also a Timer class, which we will use when we attempt to read the contents of the updated database. Since only one SQL statement can be executing at any given point in time, the Timer class gives us the ability to "try again later" (measured in milliseconds).

```
// sqlconn holds the database connection
public var sqlconn:SQLConnection = new SQLConnection();

// sqlstmt holds SQL commands
public var sqlstmt:SQLStatement = new SQLStatement();

// a bindable ArrayCollection and the data provider for the datagrid
[Bindable]
public var dp:ArrayCollection = new ArrayCollection();

// invoked after the application has loaded
private function start():void {
    // set 'people.db' as the file for our database (created after it's opened)
    var db:File = File.applicationStorageDirectory.resolvePath("people.db");

    // open the database in asynchronous mode
    sqlconn.openAsync(db);

    // event listeners for handling sql errors and 'result' are
    // invoked whenever data is retrieved from the database
    sqlconn.addEventListener(SQLEvent.OPEN, db_opened);
    sqlconn.addEventListener(SQLErrorEvent.ERROR, error);
    sqlstmt.addEventListener(SQLErrorEvent.ERROR, error);
```

```
    sqlstmt.addEventListener(SQLEvent.RESULT, result);
}
```

The variables `sqlconn` and `sqlstmt` enable us to get a connection to our SQLite database and also execute SQL queries. The `start()` method specifies the database name as `people.db`, and then opens an asynchronous connection. Note the various event handlers that are used for handling database-related actions as well as handling errors.

```
private function db_opened(e:SQLEvent):void {
    // specify the connection for the SQL statement
    sqlstmt.sqlConnection = sqlconn;

    // Table "person_table" contains three columns:
    // 1) id  (an autoincrementing integer)
    // 2) first_name (the first name of each person)
    // 3) last_name (the last name of each person)
  sqlstmt.text = "CREATE TABLE IF NOT EXISTS person_table
                            ( id INTEGER PRIMARY KEY AUTOINCREMENT,
                              first_name TEXT, last_name TEXT);";

    // execute the sqlstmt to update the database
    sqlstmt.execute();

    // refresh the datagrid to display all data rows
    refreshDataGrid();
}

// function to append a new row to person_table
// each new row contains first_name and last_name
private function addPerson():void {
    sqlstmt.text = "INSERT INTO person_table (first_name, last_name)
                            VALUES('"+first_name.text+"','"+last_name.text+"');";
    sqlstmt.execute();

    refreshDataGrid();
}
```

The method `db_opened()` specifies the name of the database and the table that contains our person-related data, and then executes the `refreshDataGrid()` method, which retrieves the latest contents of our database in order to display that data in the datagrid of our mobile application. Notice that after `addPerson()` has inserted a new person, the `refreshDataGrid()` method is invoked so that the datagrid will automatically display the newly added person.

```
// function to refresh the data in datagrid
private function refreshDataGrid(e:TimerEvent = null):void {
    // timer object pauses and then attempts to execute again
    var timer:Timer = new Timer(100,1);
    timer.addEventListener(TimerEvent.TIMER, refreshDataGrid);

    if ( !sqlstmt.executing ) {
      sqlstmt.text = "SELECT * FROM person_table"
      sqlstmt.execute();
    } else {
      timer.start();
```

```
   }
}

// invoked when we receive data from a sql command
private function result(e:SQLEvent):void {
  var data:Array = sqlstmt.getResult().data;

  // fill the datagrid
  dp = new ArrayCollection(data);
}

// remove a row from the table
private function removePerson():void {
  sqlstmt.text = "DELETE FROM person_table WHERE id="+dp[dg.selectedIndex].id;
  sqlstmt.execute();
  refreshDataGrid();
}

// error handling method
private function error(e:SQLErrorEvent):void {
// Alert.show(e.toString());
}
```

The method refreshDataGrid() first checks whether a SQL statement is currently being executed; if so, then it pauses the specified number of milliseconds (which is 100 in this example) and then retrieves all the rows from the person_table (which will include newly added persons). The method result() populates the variable dp with the refreshed set of data. The removePerson() method deletes the row that users selected by tapping on that row in the datagrid.

Figure 6–4 displays a set of rows that are stored in a SQLite database on a mobile device.

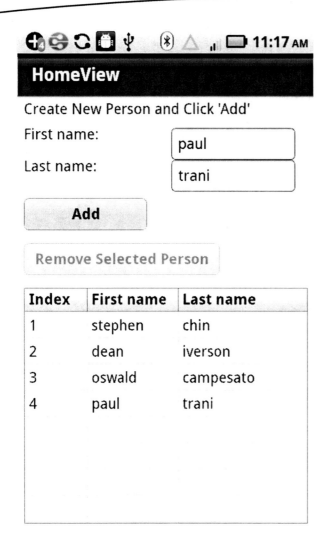

Figure 6–4. *A set of records in a SQLite database*

Learning Basic Concepts in Android

Android is an open source toolkit for developing Android mobile applications, and at the time of writing Android 3.0 ("Honeycomb") is the latest major release; the most current version of Android is 3.1. Note that Adobe AIR 2.5.1 for mobile applications requires at least Android 2.2, and you can install Adobe AIR applications on mobile devices that support Android 2.2 or higher.

The following sections provide some information about the major features of Android 3.0, where to download Android, and key concepts in Android. When you finish this section, you'll have an understanding of how to create native Android applications.

Major Features of Android 3.0

Earlier versions of Android provided support for UI components and event handlers, audio and video, managing files on the file system, graphics and animation effects, database support, web services, and telephony and messaging (SMS).

Google Android 3.0 (released in early 2011) provides backward-compatible support for the functionality in Android 2.3 (which was released in December 2010). Android 3.0 provides feature improvements over version 2.3 as well as the following new features:

- A new UI for tablets
- System bar for status and notifications
- Action bar for application control
- Customizable home screen
- Copy/paste support
- More connectivity options
- SVG support
- Universal remote function
- Google Docs integration
- Built-in remote desktop
- Improved media player
- Better GPS support
- Improved multitasking
- Tracking facility
- Battery life/power management improvements

The nice feature improvements in Android 3.0 involve longer battery life, faster graphics rendering, and richer media functionality (e.g., time-lapse video, HTTP live streaming, and DRM). Moreover, Android 3.1 supports another set of new features, including APIs for USB accessories and new input events from mice, trackballs, and joysticks. However, in this chapter we are focusing on a small subset of Android functionality that we need to understand in order to merge Adobe AIR applications with native Android applications, so we will not delve into the features of Android 3.x. Navigate to the Android home page to obtain more information about the new and improved suite of features that are supported in |Android 3.x.

Download/Installation of Android

You need to download and install Java, Eclipse, and Android in order to develop Android-based mobile applications in Eclipse. Note that Java is pre-installed on Mac OSX, and Java is also available for download via Linux-based package managers. You can download Java for your platform here: `http://java.sun.com/javase/downloads`.

If you have a Windows machine, you need to set the environment variable `JAVA_HOME` to the directory where you uncompressed the Java distribution.

The Android SDK is available for download here: `http://developer.android.com/sdk/index.html`.

For the Windows platform, the Android distribution is a file with the following type of name (this may be slightly different by the time this book is published): `android-sdk_r06-windows.zip`.

After you have completed the Java and Eclipse installation, follow the Android installation steps in order to install Android on your machine.

You also need to create an AVD (Android Virtual Device), and the step-by-step instructions for doing so are in Chapter 5.

Key Concepts in Android

Although Android applications are written in Java, the Java code is compiled into a Dalvik executable, which (along with other assets) is part of the `.apk` application file that is deployed to Android devices.

In addition to support for standard Java language features, Android applications usually involve some combination of the following Android-specific concepts:

- Activities
- Intents
- Services
- Broadcast receivers

After you have mastered the concepts in the preceding list, you can learn about `Intent Filters` and `Content Providers` (a full discussion of these two topics is beyond the scope of this chapter) and how to use them in order to provide more fine-grained Intent-based functionality as well as the ability to share data across Android applications.

The properties of every Android application are specified in the XML document `AndroidManifest.xml`, which is automatically generated during the creation of every Android application. This manifest file contains information about the Activities, `Intents`, `Services`, `Broadcast` receivers, and permissions that are part of the associated Android application.

An Android application can contain multiple Android Activities, and each Android Activity can contain multiple Intents and Intent Filters. Furthermore, an Android application can contain an Android Service and also an Android Broadcast receiver, both of which are defined as sibling elements of the Android activity elements in AndroidManifest.xml.

Listing 6–7 provides an outline of what you might find in an AndroidManifest.xml project file. In this case, the project file contains the "stubs" for two Android Activities, two Android Services, and two Android Broadcast receivers. The attributes of the XML elements have been omitted so that you can see the overall structure of an Android application, and later in this chapter you will see a complete example of the contents of AndroidManifest.xml.

Listing 6–7. *An Outline of an* AndroidManifest.xml

```
<manifest xmlns:android=http://schemas.android.com/apk/res/android>
    <application>
        <activity>
            <intent-filter>
            </intent-filter>
        </activity>
        <activity>
        </activity>
        <service>
        </service>
        <service>
            <intent-filter>
            </intent-filter>
        </service>
        <receiver>
        </receiver>
        <receiver>
            <intent-filter>
            </intent-filter>
        </receiver>
    </application>
</manifest>
```

Listing 6–7 contains two Android activity elements, two Android service elements, and two Android receiver elements. In each of these three pairs, there is one element that contains an Android intent-filter element, but keep in mind that many variations are possible for the contents of AndroidManifest.xml. The exact contents of the project file depend on the functionality of your Android application.

Android also supports Java Native Interface (JNI), which allows Java code to invoke C/C++ functions. However, you also need to download and install the Android Native Development Kit (NDK), which contains a set of tools for creating libraries that contain functions that can be called from Java code. You can use JNI if you need better performance (especially for graphics) than you can achieve through Java alone, but the details of this topic are beyond the scope of this chapter.

Android Activities

An Android Activity corresponds to a screen or a view of an application, and the main entry point of an Android application is an Android Activity that contains an onCreate() method (which overrides the same method in its superclass) that is invoked whenever you launch an Android application. When you launch your Android application, its Android Activity will be started automatically. As an example, Listing 6–8 displays the contents of HelloWorld.java, which is automatically generated when you create an Eclipse-based "Hello World" Android application later in this chapter.

Listing 6–8. *Contents of HelloWorld.java*

```
package com.apress.hello;

import android.app.Activity;
import android.os.Bundle;

public class HelloWorld extends Activity
{
    /** Called when the activity is first created. */
    @Override
    public void onCreate(Bundle savedInstanceState)
    {
        super.onCreate(savedInstanceState);
        setContentView(R.layout.main);
    }
}
```

During the project creation step for Android applications, you specify the package name and the class name; the rest of the generated code is the same for every Android project.

Notice that HelloWorld extends android.app.Activity, and it also overrides the onCreate() method. As you can probably surmise, an Android Activity is an Android class containing a set of methods (such as onCreate()) that you can override in your Android applications. An Activity contains one or more Views that belong to an Android application.

An Android View is what users see on the screen, which includes the UI widgets of the Android application. The HelloWorld Android application contains an Android class that extends the Android Activity class and overrides the onCreate() method with your custom code. Note that Android applications can also extend other Android classes (such as the Service class), and they can also create threads.

An Android application can contain more than one Android Activity, and as you already know, every Activity must be defined in the XML document AndroidManifest.xml, which is part of every Android application.

The HelloWorld Android project contains the XML document AndroidManifest.xml, in which the Android class HelloWorld is registered in the XML activity element, as shown in Listing 6–9.

Listing 6–9. *Contents of AndroidManifest.xml*

```xml
<?xml version="1.0" encoding="utf-8"?>
<manifest xmlns:android="http://schemas.android.com/apk/res/android"
        package="com.apress.hello"
        android:versionCode="1"
        android:versionName="1.0">
    <application android:icon="@drawable/icon"
                       android:label="@string/app_name">
        <activity android:name=".HelloWorld"
                     android:label="@string/app_name">
            <intent-filter>
                <action android:name="android.intent.action.MAIN" />
                <category android:name="android.intent.category.LAUNCHER" />
            </intent-filter>
        </activity>

    </application>
    <uses-sdk android:minSdkVersion="9" />
</manifest>
```

Notice the period (".") that precedes the Android `Activity` `HelloWorld` in Listing 6–9. This period is mandatory because the string `.HelloWorld` is appended to the package name `com.apress.hello` (also specified in Listing 6–9), so the fully qualified name of `HelloWorld.java` in this Android project is `com.apress.hello.HelloWorld`.

Android Intents

The Android UI (user interface) consists of `Intents` and `Views`. In abstract terms, an Android `Intent` represents the details regarding an action (often described by a verb) to perform in an Android application.

An `Intent` is essentially a notification between Android `Activities` (or `Services`). An `Intent` enables an Android `Activity` to send data to other Android `Activities` and also to receive data from other Android `Activities`.

An Android `Intent` is similar to an event handler, but Android provides additional functionality for handling multiple `Intents` and options for using existing `Intents` vs. starting a new `Intent`. Android `Intents` can start a new Android `Activity`, and they can also broadcast messages (which are processed by Android `Broadcast` receivers). The following snippet illustrates how to start a new `Activity` via an `Intent`:

```
Intent intent = new Intent(action, data);
startActivity(intent);
```

Android `Activities` and `Intents` provide a loosely coupled set of resources that is reminiscent of SOA (service-oriented architecture). The counterpart of an Android `Activity` would be a web service, and the `Intents` that the Android `Activity` can process are comparable to the "operations" or methods that the web service makes available to the world. Other Android applications can explicitly invoke one of those methods, or they can make a "general" request, in which case the "framework" determines which web services will handle that general request.

You can also broadcast `Intents` in order to send messages between components. The following snippet illustrates how to broadcast an `Intent`:

```
Intent intent = new Intent(a-broadcast-receiver-class);
sendBroadcast(intent);
```

This type of functionality provides a greater flexibility and "openness" for Android applications.

Types of Android Intents

There are several types of Android `Intents`, each of which provides slightly different functionality. A *directed* `Intent` is an `Intent` with one recipient, whereas a *broadcast* `Intent` can be received by any process. An *explicit* `Intent` specifies the Java class that needs to be invoked. An *implicit* `Intent` is an `Intent` that does not specify a Java class, which means that the Android system will determine which application will process the implicit `Intent`. If there are several applications available that can respond to an implicit `Intent`, the Android system gives users the ability to select one of those applications.

Android also has the notion of `Intent Filters`, which are used for `Intent` resolution. An `Intent Filter` indicates the `Intents` that an Android `Activity` (or Android `Service`) can "consume," and the details are specified in the XML intent-filter element. Note that if an application does not provide an `Intent Filter`, then it can be invoked only by an explicit `Intent` (and not by an implicit `Intent`).

An `Intent Filter` is specified in an Android `Activity` in the file `AndroidManifest.xml`, as shown in Listing 6–10.

Listing 6–10. *An Example of an* `Intent Filter` *in Android*

```
<intent-filter>
    <action android:name="android.intent.action.MAIN" />
    <category android:name="android.intent.category.LAUNCHER" />
</intent-filter>
```

Listing 6–10 displays a fragment from the contents of `AndroidManifest.xml`, which is shown in Listing 6–9. The XML `action` element in Listing 6–10 specifies the default value `android.intent.action.MAIN`, and the XML category element specifies `android.intent.category.LAUNCHER` (also a default value), which means that the parent `Activity` will be displayed in the application launcher.

An `Intent Filter` must contain an XML action element, and optionally contain an XML category element or an XML data element. As you can see, Listing 6–10 contains the mandatory XML action element that specifies the default action, and an optional XML category element, but not the optional XML data element.

An `Intent Filter` is a set of information that defines a specific action; the XML data element specifies the data to be acted upon, and the XML category element specifies the component that will perform the action.

There are various combinations of these three XML elements that can be specified in an `Intent Filter` because two of these elements are optional, and Android uses a priority-based algorithm to determine what will be executed for each `Intent Filter` that you define in `AndroidManifest.xml`. If you need to learn about `Intent Filters` in greater detail, consult the Android documentation for additional information.

In case you are interested in finding out about Android `Intents` that are freely available, you can visit OpenIntents, which is an open source project consisting of various Android `Intents` that have been donated by other people, and its home page is here: `www.openintents.org/en/`.

OpenIntents provides Android applications in various categories, such as utilities, business applications, education, and entertainment. The applications are available as `.apk` files, and sometimes the source code for those applications is also available for free. Moreover, OpenIntents provides links to Android libraries such as game engines, charting packages, and services such as accessing a CouchDB server, Drupal, Facebook, and many others. The OpenIntents libraries are available here: `www.openintents.org/en/libraries`.

OpenIntents also provides a registry of publicly available Android `Intents` that can be invoked by Android Activities, along with their class files, and a description of their services. Visit the OpenIntents home page for more information.

Android Services

Android `Services` are available for handling background tasks and other tasks that do not involve a visual interface. Since Android `Services` run in the main thread of the main process, Android `Services` typically start a new thread when they need to perform work without blocking the UI (which is handled in the main thread) of the Android application. Thus, an Android application can "bind" to a `Service` through a set of APIs that are exposed by that service.

An Android `Service` is defined via an XML `service` element in `AndroidManifest.xml`, as shown here:

```
<service android:name=".subpackagename.SimpleService"/>
```

Listing 6–11 displays the contents of `ServiceName.java`, which provides "skeleton" code for the definition of a custom Android Service class.

Listing 6–11. *Contents of* `SimpleService.java`

```
public class SimpleService extends Service {
   @Override
   public IBinder onBind(Intent intent) {
      return null;
   }

   @Override
   protected void onCreate() {
      super.onCreate();
      startservice(); // defined elsewhere
   }

   @Override
```

```
    protected void onCreate() {
        // insert your code here
    }

    @Override
    protected void onStart() {
        // insert your code here
    }
}
```

For example, if you need to execute something on a regular basis, you can include an instance of a `Timer` class that schedules and executes a `TimerTask` as often as required for your application needs.

Android Broadcast Receivers

The purpose of an Android Broadcast receiver is to "listen" to Android Intents. Listing 6–12 displays the definition of an Android Broadcast receiver in the `AndroidManifest.xml` file for the widget-based Android application that is discussed later in this chapter.

Listing 6–12. *Sample Entry for a Receiver in* `AndroidManifest.xml`

```
<!-- Broadcast Receiver that will process AppWidget updates -->
    <receiver android:name=".MyHelloWidget" android:label="@string/app_name">
        <intent-filter>
            <action android:name="android.appwidget.action.APPWIDGET_UPDATE" />
        </intent-filter>
        <meta-data android:name="android.appwidget.provider"
                    android:resource="@xml/hello_widget_provider" />
    </receiver>
```

Listing 6–12 contains an XML receiver element that specifies `MyHelloWidget` as the Java class for this widget. This Android receiver contains an XML `intent-filter` element with an XML `action` element that causes an action to occur when it is time to update the `AppWidget` `MyHelloWidget`, as shown here:

```
<action android:name="android.appwidget.action.APPWIDGET_UPDATE" />
```

Android Life Cycle

Earlier in this chapter, you saw the contents of `HelloWorld.java`, which contains the `onCreate()` method that overrides the same method in the superclass. In fact, `onCreate()` is one of the seven Android methods that make up the Android application life cycle.

A Google Android application contains the following methods, and this is the order in which methods are invoked during the life cycle of an Android application[1]:

- onCreate()
- onRestart()
- onStart()
- onResume()
- onPause()
- onStop()
- onDestroy()

The onCreate() method is invoked when an Activity is created, and its role is similar to init() methods in other languages. The onDestroy() method is invoked when an Activity is removed from memory, and its role is essentially that of a destructor method in C++. The onPause() method is invoked when an Activity must be paused (such as reclaiming resources). The onRestart() method is invoked when an Activity is being restarted. The onResume() method is invoked when an Activity interacts with a user. The onStart() method is invoked when an Activity becomes visible on the screen. Finally, the onStop() method is invoked in order to stop an Activity.

The methods onRestart(), onStart(), and onStop() are in the visible phase; the methods onResume() and onPause() are in the foreground phase. An Android application can pause and resume many times during the execution of that application; the details are specific to the functionality of the application (and possibly the type of user interaction as well).

Creating Android Applications

This section describes how to create an Android application in Eclipse, and a subsequent section shows you the directory structure of an Android application, followed by a discussion of the main files that are created in every Android application.

Launch Eclipse and perform the following sequence of steps in order to create a new Android application called HelloWorld:

1. Navigate to **File ➤ New ➤ Android Project**.

2. Enter "HelloWorld" for the project name.

3. Select the check box on the left of "Android 2.3" for the Build Target.

4. Enter "HelloWorld" for the Application name.

---

[1] http://developer.android.com/reference/android/app/Activity.html#Activity Lifecycle

5.   Enter "com.apress.hello" for the Package name.

6.   Enter "HelloWorld" in the Create Activity input field.

7.   Enter the digit "9" for the Min SDK Version.

8.   Click the Finish button.

Eclipse will generate a new Android project (whose structure is described in the next section). Next, launch this application by right-clicking the project name HelloWorld, and then selecting **Run As ➤ Android Application**. You must wait until the Android emulator completes its initialization steps, which can require a minute or so (but each subsequent launching of your application will be noticeably faster).

Figure 6–5 displays the output of the HelloWorld application in an Android simulator that is launched from Eclipse.

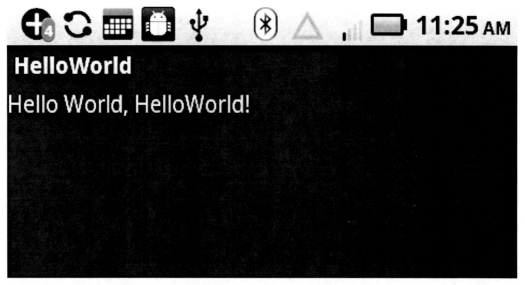

Figure 6–5. *The HelloWorld Android application*

The Structure of an Android Application

Navigate to the HelloWorld project that you created in the previous section, and right-click the project name in order to display the expanded directory structure. The next several sub-sections discuss the directory structure and the contents of the main files of every Android application.

Listing 6–13 displays the directory structure of the Android project HelloWorld.

Listing 6–13. *Structure of an Android Project*

```
+HelloWorld
  src/
    com/
      apress/
        hello/
          HelloWorld.java
  gen/
    com/
      apress/
        hello/
          R.java
  Android 2.3/
    android.jar
  assets/
  res/
    drawable-hdpi/
      icon.png
    drawable-ldpi/
      icon.png
    drawable-mdpi/
      icon.png
    layout/
      main.xml
    values/
      strings.xml
  AndroidManifest.xml
  default.properties
proguard.cfg
```

This Android application contains two Java files (HelloWorld.java and R.java), a JAR file (android.jar), an image file (icon.png), three XML files (main.xml, strings.xml, and AndroidManifest.xml), and a text file, default.properties.

The Main Files in an Android Application

The files in the HelloWorld Android application that we will discuss in this section are listed here (all files are listed relative to the project root directory):

- src/com/apress/hello/HelloWorld.java
- gen/com/apress/hello/R.java
- AndroidManifest.xml
- res/layout/main.xml
- res/values/strings.xml

Listing 6–14 displays the contents of HelloWorld.java, which is where you include all the custom Java code that is required for this Android application.

Listing 6–14. *Contents of* HelloWorld.java

```
package com.apress.hello;

import android.app.Activity;
import android.os.Bundle;

public class HelloWorld extends Activity {
    /** Called when the activity is first created. */
    @Override
    public void onCreate(Bundle savedInstanceState) {
        super.onCreate(savedInstanceState);
        setContentView(R.layout.main);
    }
}
```

Earlier in this chapter, you saw the contents of HelloWorld.java. You can think of this code as "boilerplate" code that is automatically generated during project creation, based on the user-supplied values for the package name and the class name.

Your custom code is included immediately after this statement:

```
    setContentView(R.layout.main);
```

Instead of setting the View from the file main.xml, it is also common to set the View from another XML file or from a custom class that is defined elsewhere in your Android project.

Now let's look at Listing 6–15, which displays the contents of the resources file R.java, which is automatically generated for you when you create an Android application.

Listing 6–15. *Contents of* R.java

```
/* AUTO-GENERATED FILE.  DO NOT MODIFY.
 *
 * This class was automatically generated by the
 * aapt tool from the resource data it found.  It
 * should not be modified by hand.
 */

package com.apress.hello;

public final class R {
    public static final class attr {
    }
    public static final class drawable {
        public static final int icon=0x7f020000;
    }
    public static final class layout {
        public static final int main=0x7f030000;
    }
    public static final class string {
        public static final int app_name=0x7f040001;
        public static final int hello=0x7f040000;
    }
}
```

The integer values in Listing 6–15 are essentially references that correspond to assets of an Android application. For example, the variable `icon` is a reference to the `icon.png` file that is located in a subdirectory of the `res` directory. The variable `main` is a reference to the XML file `main.xml` (shown later in this section) that is in the `res/layout` subdirectory. The variables `app_name` and `hello` are references to the XML `app_name` element and XML `hello` element that are in the XML file `strings.xml` (shown earlier in this section) that is in the `res/values` subdirectory.

Now that we have explored the contents of the Java-based project files, let's turn our attention to the XML-based files in our Android project. Listing 6–16 displays the entire contents of `AndroidManifest.xml`.

Listing 6–16. *Contents of AndroidManifest.xml*

```xml
<?xml version="1.0" encoding="utf-8"?>
<manifest xmlns:android="http://schemas.android.com/apk/res/android"
        package="com.apress.hello"
        android:versionCode="1"
        android:versionName="1.0">
    <application android:icon="@drawable/icon"
                        android:label="@string/app_name">
        <activity android:name=".HelloWorld"
                        android:label="@string/app_name">
        <intent-filter>
            <action android:name="android.intent.action.MAIN" />
            <category android:name="android.intent.category.LAUNCHER" />
        </intent-filter>
        </activity>

    </application>
    <uses-sdk android:minSdkVersion="9" />
</manifest>
```

Listing 6–16 starts with an XML declaration, followed by an XML `manifest` element that contains child XML elements, which provide information about your Android application. Notice that the XML `manifest` element contains an attribute with the package name of your Android application.

The XML `application` element in Listing 6–16 contains an `android:icon` attribute whose value is `@drawable/icon`, which refers to an image file `icon.png` that is located in the `res` subdirectory. Android supports three types of image files: high-density, medium-density, and low-density. The corresponding directories are `drawable-hdpi`, `drawable-mdpi`, and `drawable-ldpi`, all of which are subdirectories of the `res` directory under the root directory of every Android application.

The XML `application` element in Listing 6–16 also contains an `android:label` attribute whose value is `@string/app_name`, which refers to an XML element in the file `strings.xml` that is in the `res/values` subdirectory.

Listing 6–16 contains an XML `intent-filter` element, which was briefly discussed earlier in this chapter. The final part of Listing 6–10 specifies the minimum Android version number that is required for this application, as shown here:

```xml
<uses-sdk android:minSdkVersion="9" />
```

In our current example, the minimum version is 9, which is also the number that we specified during the creation step of this Android application.

Now let's take a look at Listing 6–17, which displays the contents of the XML file `strings.xml`.

Listing 6–17. *Contents of* `strings.xml`

```xml
<?xml version="1.0" encoding="utf-8"?>
<resources>
    <string name="hello">Hello World, HelloWorld!</string>
    <string name="app_name">HelloWorld</string>
</resources>
```

Listing 6–17 is straightforward: it contains an XML resources element with two XML child elements that are used to display the string "Hello World, HelloWorld!" when you launch this Android application. Note that the XML application element in the XML document `AndroidManifest.xml` references also the second XML string element, whose name attribute has the value app_name, as shown here:

```xml
<application android:icon="@drawable/icon"
                android:label="@string/app_name">
```

Now let's look at Listing 6–18, which displays the contents of the XML document `main.xml`, which contains View-related information about this Android application.

Listing 6–18. *Contents of* `main.xml`

```xml
<?xml version="1.0" encoding="utf-8"?>
<LinearLayout xmlns:android="http://schemas.android.com/apk/res/android"
    android:orientation="vertical"
    android:layout_width="fill_parent"
    android:layout_height="fill_parent"
    >
<TextView
    android:layout_width="fill_parent"
    android:layout_height="wrap_content"
    android:text="@string/hello"
    />
</LinearLayout>
```

Listing 6–18 contains an XML LinearLayout element that is the default layout for an Android application. Android supports other layout types, including AbsoluteLayout, FrameLayout, RelativeLayout, and TableLayout (none of which are discussed in this chapter).

The XML LinearLayout element contains a fill_parent attribute that indicates that the current element will be as large as the parent element (minus padding). The attributes layout_width and layout_height specify the basic values for the width and height of the View.

The XML TextView element contains the attributes layout_width and layout_height, whose values are fill_parent and wrap_content, respectively. The wrap_content attribute specifies that the size of the View will be just big enough to enclose its content (plus padding). The attribute text refers to the XML hello element that is specified in the strings.xml file (located in the res/values subdirectory), whose definition is shown here:

```
<string name="hello">Hello World, HelloWorld!</string>
```

The string "Hello World, HelloWorld!" is the text that is displayed when you launch the "Hello World" Android application in the Android simulator or in an Android device after having deployed this Android application.

Sending Notifications in Android Applications

As you already know, Adobe does not provide built-in support for notifications, which are available in native Android mobile applications. However, the example in this section will show you how to create an Adobe AIR mobile application and a native Android application that can be merged into a single .apk file, which will support the Notification-related functionality.

James Ward (who wrote the foreword for this book) contributed the socket-based code in this section, and Elad Elrom provided the step-by-step instructions for merging an Adobe AIR mobile application with a native Android application.

This section is lengthy because there is an initial setup sequence (involving six steps), two Adobe AIR source files, and also Android source files for this mobile application. The first part describes the setup sequence; the second part of this section discusses the two source files with Adobe AIR code; and the third part discusses the two source files with native Android code.

1. Download a package with the required dependencies for extending AIR for Android:

www.jamesward.com/downloads/extending_air_for_android-flex_4_5-air_2_6-v_1.zip

2. Create a regular Android project in Eclipse (do not create an Activity yet): specify a "Project name:" of FooAndroid, select Android 2.2 for the "Target name:", type "FooAndroid" for the "Application name:", enter "com.proandroidflash" for the "Package name:", type "8" for the "Min SDK Version:", and then click the Finish button.

3. Copy all of the files from the zip file you downloaded in step 1 into the root directory of the newly created Android project. You will need to overwrite the existing files, and Eclipse will prompt you about updating the launch configuration.

4. Delete the res/layout directory.

5. Add the airbootstrap.jar file to the project's build path by right-clicking the file, and then select Build Path and Add to Build Path.

6. Launch the project and confirm that you see "Hello, world" on your
    Android device. If so, then the AIR application is properly being
    bootstrapped and the Flex application in assets/app.swf is correctly
    being run.

Now that we have completed the initial setup steps, let's create a new Flex mobile
project called Foo, using the Mobile Application template, and add the code shown in
Listing 6–19.

Listing 6–19. *Receiving Data and Sending the Data to a Notification on Android*

```
<?xml version="1.0" encoding="utf-8"?>
<s:View xmlns:fx="http://ns.adobe.com/mxml/2009"
        xmlns:s="library://ns.adobe.com/flex/spark"
        title="HomeView" creationComplete="start()">

  <fx:Script source="SQLiteAccess.as"/>

  <!-- get status updates from Montastic -->
  <s:Button x="10" y="10" width="200" height="50"
          label="Get Statuses" click="invokeMontastic()">
  </s:Button>

  <s:Button x="250" y="10" width="200" height="50"
          label="Clear History" click="removeAll()">
  </s:Button>

  <s:DataGrid id="dg" left="10" right="10" top="70" bottom="100"
            dataProvider="{dp}">
    <s:columns>
      <s:ArrayList>
        <s:GridColumn headerText="ID"
                    dataField="id"
                    width="60" />
        <s:GridColumn headerText="Status"
                    dataField="status"
                    width="100" />
        <s:GridColumn headerText="URL"
                    dataField="url"
                    width="300" />
      </s:ArrayList>
    </s:columns>
  </s:DataGrid>

  <s:Button label="Create Notification" x="10" y="650" width="300" height="50">
    <s:click>
      <![CDATA[
          var s:Socket = new Socket();
          s.connect("localhost", 12345);
          s.addEventListener(Event.CONNECT, function(event:Event):void {
            trace('Client successfully connected to server');
            (event.currentTarget as Socket).writeInt(1);
            (event.currentTarget as Socket).writeUTF(allStatuses);
            (event.currentTarget as Socket).flush();
            (event.currentTarget as Socket).close();
          });
```

```
        s.addEventListener(IOErrorEvent.IO_ERROR, function(event:IOErrorEvent):void {
          trace('error sending allStatuses from client: ' + event.errorID);
        });
        s.addEventListener(ProgressEvent.SOCKET_DATA,
          function(event:ProgressEvent):void {
          trace('allStatuses sent successfully');
        });
      ]]>
    </s:click>
  </s:Button>
</s:View>
```

Listing 6–19 contains an XML Button that invokes the Montastic APIs in order to retrieve the status of the web sites that are registered in Montastic. When users click this button, the statuses of the web sites are stored in a SQLite database and the datagrid is refreshed with the new set of rows.

The second XML Button enables users to delete all the rows in the SQLite table, which is convenient because this table can quickly increase in size. If you want to maintain all the rows of this table, you probably ought to include scrolling capability for the datagrid.

When users click the third XML Button element, this initiates a client-side socket-based connection on port 12345 in order to send the latest statuses of the web sites to a server-side socket that is running in a native Android application. The Android application reads the information sent from the client and then displays the statuses in the Android notification bar.

The ActionScript3 code in Listing 6–20 is similar to Listing 6–8, so you will be able to read its contents quickly, despite the various application-specific changes to the code.

Listing 6–20. *Receiving Data and Sending the Data to a Notification on Android*

```
Import flash.data.SQLConnection;
import flash.data.SQLStatement;
import flash.events.Event;
import flash.events.IOErrorEvent;
import flash.errors.SQLErrorEvent;
import flash.events.SQLEvent;
import flash.events.TimerEvent;
import flash.filesystem.File;
import flash.net.URLLoader;
import flash.net.URLRequest;
import flash.net.URLRequestHeader;
import flash.net.URLRequestMethod;
import flash.utils.Timer;

import mx.collections.ArrayCollection;
import mx.utils.Base64Encoder;

//Montastic URL
private static const montasticURL:String =
        "https://www.montastic.com/checkpoints/show";

// sqlconn holds the database connection
public var sqlconn:SQLConnection = new SQLConnection();
```

```
// sqlstmt is a SQLStatement that holds SQL commands
public var sqlstmt:SQLStatement = new SQLStatement();

// a bindable ArrayCollection and the data provider for the datagrid
[Bindable]
public var dp:ArrayCollection = new ArrayCollection();
[Bindable]
public var allStatuses:String = "1:UP#2:UP#3:UP";

private var urlList:Array = new Array();
private var statusList:Array = new Array();
```

Listing 6–20 contains various import statements, followed by variables for opening a database connection and executing SQL statements. The `Bindable` variables provide access to the contents of the database table, as well as the URL and status of web sites that are registered with Montastic.

The variable `checkpointsXMLList` contains "live" data for the web sites that you have registered with Montastic.

```
// invoked after the application has loaded
private function start():void {
  // set 'montastic.db' as the file for our database (created after it's opened)
  var db:File = File.applicationStorageDirectory.resolvePath("montastic.db");

  // open the database in asynchronous mode
  sqlconn.openAsync(db);

  // event listeners for handling sql errors and 'result' are
  // invoked whenever data is retrieved from the database
  sqlconn.addEventListener(SQLEvent.OPEN, db_opened);
  sqlconn.addEventListener(SQLErrorEvent.ERROR, error);
  sqlstmt.addEventListener(SQLErrorEvent.ERROR, error);
  sqlstmt.addEventListener(SQLEvent.RESULT, result);
}

private function db_opened(e:SQLEvent):void {
  // specify the connection for the SQL statement
  sqlstmt.sqlConnection = sqlconn;

  // Table "montastic_table" contains three columns:
  // 1) id  (an autoincrementing integer)
  // 2) url (the url of each web site)
  // 3) status (the status of each web site)
  sqlstmt.text = "CREATE TABLE IF NOT EXISTS montastic_table ( id INTEGER PRIMARY KEY
AUTOINCREMENT, url TEXT, status TEXT);";

  // execute the sqlstmt to update the database
  sqlstmt.execute();

  // refresh the datagrid to display all data rows
  refreshDataGrid();
}
```

The methods `start()` and `db_opened()` are similar to the example earlier in this chapter, except that the database name is now `montastic.db` and the database table `montastic_table` is updated when users tap the associated `Button` in the mobile application. Note that the `montastic_table` contains the columns `id`, `url`, and `status` instead of the columns `id`, `first_name`, and `last_name`.

```
// function to append new rows to montastic table
// use a begin/commit block to insert multiple rows
private function addWebsiteInfo():void {
  allStatuses = "";
  sqlconn.begin();

  for (var i:uint = 0; i < urlList.length; i++) {
     var stmt:SQLStatement = new SQLStatement();
     stmt.sqlConnection = sqlconn;

     stmt.text = "INSERT INTO montastic_table (url, status) VALUES(:url, :status);";
     stmt.parameters[":url"] = urlList[i];
     stmt.parameters[":status"] = statusList[i];

     stmt.execute();
  }

  // insert the rows into the database table
  sqlconn.commit();

  refreshDataGrid();
}

// refresh the Montastic data in the datagrid
private function refreshDataGrid(e:TimerEvent = null):void {
    // timer object pauses and then attempts to execute again
    var timer:Timer = new Timer(100,1);
    timer.addEventListener(TimerEvent.TIMER, refreshDataGrid);

    if (!sqlstmt.executing) {
        sqlstmt.text = "SELECT * FROM montastic_table"
        sqlstmt.execute();
    } else {
        timer.start();
    }
}

// invoked when we receive data from a sql command
//this method is also called for sql statements to insert items
// and to create our table but in this case sqlstmt.getResult().data
// is null
private function result(e:SQLEvent):void {
   var data:Array = sqlstmt.getResult().data;

   // fill the datagrid with the latest data
   dp = new ArrayCollection(data);
}

// remove all rows from the table
private function removeAll():void {
  sqlstmt.text = "DELETE FROM montastic_table";
  sqlstmt.execute();

  refreshDataGrid();
```

```
}
```

The method addWebsiteInfo() is the "counterpart" to the addPerson() method, and the database insertion is performed inside a begin/end block in order to perform multiple row insertions in one SQL statement. This technique enables us to use the same logic that is used by the two methods refreshDataGrid() and result() for retrieving the latest data from the database without contention errors.

Note that instead of the method remove(), which removes a selected row from the datagrid, we now have a method, removeAll(), that removes all the rows from the database table.

```
// functions for Montastic
public function invokeMontastic():void {
   var loader:URLLoader = new URLLoader();
   loader.addEventListener(Event.COMPLETE, completeHandler);
   loader.addEventListener(IOErrorEvent.IO_ERROR, ioErrorHandler);

   var request:URLRequest = new URLRequest( montasticURL );
   request.method = URLRequestMethod.GET;

   var encoder:Base64Encoder = new Base64Encoder();
   encoder.encode("yourname@yahoo.com:insert-your-password-here");
   request.requestHeaders.push(new URLRequestHeader("Authorization",
                                         "Basic " + encoder.toString()));
   request.requestHeaders.push(new URLRequestHeader("pragma", "no-cache"));
   request.requestHeaders.push(new URLRequestHeader("Accept",
                                         "application/xml"));
   request.requestHeaders.push(new URLRequestHeader("Content-Type",
                                         "application/xml"));

   loader.load(request);
}

private function completeHandler(event:Event):void {
   var loader:URLLoader = URLLoader(event.target);
   checkpointsXMLList = new XML(loader.data);

   urlList = new Array();
   statusList = new Array();

   for each (var checkpoint:XML in checkpointsXMLList.checkpoint) {
      statusList.push(checkpoint.status.toString());
      urlList.push(checkpoint.url.toString());
   }

   allStatuses = "1="+statusList[0]+"#2="+statusList[1];

   addWebsiteInfo();
}
```

When users tap on the associated Button (whose label is "Get Statuses"), the method invokeMontastic() is executed, which in turn invokes the Montastic APIs that return XML containing status-related information regarding the web sites that the users have registered with Montastic.

Notice that the method `completeHandler()` is invoked after the asynchronous request to the Montastic web site has returned the XML-based data.

The `allStatuses` variable is updated appropriately (we need to send this string to the server socket), and then the method `addWebsiteInfo()` is executed, which updates the database table `montastic_table` with the data that we received from Montastic.

```
private function ioErrorHandler(event:IOErrorEvent):void {
   trace("IO Error" + event);
}
private function sqlError(event:SQLErrorEvent):void {
   trace("SQL Error" + event);
}
```

The functions `ioErrorHandler()` and `sqlError()` are invoked when a related error occurs, and in a production environment, you can add additional error messages that provide helpful debugging information.

As you saw earlier, we are using a hard-coded XML string that contains a sample of the information for web sites that you have registered with Montastic. Currently you can retrieve the XML-based status information about your web sites by invoking the "curl" program from the command line, as shown here (invoked as a single line):

```
curl -H 'Accept: application/xml' -H 'Content-type: application/xml' -u
yourname@yahoo.com:yourpassword https://www.montastic.com/checkpoints/index
```

Now that we have discussed the AIR-specific code, let's focus on the socket-based native Android code that processes the information from the client. The socket code is part of an Android application that we will name FooAndroid.

Before we discuss the Java code for this application, let's look at Listing 6–21, which contains the file `AndroidManifest.xml` for our Android application. Note that Listing 6–21 displays the final version of this configuration file, and not the contents that are generated during the creation step of the Android project FooAndroid.

Listing 6–21. *AndroidManifest.xml* *for the Native Android Application*

```
<?xml version="1.0" encoding="utf-8"?>
<manifest xmlns:android="http://schemas.android.com/apk/res/android"
        package="com.proandroidflash"
        android:versionCode="1"
        android:versionName="1.0">

    <uses-permission android:name="android.permission.INTERNET" />

    <application android:icon="@drawable/icon"
              android:label="@string/app_name">
    <activity android:name=".MainApp"
            android:label="@string/app_name"
            android:theme="@android:style/Theme.NoTitleBar"
            android:launchMode="singleTask"
            android:screenOrientation="nosensor"
            android:configChanges="keyboardHidden|orientation"
            android:windowSoftInputMode="stateHidden|adjustResize">
        <uses-permission android:name="android.permission.INTERNET" />
```

```
        <intent-filter>
            <action android:name="android.intent.action.MAIN" />
            <category android:name="android.intent.category.LAUNCHER" />
        </intent-filter>
    </activity>
    <service android:enabled="true" android:name="TestService" />
  </application>
</manifest>
```

Listing 6–21 specifies MainApp.java as the Android Activity for our Android application. As you will see, the Java class MainApp.java (which contains some custom Java code) extends the Android Activity AppEntry.java that is a subclass of the Android Activity class. Notice that Listing 6–21 specifies an Android Service class called TestService.java, which contains socket-based custom code that processes information that is received from the Adobe AIR client.

Now create a native Android application in Eclipse called FooAndroid with a Java class MainApp that extends the class AppEntry. The Java class AppEntry.java is a simple, pre-built Java Activity that is an intermediate class between the Android Activity class and our custom Java class, MainApp. Listing 6–22 displays the contents of the Java class MainApp.

Listing 6–22. *Main Android* Activity *Class*

```java
package com.proandroidflash;

import android.app.Activity;
import android.content.Intent;
import android.os.Bundle;

public class MainApp extends AppEntry {
    /** Called when the activity is first created. */

    @Override
    public void onCreate(Bundle savedInstanceState)
    {
      super.onCreate(savedInstanceState);

      try {
          Intent srv = new Intent(this, TestService.class);
          startService(srv);
      }
      catch (Exception e)
      {
          // service could not be started
      }
    }
}
```

The Java class MainApp (which is an indirect subclass of the Android Activity class) is executed when our Android application is launched; the onCreate() method in MainApp launches our custom Java class TestService.java (discussed later) that launches a server-side socket in order to handle data requests from the Adobe AIR client.

As you can see, the onCreate() method invokes the startService() method that is a method in the Android Activity class, in order to launch the TestService Service. This functionality is possible because MainApp is a subclass of the Android Activity class.

Now create the second Java class, TestServiceApp.java, in the com.proandroidflash package, and insert the code in Listing 6–23.

Listing 6–23. *An Android Service Class That Processes Data from an AIR Client*

```
package com.proandroidflash;

import java.io.BufferedInputStream;
import java.io.DataInputStream;
import java.io.IOException;
import java.net.ServerSocket;
import java.net.Socket;

import android.app.Notification;
import android.app.NotificationManager;
import android.app.PendingIntent;
import android.app.Service;
import android.content.Context;
import android.content.Intent;
import android.os.IBinder;
import android.os.Looper;
import android.util.Log;

public class TestService extends Service {
    private boolean stopped=false;
    private Thread serverThread;
    private ServerSocket ss;

    @Override
    public IBinder onBind(Intent intent) {
      return null;
    }
```

The initial portion of FooAndroid contains various import statements, private socket-related variables, and the onBind() method. This method can be used for other functionality that is supported by Android Service classes (which is beyond the scope of this example), and for our purposes this method simply returns null.

The next portion of Listing 6–23 contains a lengthy onCreate() method, which starts a server-side socket for handling Adobe AIR client requests.

Listing 6–23. *(Cont.) An Android Service Class That Processes Data from an AIR Client*

```
    @Override
    public void onCreate() {
      super.onCreate();

      Log.d(getClass().getSimpleName(), "onCreate");

      serverThread = new Thread(new Runnable() {
          public void run() {
              try {
                  Looper.prepare();
```

```
            ss = new ServerSocket(12345);
            ss.setReuseAddress(true);
            ss.setPerformancePreferences(100, 100, 1);

            while (!stopped) {
                Socket accept = ss.accept();
                accept.setPerformancePreferences(10, 100, 1);
                accept.setKeepAlive(true);

                DataInputStream _in = null;

                try {
                    _in = new DataInputStream(new BufferedInputStream(
                        accept.getInputStream(),1024));
                }
                catch (IOException e2) {
                  e2.printStackTrace();
                }

                int method = _in.readInt();

                switch (method) {
                    // send a notification?
                    case 1: doNotification(_in);
                            break;
                }
            }
        }
        catch (Throwable e) {
            e.printStackTrace();
            Log.e(getClass().getSimpleName(), "** Error in Listener **",e);
        }

        try {
          ss.close();
        }
        catch (IOException e) {
            Log.e(getClass().getSimpleName(), "Could not close serversocket");
        }
    }
  },"Server thread");

  serverThread.start();
}
```

The onCreate() method starts a Java Thread whose run() method launches a server-side socket on port 12345 (which is the same port as the client-side socket). The onCreate() method contains a while loop that waits for client-side requests and then processes them in the try/catch block.

If the first character in a client-side request is the digit "1", then we know that the client request is from our AIR application, and the code in the try/catch block invokes the method doNotification(). If necessary, you could enhance onCreate() (i.e., handle the occurrence of other numbers, text strings, and so forth) so that the server-side code can process other client-side requests.

```java
private void doNotification(DataInputStream in) throws IOException {
    String id = in.readUTF();
    displayNotification(id);
}

public void displayNotification(String notificationString)
{
    int icon = R.drawable.mp_warning_32x32_n;

    CharSequence tickerText = notificationString;
    long when = System.currentTimeMillis();
    Context context = getApplicationContext();
    CharSequence contentTitle = notificationString;
    CharSequence contentText = "Hello World!";

    Intent notificationIntent = new Intent(this, MainApp.class);
    PendingIntent contentIntent = PendingIntent.getActivity(this, 0,
                                          notificationIntent, 0);

    Notification notification = new Notification(icon, tickerText, when);
    notification.vibrate = new long[] {0,100,200,300};

    notification.setLatestEventInfo(context, contentTitle,
                          contentText, contentIntent);

    String ns = Context.NOTIFICATION_SERVICE;
    NotificationManager mNotificationManager =
                    (NotificationManager) getSystemService(ns);

    mNotificationManager.notify(1, notification);
}

@Override
public void onDestroy() {
    stopped = true;

    try {
        ss.close();
    }
    catch (IOException e) {}

    serverThread.interrupt();

    try {
        serverThread.join();
    }
    catch (InterruptedException e) {}
}

}
```

The doNotification() method simply reads the next character string in the input stream (which was sent from by the client) and then invokes the method displayNotification(). In our case, this character string will be a concatenated string that contains the status ("UP" or "DOWN") for each registered web site.

As you have probably surmised, the displayNotification() method contains the Android code for displaying a notification in the Android notification bar. The key point to notice is that this method creates an Android Intent with the Java class MainApp.java. The new Intent enables us to create an Android PendingIntent, which in turn allows us to create an Android Notification instance. The final line of code in displayNotification() launches our notification, which displays the status of the registered web sites in the Android notification bar.

The last part of the code is the onDestroy() method, which stops the server-side socket that was launched on the onCreate() method.

Now that we have completed the Java code for this application, we need to take care of the XML-related files for this application. First, make sure that the contents of AndroidManifest.xml in your application are the same as Listing 6–21. Second, include the following strings in the XML file strings.xml:

```
<string name="button_yes">Yes</string>
<string name="button_no">No</string>
<string name="dialog_title"><b>Adobe AIR</b></string>
<string name="dialog_text">This application requires that you first install Adobe
AIR®.\n\nDownload it free from Android Market now?</string>
```

Now that we have completed all the Adobe AIR code and the native Android code, we're ready to merge the files into one mobile application, and the steps for doing so are shown in the next section in this chapter.

You can see an example of invoking the sample application in this section displayed in Figure 6–6, which shows a set of records consisting of URLs and their statuses that are stored in a SQLite database on a mobile device.

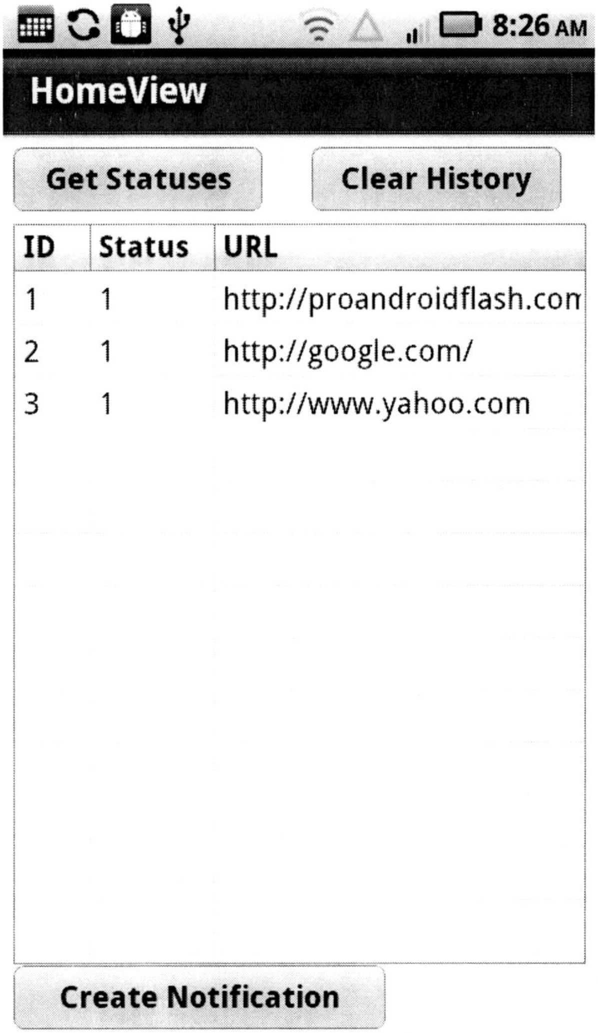

Figure 6–6. *A set of status records for registered web sites*

Adobe AIR and Native Android Integration

This section contains a process by which you can integrate native Android functionality (such as the examples in this chapter) into an Adobe AIR mobile application. Please note that the process by which this can be done is not supported by Adobe, and the actual steps could change by the time this book is published. This information was provided courtesy of Elad Elrom.

The commands in Listing 6–24 use the utilities adt, apktool, and adb to merge the contents of an Adobe AIR application, MyAIRApp, with the contents of a native Android application, AndroidNative.apk, in order to create the Adobe AIR mobile application MergedAIRApp.apk.

Listing 6–24 displays the actual commands that you need to invoke in order to create a new .apk file that comprises the code from an Adobe AIR mobile application and a native Android mobile application. Make sure that you update the value of the variable APP_HOME so that it reflects the correct value for your environment.

Listing 6–24. *Creating a Merged Application with Adobe AIR and Native Android Code*

```
APP_HOME="/users/ocampesato/AdobeFlashBuilder/MyAIRApp"
cd $APP_HOME/bin-debug
adt -package -target apk -storetype pkcs12 -keystore certificate.p12 -storepass Nyc1982
out.apk MyAIRApp-app.xml MyAIRApp.swf
apktool d -r out.apk air_apk
apktool d -r AndroidNative.apk native_apk
mkdir native_apk/assets
cp -r air_apk/assets/* native_apk/assets
cp air_apk/smali/app/AIRApp/AppEntry*.smali native_apk/smali/app/AIRApp
apktool b native_apk
cd native_apk/dist
jarsigner -verbose -keystore ~/.android/debug.keystore -storepass android out.apk
androiddebugkey
zipalign -v 4 out.apk out-new.apk
cd ../../
cp native_apk/dist/out-new.apk MergedAIRApp.apk
rm -r native_apk
rm -r air_apk
rm out.apk
adb uninstall app.AIRApp
adb install -r MergedAIRApp.apk
```

The commands in Listing 6–24 are straightforward if you are familiar with Linux or Unix. If you prefer to work in a Windows environment, you can convert the commands in Listing 6–24 to a corresponding set of DOS commands by making the following changes:

- Use "set" when defining the APP_HOME variable.

- Use DOS-style variables (example: %abc% instead of $abc).

- Replace cp with copy and replace rm with erase.

- Replace forward slashes ("/") with backward slashes ("\").

One important detail to keep in mind: you must obtain the correct self-signed certificate (which is called certificate.p12 in Listing 6–24) for the preceding merging process to work correctly. You can generate a certificate for your Flex-based application as follows:

- Select your project in FlashBuilder.

- Click Export Release Build.

- Specify a location for "Export to folder:" (or click Next).

- Click the "Create:" button.

- Provide values for the required fields.

- Specify a value in the "Save as:" input field.

- Click the OK button.

- Click "Remember password for this session" (optional).

- Click the Finish button.

After generating the self-signed certificate, copy this certificate into the directory where you execute the shell script commands that are shown in Listing 6–24, and if you have done everything correctly, you will generate a merged application that can be deployed to an Android-based mobile device.

This section concludes the multi-step process for creating and then merging Adobe AIR applications with native Android applications. As you can see, this integration process is non-trivial, and arguably non-intuitive as well, so you are bound to stumble during this process (and don't be discouraged when you do). The thing to remember is that the addition of native Android support to an Adobe AIR application could be the sort of thing that can differentiate your application from similar applications that are available in the marketplace.

Summary

In this chapter, you learned how to launch native browsers, access databases, and combine AIR mobile applications with native Android code. More specifically, you learned about the following:

- Launching a native web browser from a string containing the actual HTML code for a web site

- Enabling users to specify a URL and then launching that URL in an AIR application

- Using a SQLite database to create, update, and delete user-specific data, and also how to automatically refresh the display of the updated data

- Creating native Android applications in Eclipse

- Integrating the functionality of an external API, a SQLite database, and a native Android notification into one mobile application

The specific sequence of steps for merging an Adobe AIR application with a native Android application.

Chapter 7

Taking Advantage of Hardware Inputs

You saw in the previous chapter how to integrate your Android Flash application with the native software services provided by the Android OS. In this chapter, you will learn how to make use of the hardware sensors included in Android-powered devices. By the end of this chapter, you will be able to capture sound, images, and video; tap into geolocation services to read the device's location; and read accelerometer data to determine the orientation of the device—all from within your Flash application.

Modern mobile devices have an amazing array of hardware sensors—from accelerometers to cameras to GPS receivers. Effective mobile applications should be able to take advantage of these features when the need arises. The AIR runtime provides classes that allow you to access these native hardware resources. Some of these classes, such as `Microphone` and `Camera`, may be familiar to experienced Flash developers. Others, such as `CameraUI` and `CameraRoll`, are new additions that allow AIR applications to take advantage of features commonly found on Android devices.

Microphone

A phone wouldn't be very useful without a microphone, so we will start with this most basic of inputs. Flash has supported capturing sound with the `Microphone` class for a long time, and this class is fully supported on AIR for Android as well. As with all of the hardware support classes you will see in this chapter, the first step is to check the static `isSupported` property of the class to ensure that it is supported on the user's device. All phones will, of course, have a microphone, but this is not necessarily true of tablets and TVs. Since you will want to support a wide range of current and future devices, it is a best practice to always check the `isSupported` property of `Microphone` and the other classes we will cover in this chapter.

If `Microphone` is supported, you can then proceed to retrieve a `Microphone` instance, set your capture parameters, and attach an event listener to enable you to receive the sound data coming from the device's microphone.

Listing 7–1 shows these steps in an excerpt from the MicrophoneBasic example project located in the examples/`chapter-07` directory of this book's sample code.

Listing 7–1. *Initializing and Reading Samples from the Microphone*

```
private var activityLevel: uint;

private function onCreationComplete():void {
  if (Microphone.isSupported) {
    microphone = Microphone.getMicrophone();

    microphone.setSilenceLevel(0)
    microphone.gain = 100;
    microphone.rate = 22;
    microphone.addEventListener(SampleDataEvent.SAMPLE_DATA, onSample);

    initGraphics();
    showMessage("Speak, I can hear you...");
  } else {
    showMessage("flash.media.Microphone is unsupported on this device.");
  }
}

private function onSample(event:SampleDataEvent):void {
  if (microphone.activityLevel > activityLevel) {
    activityLevel = Math.min(50, microphone.activityLevel);
  }
}

private function showMessage(msg:String):void {
  messageLabel.text = msg;
}
```

The microphone initialization code is located inside the View's `creationComplete` handler. If `Microphone` is unsupported, the `onCreationComplete()` function calls the `showMessage()` function to display a message to the user. The `showMessage()` function simply sets the text property of a Spark Label that is positioned at the top of the view. If `Microphone` is supported, however, then a call is made to the static function `Microphone.getMicrophone()`, which returns an instance of a Microphone object. You then set the gain and rate properties of the object. A setting of 100 is the maximum gain setting for the microphone, and a rate of 22 specifies the maximum sample frequency of 22 kHz. This will ensure that even soft sounds are captured at a reasonable sampling rate. You should note that `Microphone` supports capturing at rates up to 44.1 kHz, which is the same sample rate used on compact discs. However, the quality of the recording is limited to what the underlying hardware can support. A cell phone microphone will likely capture audio at much lower rates. Although Flash will convert the captured audio to the sampling rate you requested, this does not mean that you will end up with CD-quality audio.

Finally, we add a listener for the SampleDataEvent.SAMPLE_DATA event. The application will begin receiving sound data once this listener is attached. The event has two properties of particular interest:

- position: A Number indicating the position of the data in the audio stream

- data: A ByteArray containing the audio data captured since the last SAMPLE_DATA event

An application will typically just copy the data bytes into a ByteArray created by the application to hold the entire audio clip until it can be played back, stored, or sent on to a server. See Chapter 8 for more details about capturing and playing back audio data. The MicrophoneBasic example application simply displays visual feedback about the audio data coming from the microphone by checking the activityLevel property, as shown in Listing 7–1.

One important thing to remember is to set the android.permission.RECORD_AUDIO setting in your application descriptor XML file. You will not be able to read microphone data on an Android device without this permission. The manifest section from the example project is shown in the following code snippet.

```
<android>
    <manifestAdditions>
        <![CDATA[
        <manifest>
            <!-- For debugging only -->
            <uses-permission android:name="android.permission.INTERNET"/>
            <uses-permission android:name="android.permission.RECORD_AUDIO"/>
        </manifest>
        ]]>
    </manifestAdditions>
</android>
```

Flash's support for capturing audio samples is actually quite sophisticated. You are even able to set a "zero" level using setSilenceLevel() or enable echo suppression using setUseEchoSuppression(). We encourage you to check out Adobe's excellent online documentation[1].

Figure 7–1 shows what the MicrophoneBasic application looks like when it is running on an actual phone.

---

[1] http://help.adobe.com/en_US/FlashPlatform/reference/actionscript/3/flash/media/Microphone.html

Figure 7–1. *The MicrophoneBasic example application running on an Android phone*

Camera and CameraUI

You will find a camera (or sometimes two) on most mobile devices. An Android Flash application can use the camera to capture still images as well as full motion video. Some devices are even capable of capturing high-definition video.

There are two different ways to access a device's camera. The flash.media.Camera class will give you access to the raw video stream coming from the camera. This allows you to do real-time processing on the images as they are captured from the main camera on the device.

> **NOTE:** As of AIR 2.5.1, the `flash.media.Camera` class did not support the ability to capture from more than one camera on an Android device. The ability to select which camera to use during video capture is expected in a future release of AIR for Android.

The alternative is to use `flash.media.CameraUI` to capture high-quality images and video. `CameraUI` is ideal for applications that just need to capture an image or a video with minimal hassle. It uses the native Android camera interface to handle the heavy lifting. This means the user of your application will have access to every feature that Android supports natively on a given device, including multiple cameras and the ability to adjust the white balance, geo-tagging features, focus, exposure, and flash settings.

Android also provides a standard interface for browsing the images and video that have been captured on the device. AIR provides access to this service through the `flash.media.CameraRoll` class. `CameraRoll` provides a simple way to save images to the device. It also allows the user to browse previously captured images and will inform your application if the user selects an image or video file. Like `CameraUI`, `CameraRoll` is a wrapper around the native Android media browser interface. Users like applications that feel familiar and look like the other native applications they use. It is a good thing, then, that AIR provides easy access to the native interfaces for camera functionality. They should be your first choice if they meet the needs of your application.

In the next sections, we will explore these three classes in more depth. We'll first introduce you to the basic `Camera` class and then show an example that applies some of the powerful Flash filter effects to the live video stream. Real-time video processing on a phone! How cool is that? After that, we'll take you on a guided tour of the `CameraRoll` and `CameraUI` classes and show you how to use them to capture, save, and browse media using Android's native interfaces. Let the fun begin!

Camera

The APIs that make up the Flash and Flex SDKs are generally well designed. The video capture feature is no exception. The responsibilities for this complex process are divided between two easy-to-use classes. The `flash.media.Camera` class is responsible for low-level video capture, and the `flash.media.Video` class is a `DisplayObject` that is used to show the stream to the user. So gaining access to a camera's video feed is a simple three-step process.

1. Call `Camera.getCamera()` to get a reference to a `Camera` instance.

2. Create a `flash.media.Video` object, and attach the camera to it.

3. Add the `Video` object to a `DisplayObjectContainer`, such as `UIComponent`, so that it is visible on the stage.

The code in Listing 7–2 illustrates these basic steps. You can create a new Flex mobile project in Flash Builder 4.5, and copy the code in Listing 7–2 into the `View` class that is created as part of the project. Or you can follow along by looking at the CameraBasic project in the `examples/chapter-07` directory if you have downloaded the example code for this book.

The `View` sets the visibility of its action bar to `false` in order to maximize the screen space for the video display. All of the initialization work is done in the `creationComplete` handler. As mentioned in step 3 earlier, a `UIComponent` can be used as the container for the video stream to make it visible on the stage. The `Camera`, `Video`, and `UIComponent` are all set to be the same size as the view itself.

Listing 7–2. *Basic Image Capture in a Mobile* `View` *Class*

```
<?xml version="1.0" encoding="utf-8"?>
<s:View xmlns:fx="http://ns.adobe.com/mxml/2009"
        xmlns:s="library://ns.adobe.com/flex/spark"
        xmlns:mx="library://ns.adobe.com/flex/mx"
        actionBarVisible="false"
        creationComplete="onCreationComplete()">

  <fx:Script>
    <![CDATA[
      private var camera:Camera;

      private function onCreationComplete():void {
        if (Camera.isSupported) {
          var screenWidth:Number = Screen.mainScreen.bounds.width;
          var screenHeight:Number = Screen.mainScreen.bounds.height;

          camera = Camera.getCamera();
          camera.setMode(screenWidth, screenHeight, 15);

          var video: Video = new Video(screenWidth, screenHeight);
          video.attachCamera(camera);

          videoContainer.addChild(video);
        } else {
          notSupportedLabel.visible = true;
        }
      }
    ]]>
  </fx:Script>

  <mx:UIComponent id="videoContainer" width="100%" height="100%"/>
  <s:Label id="messageLabel" visible="false" top="0" right="0"
           text="flash.media.Camera is not supported on this device."/>
</s:View>
```

Checking for Camera Support

The view also contains a label component in the foreground that displays a message to the user if the camera is not supported for some reason. Using a text component such as a label is an easy way to display status and error messages to the user on the small screen of a mobile device. Here you see the second (of several) occurrences of a static `isSupported` property, this time on the `Camera` class. It is a good practice to check

Camera's isSupported property to ensure that the feature is supported on the user's device. For example, Camera is not currently supported on mobile browsers.

> **CAUTION:** Camera is also not currently supported on AIR for TV devices. However, Adobe's documentation points out that isSupported still returns true in that environment even though getCamera always returns null. To deal with this situation, you can change the isSupported check in the previous example to
>
> if (Camera.isSupported && (camera = Camera.getCamera()) != null) { … }.

Initializing the Camera

Taking a closer look at the camera initialization code, you can see that after the Camera instance is obtained by calling the static getCamera method, there is a call to the setMode method. Without this call, the camera would default to capturing video at 160 x 120 pixels, which would look very pixilated when displayed on a modern phone where resolutions are typically 800 x 480 or more. The first and second parameters of the setMode method specify the width and height at which you would like to capture video. The third parameter of setMode stipulates the frame rate at which video should be captured in frames per second, also known as FPS.

What you request is not necessarily what you get, though. The camera will be put into whichever of its native modes matches your request parameters most closely. There is a fourth optional parameter of the setMode call that controls whether preference is given to your resolution (width and height) or to your FPS request when picking a native camera mode. By default, the camera will try to match your resolution request even if it means that your FPS request cannot be met.

Therefore we call setMode and request a video capture resolution that matches the resolution of the View—essentially using this.width and this.height. This is the same as the resolution of the device's screen since the application is running in full-screen mode, as we will describe in the next section. We also request that the video be captured at 15 frames per second. This is a reasonable rate for video while not being too much of a drain on performance and therefore battery life. You may want to decrease your FPS request on slower devices.

On a Nexus S phone with 800 x 480 screen resolution, this request results in the camera being set to capture frames at 720 x 432. On the Motorola Droid with 854 x 480 resolution, the camera captures at 848 x 477. In both cases, the camera selects a mode that is as close as possible to the requested resolution *while preserving the requested aspect ratio*.

For more details on configuration and usage, consult the documentation of flash.media.Camera and flash.media.Video on Adobe's web site at http://help.adobe.com/en_US/FlashPlatform/reference/actionscript/3/.

Application Settings and Android Permissions

The video stream coming from Flash's Camera class assumes a landscape orientation. You will get the best result by locking your application to landscape mode. Otherwise all of the video will look like it has been rotated by 90 degrees. The options that control this behavior can be found in the initialWindow section of the application descriptor XML file associated with your project. In the CameraBasic project, the file is called CameraBasic-app.xml and is located in the project's src folder. You will need to set aspectRatio to landscape and autoOrients to false. Note that unchecking the Automatically Reorient check box when you create a mobile project in Flash Builder 4.5 will set autoOrients to false when the application descriptor file is created.

Listing 7–3 shows the final application descriptor for the CameraBasic project. Comments and unused settings have been removed from the generated file for clarity. As previously mentioned, the application was also specified to be a full-screen application when the project was created. This causes the initialWindow setting of fullScreen to be set to true and results in the application taking up the entire screen when running, hiding the Android indicator bar at the top of the screen.

Listing 7–3. *The* CameraBasic-app.xml *Application Descriptor File from the CameraBasic Project*

```xml
<?xml version="1.0" encoding="utf-8" standalone="no"?>
<application xmlns="http://ns.adobe.com/air/application/2.5">
    <id>CameraBasic</id>
    <filename>CameraBasic</filename>
    <name>CameraBasic</name>
    <versionNumber>0.0.1</versionNumber>

    <initialWindow>
        <content>[This value will be overwritten by Flash Builder…]</content>
        <autoOrients>false</autoOrients>
        <aspectRatio>landscape</aspectRatio>
        <fullScreen>true</fullScreen>
        <visible>false</visible>
    </initialWindow>

    <android>
        <manifestAdditions><![CDATA[
            <manifest>
                <uses-permission android:name="android.permission.CAMERA" />
            </manifest>
        ]]></manifestAdditions>
    </android>
</application>
```

You will need to specify the Android camera permission in the APK file's manifest in order to gain access to the device's camera. As you can see in Listing 7–3, the application descriptor's Android manifest section includes the android.permission.CAMERA permission. Specifying this permission implies that the android.hardware.camera and android.hardware.camera.autofocus features are used. Therefore, they aren't specifically listed in the manifest additions.

Manipulating the Camera's Video Stream

The advantage of using `Camera` instead of `CameraUI` is that you get access to the video stream as it is captured. You can apply several types of image filter effects to the video stream: blurs, glows, bevels, color transforms, displacement maps, and convolutions. Some of these are relatively inexpensive while others, like a `ConvolutionFilter`, can be processor-intensive and will therefore decrease the frame rate of the captured video stream. The simple blur, glow, and bevel filters are pretty straightforward to use, so this example will use some of the more complex filters: the `ColorMatrixFilter`, the `DisplacementMapFilter`, and the `ConvolutionFilter`.

Listing 7–4 shows the code for the default view of the CameraFilter example project. It can be found in the `examples/chapter-07` directory if you have downloaded the book's accompanying source code.

Listing 7–4. The `VideoFilterView.mxml` File from the CameraFilter Example Project

```
<?xml version="1.0" encoding="utf-8"?>
<s:View xmlns:fx="http://ns.adobe.com/mxml/2009"
        xmlns:s="library://ns.adobe.com/flex/spark"
        xmlns:mx="library://ns.adobe.com/flex/mx"
        actionBarVisible="false" creationComplete="onCreationComplete()">

    <fx:Script source="VideoFilterViewScript.as"/>

    <fx:Declarations>
      <s:NumberFormatter id="fpsFormatter" fractionalDigits="1"/>
    </fx:Declarations>

    <s:viewMenuItems>
      <s:ViewMenuItem label="No Filter" click="onFilterChange(event)"/>
      <s:ViewMenuItem label="Night Vision" click="onFilterChange(event)"/>
      <s:ViewMenuItem label="Pencil" click="onFilterChange(event)"/>
      <s:ViewMenuItem label="Ripples" click="onFilterChange(event)"/>
      <s:ViewMenuItem label="Funny Face" click="onFilterChange(event)"/>
    </s:viewMenuItems>

    <mx:UIComponent id="videoContainer" width="100%" height="100%"/>
    <s:Label id="messageLabel" top="0" right="0"/>
</s:View>
```

You can see in Listing 7–4 that we've separated the ActionScript code into its own file since the code associated with this example grew much larger compared to the previous example. We've included the script file using the `source` attribute of the `<fx:Script>` tag. It is a little inconvenient to write code that spans two files like this, but doing it this way keeps both files to a more manageable size. You will also note the addition of a `<fx:Declarations>` element that declares a `NumberFormatter` that is used to format the frames per second value.

You can imagine that if there will be multiple filters that can be applied to the video stream, then there will need to be a way for the user to select which filter should be active. The `ViewMenuItems` shown in Listing 7–4 give the user an easy way to accomplish this. Clicking a `ViewMenuItem` results in a call to the `onFilterChange` handler, which will handle setting up the newly selected filter effect. The resulting application is shown in Figure 7–2 with the menu visible.

Figure 7–2. *The menu that allows users to select which filter effect to apply*

So now that the menu is working, it is time to take a look at creating and attaching image filter effects to the video stream.

> **TIP:** An AIR for Android application is not notified when the user presses the "home" button since that is used by Android itself. However, you can listen for Android's "back" and "search" buttons by checking for `Keyboard.BACK` and `Keyboard.SEARCH` in your `KeyboardEvent` listener. In those two cases, it is probably a good idea to call `event.preventDefault()` to prevent any potential default action the system would take in response to those button presses.

Creating Image Filter Effects

As would be expected, Flash provides sophisticated image processing effects that are easy to use. Applying filter effects to a video stream is not the main point of this chapter, so we will only briefly describe the filters and present the relevant code with little comment. Adobe's excellent online documentation can be consulted for the details about the filters included in the `flash.filters` package. If you are already familiar with the filter effects in Flash, you can browse the code and move on quickly to the next section.

The first step is to create the filters. Listing 7–5 shows the initialization code. The `onCreationComplete()` method, just as in the previous example, is the view's `creationComplete` handler. The first thing that `onCreationComplete()` does is call the `initFilters()` method, which encapsulates all of the filter initialization code. The three filter effects used by this example are `ColorMatrixFilter`, `ConvolutionFilter`, and `DisplacementMapFilter`.

Listing 7–5. *Creating the Image Filter Instances*

```
private function onCreationComplete():void {
  var screenWidth:Number = Screen.mainScreen.bounds.width;
  var screenHeight:Number = Screen.mainScreen.bounds.height;

  initFilters(screenWidth, screenHeight);

  if (Camera.isSupported) {
    // The same Camera and Video initialization as before…
  } else {
    showNotSupportedMsg();
  }
}

private function initFilters(screenWidth:Number, screenHeight:Number):void {
  var colorMat: Array = [
    .5,  0,  0,  0,  0,
     0, 10,  0,  0,  0,
     0,  0, .5,  0,  0,
     0,  0,  0,  1,  0
  ];

  nightVisionFilter = new ColorMatrixFilter(colorMat);

  var sharpMat: Array = [
     0, -5,  0,
    -5, 20, -5,
     0, -5,  0
  ];

  ultraSharpFilter = new ConvolutionFilter(3, 3, sharpMat);

  var bmpData: BitmapData = new BitmapData(screenWidth, screenHeight, false);
  var pt: Point = new Point(0, 0);

  displacementFilter = new DisplacementMapFilter(bmpData, pt,
    BitmapDataChannel.RED, BitmapDataChannel.RED, 40, 40);
}
```

A `ColorMatrixFilter` uses a 4 x 5 matrix whose values are multiplied by the color channels of each pixel. For example, the entries in the first row of the matrix are multiplied by the red, green, blue, and alpha components of the unfiltered pixel, and the results are summed, along with the fifth value in the row, and assigned to be the red component of the final filtered pixel. The green, blue, and alpha components of the filtered pixel are computed similarly using the second, third, and fourth rows of the matrix respectively. This is done for each pixel in the source image to produce the final filtered image. A `ColorMatrixFilter` is capable of many complex color manipulation effects, including saturation changes, hue rotation, luminance to alpha transposition (the brighter the pixel in the source image, the more translucent it will be in the filtered image), and others. As you can see, this example program uses the `ColorMatrixFilter` to produce a pseudo night vision effect by boosting the green channel and dampening the red and blue channels. The alpha channel is left unchanged.

The ConvolutionFilter is the workhorse of image processing filters. It works by defining a matrix whose elements are multiplied by a block of pixels. The results of this multiplication are then summed to get the final value of the pixel. We are using a 3x3 matrix in this example, and from its values you can see that the red, green, blue, and alpha components of each pixel in the source image are multiplied by a factor of 20, while at the same time the pixels directly to the north, south, east, and west of the source pixel are all multiplied by a factor of -5. These results are then summed to get the final value of the filtered pixel. The zeros in the corners of the matrix mean that the pixels to the northwest, northeast, southwest, and southeast of the source pixel are completely removed from the equation. Since the negative factors balance out the positive factor, the overall luminance of the image remains unchanged. The matrix we've defined here implements a basic edge detection algorithm. And the multiplication factors are large enough that the resulting image will be mostly black with the edges in white. The filtered image looks a bit like it was drawn with a white pencil on a black page, hence the name we used for the filter: Pencil.

A DisplacementFilter uses the pixel values in one bitmap to offset the pixels in the source image. The resulting image will therefore be warped in some way as compared to the original image. This results in all sorts of fun and interesting effects. The code in the initFilters() method simply initializes the displacement filter with an empty bitmap. The choice of displacement map is actually set when the user selects either the Funny Face filter or the Ripples filter. The displacement maps used by this example are shown in Figure 7–3. For your own sanity, don't stare at these images for too long!

The displacement filter is configured to use the displacement map's red color channel when calculating both the x and y displacement values. Therefore the Funny Face map on the left in Figure 7–3 is simply a red dot centered on a gray background. This will leave the surrounding pixels unchanged but expand the pixels in the center of the image to produce a bulbous effect. The Ripples map is just alternating circles of red and black that result in positive and negative pixel offsets (expanding and contracting), giving the impression that the source image is being viewed through rippling water, although this ripple appears frozen in time and space (hmm, sounds like a bad *Star Trek* episode).

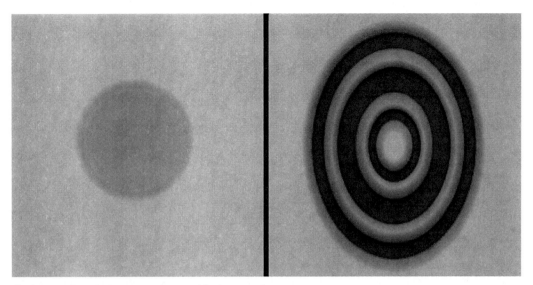

Figure 7–3. *The displacement maps used in the example program*

Listing 7–6 shows the code that sets these displacement maps on the displacement filter in response to the corresponding menu button clicks. When the ripple or funny face effect is selected, the appropriate bitmap (which was loaded at startup from an embedded resource) is drawn into the displacement filter's `mapBitmap`.

Listing 7–6. *Selecting Filters and Setting the Displacement Maps*

```
[Embed(source="funny_face.png")]
private var FunnyFaceImage:Class;

[Embed(source="ripples.png")]
private var RippleImage:Class;

private var rippleBmp:Bitmap = new RippleImage() as Bitmap;
private var funnyFaceBmp:Bitmap = new FunnyFaceImage() as Bitmap;

// This function is the click handler for all buttons in the menu.  videoContainer
// is a UIComponent that is displaying the video stream from the camera.
private function onFilterChange(event:Event):void {
  var btn: Button = event.target as Button;
  switch (btn.id) {
    case "noFilterBtn":
      videoContainer.filters = [];
      break;

    case "nightVisionBtn":
      videoContainer.filters = [nightVisionFilter];
      break;

    case "sharpBtn":
      videoContainer.filters = [ultraSharpFilter];
      break;

    case "rippleBtn":
```

```
        showDisplacementFilter(true);
        break;

      case "funnyFaceBtn":
        showDisplacementFilter(false);
        break;
  }

  toggleMenu();
}

private function showDisplacementFilter(ripples:Boolean):void {
  var bmp: Bitmap = ripples ? rippleBmp : funnyFaceBmp;

  var mat: Matrix = new Matrix();
  mat.scale(width / bmp.width, height / bmp.height);

  displacementFilter.mapBitmap.draw(bmp, mat);

  videoContainer.filters = [displacementFilter];
}
```

Figure 7–4 shows some images captured using these filters. From the top left and going counterclockwise, you can see an image with no filtering, the funny face filter, the pencil filter, and the night vision filter.

Figure 7–4. *The output of some of the filters used in this example captured on a Nexus S mobile phone*

It should be noted that while the displacement map and the color matrix filter are relatively inexpensive in performance terms, the convolution filter is a real performance killer on the Android devices on which we tested it. This serves as an important reminder that processor cycles are not plentiful like they are on desktop systems. Always test your performance assumptions on your target hardware!

Displaying an FPS Counter

One easy way to monitor performance on the target hardware is to display an ongoing count of the frames per second. Listing 7–7 shows code that displays the camera's FPS count in a Label control. The FPS value is formatted and updated every two seconds by a timer that is running in the background. The FPS count comes directly from the camera but does take into account the time taken by the filters. As you apply filters, you will see the frame rate drop since that will slow down the entire program, including the video capture process. The performance counter can be hidden and redisplayed by tapping anywhere on the screen. This is accomplished by adding a click handler to the UIComponent that is displaying the video stream.

Listing 7–7. *Showing a Performance Counter on the Screen*

```
private var timer: Timer;
private var fpsString: String;

private function onCreationComplete(): void {
  var screenWidth:Number = Screen.mainScreen.bounds.width;
  var screenHeight:Number = Screen.mainScreen.bounds.height;

  initFilters(screenWidth, screenHeight);

  if (Camera.isSupported) {
    // The same Camera and Video initialization as before…

    videoContainer.addEventListener(MouseEvent.CLICK, onTouch);
    fpsString = " FPS ("+camera.width+"x"+camera.height+")";

    timer = new Timer(2000);
    timer.addEventListener(TimerEvent.TIMER, updateFPS);
    timer.start();
  } else {
    showNotSupportedMsg();
  }
}

private function updateFPS(event:TimerEvent):void {
  messageLabel.text = fpsFormatter.format(camera.currentFPS) + fpsString;
}

private function onTouch(event:MouseEvent):void {
  if (messageLabel.visible) {
    timer.stop();
    messageLabel.visible = false;
  } else {
    timer.start();
    messageLabel.visible = true;
  }
}
```

Now that the application has the ability to create interesting images from the video stream, the next logical step is to capture a frame of video and save it on the device.

Capturing and Saving Images from the Video Stream

The culmination of our series of example projects dealing with the Camera class is CameraFunHouse. This final app finishes the series by incorporating support for capturing an image from the video stream and saving it on the device. You must use AIR for Android's new CameraRoll class to save images on a device. Fortunately, this is an easy process that will be demonstrated at the end of this section.

Capturing an image from the video stream uses nothing more than good old-fashioned Flash and Flex functionality. You start with a few additions to the View's MXML file as shown in Listing 7–8. The new additions are highlighted for your convenience. They consist of a new UIComponent that will display the bitmap of the still image captured from the video stream. This bitmap will be shown as a preview so the user can decide if the image should be saved. The other new additions are buttons that the user can tap to capture an image and then either save or discard it.

Listing 7–8. *View Enhancements to Support Image Capture and Saving*

```
<?xml version="1.0" encoding="utf-8"?>
<s:View xmlns:fx="http://ns.adobe.com/mxml/2009"
        xmlns:s="library://ns.adobe.com/flex/spark"
        xmlns:mx="library://ns.adobe.com/flex/mx"
        actionBarVisible="false"
        creationComplete="onCreationComplete()">

  <fx:Script source="FunHouseVideoViewScript.as"/>

  <fx:Declarations>
    <!-- Same as before -->
  </fx:Declarations>

  <s:viewMenuItems>
    <!-- Same as before -->
  </s:viewMenuItems>

  <mx:UIComponent id="videoContainer" width="100%" height="100%"/>
  <mx:UIComponent id="bitmapContainer" width="100%" height="100%"/>

  <s:Button id="captureButton" width="100%" bottom="0" label="Capture Image"
          alpha="0.75" click="onCaptureImage()"/>

  <s:Button id="saveButton" width="40%" right="0" bottom="0"
          label="Save Image" alpha="0.75" click="onSaveImage()"/>
  <s:Button id="discardButton" width="40%" left="0" bottom="0"
          label="Discard Image" alpha="0.75" click="onDiscardImage()"/>

  <s:Label id="messageLabel" top="0" right="0"/>
</s:View>
```

The Capture Image button will always be visible while the application is in capture mode. The button is translucent so the user can see the video stream behind the button. Once the user has tapped the capture button, the application will grab and display the image, hide the capture button, and show the Save Image and Discard Image buttons. This logic is controlled by code that has been added to the ActionScript file along with the three new click handlers: onCaptureImage(), onSaveImage(), and onDiscardImage(). These additions are shown in Listing 7–9.

Listing 7–9. *Additions and Changes to the ActionScript Code to Support Image Capture and Save*

```
private function onCreationComplete():void {
  var screenWidth:Number = Screen.mainScreen.bounds.width;
  var screenHeight:Number = Screen.mainScreen.bounds.height;

  initFilters(screenWidth, screenHeight);
  setCaptureMode(true);

  // The rest of the method is the same as before…
}

// Determines which controls are visible
private function setCaptureMode(capture: Boolean): void {
  videoContainer.visible = capture;
  bitmapContainer.visible = !capture;

  captureButton.visible = capture;
  saveButton.visible = !capture;
  discardButton.visible = !capture;
}

private function onCaptureImage():void {
  var bmp: BitmapData = new BitmapData(width, height, false, 0xffffff);
  bmp.draw(videoContainer);

  bitmapContainer.addChild(new Bitmap(bmp));
  setCaptureMode(false);
}

private function onDiscardImage():void {
  bitmapContainer.removeChildAt(0);
  setCaptureMode(true);
}

private function onSaveImage():void {
  if (CameraRoll.supportsAddBitmapData) {
    var bmp: Bitmap = bitmapContainer.removeChildAt(0) as Bitmap;
    new CameraRoll().addBitmapData(bmp.bitmapData);
    setCaptureMode(true);
  } else {
    showNotSupportedMsg(ROLL_NOT_SUPPORTED);
    saveButton.visible = false;
  }
}
```

The onCaptureImage() function just draws the contents of the videoContainer into a new bitmap and displays it in the bitmapContainer as a preview. The call to setCaptureMode(false) at the end of the method takes care of setting the visibility of all the appropriate controls. Likewise, the onDiscardImage() handler removes the preview bitmap and puts the application back into capture mode.

The CameraRoll class comes into play when the user wants to save the image. As you can see, it follows the familiar pattern of checking for support before using the class. You should first ensure that the device supports saving images by using the CameraRoll.supportsAddBitmapData property. Assuming that adding an image is supported, the onSaveImage() function creates a new CameraRoll instance and calls its addBitmapData method, passing a reference to the BitmapData object that holds the preview image. CameraRoll will issue events when the image has been successfully saved or if an error occurs that prevents the save operation. The PhotoCollage example that is covered in the next section will show an example of using these events. Figure 7–5 shows the completed CameraFunHouse application capturing an image of a cooperative canine.

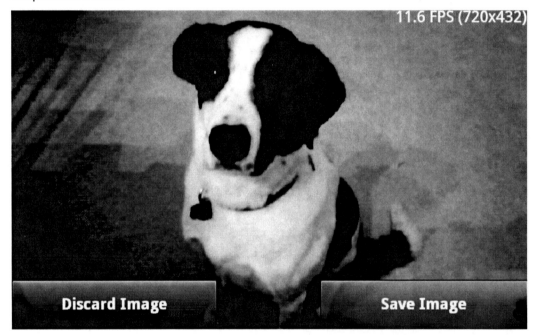

Figure 7–5. *Our model gladly gave permission for her likeness to be used in exchange for a treat.*

The CameraRoll class also lets the user browse and select images that have been saved on the device as well as those that have been stored by the user in photo albums on the Internet! This feature will be explained in the next section.

CameraRoll

Browsing photos on an Android device with CameraRoll is almost as easy as saving them. We will illustrate this feature in the context of a new example program named PhotoCollage. This program lets you select images that have been stored on the device and arrange them in a collage. You are able to drag, zoom, and rotate the images using multitouch gestures. When the images are arranged to your liking, you can then save the new image back to the camera roll. This example can be found in the examples/chapter-

07 directory of the book's source code. Listing 7–10 shows the MXML file of the application's home view.

Listing 7–10. *The Home View of the PhotoCollage Application—PhotoCollageHome.mxml*

```
<?xml version="1.0" encoding="utf-8"?>
<s:View xmlns:fx="http://ns.adobe.com/mxml/2009"
        xmlns:s="library://ns.adobe.com/flex/spark"
        xmlns:mx="library://ns.adobe.com/flex/mx"
        actionBarVisible="false"
        creationComplete="onCreationComplete()" >

  <fx:Script source="PhotoCollageHomeScript.as"/>

  <s:viewMenuItems>
    <s:ViewMenuItem label="Browse" click="onBrowse()"/>
    <s:ViewMenuItem label="Clear" click="onClear()"/>
    <s:ViewMenuItem label="Save" click="onSave()"/>
  </s:viewMenuItems>

  <mx:UIComponent id="photoContainer" width="100%" height="100%"/>
  <s:Label id="messageLabel" top="0" left="0" mouseEnabled="false"/>
</s:View>
```

You can see that just as in the previous examples, a menu has been declared for this view. And we have once again separated the view's associated script code into its own file. The view has two child components: a UIComponent to act as a container for the images that are being arranged and a Label to provide a way to show messages from the application. Note that the label's mouseEnabled property is set to false. This will prevent the label from interfering with the user's touch gestures. See the section titled "A Debugging Aside" for more details about how the messageLabel is used to provide feedback on the running program.

The code to add a KeyboardEvent listener to the stage is the same as in the previous examples, so we will not repeat it here.

Image Browsing

As you saw in Listing 7–10, the onBrowse handler is called when the user taps the Browse button. This sets off a series of actions that allows the user to browse for an image using the native Android image browser and, if an image is selected, culminates with the image appearing in the application's view. Listing 7–11 shows the relevant source code.

Listing 7–11. *The Code That Initiates a Browse Action and Displays the Selected Image*

```
private static const BROWSE_UNSUPPORTED: String = "Browsing with " +
    "flash.media.CameraRoll is unsupported on this device.";

private var cameraRoll: CameraRoll = new CameraRoll();

private function onCreationComplete():void {
  cameraRoll.addEventListener(MediaEvent.SELECT, onSelect);
  cameraRoll.addEventListener(Event.CANCEL, onSelectCanceled);
  cameraRoll.addEventListener(ErrorEvent.ERROR, onCameraRollError);
```

```
      cameraRoll.addEventListener(Event.COMPLETE, onSaveComplete);

      // …
    }

    private function onBrowse():void {
      if (CameraRoll.supportsBrowseForImage) {
        cameraRoll.browseForImage();
      } else {
        showMessage(BROWSE_UNSUPPORTED);
      }
      toggleMenu();
    }

    private function onSelect(event:MediaEvent):void {
      var loader: Loader = new Loader();
      loader.contentLoaderInfo.addEventListener(Event.COMPLETE, onLoaded);
      loader.load(new URLRequest(event.data.file.url));
    }

    private function onLoaded(event:Event):void {
      var info: LoaderInfo = event.target as LoaderInfo;
      var bmp: Bitmap = info.content as Bitmap;

      scaleContainer(bmp.width, bmp.height);

      var sprite: Sprite = new Sprite();

      sprite.addEventListener(TransformGestureEvent.GESTURE_ZOOM, onZoom);
      sprite.addEventListener(TransformGestureEvent.GESTURE_ROTATE, onRotate);
      sprite.addEventListener(MouseEvent.MOUSE_DOWN, onMouseDown);
      sprite.addEventListener(MouseEvent.MOUSE_UP, onMouseUp);
      sprite.addChild(bmp);

      photoContainer.addChild(sprite);
    }

    private function onSelectCanceled(event:Event):void {
      showMessage("Select canceled");
    }

    private function onCameraRollError(event:ErrorEvent):void {
      showMessage("Error: "+event.text);
    }

    private function onSaveComplete(event:Event):void {
      showMessage("CameraRoll operation complete");
    }
```

The onCreationComplete() function attaches handlers for all of the CameraRoll events that matter to this application. MediaEvent.SELECT and Event.CANCEL are the two possible successful results of the browse operation. The ErrorEvent.ERROR is sent if an error occurs either during browsing or during saving. And finally, the Event.COMPLETE event is triggered when a save is completed successfully. The onSelectCanceled(), onCameraRollError(), and onSaveComplete() handler functions simply call the showMessage function to display a message on the screen.

Now that the application is listening to all of the necessary events, it is ready to handle the onBrowse callback. As always, the first thing you should do is to check if browsing is supported using the CameraRoll.supportsBrowseForImage property. If this property is true, you can call the browseForImage() instance method on the cameraRoll object. This triggers the native Android image browser to be shown to the user. If a user selects an image, the application's onSelect() handler will be called. The MediaEvent object that is passed as a parameter to this function contains a property called data that is an instance of a MediaPromise object. The key piece of information in the MediaPromise object is the file property. You can use the URL of the file to load the selected image. So, as shown earlier, what you are really after is the event.data.file.url property. This property is passed to a Loader object that handles loading the image data. When the load is complete, it triggers the onLoaded callback that is responsible for taking the resulting bitmap and placing it inside a Sprite so it can be manipulated by the user. This Sprite is then added to the photoContainer so it can be displayed on the screen.

Using a Loader is not the only way to read the data, of course. If you are simply interested in displaying the photo rather than manipulating it with touch gestures, it is easier to use a Spark BitmapImage or a halo Image. In those two cases, you only need to set the source property of the Image or BitmapImage to the event.data.file.url and then add it to your stage. Everything else will be handled automatically. Figure 7–6 shows the PhotoCollage application running on an Android device.

Figure 7–6. *The PhotoCollage program running on a Nexus S*

A Debugging Aside

The on-device debugger that comes with Flash Builder 4.5 is a wonderful tool. But sometimes it is quicker to use good old-fashioned debug output to get a feel for what is going on with the program. The traditional method of adding such output in Flash has been through the use of the trace() function. This function will print messages only when the application is run in debug mode. Flash Builder's debugger connects to the

Flash player and will display the `trace` messages in the debugger's console window. This method works when debugging on a mobile device as well.

There are times when you may want to write output directly to the screen, either as part of the debugging process or just to present extra information to the user. Fortunately this is very easy to set up in an AIR for Android program. Listing 7–12 shows the small amount of code that is required to provide your application with a workable output log right on the device's screen. The listing includes the declaration of `messageLabel` from the MXML file previously shown just as a reminder. The `messageLabel` is a simple Spark `Label` that sits in the top left-hand corner of the view. It sits on top of all of the other display objects, so its mouse interaction has to be disabled so it won't interfere with user input.

Listing 7–12. *Adding Debug Output to an AIR for Android Application*

```
// From PhotoCollageHome.mxml
<s:Label id="messageLabel" top="0" left="0" mouseEnabled="false"/>

// From PhotoCollageHomeScript.as
private function onCreationComplete():void {
  // CameraRoll event listener initialization…

  // Make sure the text messages stay within the confines
  // of our view's width.
  messageLabel.maxWidth = Screen.mainScreen.bounds.width;
  messageLabel.maxHeight = Screen.mainScreen.bounds.height;

  // Multitouch initialization…
}

private function showMessage(msg:String):void {
  if (messageLabel.text && messageLabel.height < height) {
    messageLabel.text += "\n" + msg;
  } else {
    messageLabel.text = msg;
  }
}
```

In the `onCreationComplete()` function, the `messageLabel`'s `maxWidth` and `maxHeight` properties are set to the width and height of the screen. This will prevent the label's text from being drawn outside the bounds of the screen. The final piece is a small `showMessage` function that takes a message string as a parameter. If the `messageLabel.text` property is currently empty or if the `messageLabel` is growing too large, then the text property is set to the message string, effectively clearing the label. Otherwise the new message is just appended to the existing text along with a newline character. The result is a message buffer that expands down the screen until it gets to the bottom, at which time the existing messages will be erased and the new messages will start again at the top. It's not a full-featured application log and it has to be reimplemented for each `View` in your application, but it's hard to beat as a simple way to display debugging messages on the screen.

You should now be familiar with using the `CameraRoll` class to browse and save images on an Android device. You can find the complete source code in the

PhotoCollageHomeScript.as file in the PhotoCollage example project. The ActionScript file includes portions that were not shown previously, such as the handling of the multitouch zoom and rotate gestures as well as touch dragging. This code should give you a good idea of how to handle this sort of user input. You can also refer back to the "Multitouch and Gestures" section of Chapter 2 if you need more details on these topics.

The final aspect of Flash's camera support that will be covered in this chapter is using the native Android media capture interface via the CameraUI class. That will be the subject of the next section.

CameraUI

The CameraUI class gives you the ability to harness the power of the native Android media capture interface to capture high-quality, high-resolution images and video. Usage of this class involves the now familiar three steps: ensure the functionality is supported, call a method to invoke the native interface, and register a callback to be notified when the image or video has been captured so that you can display it in your application. Listing 7–13 shows the CaptureView of the CameraUIBasic example project. This short program illustrates the three steps just listed.

Listing 7–13. *Basic Image Capture Using* CameraUI

```
<?xml version="1.0" encoding="utf-8"?>
<s:View xmlns:fx="http://ns.adobe.com/mxml/2009"
         xmlns:s="library://ns.adobe.com/flex/spark"
         actionBarVisible="false" creationComplete="onCreationComplete()">

<fx:Script>
    <![CDATA[
      private var cameraUI:CameraUI;

      private function onCreationComplete():void {
        if (CameraUI.isSupported) {
          cameraUI = new CameraUI();
          cameraUI.addEventListener(MediaEvent.COMPLETE, onCaptureComplete);
        }

        captureButton.visible = CameraUI.isSupported;
        notSupportedLabel.visible = !CameraUI.isSupported;
      }

      private function onCaptureImage():void {
        cameraUI.launch(MediaType.IMAGE);
      }

      private function onCaptureComplete(event:MediaEvent):void {
        image.source = event.data.file.url;
      }
    ]]>
  </fx:Script>

  <s:Label id="notSupportedLabel" width="100%" height="100%"
```

```
                verticalAlign="middle" textAlign="center"
                text="CameraUI is not supported on this device."/>

    <s:Image id="image" width="100%" height="100%"/>
    <s:Button id="captureButton" width="100%" bottom="0" label="Capture Image"
                alpha="0.75" click="onCaptureImage()"/>
</s:View>
```

The onCreationComplete() method checks for CameraUI support and creates a new cameraUI instance if it exists. An event listener is then added to the instance object so the application gets notified when the capture is complete via its onCaptureComplete callback function. When the user taps on the Capture Image button, the onCaptureImage callback calls CameraUI's launch method to show the Android capture interface. The callback function we attached to CameraUI is called when the capture is complete. It receives a MediaEvent parameter, the same event class that is used by CameraRoll as was discussed in the previous section. As before, the event contains a MediaPromise instance in its data property. Therefore you can load the captured image by using the event.data.file.url just as was done when an image is selected using the CameraRoll's browse function.

The CameraUIBasic example program displays a view with a single translucent button that has a "Capture Image" label. Android's native camera interface is launched via the CameraUI class when the user taps the button. After an image is captured, the image data is returned to the original view for display, as shown in Listing 7–13. Figure 7–7 is a sequence of images that show the native Android camera interface capturing an image of a robot and returning it to the application for display. A team of middle school students competing in the FIRST Tech Challenge robotics competition built the robot pictured in Figure 7–7.

> **NOTE:** Any photo captured with CameraUI is also automatically saved to the device's photo gallery and therefore can be retrieved later using the CameraRoll class.

That concludes our coverage of the camera functionality in AIR for Android. In the rest of this chapter, you will learn about the inhabitants of the flash.sensors package: Accelerometer and Geolocation. We hope you will find it quick and to the point.

Figure 7–7. *An image of a robot captured with the native Android camera interface and* `CameraUI`

Accelerometer

The accelerometer sensor allows you to detect the orientation of the device by measuring the acceleration due to the force of gravity experienced along its x, y, and z axes. While at rest, any object on earth will experience an approximate 9.8 m/s/s (meters per second per second) acceleration due to the force of gravity. 9.8 m/s/s is also known as 1 gravity-force or 1 g-force—or simply 1g of acceleration. So an acceleration of 10g would be ten times the force of gravity or 98 m/s/s. That is a very large g-force, normally experienced only by fighter pilots during extreme maneuvers!

Since a phone is a three-dimensional object, its orientation can be determined by looking at how that 1g of force is distributed along its three axes. The accelerometer can also tell you if the phone is being shaken or moved in some other rapid manner, since in that situation it would be experiencing significantly more or less than 1g of acceleration on its three axes. You need to know how the axes of the phone are laid out in order to glean useful information from the accelerometer values. Figure 7–8 illustrates the orientation of the phone's acceleration axes with respect to the body of the phone.

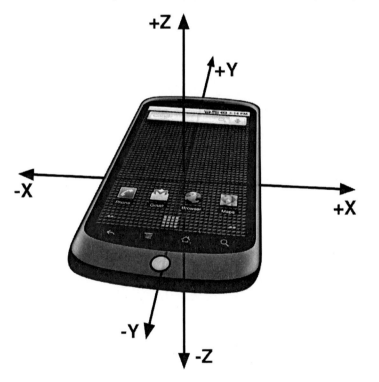

Figure 7–8. *The accelerometer axes of an Android phone*

If you align one of the marked axes in Figure 7–8 so that it is *in direct opposition* to the force of gravity, you will read 1g of acceleration on that axis. If an axis is orthogonal to the force of gravity, then it will read 0g. For example, if you lay your phone down, face up, on a flat surface, then the accelerometer will read approximately +1g on the z axis and about 0g on the x and y axes. If you then flip the phone over so that it lies face down, the accelerometer will register -1g on the z axis.

The Accelerometer and AccelerometerEvent Classes

The fine folks on the AIR team at Adobe continue their trend of making our lives easier by providing a simple class with which you can interact with the accelerometer sensor. It is unsurprisingly named Accelerometer and comes equipped with the usual static isSupported property. The class declares only one new instance method, setRequestedUpdateInterval(). This method takes a single parameter that specifies the number of milliseconds to wait between updates. A value of zero means to use the minimum supported update interval. The accelerometer will send its updates to your application using an AccelerometerEvent (of course!) of type AccelerometerEvent.UPDATE. An AccelerometerEvent instance contains four properties that tell you the current acceleration detected along each of the three axes plus the timestamp at which the values were measured. The four properties are named accelerationX, accelerationY, accelerationZ, and timestamp. The three accelerations are specified in g-forces, and the timestamp is in milliseconds as measured from when the sensor started sending events to the application. The timestamp can allow you to detect shakes and other movements by telling you if large negative and positive g-forces have been experienced within a short amount of time.

The Accelerometer class also contains a property named muted. This property is true if the user has denied the application access to the accelerometer sensor. The application can register a callback that listens for events of type StatusEvent.STATUS if it wishes to be notified when the value of the muted property changes. Listing 7–14 shows the code from the AccelerometerBasic example application that is relevant to initializing and receiving updates from the accelerometer.

Listing 7–14. *Reading the Accelerometer Sensor*

```
private var accelerometer: Accelerometer;

private function onCreationComplete():void {
  if (Accelerometer.isSupported) {
    showMessage("Accelerometer supported");

    accelerometer = new Accelerometer();
    accelerometer.addEventListener(AccelerometerEvent.UPDATE, onUpdate);
    accelerometer.addEventListener(StatusEvent.STATUS, onStatus);
    accelerometer.setRequestedUpdateInterval(100);

    if (accelerometer.muted) {
      showMessage("Accelerometer muted, access denied!");
    }
  } else {
    showMessage(UNSUPPORTED);
  }
}
```

```
private function onStatus(event:StatusEvent):void {
  showMessage("Muted status has changed, is now: "+accelerometer.muted);
}

private function onUpdate(event:AccelerometerEvent):void {
  updateAccel(xAxis, event.accelerationX, 0);
  updateAccel(yAxis, event.accelerationY, 1);
  updateAccel(zAxis, event.accelerationZ, 2);

  time.text = "Ellapsed Time: " + event.timestamp + "ms";
}

private function updateAccel(l: Label, val: Number, idx: int):void {
  var item: Object = accelData[idx];
  item.max = formatter.format(Math.max(item.max, val));
  item.min = formatter.format(Math.min(item.min, val));

  l.text = item.title +
      "\n  Current Value: " + formatter.format(val) + "g" +
      "\n  Minimum Value: " + item.min + "g" +
      "\n  Maximum Value: " + item.max + "g";
}
```

After checking to ensure the accelerometer is supported on the current device, the onCreationComplete() method creates a new instance of the Accelerometer class and attaches listeners for the update and status events. The setRequestedUpdateInterval method is called to request updates every 100ms. You should always be mindful of battery consumption when programming for mobile devices. Always set the longest update interval that still meets the requirements of your application. Once the update listener is attached, the program will start receiving events from the sensor. The data contained within these events is displayed on the screen in a series of labels: one for each axis and one for the timestamp. The program also keeps track of and displays the minimum and maximum values that have been reported by the sensor. Figure 7–9 shows the output of the AccelerometerBasic program on an Android device.

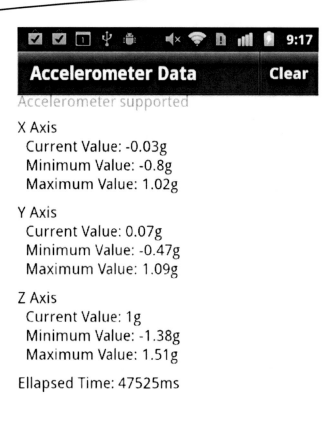

Figure 7–9. *The AccelerometerBasic program running on an Android device*

This program includes a button in its action bar that allows the user to clear the minimum and maximum values that have been recorded so far. This makes it useful for experimenting with accelerometer readings when planning your own applications. The minimum and maximum values are initialized to plus or minus 10g since it is unlikely that a phone will ever experience more acceleration than that, unless you happen to be a fighter pilot. As a final note, your application does not need to specify any special Android permission in the application descriptor in order to use the accelerometer.

You can see from the material in this section that reading the accelerometer in an AIR application is easy and allows you to accept a user's input in new and creative ways. We will next take a look at how to read another form of data that is widely used in mobile applications: geolocation data.

Geolocation

The prevalence of geolocation services in mobile devices has led to a rapid increase in the number of location-aware applications in recent years. Location data can come from cell tower triangulation, a database of known Wi-Fi access points, and of course, GPS satellites. Location data based on Wi-Fi and cell towers is not as accurate as GPS data, but it can be quicker to obtain and consumes less battery power than using the device's GPS receiver. Due to this complexity, getting an accurate location can be more complicated than you might assume.

AIR provides a way for developers to easily access location data without having to worry about most of the details involved in obtaining accurate readings. Geolocation and GeolocationEvent are the two primary classes involved in this process. The use of these classes will be familiar to you by now if you have just finished reading the previous section covering the accelerometer. As usual, you start by checking the static isSupported property of the Geolocation class. If support is available, you can optionally use the setRequestedUpdateInterval method to request updates at a certain rate. The method takes a single parameter that is the requested time interval between updates expressed in milliseconds. It is important to bear in mind that this is only a request—a hint to the device about how often you would like to receive updates. It is not a guarantee. The actual update rate could be greater or less than the requested rate. In fact, although you can request intervals of less than one second, on the devices we've tested, we have yet to see an AIR application that can receive updates quicker than one second apart.

Battery usage is an even greater concern with geolocation data since the GPS receiver can be a real drain on battery life. This is especially true if the device is in a place where the signal is weak. Therefore you should give careful thought to how often your application really needs location updates. Update intervals of one minute (60,000 milliseconds) or more are not uncommon in location-aware applications. And since heading and speed are also provided with the location data, there is a certain amount of extrapolation that can be done based on previous data. This can significantly smooth out the location updates you provide to the users of your application.

You will receive location data from a GeolocationEvent object of type GeolocationEvent.UPDATE that is passed to the event handler you will register with your Geolocation instance. The GeolocationEvent class contains several properties of interest:

- latitude: The latitude of the device in degrees; the range will be between -90 and +90 inclusive.

- longitude: The longitude of the device in degrees; the range will be between -180 and +180 inclusive, where negative numbers indicate a position to the west of the Prime Meridian (also known as the Greenwich Meridian or International Meridian) and positive longitude is to the east.

▓ horizontalAccuracy: An estimate of how accurate the location data is on the horizontal plane expressed in meters

▓ verticalAccuracy: An estimate of how accurate the location data is vertically expressed in meters

▓ speed: The speed as measured using the distance between recent location readings with respect to time; the value is in meters per second.

▓ altitude: The current altitude of the device above sea level expressed in meters

▓ timestamp: The number of milliseconds, at the time the event was sent, since the application started receiving location updates

CAUTION: Although AIR 2.5.1 supports a heading property in the GeolocationEvent, this property is not currently supported on Android devices and will always return NaN.

The Geolocation class also contains a property named muted that will be set to true if the user has disabled geolocation (or if you forgot to specify the android.permission.ACCESS_FINE_LOCATION permission in the manifest section of the application descriptor XML file!). When the value of the muted property changes, the Geolocation class will send a StatusChange event with the type StatusChange.STATUS to your listener if you have added one. Listing 7–15 shows the source code for the GeolocationBasic example project. This code illustrates the steps to receive and display geolocation data in your application.

Listing 7–15. *The Source Code for the GeolocationBasicHome View*

```
<?xml version="1.0" encoding="utf-8"?>
<s:View xmlns:fx="http://ns.adobe.com/mxml/2009"
        xmlns:s="library://ns.adobe.com/flex/spark"
        creationComplete="onCreationComplete()" title="Geolocation Data">

  <fx:Declarations>
    <s:NumberFormatter id="f" fractionalDigits="4"/>
  </fx:Declarations>

  <fx:Script>
    <![CDATA[
      import flash.sensors.Geolocation;

      private static const UNSUPPORTED: String = "flash.sensors.Geolocation "+
        "is not supported on this device.";

      private var loc: Geolocation;

      private function onCreationComplete():void {
        if (Geolocation.isSupported) {
          showMessage("Geolocation supported");

          loc = new Geolocation();
```

```
            if (!loc.muted) {
              loc.addEventListener(GeolocationEvent.UPDATE, onUpdate);
              loc.addEventListener(StatusEvent.STATUS, onStatus);
              loc.setRequestedUpdateInterval(1000);
            } else {
              showMessage("Geolocation muted");
            }
          } else {
            showMessage(UNSUPPORTED);
          }
        }

        private function onStatus(event:StatusEvent):void {
          showMessage("Geolocation status changed, muted is now " + loc.muted);
        }

        private function onUpdate(event:GeolocationEvent):void {
          geoDataLabel.text = "Geolocation" +
            "\n  Latitude: " + f.format(event.latitude) + "\u00B0" +
            "\n  Longitude: " + f.format(event.longitude) + "\u00B0" +
            "\n  Horz Accuracy: " + f.format(event.horizontalAccuracy) + " m" +
            "\n  Vert Accuracy: " + f.format(event.verticalAccuracy) + " m" +
            "\n  Speed: " + f.format(event.speed) + " m/s" +
            "\n  Altitude: " + f.format(event.altitude) + " m" +
            "\n  Timestamp: " + f.format(event.timestamp) + " ms";
        }

        private function showMessage(msg:String):void {
          if (messageLabel.text && messageLabel.height < height) {
            messageLabel.text += "\n" + msg;
          } else {
            messageLabel.text = msg;
          }
        }
      }
    ]]>
  </fx:Script>

  <s:Label id="geoDataLabel" width="100%"/>
  <s:Label id="messageLabel" top="0" left="0" mouseEnabled="false" alpha="0.5"/>
</s:View>
```

And as we referred to in passing, this code will not work unless you specify the proper Android permission in the manifest section of your application descriptor. The application descriptor for this application is shown in Listing 7–16.

Listing 7–16. *The Application Descriptor for GeolocationBasic Showing the Proper Usage of the Fine Location Permission*

```
<?xml version="1.0" encoding="utf-8" standalone="no"?>
<application xmlns="http://ns.adobe.com/air/application/2.5">
    <id>GeolocationBasic</id>
    <filename>GeolocationBasic</filename>
    <name>GeolocationBasic</name>
    <versionNumber>0.0.1</versionNumber>

    <initialWindow>
        <content>[This value will be overwritten by Flash Builder in the output
app.xml]</content>
```

```
        <autoOrients>false</autoOrients>
        <fullScreen>false</fullScreen>
        <visible>false</visible>
    </initialWindow>

    <android>
        <manifestAdditions>
            <![CDATA[
            <manifest>
                <!-- Only used for debugging -->
                <uses-permission android:name="android.permission.INTERNET"/>
                <uses-permission android:name="android.permission.ACCESS_FINE_LOCATION"/>
            </manifest>
            ]]>
        </manifestAdditions>
    </android>
</application>
```

Android uses ACCESS_COARSE_LOCATION to limit the geolocation data to using only Wi-Fi and cell towers for location information. The ACCESS_FINE_LOCATION permission that was used earlier encompasses the coarse location permission and also adds the ability to access the GPS receiver to obtain more accurate readings. Figure 7–10 shows a screen capture of the GeolocationBasic program in action.

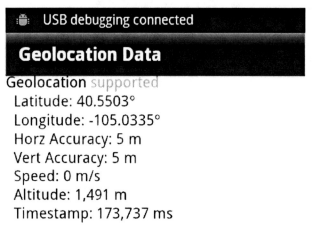

Figure 7–10. *The GeolocationBasic program running on an Android device*

Summary

This chapter has covered a variety of sensors and hardware capabilities. From microphones and cameras to media storage, accelerometers, and geolocation data, you now have all the knowledge you need to integrate your applications with the full variety of hardware services available to AIR applications. Over the course of this chapter, you have learned the following:

- How to use the microphone to receive audio input

- How to access and view real-time video streams

- How to apply various filter effects to those video streams

- How to store and browse for media on the mobile device

- How to use Android's native image and video capture interface in your own application

- How to read and interpret acceleration data from the accelerometer

- How to retrieve location data including latitude, longitude, speed, and altitude from the geolocation sensors on a device

You will continue on the path of AIR and Android discovery by exploring Flash's media playback capabilities in the next chapter.

Chapter 8

Rich Media Integration

If your users aren't using their Android device to make phone calls, then they are most likely either playing games, listening to music, or watching videos. When it comes right down to it, the consumption of audio and video may be even more important to modern consumers than the communication capabilities of their mobile devices. Fortunately, outstanding support for audio and video is one of the real strengths of the Flash platform. In fact, this is one of the primary reasons that the Flash Player has become so ubiquitous on our computers and mobile devices.

The previous chapter showed you how to capture audio and video on your Android device. This chapter builds upon those concepts and will teach you how to use the power of the Flash platform to unlock the rich media potential of an Android mobile device.

Playing Sound Effects

Sound effects are typically short sounds that you play in response to various application events such as alert pop-ups or button presses. The audio data for the sound effect should be in an MP3 file and can be embedded in your application's SWF file or downloaded from the Internet. You embed an MP3 asset in your application by using the Embed metadata tag to identify the asset, as shown in Listing 8–1.

Listing 8–1. *Embedding a Sound File with the* Embed *Metadata Tag*

```
<?xml version="1.0" encoding="utf-8"?>
<s:View xmlns:fx="http://ns.adobe.com/mxml/2009"
        xmlns:s="library://ns.adobe.com/flex/spark"
        xmlns:mx="library://ns.adobe.com/flex/mx"
        title="SoundAssets">

  <fx:Script>
    <![CDATA[
      import mx.core.SoundAsset;

      [Embed(source="mySound.mp3")]
      private var MySound:Class;
      private var sound:SoundAsset = new MySound();
```

```
      ]]>
    </fx:Script>

  <s:Button label="Play SoundAsset" click="sound.play()"/>
</s:View>
```

The Embed metadata tag will cause the compiler to transcode the MP3 file and embed it in your application's SWF file. The source attribute specifies the path and file name of the MP3 file. In this case, we have placed the file in the same package as our source file. You access the embedded sound by creating an instance of the class associated with the Embed tag, which in Listing 8–1 is a class named MySound. The MySound class is generated by the compiler and will be a subclass of mx.core.SoundAsset. Therefore it has all the necessary support for basic playback of an audio asset. In Listing 8–1, we take advantage of this support by creating an instance variable named sound and calling its play method in response to a button click.

The SoundEffect Class

Although it's nice to know what's going on behind the scenes, you typically don't need to bother with creating and instancing a SoundAsset in your Flex programs. Your tool of choice will usually be the SoundEffect class, due to its ability to easily create interesting effects during the playback of the sample. It offers simple control of looping, panning, and volume effects during playback. Since it extends the base mx.effect.Effect class, it can be used anywhere a regular effect could be used. For example, you can set a SoundEffect instance as a Button's mouseDownEffect or as the creationCompleteEffect of an Alert dialog. Listing 8–2 shows how you can do this, as well as how to play a SoundEffect manually.

Listing 8–2. *Creating and Playing a Looping* SoundEffect

```
<?xml version="1.0" encoding="utf-8"?>
<s:View xmlns:fx="http://ns.adobe.com/mxml/2009"
        xmlns:s="library://ns.adobe.com/flex/spark"
        xmlns:mx="library://ns.adobe.com/flex/mx"
        title="SoundEffects">

  <fx:Declarations>
    <mx:SoundEffect id="mySound" source="{MySound}" useDuration="false"
                    loops="2"/>
  </fx:Declarations>

  <fx:Script>
    <![CDATA[
      [Bindable]
      [Embed(source="mySound.mp3")]
      private var MySound:Class;

      private function playEffect(event:MouseEvent):void {
        mySound.end();
        mySound.play([event.target]);
      }
    ]]>
  </fx:Script>
```

```
    <s:VGroup horizontalCenter="0" horizontalAlign="contentJustify">
      <s:Button label="Play mouseDownEffect" mouseDownEffect="{mySound}"/>
      <s:Button label="End &amp; Play SoundEffect" click="playEffect(event)"/>
    </s:VGroup>
</s:View>
```

The SoundEffect declaration that is highlighted in Listing 8–2 creates a sound effect that loops twice every time it is played. Note the useDuration attribute that is set to false. The duration of a SoundEffect is set to 500 milliseconds by default, and if useDuration is left at its default value of true, then only the first half-second of your sound will be played. Therefore you will almost always want to set this attribute to false unless you also set the duration attribute in order to play only a portion of your sound effect. The source attribute of the SoundEffect is given the class name of the embedded sound asset.

We then create two buttons to illustrate the two different ways you can play a SoundEffect. The first button simply sets the instance id of the SoundEffect as its mouseDownEffect. This plays our audio sample every time the mouse button is pressed over the button. Each time the mouse button is pressed, a new effect is created and played. If you click quickly enough, and your sound sample is long enough, it is possible to hear them playing simultaneously.

Clicking the second button will call the playEffect method, which does two things. First it will stop any instances of the effect that are currently playing by calling the end method. This ensures that the sound cannot overlap with any other instances of itself. Second, a new sound effect is played using the button as its target object. The MouseEvent's target property provides a convenient way to refer to the button that we will be using as the target of our effect. Note that the parameter to the play method is actually an array of targets. This is why we need the extra set of square brackets around the event.target parameter.

You can see that each sound you embed in this manner requires three lines of code: two metadata tags and the line that declares a class name for the sound asset. There is a way to avoid this and embed the sound into the sound effect directly.

Embedded SoundEffect Example

You can use an @Embed directive in the source attribute of a SoundEffect declaration. This technique is used in the SoundEffectBasic sample application, which can be found in the examples/chapter-08 directory of the sample code for this book. This example application also demonstrates how to adjust the volume and panning of the sound effect as it plays. Listing 8–3 shows the main View of the application.

Listing 8–3. *The Home View of the SoundEffectBasic Example Program*

```
<?xml version="1.0" encoding="utf-8"?>
<s:View xmlns:fx="http://ns.adobe.com/mxml/2009"
        xmlns:s="library://ns.adobe.com/flex/spark"
        xmlns:mx="library://ns.adobe.com/flex/mx"
        title="Code Monkey To-Do List">
```

```
<fx:Declarations>
  <mx:SoundEffect id="coffee" source="@Embed('coffee.mp3')"
                  useDuration="false" volumeFrom="1.0" volumeTo="0.0"/>
  <mx:SoundEffect id="job" source="@Embed('job.mp3')"
                  useDuration="false" panFrom="-1.0" panTo="1.0"/>
  <mx:SoundEffect id="meeting" source="@Embed('meeting.mp3')"
                  useDuration="false" volumeFrom="1.0" volumeTo="0.0"
                  volumeEasingFunction="Back.easeOut"/>
</fx:Declarations>

<fx:Script>
  <![CDATA[
    import flash.net.navigateToURL;
    import mx.effects.easing.Back;

    private static const CM_URL_STR:String = "http://www.jonathancoulton.com"+
        "/2006/04/14/thing-a-week-29-code-monkey/";

    private static const CM_URL:URLRequest = new URLRequest(CM_URL_STR);

    private function play(event:MouseEvent, effect:SoundEffect):void {
      effect.end();
      effect.play([event.target]);
    }
  ]]>
</fx:Script>

<s:VGroup horizontalCenter="0" horizontalAlign="contentJustify" top="15" >
  <s:Button label="1. Get Coffee" click="play(event, coffee)"/>
  <s:Button label="2. Go to Job"  click="play(event, job)"/>
  <s:Button label="3. Have Meeting" mouseDownEffect="{meeting}"/>
</s:VGroup>

<s:Button horizontalCenter="0" bottom="5" width="90%"
          label="About Code Monkey..." click="navigateToURL(CM_URL)"/>
</s:View>
```

The first thing to note in Listing 8–3 is the use of the @Embed statement in the source attribute of each SoundEffect declaration. This allows you to embed a sound asset and associate it with a SoundEffect in one step. Just as before, if your sound file is in a different package from your source file, then you must include the path to the sound file in the @Embed statement in order for the compiler to find it.

Each sound effect will play a short excerpt from the song "Code Monkey," by Jonathan Coulton. We have used the volumeFrom and volumeTo attributes of the SoundEffect class to fade the volume from 1.0 (maximum volume) to 0.0 (minimum volume) as the audio sample plays. Since we did not specify a volumeEasingFunction, it will be a linear fade. Similarly, the second sound effect will linearly pan the audio sample from -1.0 (left speaker) to 1.0 (right speaker) as the sample plays. If you want to use a different easing function for your pan effect, you would specify it using the panEasingFunction property of the SoundEffect class. The final SoundEffect declaration shows how to use one of Flex's built-in easers to change the volume of the sample as it plays. By using the Back easer's fadeOut method, we will fade the volume down to the target value of 0.0, overshoot it a little, and rebound back up past 0.0 again before finally settling on the end value. This creates an interesting little surge in volume at the end of the audio sample.

This example demonstrates once again the two different methods of playing sound effects. There is also a fourth button at the bottom of the screen that, when clicked, will launch Android's native web browser and take you to the "Code Monkey" web page by using the navigateToURL method that was covered in Chapter 6. The resulting application is shown in Figure 8-1.

Figure 8-1. *The Code Monkey sound effects example running on an Android device*

The SoundEffect class is perfect for playing small sound effects in response to application events. If you need more advanced control over sound in your application, then it is time to dig deeper into the functionality that the Flash platform has to offer.

Sophisticated Sound Solutions

The SoundEffect class is a convenient abstraction for that (mostly silent) majority of applications whose needs do not extend beyond the ability to occasionally prompt or notify the user. There are some applications in which sound is one of the main ingredients. If you want to record voice memos or play music, then you need to go a little deeper into the Flash sound APIs. We will start by taking a look at the Sound class and its partners: SoundChannel and SoundTransform. All three of these classes can be found in the flash.media package.

The Sound class serves as the data container for your audio file. Its main responsibilities are to provide mechanisms for loading data into its buffer and to begin playback of that data. The audio data loaded into a Sound class will typically come from either an MP3 file or from the application itself generating data dynamically. Unsurprisingly, the key methods to be aware of in this class are the load and play methods. You use the load method to provide the URL of the MP3 file that should be loaded into the Sound. Once data is loaded into a Sound, it cannot be changed. If you later want to load another MP3 file, you must create a new Sound object. Passing a URL to the constructor of the Sound object is equivalent to calling the load method. The Sound class dispatches several events during the process of loading audio data, as shown in Table 8–1.

Table 8–1. *Loading Events Dispatched by the Sound Object*

Event	Type	Dispatched when...
Open	flash.events.Event.OPEN	Loading begins.
Progress	flash.events.ProgressEvent.PROGRESS	Data is loading. Check the event's bytesLoaded and bytesTotal properties.
id3	flash.events.Event.ID3	ID3 metadata is available to be read. Check the Sound's id3 property.
ioError	flash.events.IOErrorEvent	The load operation fails. Check the event's errorID and text properties.
Complete	flash.events.Event.COMPLETE	Data has loaded successfully.

After the data has been loaded, calling the play method of the Sound class will cause the sound to begin playing. The play method returns a SoundChannel object that can be used to track the progress of the sound's playback and to stop it early. The SoundChannel also has a SoundTransform object associated with it that you can use to change the volume and panning of the sound as it plays. There are three optional parameters that can be passed to the play method. First there is the startTime parameter, which will cause the sound to begin playing at the specified number of milliseconds into the sample. You can also pass a loop count if you want the sound to play a certain number of times. And finally, it is also possible to provide a SoundTransform object as a parameter to the play method if you would like to set the initial transform of the sound when it begins playing. The transform you pass will be set as the SoundChannel's SoundTransform.

A new SoundChannel object is created and returned every time the Sound.play method is called. SoundChannel serves as your main point of interaction with the sound while it is playing. It allows you to track the current position and volume of the sound. It contains a stop method, which interrupts and terminates playback of the sound. When a sound has reached the end of its data, the SoundChannel class will notify you by dispatching a soundComplete event of type flash.events.Event.SOUND_COMPLETE. And finally, you can also use its soundTransform property to manipulate the volume of the sound and to pan the sound to the left and right speakers. Figure 8–2 illustrates the relationship between these three collaborating classes.

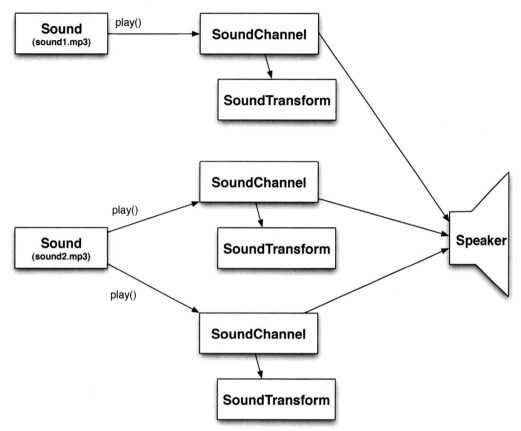

Figure 8–2. *The relationship between* Sound, SoundChannel, *and* SoundTransform

Now admittedly the path from the SoundChannel to the speaker is not as direct as Figure 8–2 implies. There are several layers (including OS drivers and digital-to-analog conversion circuitry) that exist before the audio signal reaches the speaker. There is even another class that Flash provides in the flash.media package called SoundMixer, which includes several static methods for manipulating and gathering data about the sounds being played by the application at a global level.

That wraps up our overview of the classes you need to be familiar with in order to play sound on your Android device using Flash. In the next sections, we will take a look at some examples that use these classes to play sound from in-memory buffers and from files stored on the device.

Playing Recorded Sound

We showed you in the MicrophoneBasic example application from Chapter 7 how to record audio data from the device's microphone. Expanding on that example will provide a convenient starting point for a more in-depth exploration of Flash's audio support. You may recall that we attached an event handler to the Microphone object to handle its sampleData event. The handler was called each time the microphone had data for our application. We didn't actually do anything with the microphone data in that example, but it would have been a simple thing to just copy the data into a ByteArray for later playback. The question is: how do we play sound data from a ByteArray?

Generating Sound Data on the Fly

If you call the play() method on a Sound object that has nothing loaded into it, the object is forced to go looking for sound data to play. It does so by dispatching sampleData events to request sound samples. The event's type is SampleDataEvent.SAMPLE_DATA, and it is found in the flash.events package. This happens to be the same type of event the Microphone class uses to notify us that samples are available. The answer to our previous question is simple, then: you just attach a handler for the Sound's sampleData event and start copying bytes into the event's data property.

Therefore our enhanced application will have two separate handlers for the sampleData event. The first will copy data to a ByteArray when the microphone is active, and the second will copy the data from that same ByteArray to the Sound object when we are playing it back. The source code for the new application can be found in the SoundRecorder application located in the examples/chapter-08 directory. Listing 8–4 shows the sampleData event handler for the microphone data.

Listing 8–4. *The Setup Code and Event Handler for the Microphone's Data Notifications*

```
private static const SOUND_RATE:uint = 44;
private static const MICROPHONE_RATE:uint = 22;

// Handles the View's creationComplete event
private function onCreationComplete():void {
  if (Microphone.isSupported) {
    microphone = Microphone.getMicrophone();
    microphone.setSilenceLevel(0)
    microphone.gain = 75;
    microphone.rate = MICROPHONE_RATE;

    sound = new Sound();
    recordedBytes = new ByteArray();
  } else {
    showMessage("microphone unsupported");
  }
}

// This handler is called when the microphone has data to give us
```

```
private function onMicSample(event:SampleDataEvent):void {
  if (microphone.activityLevel > activityLevel) {
    activityLevel = Math.min(50, microphone.activityLevel);
  }

  if (event.data.bytesAvailable) {
    recordedBytes.writeBytes(event.data);
  }
}
```

The onCreationComplete handler is responsible for detecting the microphone, initializing it, and creating the ByteArray and Sound objects the application uses to store and play sound. Note that the microphone's rate is set to 22 kHz. This is adequate quality for capturing a voice recording and takes up less space than does recording at the full 44 kHz.

This handler is simple. Just as before, the Microphone object's activityLevel property is used to compute a number that is later used to determine the amplitude of the animated curves drawn on the display to indicate the sound level. Then the event's data property, which is a ByteArray, is used to determine if any microphone data is available. If the bytesAvailable property is greater than zero, then the bytes are copied from the data array to the recordedBytes array. This will work fine for normal recordings. If you need to record hours of audio data, then you should either stream the data to a server or write it to a file on the device.

Since we are working with raw audio data, it is up to the program to keep track of what format the sound is in. In this case, we have a microphone that is giving us 22 kHz mono (1-channel) sound samples. The Sound object expects 44 kHz stereo (left and right channel) sound. This means that each microphone sample will have to be written to the Sound data twice to convert it from mono to stereo and then twice more to convert from 22 kHz to 44 kHz. So each microphone sample will nominally be copied to the Sound object's data array four times in order to play the recording back using the same rate at which it was captured. Listing 8–5 shows the Sound's sampleData handler that performs the copy.

Listing 8–5. *The Event Handler for the Sound Object's Data Requests*

```
// This handler is called when the Sound needs more data
private function onSoundSample(event:SampleDataEvent):void {
  if (soundChannel) {
    var avgPeak:Number = (soundChannel.leftPeak + soundChannel.rightPeak) / 2;
    activityLevel = avgPeak * 50;
  }

  // Calculate the number of stereo samples to write for each microphone sample
  var sample:Number = 0;
  var sampleCount:int = 0;
  var overSample:Number = SOUND_RATE / MICROPHONE_RATE * freqMultiplier;

  while (recordedBytes.bytesAvailable && sampleCount < 2048/overSample) {
    sample = recordedBytes.readFloat();
    for (var i:int=0; i<overSample; ++i) {
      // Write the data twice to convert from mono to stereo
      event.data.writeFloat(sample);
```

```
        event.data.writeFloat(sample);
      }
      ++sampleCount;
    }
  }
}
```

Since the curves on the display should be animated during playback as well as recording, the first thing that is done in the handler is to compute the `activityLevel` that is used in drawing the curves. From our overview of the sound-related classes in the last section, we know that the `SoundChannel` class is where we need to look for information about a sound that is playing. This class has a `leftPeak` and a `rightPeak` property that indicate the amplitude of the sound. Both of these values range from 0.0 to 1.0, where 0.0 is silence and 1.0 is maximum volume. The two values are averaged and multiplied by 50 to compute an `activityLevel` that can be used to animate the waveform display.

Now we arrive at the interesting bits: transferring the recorded data to the sound's data array. The `overSample` value is calculated first. It accounts for the difference in capture frequency vs. playback frequency. It is used in the inner `for` loop to control how many stereo samples are written (remember that `writeFloat` is called twice because each sample from the microphone is used for both the right and left channels during playback). Normally the value of the `overSample` variable will be two (44 / 22), which when multiplied by the two calls to `writeFloat` will give us the four playback samples for each microphone sample that we calculated earlier. You no doubt have noticed an extra frequency multiplier factor has also been included. This multiplier will give us the ability to speed up (think chipmunks) or slow down the frequency of the playback. The value of the `freqMultiplier` variable will be limited to 0.5, 1.0, or 2.0, which means that the value of `overSample` will be 1, 2, or 4. A value of 1 will result in only half as many samples being written as compared to the normal value of 2. That means the frequency would be doubled and we'll hear chipmunks. An `overSample` value of 4 will result in a slow-motion audio playback.

The next question to be answered is: how much of our `recordedBytes` array should be copied to the `Sound` each time it asks for data? The rough answer is "between 2048 and 8192 samples." The exact answer is "it depends." Don't you hate that? But in this one case the universe has shown us mercy in that the dependency is very easy to understand. Write more samples for better performance, and write fewer samples for better latency. So if your application simply plays back a sound exactly as it was recorded, use 8192. If you have to generate the sound or change it dynamically, say, to change the playback frequency, then use something closer to 2048 to reduce the lag between what users see on the screen and what they hear from the speaker. If you write fewer than 2048 samples to the buffer, then the `Sound` treats that as a sign that there is no more data, and playback will end after those remaining samples have been consumed. In Listing 8–5, the `while` loop ensures that 2048 samples are always written as long as there is enough data available in the `recordedBytes` array.

We now have the ability to both record and play back voice samples. All the application lacks is a way to transition between the two modes.

Handling the State Transitions

The application has four states: stopped, recording, readyToPlay, and playing. Tapping somewhere on the screen will cause the application to transition from one state to the next. Figure 8–3 illustrates this process.

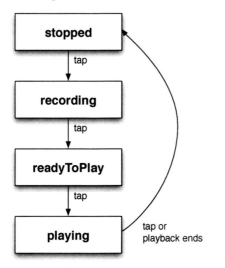

Figure 8–3. *The four states of the SoundRecorder application*

The application starts in the stopped state. When the user taps the screen, the application transitions to the recording state and begins recording his or her voice. Another tap stops the recording and transitions to the readyToPlay state. Another tap begins playback in the playing state when the user is ready to hear the recording. The user can then tap a fourth time to stop the playback and return to the stopped state, ready to record again. The application should also automatically transition to the stopped state if the playback ends on its own. Listing 8–6 shows the MXML for the one and only View of this application.

Listing 8–6. *The Home View of the SoundRecorder Application*

```xml
<?xml version="1.0" encoding="utf-8"?>
<s:View xmlns:fx="http://ns.adobe.com/mxml/2009"
        xmlns:s="library://ns.adobe.com/flex/spark"
        actionBarVisible="false"
        creationComplete="onCreationComplete()">

  <fx:Script source="SoundRecorderHomeScript.as"/>

  <s:states>
    <s:State name="stopped"/>
    <s:State name="recording"/>
    <s:State name="readyToPlay"/>
    <s:State name="playing"/>
  </s:states>
```

```
    <s:transitions>
      <s:Transition toState="stopped">
        <s:Parallel>
          <s:Scale target="{stopLabel}" scaleXBy="4" scaleYBy="4"/>
          <s:Fade target="{stopLabel}" alphaFrom="1" alphaTo="0"/>
          <s:Scale target="{tapLabel}" scaleXFrom="0" scaleXTo="1"
                   scaleYFrom="0" scaleYTo="1"/>
          <s:Fade target="{tapLabel}" alphaFrom="0" alphaTo="1"/>
        </s:Parallel>
      </s:Transition>

      <s:Transition toState="readyToPlay">
        <s:Parallel>
          <s:Scale target="{stopLabel}" scaleXBy="4" scaleYBy="4"/>
          <s:Fade target="{stopLabel}" alphaFrom="1" alphaTo="0"/>
          <s:Scale target="{tapLabel}" scaleXFrom="0" scaleXTo="1"
                   scaleYFrom="0" scaleYTo="1"/>
          <s:Fade target="{tapLabel}" alphaFrom="0" alphaTo="1"/>
        </s:Parallel>
      </s:Transition>

      <s:Transition toState="*">
        <s:Parallel>
          <s:Scale target="{tapLabel}" scaleXBy="4" scaleYBy="4"/>
          <s:Fade  target="{tapLabel}" alphaFrom="1" alphaTo="0"/>
          <s:Scale target="{stopLabel}" scaleXFrom="0" scaleXTo="1"
                   scaleYFrom="0" scaleYTo="1"/>
          <s:Fade  target="{stopLabel}" alphaFrom="0" alphaTo="1"/>
        </s:Parallel>
      </s:Transition>
    </s:transitions>

    <s:Group id="canvas" width="100%" height="100%" touchTap="onTouchTap(event)"/>
    <s:Label id="messageLabel" top="0" left="0" mouseEnabled="false" alpha="0.5"
             styleName="label"/>

      <s:Label id="tapLabel" bottom="100" horizontalCenter="0" mouseEnabled="false"
               text="Tap to Record" includeIn="readyToPlay, stopped"
               styleName="label"/>
    <s:Label id="stopLabel" bottom="100" horizontalCenter="0" mouseEnabled="false"
             text="Tap to Stop" includeIn="playing, recording"
             styleName="label"/>

      <s:Label id="speedLabel" top="100" horizontalCenter="0" mouseEnabled="false"
               text="{1/freqMultiplier}x" fontSize="48" includeIn="playing"
               styleName="label"/>
</s:View>
```

This code includes the source file that contains the ActionScript code for this View, declares the four states of the View and the transitions between them, and lastly declares the UI components displayed in the View. The UI components include a Group that serves as both the drawing canvas for the animated waveform and the handler for the tap events that trigger the state transitions. There is also a Label for displaying error messages to the user, two Labels that display state messages to the user, and a Label that indicates the frequency of the playback.

Now the table is set; our user interface and application states are defined. The next step will be to look at the code that controls the state changes and UI components. Listing 8–7 shows the ActionScript code that controls the transitions from one state to the next.

Listing 8–7. *Controlling the State Transition Order of the SoundRecorder Application*

```
private function onTouchTap(event:TouchEvent):void {
  if (currentState == "playing" && isDrag) {
    return;
  }

  incrementProgramState();
}

private function onSoundComplete(event:Event):void {
  incrementProgramState();
}

private function incrementProgramState():void {
  switch (currentState) {
    case "stopped":
      transitionToRecordingState();
      break;
    case "recording":
      transitionToReadyToPlayState();
      break;
    case "readyToPlay":
      transitionToPlayingState();
      break;
    case "playing":
      transitionToStoppedState();
      break;
  }
}
```

You can see that the application state will be changed when the user taps the screen or when the recorded sound has finished playing. The onTouchTap function also performs checks to make sure that the tap event was not generated as part of a drag (which is used to control playback frequency). The incrementProgramState function simply uses the value of the currentState variable to determine which state should be entered next and calls the appropriate function to perform the housekeeping associated with entering that state. These functions are shown in Listing 8–8.

Listing 8–8. *The State Transition Functions of the SoundRecorder Application*

```
private function transitionToRecordingState():void {
  recordedBytes.clear();
  microphone.addEventListener(SampleDataEvent.SAMPLE_DATA, onMicSample);
  currentState = "recording";
}

private function transitionToReadyToPlayState():void {
  microphone.removeEventListener(SampleDataEvent.SAMPLE_DATA, onMicSample);
  tapLabel.text = "Tap to Play";
  currentState = "readyToPlay";
}
```

```
private function transitionToPlayingState():void {
  freqMultiplier = 1;
  recordedBytes.position = 0;

  canvas.addEventListener(TouchEvent.TOUCH_BEGIN, onTouchBegin);
  canvas.addEventListener(TouchEvent.TOUCH_MOVE, onTouchMove);

  sound.addEventListener(SampleDataEvent.SAMPLE_DATA, onSoundSample);
  soundChannel = sound.play();
  soundChannel.addEventListener(Event.SOUND_COMPLETE, onSoundComplete);

  currentState = "playing";
}

private function transitionToStoppedState():void {
  canvas.removeEventListener(TouchEvent.TOUCH_BEGIN, onTouchBegin);
  canvas.removeEventListener(TouchEvent.TOUCH_MOVE, onTouchMove);

  soundChannel.stop()
  soundChannel.removeEventListener(Event.SOUND_COMPLETE, onSoundComplete);
  sound.removeEventListener(SampleDataEvent.SAMPLE_DATA, onSoundSample);

  tapLabel.text = "Tap to Record";
  currentState = "stopped";
}
```

The transitionToRecordingState function clears any existing data from the
recordedBytes array, adds the sampleData listener to the microphone so that it will start
sending data samples, and finally sets the currentState variable to trigger the animated
state transition. Similarly, the transitionToReadyToPlayState is called when recording is
finished. It is responsible for removing the sampleData listener from the microphone,
changing the Label in the UI to read "Tap to Play", and once again setting the
currentState variable to trigger the animated transition.

The transitionToPlayingState function is called when the user taps the screen to start
the playback of the recorded sample. It first resets the playback frequency to 1 and
resets the read position of the recordedBytes array to the beginning of the array. Next, it
adds touch event listeners to the canvas Group in order to listen for the gestures that
control the frequency multiplier during playback. It also installs a handler for the Sound's
sampleData event so the application can provide data for the Sound during playback. The
play method is then called to start the playback of the sound. Once we have a reference
to the soundChannel that controls playback, we can add a handler for the soundComplete
event so we know if the sound finishes playing, so we can transition automatically back
to the stopped state. And finally, the value of the View's currentState variable is
changed to trigger the animated state transition.

The last transition is the one that takes the application back to the stopped state. The
transitionToStoppedState function is responsible for stopping the playback (this has no
effect if the sound has finished playing) and removing all of the listeners that were added
by the transitionToPlayingState function. It finally resets the text property of the Label
and changes the value of the currentState variable to trigger the state transition
animation.

The remaining piece of functionality to be covered is the frequency multiplier. Listing 8–9 shows the code that handles the touch events that control this variable.

Listing 8–9. *Controlling the Frequency of the Playback with Touch Gestures*

```
private function onTouchBegin(event:TouchEvent):void {
  touchAnchor = event.localY;
  isDrag = false;
}

private function onTouchMove(event:TouchEvent):void {
  var delta:Number = event.localY - touchAnchor;
  if (Math.abs(delta) > 75) {
    isDrag = true;
    touchAnchor = event.localY;
    freqMultiplier *= (delta > 0 ? 2 : 0.5);
    freqMultiplier = Math.min(2, Math.max(0.5, freqMultiplier));
  }
}
```

The onTouchBegin handler is called when the user first initiates a touch event. The code makes note of the initial y-location of the touch point and resets the isDrag flag to false. If a touch drag event is received, the onTouchMove handler checks to see if the movement is large enough to trigger a drag event. If so, the isDrag flag is set to true so the rest of the application knows that a frequency multipler adjustment is in progress. The direction of the drag is used to determine whether the frequency multipler should be halved or doubled. The value is then clamped to be between 0.5 and 2.0. The touchAnchor variable is also reset so the computation can be run again in the event of further movement. The result is that during playback the user can drag a finger either up or down on the screen to dynamically change the frequency of the playback.

Figure 8–4 shows the SoundRecorder sample application running on an Android device. The image on the left shows the application in recording state, while the image on the right shows the animated transition from the readyToPlay state to the playing state.

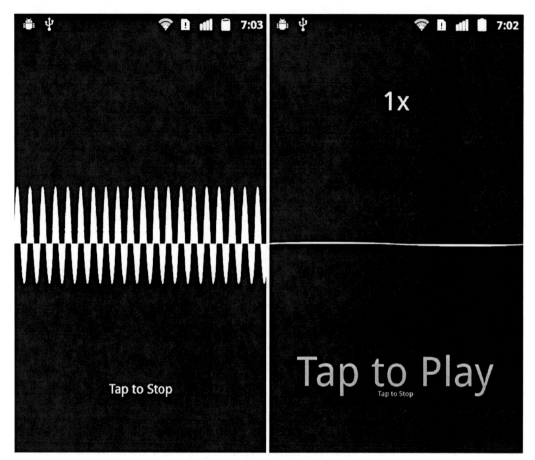

Figure 8–4. *The SoundRecorder application running on an Android device*

We have now shown you how to play and manipulate data that was stored in a ByteArray. It should be noted that this technique would also work if you needed to manipulate data stored in a Sound object rather than a ByteArray. You can use the extract method of the Sound class to access the raw sound data, manipulate it in some way, and then write it back to another Sound object in its sampleData handler.

Another common use for sound capabilities is in playing music, either streamed over the Internet or stored on the device in MP3 files. If you think the Flash platform would be a good fit for this type of application, you are right! The next section will show you how to write a mobile music player in Flash.

A Flash Music Player

Playing sound from MP3 files on a device is rather uncomplicated. There is more to a music player than simply playing a sound, however. This section will start by showing you how to play an MP3 file with Flash's sound API. Once that is out of the way, we will look at the additional considerations that you will have to take into account when creating a mobile application.

Playing MP3 Files

Loading an MP3 file into a Sound object is as simple as using a URL that begins with the `file` protocol. Listing 8–10 shows how it can be accomplished.

Listing 8–10. *Loading and Playing an MP3 File from the Filesystem*

```
<?xml version="1.0" encoding="utf-8"?>
<s:View xmlns:fx="http://ns.adobe.com/mxml/2009"
        xmlns:s="library://ns.adobe.com/flex/spark"
        creationComplete="onCreationComplete()"
        title="Sound Loading">

  <fx:Script>
    <![CDATA[
      private var sound:Sound;

      private function onCreationComplete():void {
        var path:String = "file:///absolute/path/to/the/file.mp3";
        sound = new Sound(new URLRequest(path));
        sound.play();
      }
    ]]>
  </fx:Script>
</s:View>
```

The three lines shown in bold are all that's needed to play the MP3 file. Note the third forward slash after `file://` that is used to indicate that this is an absolute path to the MP3 file. You would obviously not want to use a constant path like this in a real application. We will look at strategies for handling filesystem paths in a more elegant manner later in the chapter, when we discuss the considerations that go into making real-world applications.

Reading ID3 Metadata

Playing the music file is a good start; it's the essence of a music player, after all. Another thing that all music players do is to read the metadata embedded in the ID3 tags of the file.[1] This metadata includes things like the name of the artist and the album, the year it was recorded, and even the genre and track number of the song. The Sound class provides built-in support for reading these tags. Listing 8–11 shows how to add this functionality to our fledgling music player. The lines in bold indicate the new additions to the source code from Listing 8–10.

---

[1] `www.id3.org/`

Listing 8–11. *Reading ID3 Metadata from an MP3 file*

```
<?xml version="1.0" encoding="utf-8"?>
<s:View xmlns:fx="http://ns.adobe.com/mxml/2009"
        xmlns:s="library://ns.adobe.com/flex/spark"
        creationComplete="onCreationComplete()"
        title="Sound Loading">

  <fx:Script>
    <![CDATA[
      private var sound:Sound;

      private function onCreationComplete():void {
        var path:String = "file:///absolute/path/to/the/file.mp3";
        sound = new Sound(new URLRequest(path));
        sound.addEventListener(Event.ID3, onID3);
        sound.play()
      }

      private function onID3(event:Event):void {
        metaData.text = "Artist: "+sound.id3.artist+"\n"+
                        "Year: "+sound.id3.year+"\n";
      }
  </fx:Script>

  <s:Label id="metaData" width="100%" textAlign="center"/>
</s:View>
```

The onID3 handler was added as a listener for the Event.ID3 event. This handler is called when the metadata has been read from the MP3 file and is ready to be used. There are several predefined properties in the ID3Info class that correspond to the more commonly used ID3 tags. Things like album name, artist name, song name, genre, year, and track number all have properties defined in the class. Further, you can also access any of the other text information frames defined by version 2.3 of the ID3 specification.[2] For example, to access the TPUB frame that contains the name of the publisher, you would use sound.id3.TPUB.

One thing that is not supported is reading images, such as album covers, from the ID3 tags. You will learn how to accomplish this using an open source ActionScript library later in this chapter.

Implementing Pause Functionality

The SoundChannel class has no direct support for pausing the playback of the sound data. However, it is easy to implement a pause feature using a combination of the class's position property and its stop method. Listing 8–12 shows one possible technique for implementing a play/pause toggle. Once again the new code additions are shown in bold type.

---

[2] www.id3.org/id3v2.3.0

Listing 8–12. *Implementing a Play/Pause Toggle*

```
<?xml version="1.0" encoding="utf-8"?>
<s:View … >

  <fx:Script>
    <![CDATA[
      private var sound:Sound;
      private var channel:SoundChannel;
      private var pausePosition:Number = 0;

      [Bindable] private var isPlaying:Boolean = false;

      private function onCreationComplete():void {
        var path:String = "file:///absolute/path/to/the/file.mp3";
        sound = new Sound(new URLRequest(path));
        sound.addEventListener(Event.ID3, onID3);
      }

      private function onID3(event:Event):void { /* same as before */ }

      private function onClick():void {
        if (isPlaying) {
          pausePosition = channel.position;
          channel.stop();
          channel.removeEventListener(Event.SOUND_COMPLETE, onSoundComplete);
          isPlaying = false;
        } else {
          channel = sound.play(pausePosition);
          channel.addEventListener(Event.SOUND_COMPLETE, onSoundComplete);
          isPlaying = true;
        }
      }

      private function onSoundComplete(event:Event):void {
        isPlaying = false;
        pausePosition = 0;
      }
    ]]>
  </fx:Script>

  <s:VGroup top="5" width="100%" horizontalAlign="center" gap="20">
    <s:Label id="metaData" width="100%" textAlign="center"/>
    <s:Button label="{isPlaying ? 'Pause' : 'Play'}" click="onClick()"/>
  </s:VGroup>
</s:View>
```

The Sound's play method is no longer called in the onCreationComplete handler. Instead, a button has been added to the interface whose Label is either "Play" or "Pause" depending on the value of the isPlaying flag. A tap on the button triggers a call to the onClick handler. If the sound is currently playing, the channel's position is saved in the pausePosition instance variable, the sound is stopped, and the soundComplete event listener is removed from the channel. When the sound is next played, a new SoundChannel object will be created. Therefore, failure to remove our listener from the old SoundChannel would result in a memory leak.

If the sound is not currently playing, it is started by a call to the Sound's play method. The pausePosition is passed as an argument to the play method so that the sound will play from the same location at which it was last stopped. A listener for the soundComplete event is attached to the new SoundChannel object returned by the play method. The handler for this event is called when the sound has finished playing all the way through to the end. When this happens, the handler will reset the values of the isPlaying flag to false and the pausePosition to zero. That way the song will be played from the beginning the next time the play button is tapped.

Adjusting the Volume

The ability to adjust the volume of the song while it is playing must surely be added to our music player as well. This is a job for the SoundTransform object that is associated with the SoundChannel of the song when it is played. Listing 8–13 illustrates how to use the SoundTransform to change both the volume and the pan of the sound while it is playing.

Listing 8–13. *Implementing Volume and Panning Adjustments*

```
<?xml version="1.0" encoding="utf-8"?>
<s:View …>
  <fx:Script>
    <![CDATA[
      /* All other code is unchanged… */

      private function onClick():void {
        if (isPlaying) {
          /* Same as before */
        } else {
          channel = sound.play(pausePosition);
          channel.addEventListener(Event.SOUND_COMPLETE, onSoundComplete);
          onVolumeChange();
          onPanChange();
          isPlaying = true;
        }
      }

      private function onVolumeChange():void {
        if (channel) {
          var xform:SoundTransform = channel.soundTransform;
          xform.volume = volume.value / 100;
          channel.soundTransform = xform;
        }
      }

      private function onPanChange():void {
        if (channel) {
          var xform:SoundTransform = channel.soundTransform;
          xform.pan = pan.value / 100;
          channel.soundTransform = xform;
        }
    ]]>
  </fx:Script>
```

```
<s:VGroup top="5" width="100%" horizontalAlign="center" gap="20">
  <s:Label id="metaData" width="100%" textAlign="center"/>
  <s:Button label="{isPlaying ? 'Pause' : 'Play'}" click="onClick()"/>
  <s:HSlider id="volume" minimum="0" maximum="100" value="100"
          change="onVolumeChange()"/>
  <s:HSlider id="pan" minimum="-100" maximum="100" value="0"
          change="onPanChange()"/>
</s:VGroup>
</s:View>
```

We have added two horizontal sliders that can be used to adjust volume and panning of the sound as it plays. There may not be a good reason for a music player on a mobile device to worry about panning, but it is shown here for completeness. Perhaps this music player will someday grow into a mini mobile mixing studio. If that happens, you will have a head start on this piece of functionality!

The change event handlers are called when the sliders are moved. Note the pattern required for adjusting the SoundTransform settings. You first get a reference to the existing transform so that you start with all of the current settings. You then change the setting you're interested in and set the transform object on the channel again. Setting the soundTransform property triggers the channel to update its settings. This way you can batch several transform changes together and pay the cost of resetting the channel's transform only once.

The volume property of the SoundTransform expects a value between 0.0 (silence) and 1.0 (maximum volume). Similarly the pan property expects a value between -1.0 (left) and 1.0 (right). The change handlers are responsible for adjusting the slider's values to the appropriate range. The last thing to note is that onVolumeChange and onPanChange are also called when the sound begins playing. Once again, this is necessary since a new channel is created by every call to the Sound's play method. This new channel object will not have the new settings until those calls to onVolumeChange and onPanChange.

That wraps up our quick overview of basic music player functionality. There is no need to read any further if that is all the information you needed to know, so feel free to skip ahead to the "Playing Video" section instead. However, if you are interested in seeing all of the considerations that go into taking this minimalistic music player and turning it into a real Android application, then the next section is for you.

From Prototype to Application

We have covered the basic techniques required to play music in Flash, but it will take a lot more effort to create a real music player application. This section will talk about some of the things that will need to be done, including the following:

- Creating code that is testable, maintainable, and reusable

- Dealing with different screen densities

- Incorporating third-party libraries to provide functionality missing from Flash

- Creating a custom control to add a little more visual flair

- Handling activate and deactivate events for the application and Views

- Persisting data when the application is deactivated

We will start by looking at an architectural pattern that helps you separate a View's logic from its presentation in order to create code that is more reusable and testable. You can follow along with this discussion by consulting the MusicPlayer sample application found in the examples/chapter-08 directory of the book's source code.

A Better Pattern: The Presentation Model

When we have previously wanted to separate a View's logic from its presentation, we have relied on simply moving the ActionScript code to a separate file. This file is then included in the MXML View using the source attribute of the `<fx:Script>` tag. This works, but you end up with script logic that is strongly coupled to the View it was written for and therefore not very reusable. There are much better options for achieving a separation of responsibilities in your user interface.

In 2004, Martin Fowler published an article that detailed a design pattern called the Presentation Model.[3] This pattern is a slight modification of the popular MVC pattern,[4] and is particularly well suited to modern frameworks, like Flash, Silverlight, WPF, and JavaFX, that include features such as data binding. Implementing this pattern typically requires three classes that work together: the data model, the presentation model, and the View. It is worth noting that the data model is usually just called the "model" or sometimes the "domain model." Each presentation model has access to one or more data models whose contents it presents to the View for display. Although not part of the original pattern description, it is extremely common to see service classes included as a fourth component in rich Internet applications. A service class encapsulates the logic needed to access web services (or any other kind of service). A service class and a presentation model will typically pass data model objects back and forth.

This common application structure is illustrated in Figure 8–5 with a design we will implement later in our music player application. The SongListView is our MXML file that declares a View to display a list of objects. The SongListView knows only about its presentation model, the SongListViewModel. The presentation model has no knowledge about the View or Views that are using it. Its job is to collaborate with the MusicService to present a list of MusicEntry objects for display. There is a clear separation of responsibilities, and each class has limited knowledge of the rest of the system. In software engineering terms, the design has low coupling and high cohesion. This should be the goal in any application you design.

---

[3] Martin Fowler, "Presentation Model,"
http://martinfowler.com/eaaDev/PresentationModel.html, July 19, 2004

[4] Martin Fowler, "Model View Controller,"
http://martinfowler.com/eaaCatalog/modelViewController.html

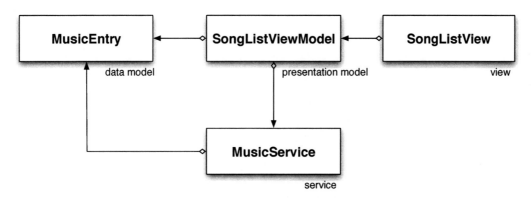

Figure 8–5. *A common implementation of the Presentation Model pattern*

In summary, use of the Presentation Model pattern has two main benefits:

1. The View knows about the presentation model, but the presentation model knows nothing of the View. This makes it easy for multiple Views to share the same presentation model. This is one way in which the Presentation Model pattern makes it easier to reuse code.

2. Most logic is moved out of the View and into the presentation model. The View can bind to properties of the presentation model in order to present data to the user. Actions such as button presses are ideally passed directly to the presentation model rather than handled in the View. This means that most of the code worth testing is in the presentation model and you don't have to worry as much about testing UI code.

Creating the ViewNavigatorApplication

Now that the basic building blocks of the application design are understood, it is time to create a new Flex mobile project. This application will be a ViewNavigatorApplication since we will need to navigate between two different Views: a View containing a list of songs, artists, or albums, and a View containing the controls for playing a song. Once the project is created, we can set up the application's package structure. There will be one package each for the assets, views, viewmodels, models, and services. This makes it easy to organize the various classes in the application by their responsibility. The assets package is where all of the application's graphical assets, such as icons and splash screens, will be placed.

The main job of the ViewNavigatorApplication is to create and display the first View. This is normally done by setting the firstView attribute of the <s:ViewNavigatorApplication> tag. It will be done a little differently in this application since each View's presentation model will be passed to it in its data property. To accomplish this, a handler is assigned to the initialize event of the ViewNavigatorApplication. In this onInitialize handler, the MusicService and the initial presentation model will be created and passed to the first View. Listing 8–14 shows the MXML for the application.

Listing 8–14. *The MXML for the Main* ViewNavigatorApplication

```
<?xml version="1.0" encoding="utf-8"?>
<s:ViewNavigatorApplication xmlns:fx="http://ns.adobe.com/mxml/2009"
                    xmlns:s="library://ns.adobe.com/flex/spark"
                    splashScreenImage="@Embed('assets/splash.png')"
                    initialize="onInitialize()"
                    applicationDPI="160">

<fx:Script>
    <![CDATA[
        import services.LocalMusicService;
        import services.MusicService;
        import views.SongListView;
        import viewmodels.SongListViewModel;

        private function onInitialize():void {
            var service:MusicService = new LocalMusicService();
            navigator.pushView(SongListView, new SongListViewModel(service));
        }
    ]]>
</fx:Script>
</s:ViewNavigatorApplication>
```

The concrete implementation of the MusicService interface being used in this application is a class named LocalMusicService that reads files from the device's local filesystem. This service instance is then used to construct the presentation model, which in this case is an instance of SongListViewModel. Passing the service to the presentation model like this is preferred over letting the presentation model construct the service internally. This makes it easy to give the presentation models different versions of the service during testing or if the program's feature set is expanded to include other types of music services. But we are getting ahead of ourselves. We will look at these classes in more detail in the next section.

> **NOTE:** Some people prefer to let the View class create its own presentation model rather than passing it in as we did here by using the data property. We prefer to pass the presentation models to the Views since, everything else being equal, you should always prefer less coupling between your classes. However, either way works well in practice.

One final thing to be noted in Listing 8–14 is the declaration of the applicationDPI attribute of the ViewNavigatorApplication. We have set it to 160 to indicate that the application's UI will be designed for a screen with 160 dpi. If the application is run on a higher-dpi screen, the UI will be scaled accordingly. Refer back to the "Density in Flex Applications" section of Chapter 2 for more details.

Implementing the MusicService

It is a good idea to define your service classes as an `interface`. Then your presentation model has a dependency only on the `interface` class instead of on any one concrete service implementation. This makes it possible to use different service implementations in your presentation model. For instance, you could create one implementation of the music service that reads music files from the device's local storage, while another implementation could be used for streaming music over the Internet.

There is an even better reason for using a service interface, however; it makes it easy to unit test your presentation models. Say that you normally run your application with a `MusicService` implementation that reads music files from an Internet web service. If your presentation model is hardwired to use this version, then you cannot test the presentation model in isolation. You need to make sure you have a live Internet connection and that the web service is up and running, or your tests will fail. Making the presentation model depend only on the interface makes it trivial to swap in a mock service that returns a predefined list of `MusicEntry` objects to your presentation model. This makes your unit tests reliable and repeatable. It also makes them run a lot faster since you don't have to download data from the web service in every test!

The job of the `MusicService` is simply to provide a list of `MusicEntry` objects given a URL path. The `interface` class will therefore contain a single method, as shown in Listing 8–15.

Listing 8–15. *The* `MusicService` *Interface*

```
package services
{
  import mx.collections.ArrayCollection;

  public interface MusicService {
    /**
     * A MusicService implementation knows how to use the rootPath to find
     * the list of MusicEntry objects that reside at that path.
     *
     * @return An ArrayCollection of MusicEntry objects.
     * @see models.MusicEntry
     */
    function getMusicEntries(rootPath:String = null):ArrayCollection;
  }
}
```

A `MusicEntry` object can represent either a song or a container that holds one or more other songs. In this way, we can navigate through a hierarchical list of artists, albums, and songs using multiple lists of `MusicEntry` objects. As with most data models, this class is a collection of properties with very little, if any, logic. The `MusicEntry` object is shown in Listing 8–16.

Listing 8–16. *The* `MusicEntry` *Data Model*

```
package models
{
  import flash.utils.IDataInput;
```

```
/**
 * This class represents an object that can be either a song or a container
 * of other songs.
 */
public class MusicEntry {
  private var _name:String;
  private var _url:String;
  private var _streamFunc:Function;

  public function MusicEntry(name:String, url:String, streamFunc:Function) {
    _name = name;
    _url = url;
    _streamFunc = streamFunc;
  }

  public function get name():String {
    return _name;
  }

  public function get url():String {
    return _url;
  }

  /**
   * @return A stream object if this is a valid song.  Null otherwise.
   */
  public function get stream():IDataInput {
    return _streamFunc == null ? null : _streamFunc();
  }

  public function get isSong():Boolean {
    return _streamFunc != null;
  }
 }
}
```

The MusicEntry contains properties for the name of the entry, a url that identifies the location of the entry, a stream that can be used to read the entry if it is a song, and an isSong property that can be used to tell the difference between an entry that represents a song versus one that represents a container of songs. Since we don't know in advance what kind of stream we will need to read the song, we rely on ActionScript's functional programming capabilities. This allows the creator of a MusicEntry object to pass a function object to the class's constructor that, when called, takes care of creating the appropriate type of stream.

This application will play music files from the device's local storage, so our service will provide MusicEntry objects read from the filesystem of the device. Listing 8–17 shows the LocalMusicService implementation.

Listing 8–17. *An Implementation of a MusicService That Reads Songs from the Local Filesystem*

```
package services
{
  import flash.filesystem.File;
  import flash.filesystem.FileMode;
  import flash.filesystem.FileStream;
```

```
import flash.utils.IDataInput;
import mx.collections.ArrayCollection;
import models.MusicEntry;

public class LocalMusicService implements MusicService {
  private static const DEFAULT_DIR:File = File.userDirectory.resolvePath("Music");

  /**
   * Finds all of the files in the directory indicated by the path variable
   * and adds them to the collection if they are a directory or an MP3 file.
   *
   * @return A collection of MusicEntry objects.
   */
  public function getMusicEntries(rootPath:String=null):ArrayCollection {
    var rootDir:File = rootPath ? new File(rootPath) : DEFAULT_DIR;
    var songList:ArrayCollection = new ArrayCollection();

    if (rootDir.isDirectory) {
      var dirListing:Array = rootDir.getDirectoryListing();

      for (var i:int = 0; i < dirListing.length; i++) {
        var file:File = dirListing[i];

        if (!shouldBeListed(file))
          continue;

        songList.addItem(createMusicEntryForFile(file));
      }
    }

    return songList;
  }

  /**
   * @return The appropriate type of MusicEntry for the given file.
   */
  private function createMusicEntryForFile(file:File):MusicEntry {
    var name:String = stripFileExtension(file.name);
    var url:String = "file://" + file.nativePath;
    var stream:Function = null;

    if (!file.isDirectory) {
      stream = function():IDataInput {
        var stream:FileStream = new FileStream();
        stream.openAsync(file, FileMode.READ);
        return stream;
      }
    }

    return new MusicEntry(name, url, stream);
  }

  // Other utility functions removed for brevity…
  }
}
```

It is unsurprising that this type of service relies heavily on the classes found in the flash.filesystem package. You should always try to use the path properties defined in the File class when working with filesystem paths. The DEFAULT_DIR constant uses the File.userDirectory as the basis of its default path, which on Android points to the /mnt/sdcard directory. Therefore this service will default to looking in the /mnt/sdcard/Music directory for its files. This is a fairly standard location for music files on Android devices.

> **NOTE:** File.userDirectory, File.desktopDirectory, and
> File.documentsDirectory all point to /mnt/sdcard on an Android device.
> File.applicationStorageDirectory points to a "Local Store" directory that is specific to
> your application. File.applicationDirectory is empty.

The getMusicEntries implementation in LocalMusicPlayer converts the provided rootPath string to a File, or uses the default directory if rootPath is not provided, and then proceeds to iterate through the files located at that path. It creates a MusicEntry object for any File that is either a directory (a container of other songs) or an MP3 file (a song). If the File is a song rather than a directory, the createMusicEntryForFile function creates a function closure that, when called, opens an asynchronous FileStream for reading. This function closure is then passed to the constructor of the MusicEntry object to be used if the song is played. You may recall from Listing 8–16 that the value of this closure object—regardless of whether it is null—is used to determine the type of MusicEntry the object represents.

The SongListView

Listing 8–14 showed that the first View created by the application is the SongListView. The application's onInitialize handler instantiates the appropriate type of MusicService and uses it to construct the SongListViewModel for the View. The SongListViewModel is then passed to the View by using it as the second parameter to the navigator.pushView function. This will put a reference to the model instance in the View's data property.

The job of the SongListViewModel is pretty straightforward. It uses the MusicService it is given to retrieve a list of MusicEntry objects for the SongListView to display. Listing 8–18 shows the source code of this presentation model.

Listing 8–18. *The Presentation Model for the* SongListView

```
package viewmodels
{
  import models.MusicEntry;
  import mx.collections.ArrayCollection;
  import services.LocalMusicService;
  import services.MusicService;

  [Bindable]
  public class SongListViewModel {
```

```
    private var _entries:ArrayCollection = new ArrayCollection();
    private var _musicEntry:MusicEntry;
    private var _musicService:MusicService;

    public function SongListViewModel(service:MusicService = null,
                                      entry:MusicEntry = null ) {
      _musicEntry = entry;
      _musicService = service;

      if (_musicService) {
        var url:String = _musicEntry ? _musicEntry.url : null;
        entries = _musicService.getMusicEntries(url);
      }
    }

    public function get entries():ArrayCollection {
      return _entries;
    }

    public function set entries(value:ArrayCollection):void {
      _entries = value;
    }

    public function cloneModelForEntry(entry:MusicEntry):SongListViewModel {
      return new SongListViewModel(_musicService, entry);
    }

    public function createSongViewModel(selectedIndex:int):SongViewModel {
      return new SongViewModel(entries, selectedIndex);
    }
  }
}
```

The class is annotated with `Bindable` so the `entries` property can be bound to the UI component in the `View` class.

The constructor will store the references to the `MusicService` and `MusicEntry` instances that are passed in. If the service reference is not null, then the collection of entries is retrieved from the `MusicService`. If the service is null, then the `entries` collection will remain empty.

There are two additional public functions in the class. The `cloneModelForEntry` function will create a new `SongListViewModel` by passing along the `MusicService` reference it was given. The `createSongViewModel` will create a new presentation model for the `SongView` using this model's `entries` collection and the index of the selected entry. This is the logical place for these functions since this presentation model has references to the data required to create new presentation models. For this reason, it is common for one presentation model to create another.

With this in mind, it is time to see how the `View` uses its presentation model. The source code for `SongListView` is shown in Listing 8–19.

Listing 8–19. *The SongListView*

```xml
<?xml version="1.0" encoding="utf-8"?>
<s:View xmlns:fx="http://ns.adobe.com/mxml/2009"
        xmlns:s="library://ns.adobe.com/flex/spark"
        initialize="onInitialize()"
        title="Music Player">

  <fx:Script>
    <![CDATA[
      import spark.events.IndexChangeEvent;
      import models.MusicEntry;
      import viewmodels.SongListViewModel;

      [Bindable]
      private var model:SongListViewModel;

      private function onInitialize():void {
        model = data as SongListViewModel;
      }

      private function onChange(event:IndexChangeEvent):void {
        var list:List = List(event.target);
        var selObj:MusicEntry = list.selectedItem as MusicEntry;

        if (selObj.isSong) {
          var index:int = list.selectedIndex;
          navigator.pushView(SongView, model.createSongViewModel(index));
        } else {
          navigator.pushView(SongListView, model.cloneModelForEntry(selObj));
        }
      }
    ]]>
  </fx:Script>

  <s:List width="100%" height="100%" change="onChange(event)"
          dataProvider="{model.entries}">
    <s:itemRenderer>
      <fx:Component>
        <s:IconItemRenderer labelField="name" decorator="{chevron}">
          <fx:Declarations>
            <s:MultiDPIBitmapSource id="chevron"
                              source160dpi="@Embed('assets/chevron160.png')"
                              source240dpi="@Embed('assets/chevron240.png')"
                              source320dpi="@Embed('assets/chevron320.png')"/>
          </fx:Declarations>
        </s:IconItemRenderer>
      </fx:Component>
    </s:itemRenderer>
  </s:List>
</s:View>
```

The onInitialize handler initializes the View's model reference from the data property. The model is then used to access the entries that serve as the List's dataProvider. It is also used in the List's onChange handler. If the selected MusicEntry is a song, the model is used to create a new SongViewModel and the navigator.pushView function is used to display a SongView. Otherwise, a new SongListViewModel is created and a new

SongListView is displayed using the selected MusicEntry as the path for the new collection of MusicEntry objects.

A custom IconItemRenderer is also declared for the List component. This was done in order to add a chevron to the item renderer to indicate that selecting an item leads to a new View. A MultiDPIBitmapSource was used to reference the three pre-scaled versions of the chevron image. Note that the chevron bitmap source must be contained inside the <fx:Declaration> tag that is a child element of the <s:IconItemRenderer> tag. The bitmap source will not be visible to the IconItemRenderer if it is declared as a child of the View's <fx:Declaration> tag.

The chevron160.png file is the base size, while chevron240.png is 50% larger, and chevron320.png is twice as large. The optimal size of the chevron bitmap will be selected based on the screen properties of the device on which the program is run. Figure 8–6 shows the SongListView running on a low- and medium-dpi device. Note that the chevron has no pixilated artifacts from being scaled, as would be the case if we used the same bitmap on both screens.

Figure 8–6. *The SongListView running on devices with different dpi classifications*

> **CAUTION:** You can also use an FXG graphic as the icon or decorator of an `IconItemRenderer` by declaring it in the same way as the `MultiDPIBitmapSource` previously. Unfortunately, since the icon and decorator will be converted into a bitmap and then scaled, you will lose the benefits of using a vector graphic in the first place. For this reason, it is our recommendation that you use `MultiDPIBitmapSource` objects with your custom `IconItemRenderers`.

The SongView

That brings us to the real heart of the application: the view that lets users play music! We want this interface to have the same functionality as most other music players. We will display the song title and the album cover. It should have controls that allow the user to skip to the next or previous song, play and pause the current song, adjust the position of the current song as well as the volume and the panning (just for fun). The resulting interface is shown in Figure 8–7.

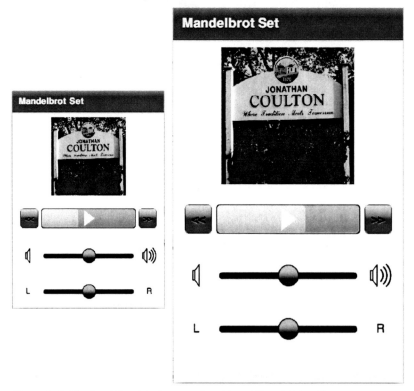

Figure 8–7. *The SongView interface running at two different dpi settings*

You can see from Figure 8–7 that this interface is a little more complicated than the list view. It even includes a custom control that serves not only as a play/pause button but also as a progress indicator for the play position of the current song. In addition, you can swipe your finger back and forth across the button to control the position of the song. Writing this custom control is just one of the topics that will be covered in this section.

Listing 8–20 shows part of the MXML file that defines this View. Since this is a larger interface declaration, we will break it down into smaller, more digestible pieces.

Listing 8–20. *The States and the Script Sections of the* SongView *MXML File*

```
<?xml version="1.0" encoding="utf-8"?>
<s:View xmlns:fx="http://ns.adobe.com/mxml/2009"
        xmlns:s="library://ns.adobe.com/flex/spark"
        xmlns:assets="assets.*"
        xmlns:views="views.*"
        initialize="onInitialize()"
        viewDeactivate="onViewDeactivate()"
        title="{model.songTitle}" >

    <s:states>
      <s:State name="portrait"/>
      <s:State name="landscape"/>
    </s:states>

    <fx:Script>
      <![CDATA[
        import viewmodels.SongViewModel;

        [Bindable]
        private var model:SongViewModel;

        private function onInitialize():void {
          model = data as SongViewModel;
          model.addEventListener(SongViewModel.SONG_ENDED, onSongEnded);
        }

        private function onViewDeactivate():void {
          model.removeEventListener(SongViewModel.SONG_ENDED, onSongEnded);
          if (model.isPlaying)
            model.onPlayPause();
        }

        private function onSongEnded(event:Event):void {
          progressButton.stop();
        }
      ]]>
    </fx:Script>
    <!-- UI components removed for now… -->
</s:View>
```

The <s:states> section of the file declares states for the portrait and landscape orientation of the interface. Remember from Chapter 2 that by explicitly declaring the names for these states in the View, Flex will set the state of our View appropriately when the orientation of the device changes. Having done this, you can take advantage of these state names to adjust the layout of your interface when the orientation changes.

As in the SongListView, the onInitialize handler initializes the presentation model reference from the data property. It also attaches a handler for the model's SONG_ENDED event so the onSongEnded handler can adjust the interface appropriately when a song finishes playing. A handler for the View's viewDeactivate event is also declared. This allows the View to stop the playback of the song when the user leaves the View.

We will now examine the UI components of this View one snippet at a time.

```
<s:Rect width="100%" height="100%">
  <s:fill>
    <s:LinearGradient rotation="90">
      <s:GradientEntry color="0xFFFFFF" ratio="0.40"/>
      <s:GradientEntry color="0xe2e5f4" ratio="1.00"/>
    </s:LinearGradient>
  </s:fill>
</s:Rect>
```

This first piece of MXML declares the background gradient that fades from white to a light blue at the bottom of the screen. The rectangle's width and height are set to 100% so that it will automatically fill the screen no matter what orientation the device is in.

```
<s:Group width="100%" height="100%">
  <s:layout.landscape>
    <s:HorizontalLayout verticalAlign="middle" paddingLeft="10"/>
  </s:layout.landscape>
  <s:layout.portrait>
    <s:VerticalLayout horizontalAlign="center" paddingTop="10"/>
  </s:layout.portrait>
```

The foregoing snippet creates the Group that serves as the container for the rest of the interface. Once again, its width and height are set so that it always fills the screen. The Group uses a HorizontalLayout in landscape mode and a VerticalLayout in portrait mode. The state syntax ensures that the correct layout is used when the device is reoriented. Figure 8–8 shows the SongView interface on a device held in landscape orientation.

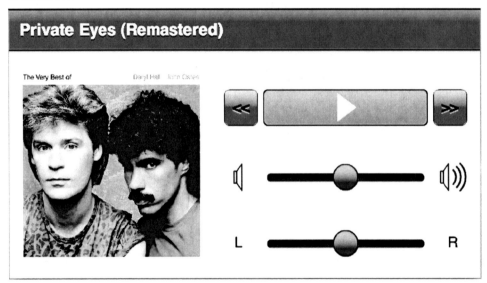

Figure 8–8. *The music player interface in landscape orientation*

The Group in the next bit of code is the container for the image of the album cover. The size of the Group is adjusted dynamically based on the orientation, but the width and height are always kept equal—it always forms a square.

```
<s:Group width.portrait="{height*0.4}" height.portrait="{height*0.4}"
         width.landscape="{width*0.4}" height.landscape="{width*0.4}">
  <s:BitmapImage id="albumCover" width="100%" height="100%"
                 source="{model.albumCover}"
                 visible="{model.albumCover != null}"/>

  <assets:DefaultAlbum id="placeHolder" width="100%" height="100%"
                       visible="{!model.albumCover}" />
</s:Group>
```

The source of the albumCover bitmap is bound to the model's albumCover property. This bitmap is visible only if there actually is an albumCover image in the model. If there is not, a placeholder graphic is shown instead. The placeholder is an FXG image that is located in the application's assets package. You can see that it is trivial to use FXG graphics in your MXML declarations. They also scale well for different screen densities since they are vector graphics.

After the album cover, we arrive at the VGroup that contains the controls for this View. This VGroup is actually made up of three separate HGroup containers. The first contains the previous song button, the custom ProgressButton control, and a next song button. The next HGroup container holds the horizontal volume slider, along with its FXG icons to indicate low and high volume levels on each side of the slider. The final HGroup contains the horizontal pan slider, along with Labels that show which direction is left and which is right. Note that the model's volume, pan, and percentComplete properties are bound to the interface components with a two-way binding. This means that either side of the binding can set the value of the property and the other will be updated.

```
<s:VGroup id="controls" horizontalAlign="center" width="100%"
          paddingTop="20" gap="40">
  <s:HGroup width="90%">
    <s:Button label="&lt;&lt;" height="40" click="model.previousSong()"/>
    <views:ProgressButton id="progressButton" width="100%" height="40"
                   click="model.onPlayPause()"
                   percentComplete="@{model.percentComplete}"
                   skinClass="views.ProgressButtonSkin"/>
    <s:Button label="&gt;&gt;" height="40" click="model.nextSong()"/>
  </s:HGroup>

  <s:HGroup verticalAlign="middle" width="90%">
    <assets:VolLow id="volLow" width="32" height="32"/>
    <s:HSlider width="100%" maximum="1.0" minimum="0.0" stepSize="0.01"
            snapInterval="0.01" value="@{model.volume}" showDataTip="false"/>
    <assets:VolHigh id="volHigh" width="32" height="32"/>
  </s:HGroup>

  <s:HGroup verticalAlign="middle" width="90%" >
    <s:Label text="L" width="32" height="32" verticalAlign="middle"
            textAlign="center"/>
    <s:HSlider width="100%" maximum="1.0" minimum="-1.0" stepSize="0.01"
            snapInterval="0.01" value="@{model.pan}" showDataTip="false"/>
    <s:Label text="R" width="32" height="32" verticalAlign="middle"
```

```
                        textAlign="center"/>
            </s:HGroup>
          </s:VGroup>
        </s:Group>
    </s:View>
```

Notice that there is virtually no logic in the View. It is all declarative presentation code, just as it should be. All of the hard work is delegated to the presentation model.

Unfortunately, the SongViewModel class is too large to list in its entirety, so we will limit ourselves to looking at only a few choice sections of the class. Remember that the basic functionality required to play a music file was already covered earlier in the chapter, and if you want to examine the complete source code of the class, you can refer to the MusicPlayer project included with the book's example code. Listing 8–21 shows the declaration and the constructor for the SongViewModel class.

Listing 8–21. *The Declaration of the SongViewModel Class*

```
package viewmodels
{
  // import statements…

  [Event(name="songEnded", type="flash.events.Event")]

  [Bindable]
  public class SongViewModel extends EventDispatcher {
    public static const SONG_ENDED:String = "songEnded";

    public var albumCover:BitmapData;
    public var albumTitle:String = "";
    public var songTitle:String = "";
    public var artistName:String = "";
    public var isPlaying:Boolean = false;

    private var timer:Timer;

    public function SongViewModel(songList:ArrayCollection, index:Number) {
      this.songList = songList;
      this.currentIndex = index;

      timer = new Timer(500, 0);
      timer.addEventListener(TimerEvent.TIMER, onTimer);

      loadCurrentSong();
    }
  }
}
```

The class extends EventDispatcher so that it can notify any Views that might be listening when a song ends. The model dispatches the SONG_ENDED event when this happens. This model is also annotated with Bindable to ensure that Views can easily bind to properties such as the albumCover bitmap, the albumTitle, songTitle, artistName, and the isPlaying flag. The constructor takes a collection of MusicEntries and the index of the song from that collection that should be played. These parameters are saved into instance variables for later reference, as they are used when the user wants to skip to the previous or next song in the collection. The constructor also initializes a timer that goes off every 500 milliseconds. This timer reads the current position of the song and updates the class's `percentComplete` variable. And lastly, the constructor causes the current song to be loaded. The next two sections present more details regarding the handling of `percentComplete` updates and the `loadCurrentSong` method.

Special Considerations for Two-Way Binding

When looking at the MXML declaration of `SongView`, we noted that two-way bindings were used with the model's `volume`, `pan`, and `percentComplete` variables. This means that their values can be set from outside the model class. This extra bit of complexity requires some special handling in the model class. Listing 8–22 shows the code related to these properties in `SongViewModel`.

Listing 8–22. *Handling Two-Way Binding in the Presentation Model*

```
private var _volume:Number = 0.5;
private var _pan:Number = 0.0;
private var _percentComplete:int = 0;

public function get volume():Number { return _volume; }
public function set volume(val:Number):void {
  _volume = val;
  updateChannelVolume();
}

public function get pan():Number { return _pan; }
public function set pan(val:Number):void {
  _pan = val;
  updateChannelPan();
}

public function get percentComplete():int { return _percentComplete; }

/**
 * Setting this value causes the song's play position to be updated.
 */
public function set percentComplete(value:int):void {
  _percentComplete = clipToPercentageBounds(value)
  updateSongPosition();
}

/**
 * Clips the value to ensure it remains between 0 and 100 inclusive.
 */
private function clipToPercentageBounds(value:int):int {
  return Math.max(0, Math.min(100, value));
}

/**
 * Set the position of the song based on the percentComplete value.
 */
private function updateSongPosition():void {
  var newPos:Number = _percentComplete / 100.0 * song.length;
  if (isPlaying) {
```

```
      pauseSong()
      playSong(newPos);
    } else {
      pausePosition = newPos;
    }
  }
}
```

The public get and set functions of the volume, pan, and percentComplete properties ensure that they can be bound in the View. Simply declaring the variables as public will not work here since we need to do some extra work when they are set from outside the class. When the volume and pan properties are set, we only need to call functions that update the values in the SoundTransform, as was shown earlier in the chapter. Handling percentageComplete updates is a little more involved: we need to stop the song if it is playing and then restart it at its new position. We use the private pauseSong and playSong utility methods to handle the details. If the song is not currently playing, we only have to update the private pausePosition variable so that it begins at the updated location the next time the song begins playing.

That covers the handling of percentComplete updates from outside the class, but what about updates that come from within the class? Recall that there is a timer that reads the song's position every half-second and then updates the value of percentComplete. In this case, we still need to notify the other side of the binding that the value of percentComplete has been changed, but we cannot use the set method to do so because we do not want to stop and restart the song every half-second. We need an alternative update path, as shown in Listing 8–23.

Listing 8–23. *Updating* percentComplete *During Timer Ticks*

```
/*
 * Update the song's percentComplete value on each timer tick.
 */
private function onTimer(event:TimerEvent):void {
  var oldValue:int = _percentComplete;

  var percent:Number = channel.position / song.length * 100;
  updatePercentComplete(Math.round(percent));
}


/**
 * Updates the value of _percentComplete without affecting the playback
 * of the current song (i.e. updateSongPosition is NOT called).  This
 * function will dispatch a property change event to inform any clients
 * that are bound to the percentComplete property of the update.
 */
private function updatePercentComplete(value:int):void {
  var oldValue:int = _percentComplete;
  _percentComplete = clipToPercentageBounds(value);

  var pce:Event = PropertyChangeEvent.createUpdateEvent(this,
        "percentComplete", oldValue, _percentComplete);
  dispatchEvent(pce);
}
```

The solution presented here is to update the value of _percentComplete directly and then manually dispatch the PropertyChangeEvent to inform the other side of the binding that the value has changed.

Integrating the Metaphile Library

It would be really nice to display the image of the album cover if one is embedded in the metadata of the MP3 file. However, the Flash's ID3Info class does not support reading image metadata from sound files. Luckily, there is a vibrant development community that has grown around the Flex and Flash platforms over the years. This community has given birth to many third-party libraries that help fill in functionality missing from the platform. One such library is the open source Metaphile library.[5] This small but powerful ActionScript library provides the ability to read metadata—including images—from many popular file formats.

Using the library is as simple as downloading the latest code from the project's web site, compiling it into an .swc file, and placing that file in your project's libs directory. The library provides an ID3Reader class that can be used to read MP3 metadata entries, as shown in Listing 8–24. While the Sound class uses the URL provided by the current song's MusicEntry instance, Metaphile's ID3Reader class is set up to read its metadata. An onMetaData event handler is notified when the metadata has been parsed. The class's autoLimit property is set to -1 so that there is no limit on the size of the metadata that can be parsed, and the autoClose property is set to true to ensure that the input stream will be closed once ID3Reader is finished reading the metadata. The final step is to call the read function of ID3Reader with the input stream created by accessing the MusicEntry's stream property passed in as the parameter.

Listing 8–24. *Loading an MP3 File and Reading Its Metadata*

```
/**
 * Loads the song data for the entry in the songList indicated by
 * the value of currentSongIndex.
 */
private function loadCurrentSong():void {
  try {
    var songFile:MusicEntry = songList[currentIndex];

    song = new Sound(new URLRequest(songFile.url));

    var id3Reader:ID3Reader = new ID3Reader();
    id3Reader.onMetaData = onMetaData;
    id3Reader.autoLimit = -1;
    id3Reader.autoClose = true;

    id3Reader.read(songFile.stream);
  } catch (err:Error) {
    trace("Error while reading song or metadata: "+err.message);
  }
```

---

[5] http://code.google.com/p/metaphile/

```
    }
    /**
     * Called when the song's metadata has been loaded by the Metaphile
     * library.
     */
    private function onMetaData(metaData:IMetaData):void {
      var songFile:MusicEntry = songList[currentIndex];
      var id3:ID3Data = ID3Data(metaData);

      artistName = id3.performer ? id3.performer.text : "Unknown";
      albumTitle = id3.albumTitle ? id3.albumTitle.text : "Unknown";
      songTitle = id3.songTitle ? id3.songTitle.text : songFile.name;

      if (id3.image) {
        var loader:Loader = new Loader();
        loader.contentLoaderInfo.addEventListener(Event.COMPLETE,
                                        onLoadComplete)
        loader.loadBytes(id3.image);
      } else {
        albumCover = null;
      }
    }

    /**
     * Called when the album image is finished loading from the metadata.
     */
    private function onLoadComplete(e:Event):void  {
      albumCover = Bitmap(e.target.content).bitmapData
    }
```

The onMetaData handler is passed a parameter that conforms to the Metaphile library's
IMetaData interface. Since this handler is attached to an ID3Reader object, we know it is
safe to cast the passed-in metaData object to an instance of an ID3Data object. Doing so
gives us easy access to properties of the ID3Data class such as performer, albumTitle,
and songTitle. If there is image data present in the image property of the ID3Data class,
a new instance of flash.display.Loader is created to load the bytes into a
DisplayObject. When the image bytes are loaded, the onLoadComplete handler uses the
DisplayObject stored in the Loader's content property to initialize the albumCover
BitmapData object. Since the View is bound to the albumCover property, it will display the
album cover image as soon as it is updated.

Creating a Custom Component

Creating custom mobile components is much like creating any other custom Spark
component in Flex 4. You create a component class that extends SkinnableComponent
and a Skin to go along with it. As long as your graphics are not too complex, you can
use a regular MXML Skin. If you encounter performance problems, you may need to
write your Skin in ActionScript instead. See Chapter 11 for more information about
performance tuning your mobile application.

The custom component we will write is the ProgressButton. To save space in our user
interface, we want to combine the functionality of the play/pause button with that of a

progress monitor that indicates the current play position of the song. The control will also let the user adjust that playback position if desired. So if the user taps the control, we will treat it as a toggle of the button. If the user touches the control and then drags horizontally, it will be treated as a position adjustment.

The control will therefore have two graphical elements: an icon that indicates the state of the play/pause functionality and a progress bar that shows the playback position of the song. Figure 8–9 shows the control in its various states.

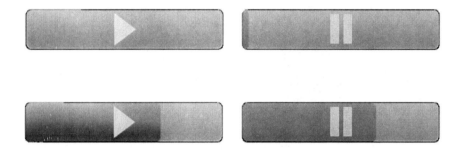

Figure 8–9. *The custom* `ProgressButton` *control*

When creating custom Spark controls, you can think of the Skin as your View and the SkinnableComponent as your model. Listing 8–25 shows the ProgressButton class, which extends SkinnableComponent and therefore acts as the control's model.

Listing 8–25. *The Declaration of the Component Portion of the* `ProgressButton`

```
package views
{
  // imports removed…

  [SkinState("pause")]
  public class ProgressButton extends SkinnableComponent
  {
    [SkinPart(required="true")]
    public var playIcon:DisplayObject;

    [SkinPart(required="true")]
    public var pauseIcon:DisplayObject;

    [SkinPart(required="true")]
    public var background:Group;

    [Bindable]
    public var percentComplete:Number = 0;

    private var mouseDownTime:Number;
    private var isMouseDown:Boolean;

    public function ProgressButton() {
```

```
        // Make sure the mouse doesn't interact with any of the skin parts
        mouseChildren = false;

        addEventListener(MouseEvent.MOUSE_DOWN, onMouseDown);
        addEventListener(MouseEvent.MOUSE_MOVE, onMouseMove);
        addEventListener(MouseEvent.MOUSE_UP, onMouseUp);
        addEventListener(MouseEvent.CLICK, onMouseClick);
    }

    override protected function getCurrentSkinState():String {
        if (isPlaying()) {
            return "play";
        } else {
            return "pause";
        }
    }

    override protected function partAdded(partName:String, instance:Object):void {
        super.partAdded(partName, instance);

        if (instance == pauseIcon) {
            pauseIcon.visible = false;
        }
    }

    override protected function partRemoved(partName:String, instance:Object):void {
        super.partRemoved(partName, instance);
    }

    // Consult Listing 8-26 for the rest of this class
    }
}
```

The component has two states that every Skin must support: play and pause. The component class is annotated with SkinState("pause") to set the default state of its Skin to the pause state. Although a Skin may declare as many parts as needed, the component requires every Skin to define at least the playIcon, the pauseIcon, and a background. The final component of the interface contract between the component and the Skin is the bindable percentComplete property that the Skin uses to draw the progress bar. The component's constructor disables mouse interaction with any child components contained in the Skin and attaches listeners for the mouse events that it needs to handle.

There are three methods that most components will need to implement to ensure correct behavior of the custom control: getCurrentSkinState, partAdded, and partRemoved. The Skin calls the getCurrentSkinState function when it needs to update its display. The ProgressButton component overrides this function to return the state name based on the current value of the isPlaying flag. The partAdded and partRemoved functions give the component the chance to perform initialization and cleanup tasks when Skin parts are added and removed. In this case, both of these functions make sure to call their corresponding functions in the super class, and the only specialization done for ProgressButton is to make sure the pauseIcon is invisible when it is added.

Listing 8–26 shows the remainder of the functions defined in the `ProgressButton` class. It shows the functions that make up the rest of the class's public interface, its mouse event handlers, and its private utility functions. `SongView`, for instance, calls the `stop` function when it has been notified that the current song has finished playing.

Listing 8–26. *The Remaining Functionality of the* `ProgressButton` *Component Class*

```
/**
 * If in "play" state, stops the progress and changes the control's
 * state from "play" to "pause".
 */
public function stop():void {
  if (isPlaying()) {
    togglePlayPause();
  }
}

/**
 * @return True if the control is in "play" state.
 */
public function isPlaying():Boolean {
  return pauseIcon && pauseIcon.visible;
}

private function onMouseDown(event:MouseEvent):void {
  mouseDownTime = getTimer();
  isMouseDown = true;
}

private function onMouseMove(event:MouseEvent):void {
  if (isMouseDown && getTimer() - mouseDownTime > 250) {
    percentComplete = event.localX / width * 100;
  }
}

private function onMouseUp(event:MouseEvent):void {
  isMouseDown = false;
}

private function onMouseClick(event:MouseEvent):void {
  if (getTimer() - mouseDownTime < 250) {
    togglePlayPause();
  } else {
    event.stopImmediatePropagation();
  }
}

private function togglePlayPause():void {
  if (playIcon.visible) {
    playIcon.visible = false;
    pauseIcon.visible = true;
  } else {
    playIcon.visible = true;
    pauseIcon.visible = false;
  }
}
```

The MouseEvent handlers take care of distinguishing a tap from a drag gesture. If the control is pressed for less than 250 milliseconds, the gesture will be interpreted as a button press and no dragging will occur. Any touch that lasts longer than 250 milliseconds will be interpreted as a drag rather than a touch and the value of the percentComplete value will be adjusted according to the location of the mouse relative to the origin of the control. The togglePlayPause function is used by some of the other functions in the class to toggle the visibility of the icons, which then determines the state of the control.

The last step in creating a custom control is to define a Skin class. This is simply a matter of creating a new MXML Skin component. The Skin used for the ProgressButton in the MusicPlayer application is shown in Listing 8–27. Every Skin must include a metadata tag that specifies the HostComponent for which the Skin was designed. A reference to the HostComponent specified in the metadata tag is available to the Skin via its hostComponent property. Another requirement is that the Skin must declare all of the states in which it is interested. Further, the names of the states must correspond to those defined by the host component for the Skin to function correctly.

Listing 8–27. *The ProgressButtonSkin Declaration*

```
<?xml version="1.0" encoding="utf-8"?>
<s:Skin xmlns:fx="http://ns.adobe.com/mxml/2009"
        xmlns:s="library://ns.adobe.com/flex/spark"
        xmlns:assets="assets.*"
        minWidth="20" minHeight="20">

  <fx:Metadata>
    [HostComponent("views.ProgressButton")]
  </fx:Metadata>

  <s:states>
    <s:State name="play"/>
    <s:State name="pause"/>
  </s:states>

  <s:Group id="background" width="{hostComponent.width}"
           height="{hostComponent.height}">

    <s:Rect top="0" right="0" bottom="0" left="0" radiusX="5" radiusY="5">
      <s:fill>
        <s:SolidColor color="0x1A253C" />
      </s:fill>
    </s:Rect>

    <s:Rect top="1" right="1" bottom="1" left="1" radiusX="5" radiusY="5">
      <s:fill>
        <s:LinearGradient rotation="90">
          <s:GradientEntry color="0xa0b8f0" ratio="0.00"/>
          <s:GradientEntry color="0x81A1E0" ratio="0.48"/>
          <s:GradientEntry color="0x6098c0" ratio="0.85"/>
        </s:LinearGradient>
      </s:fill>
    </s:Rect>

    <s:Rect  top="1" bottom="1" left="1" right="1" radiusX="5" radiusY="5">
```

```
      <s:stroke>
        <s:SolidColorStroke color="0xa0b8f0" weight="1"/>
      </s:stroke>
    </s:Rect>

    <s:Rect radiusX="5" radiusY="5" top="1" bottom="1" x="1"
        width="{(hostComponent.width-2)*hostComponent.percentComplete/100.0}">
      <s:fill>
        <s:LinearGradient rotation="90">
          <s:GradientEntry color="0xFFE080" ratio="0.00"/>
          <s:GradientEntry color="0xFFc860" ratio="0.48"/>
          <s:GradientEntry color="0xE0a020" ratio="0.85"/>
        </s:LinearGradient>
      </s:fill>
    </s:Rect>

    <assets:Play id="playIcon" verticalCenter="0" horizontalCenter="0"
                 width="{hostComponent.height-4}"
                 height="{hostComponent.height-4}"/>
    <assets:Pause id="pauseIcon" verticalCenter="0" horizontalCenter="0"
                 width="{hostComponent.height-4}"
                 height="{hostComponent.height-4}"/>

  </s:Group>
</s:Skin>
```

The background Group serves as a container for the rest of the graphics of the Skin. It is bound to the width and height of the hostComponent. The next three rectangles declared by the Skin serve as the borders and background fill of the component. The fourth rectangle draws the progress bar. Its width is based on a calculation involving the width of the hostComponent and its percentComplete property. It is declared after the three background and border rectangles so that it will be drawn on top of them. The final parts to be added to the Skin are the FXG graphics for the playIcon and the pauseIcon. FXG files are just as easy to use in Skin classes as they are in any other MXML file. FXG files are compiled to an optimized format and drawn as vector graphics. For this reason, they not only are fast to render but also scale nicely. You don't have to worry about them looking bad at different resolutions and screen densities (except when used in IconItemRenderers, as noted previously!).

That concludes our look at playing sound in Flash and at creating a MusicPlayer that goes somewhat beyond a trivial example application by exploring the issues that you will have to deal with when writing real Android applications. For the rest of this chapter, we will be exploring video playback, a feature that made Flash into a household word.

Playing Video

Some recent estimates have Flash responsible for as much as 75% of the Web's video.[6] Whether video is in the On2 VP6 format or in the widely used H.264 format, rest assured that it can be played in your mobile Flash and Flex applications. There are, however, some things that must be taken into account when dealing with mobile devices. Although mobile devices are growing in CPU and graphical power at an incredible rate, they are still much slower than an average desktop or notebook computer. Recent high-end mobile devices have support for hardware-accelerated decoding and rendering of H.264 video, but many do not. And new features in Flash, like Stage Video, which gives your Flash applications access to hardware-accelerated video rendering on the desktop and TV, are not yet available on Android devices—although it is only a matter of time. Until then, you must make some compromises when playing video on mobile devices. This starts with encoding, which is where our examination of mobile Flash video will begin.

Optimizing Video for Mobile Devices

Video encoding is half science and half black art. There are some great resources available that explore the topic in all of its glorious detail.[7] Therefore we will only summarize some of the recent recommended best practices, while advising that you examine the sources cited in the footnotes of this page for an in-depth treatment of the subject. The main things to keep in mind when you are encoding video for mobile devices are that you are dealing with more limited hardware and you will have to cope with bandwidth that fluctuates between 3G, 4G, and Wi-Fi networks.

Adobe recommends that when encoding new video, you prefer the H.264 format at a maximum frame rate of 24 fps (frames per second) and with 44.1 kHz AAC-encoded stereo audio. If you must use the On2 VP6 format, then the same recommendation applies to frame rate and audio sampling, only with audio in MP3 format rather than AAC. If you are encoding with H.264, you will want to stick with the baseline profile if you want good performance across the greatest number of devices. If your source footage is at a frame rate that is higher than 24, you may want to consider halving it until you are below that target. For example, if your footage is at 30 fps, then you will get the best results by encoding it at 15 fps since the encoder won't have to interpolate any of the video data.

---

[6]Adobe, Inc., "Delivering video for Flash Player 10.1 on mobile devices," www.adobe.com/devnet/devices/articles/delivering_video_fp10-1.html, February 15, 2010

[7]Adobe, Inc., "Video encoding guidelines for Android mobile devices," www.adobe.com/devnet/devices/articles/encoding-guidelines-android.html, December 22, 2010

Table 8–2 shows encoding recommendations gathered from recent publications from Adobe and conference sessions at Adobe Max and 360|Flex. All of these numbers assume H.264 encoding in the baseline profile. Keep in mind that these are only recommendations—they change rapidly as faster hardware becomes available, and they may not apply to your specific situation. Also, these recommendations are targeting the largest number of devices possible. If your application is specifically targeted at high-end devices running the latest versions of Android, then these numbers may be a little too conservative for your needs.

Table 8–2. *Encoding Recommendations for Mobile Devices*

	Wi-Fi	4G	3G
Resolution	640x480 (4:3)	512x384 (4:3)	480x360 (4:3)
	640x360 (16:9)	512x288 (16:9)	480x272 (16:9)
Video Bit Rate	500–700 kbps	350–500 kbps	Up to 350 kbps
Audio Bit Rate	Up to 160 kbps	Up to 128 kbps	Up to 64 kbps

There are also several steps you can take in your application to ensure that you are getting the best performance. You should avoid the use of transforms: rotation, perspective projections, and color transforms. Avoid drop shadows, filter effects, and Pixel Bender effects. And you should avoid transparency and blending the video object with other graphics as much as possible.

It is also best to try to avoid excessive ActionScript processing. For example, if you have a timer that is updating your playhead, do not have it updating multiple times per second if it's really not necessary that it do so. The goal is to always dedicate as much processing time as possible to rendering and minimize the amount needed for program logic while playing video. For this same reason, you should also try to avoid stretching or compressing the video if at all possible. It is a better idea to use the Capabilities class, or the size of your View, to determine the size of your display area and then select the closest match. That assumes you have multiple formats of the video to choose from. If you do not, then it is best to include options in your application that will let the user determine whether to play the video at its natural resolution or to stretch it to fill the screen (and remember that with video, you nearly always want to maintain aspect ratio when stretching).

Spark VideoPlayer

The topic of playing video is too large to fit in one section, or even one chapter, of a book. We will not go into installing or connecting to a streaming server such as the Red5 Media Server or Adobe's Flash Media Server. We will not cover topics such as DRM (digital rights management)[8] or CDNs (content delivery networks). Instead, we will cover the basic options for playing video in your applications. All of these options will work with either progressive downloads or with streaming servers. It is our intention to get you started in the right direction so that you know where to begin. If you then need more advanced features such as those mentioned previously, Adobe's documentation is more than adequate.

The first option we will look at is the Spark `VideoPlayer` component that was introduced with Flex 4. This component is built on top of the Open Source Media Framework (OSMF), a library designed to handle all of the "behind the scenes" tasks required by a full-featured video player. The idea is that you write your cool video player GUI, wire it to the functionality provided by OSMF, and you are ready to go. We'll look at OSMF in more depth later in the chapter.

So the Spark `VideoPlayer`, then, is a pre-packaged video player UI built on top of the pre-packaged OSMF library. It is the ultimate in convenience (and laziness) since you can add video playback functionality to your app with just a few lines of code. Listing 8–28 shows how to instantiate a `VideoPlayer` in a `View` MXML file.

Listing 8–28. *Using the Spark* `VideoPlayer` *in a Mobile Application*

```
<?xml version="1.0" encoding="utf-8"?>
<s:View xmlns:fx="http://ns.adobe.com/mxml/2009"
        xmlns:s="library://ns.adobe.com/flex/spark"
        viewDeactivate="onViewDeactivate()"
        actionBarVisible="false">

   <fx:Script>
     <![CDATA[
       private static const sourceURL:String = "http://ia600408.us.archive.org"+
          "/26/items/BigBuckBunny_328/BigBuckBunny_512kb.mp4";

       private function onViewDeactivate():void {
         player.stop();
       }
     ]]>
   </fx:Script>

   <s:VideoPlayer id="player" width="100%" height="100%" source="{sourceURL}"
                  skinClass="views.MobileVideoPlayerSkin"/>
</s:View>
```

This application is set to full screen, and the `View`'s `ActionBar` has been disabled to allow the `VideoPlayer` to take up the entire screen of the device. All the component needs is a source URL, and it will automatically begin playback as soon as sufficient data has been buffered. It truly does not get any easier. We did take care to stop the playback when the `View` is deactivated. It's a small thing, but there is no reason to continue buffering and playing any longer than is strictly necessary.

---

[8] http://help.adobe.com/en_US/as3/dev/WS5b3ccc516d4fbf351e63e3d118676a5be7-8000.html

If you use Flash Builder or consult the docs for the VideoPlayer class, you may see an ominous warning about VideoPlayer not being "optimized for mobile," but it turns out that in this case what they really mean is "warning: no mobile skin defined yet!" You can use VideoPlayer as is, but when you run your app on a medium- or high-dpi device, the video controls will be teeny tiny (yes, that's the technical term) and hard to use. The solution is to do what we've done in this example and create your own MobileVideoPlayerSkin.

In this case, we have just used Flash Builder to create a new Skin based on the original VideoPlayerSkin and then modified it a little. We removed the drop shadow, scaled the controls a bit, and adjusted the spacing. The modified Skin can be found in the VideoPlayers sample project located in the examples/chapter-08 directory of the book's source code. The result can be seen in Figure 8–10, where we are playing that famous workhorse of example video clips: Big Buck Bunny. These images were taken from a Nexus S where the controls are now large enough to be useable.

Figure 8–10. *The Spark VideoPlayer running on a Nexus S in regular (top) and full-screen (bottom) modes*

This was just a quick modification of the current `VideoPlayerSkin`, but of course you can get as fancy with your new mobile `Skin` as you want thanks to the skinning architecture of the Spark components introduced in Flex 4. Just remember some of the performance constraints you will face in a mobile environment.

Video with NetStream

Having a convenient, pre-packaged solution such as `VideoPlayer` is nice, but there are times when you really need something that is customized. Or perhaps you don't want all of the baggage that comes with an "everything's included" library like OSMF. That's where the `NetConnection`, `NetStream`, and `Video` classes come in. These classes allow you to build a lightweight or full-featured and fully customized video player.

In short, `NetConnection` handles the networking; `NetStream` provides the programmatic interface that controls the streaming, buffering, and playback of the video; and `Video` provides the display object where the decoded video ultimately appears. In this scenario, you are the one responsible for supplying the user interface for the video player. Listing 8–29 shows a very minimalistic MXML declaration for a `NetStream`-based video player.

Listing 8–29. *The MXML File for the NetStreamVideoView*

```
<?xml version="1.0" encoding="utf-8"?>
<s:View xmlns:fx="http://ns.adobe.com/mxml/2009"
        xmlns:s="library://ns.adobe.com/flex/spark"
        xmlns:mx="library://ns.adobe.com/flex/mx"
        initialize="onInitialize()"
        viewDeactivate="onViewDeactivate()"
        actionBarVisible="false"
        backgroundColor="black">

  <fx:Script source="NetStreamVideoViewScript.as"/>

  <mx:UIComponent id="videoContainer" width="100%" height="100%"/>

  <s:Label id="logger" width="100%" color="gray"/>

  <s:HGroup bottom="2" left="30" right="30" height="36" verticalAlign="middle">
    <s:ToggleButton id="playBtn" click="onPlayPause()" selected="true"
      skinClass="spark.skins.spark.mediaClasses.normal.PlayPauseButtonSkin"/>
    <s:Label id="timeDisplay" color="gray" width="100%" textAlign="right"/>
  </s:HGroup>
</s:View>
```

We have declared a `UIComponent` that serves as the eventual container for the `Video` display object. Other than that, there are just two other visible controls. The first is a `ToggleButton` that "borrows" the `PlayPauseButtonSkin` from the Spark `VideoPlayer` component (OK, we admit it, we flat-out stole the `Skin` and we're not even a little bit sorry). This gives us an easy way to display a button with the traditional triangle play icon and the double-bar pause icon. The other control is simply a `Label` that will display the duration of the video clip and the current play position.

There are various ActionScript functions mentioned in the MXML declaration as event handlers for the View's initialize and viewDeactivate events as well as for the Button's click event. The ActionScript code has been moved to a separate file and included with a <fx:Script> tag. Listing 8–30 shows the code for the View's onInitialize and onViewDeactivate handlers.

Listing 8–30. *The View Event Handlers for the* NetStreamVideoView

```
private static const SOURCE:String = "http://ia600408.us.archive.org/"+
  "26/items/BigBuckBunny_328/BigBuckBunny_512kb.mp4";

private var video:Video;
private var ns:NetStream;
private var isPlaying:Boolean;
private var timer:Timer;
private var duration:String = "";

private function onInitialize():void {
  video = new Video();
  videoContainer.addChild(video);

  var nc:NetConnection = new NetConnection();
  nc.connect(null);

  ns = new NetStream(nc);
  ns.addEventListener(NetStatusEvent.NET_STATUS, onNetStatus);
  ns.client = {
    onMetaData: onMetaData,
    onCuePoint: onCuePoint,
    onPlayStatus: onPlayStatus
  };

  ns.play(SOURCE);
  video.attachNetStream(ns);

  timer = new Timer(1000);
  timer.addEventListener(TimerEvent.TIMER, onTimer);
  timer.start();
}

private function onViewDeactivate():void {
  if (ns) {
    ns.close();
  }
}
```

The onInitialize handler takes care of all of the setup code. The Video display object is created and added to its UIComponent container. Next, a NetConnection is created, and its connect method is called with a null value. This tells the NetConnection that it will be playing an MP3 or video file from the local filesystem or from a web server. NetConnection can also be used for Flash Remoting or to connect to Flash Media Servers if different parameters are passed to its connect method.

The next step is to create the NetStream object by passing it a reference to the NetConnection in its constructor. There are several events that you may be interested in receiving from the NetStream object depending on the sophistication of your player. The

NET_STATUS event will give you notifications about buffer status, playback status, and error conditions. There are also metaData, cuePoint, and playStatus events that are attached to the NetStream's client property. The client is just an Object that defines certain properties; it doesn't have to be of any particular type. In the foregoing listing, we just used an object literal to declare an anonymous object with the desired properties.

The metaData event will give you important information such as the width, height, and duration of the video. The cuePoint event will notify you whenever a cue point that was embedded in the video has been reached. Handling the playStatus will even let you know when the video has reached its end. These event handlers are shown in Listing 8–31.

The final steps are to begin playing the NetStream, attach it to the Video display object, and to create and start the timer that will update the time display once per second.

Listing 8–31. *The NetStream Event Handlers*

```
private function onMetaData(item:Object):void {
  video.width = item.width;
  video.height = item.height;

  video.x = (width - video.width) / 2;
  video.y = (height - video.height) / 2;

  if (item.duration)
    duration = formatSeconds(item.duration);
}

private function onCuePoint(item:Object):void {
  // Item has four properties: name, time, parameters, type
  log("cue point "+item.name+" reached");
}

private function onPlayStatus(item:Object):void {
  if (item.code == "NetStream.Play.Complete") {
    timer.stop();
    updateTimeDisplay(duration);
  }
}

private function onNetStatus(event:NetStatusEvent):void {
  var msg:String = "";

  if (event.info.code)
    msg += event.info.code;

  if (event.info.level)
    msg += ", level: "+event.info.level;

  log(msg);
}

private function log(msg:String, showUser:Boolean=true):void {
  trace(msg);
  if (showUser)
    logger.text += msg + "\n";
}
```

The onMetaData handler uses the width and height of the video to center it in the View. It also saves the duration of the video to be used in the time display Label. In the onPlayStatus handler, we check to see if this is a NetStream.Play.Complete notification and, if so, stop the timer that has been updating the time display. The onCuePoint and onNetStatus handlers are there only for demonstration purposes, and their output is simply logged to the debug console and optionally to the screen.

Listing 8–32 shows the remaining code associated with the NetStreamVideoView. The onPlayPause function serves as the ToggleButton's click handler. Depending on the selected state of the ToggleButton, it will either pause or resume the NetStream and start or stop the timer that updates the timeDisplay Label. The onTimer function is the handler for that Timer. It will use the NetStream's time property, formatted as a minutes:seconds string, to update the Label.

Listing 8–32. *Playing, Pausing, and Reading Properties from the* NetStream

```
private function onPlayPause():void {
  if (playBtn.selected) {
    ns.resume();
    timer.start();
  } else {
    ns.pause();
    timer.stop();
  }
}

private function onTimer(event:TimerEvent):void {
  updateTimeDisplay(formatSeconds(ns.time));
}

private function updateTimeDisplay(time:String):void {
  if (duration)
    time += " / "+duration;

  timeDisplay.text = time;
}

private function formatSeconds(time:Number):String {
  var minutes:int = time / 60;
  var seconds:int = int(time) % 60;

  return String(minutes+":"+(seconds<10 ? "0" : "")+seconds);
}
```

Figure 8–11 shows the result of all of this code running on a low-dpi Android device. A minimal player such as this one is more appropriate for this type of screen.

Figure 8–11. *A minimal* NetStream-*based video player running on a low-dpi device*

As you can see, there was a lot more code involved in creating our minimalistic NetStream-based video player. But if you need ultimate flexibility in a lightweight video player implementation, the combination of the NetStream and Video classes will provide all of the power you need.

We mentioned Stage Video briefly at the beginning of this section on playing video. Once supported on Android, it will allow your NetStream-based video players to take advantage of hardware-accelerated decoding and rendering of H.264 video. Adobe provides a very helpful "getting started" guide to help you convert your NetStream code to use Stage Video rather than the Video display object.[9] If you prefer to future-proof yourself with very little effort, you can take advantage of the third option for writing a video player on Android: the OSMF library. It is the subject of our next section, and it will automatically take advantage of Stage Video when it becomes available on Android.

Playing Video with OSMF

The Open Source Media Framework is a project started by Adobe to create a library that captures best practices when it comes to writing Flash-based media players. It is a full-featured media player abstracted into a handful of easy-to-use classes. The library allows you to quickly create high-quality video players for use in your Flex and Flash applications. OSMF is included with the Flex 4 SDK, but you can also download the latest version from the project's web site.[10] Listing 8–33 shows the MXML code for the OSMFVideoView. The user interface code shown here is almost exactly the same as the

---

[9]Adobe, Inc., "Getting started with stage video," www.adobe.com/devnet/flashplayer/articles/stage_video.html, February 8, 2011

[10]http://sourceforge.net/projects/osmf.adobe/files/

code in Listing 8–29 for the `NetStreamVideoView`. In essence we're just replacing the NetStream-based back end with an OSMF-based `MediaPlayer` implementation.

Listing 8–33. *The MXML Declaration for the* `OSMFVideoView`

```
<?xml version="1.0" encoding="utf-8"?>
<s:View xmlns:fx="http://ns.adobe.com/mxml/2009"
        xmlns:s="library://ns.adobe.com/flex/spark"
        xmlns:mx="library://ns.adobe.com/flex/mx"
        initialize="onInitialize()"
        viewDeactivate="onViewDeactivate()"
        actionBarVisible="false"
        backgroundColor="black">

  <fx:Script source="OSMFVideoViewScript.as"/>

  <mx:UIComponent id="videoContainer" width="100%" height="100%"/>
  <s:HGroup bottom="2" left="30" right="30" height="36" verticalAlign="middle">
    <s:ToggleButton id="playBtn" click="onPlayPause()" selected="true"
skinClass="spark.skins.spark.mediaClasses.normal.PlayPauseButtonSkin"/>
    <s:Label id="timeDisplay" color="gray" width="100%" textAlign="right"/>
  </s:HGroup>
</s:View>
```

Listing 8–34 shows the initialization code for the OSMF classes that will be used to implement the video player. We pass an instance of `URLResource` that contains the URL of our movie to the `LightweightVideoElement` constructor. An OSMF `MediaElement` is an interface to the type of media being played. `LightweightVideoElement` is a specialization that represents a video and supports both progressive download and simple RTMP streaming. There is also a class named `VideoElement` that supports more streaming protocols, but for our purposes the `LightweightVideoElement` has all of the functionality that is required.

Once the `LightweightVideoElement` is created, it is passed to the constructor of the OSMF `MediaPlayer` class. `MediaPlayer` is the class through which you will control the playback of the video. It is capable of dispatching many different events that can be used to get information about the state and status of the `MediaPlayer`. In the example code shown next, we handle the `mediaSizeChange` event to center the video display on the View, the `timeChange` and `durationChange` events to update the `timeDisplay` Label, and the `complete` event to inform us when the video has finished playing.

The `MediaPlayer` is not a display object itself. Instead it provides a `displayObject` property that can be added to the display list. In this case, it is being added as a child of the `videoContainer` UIComponent. The final bit of initialization we do is to use the `currentTimeUpdateInterval` property to request that we be given updates on the `currentTime` of the video player only once per second instead of the default value of every 250 milliseconds. The video will begin playing automatically since the default value of the `MediaPlayer`'s `autoPlay` property is true.

Listing 8–34. *Initialization Code for the OSMF-Based* `MediaPlayer`

```
import org.osmf.elements.VideoElement;
import org.osmf.events.DisplayObjectEvent;
import org.osmf.events.MediaElementEvent;
import org.osmf.events.TimeEvent;
import org.osmf.media.MediaPlayer;
import org.osmf.media.URLResource;
import org.osmf.net.NetLoader;

private static const sourceURL:String = "http://ia600408.us.archive.org"+
  "/26/items/BigBuckBunny_328/BigBuckBunny_512kb.mp4";

private var player:MediaPlayer;
private var duration:String;

private function onInitialize():void {
  var element:LightweightVideoElement;
  element = new LightweightVideoElement(new URLResource(sourceURL));

  player = new MediaPlayer(element);
  videoContainer.addChild(player.displayObject);

  player.addEventListener(DisplayObjectEvent.MEDIA_SIZE_CHANGE, onSize);
  player.addEventListener(TimeEvent.CURRENT_TIME_CHANGE, onTimeChange);
  player.addEventListener(TimeEvent.DURATION_CHANGE, onDurationChange);
  player.addEventListener(TimeEvent.COMPLETE, onVideoComplete);
  player.currentTimeUpdateInterval = 1000;
}

private function onViewDeactivate():void {
  if (player)
    player.stop();
}

private function onPlayPause():void {
  if (player.playing) {
    player.play();
  } else {
    player.pause();
  }
}
```

In the `onViewDeactivate` handler just shown, we make sure to stop the player when the View is deactivated. You can also see the `click` handler for the play/pause `ToggleButton`. It simply calls the `MediaPlayer`'s play and pause methods, depending on whether the player is currently playing.

Listing 8–35 continues the listing of the script code for the `OSMFVideoView` by showing the `MediaPlayer` event handlers. The `onSize` handler is called whenever the media changes size. We use this handler to center the `MediaPlayer`'s `displayObject` on the View. The `onDurationChange` handler is called when the player learns the total duration of the video being played. We use this handler to store the duration as a formatted string that is later used by the `timeDisplay` Label. The `onTimeChange` handler is called once per second—as we requested during initialization—so we can update the `timeDisplay`

Label. And finally, onVideoComplete is included for demonstration purposes. Our implementation just prints a message to the debug console.

Listing 8–35. *The OSMF Event Handlers*

```
private function onSize(event:DisplayObjectEvent):void {
  player.displayObject.x = (width - event.newWidth) / 2;
  player.displayObject.y = (height - event.newHeight) / 2;
}

private function onDurationChange(event:TimeEvent):void {
  duration = formatSeconds(player.duration);
}

private function onTimeChange(event:TimeEvent):void {
  updateTimeDisplay(formatSeconds(player.currentTime));
}

private function onVideoComplete(event:TimeEvent):void{
  trace("The video played all the way through!");
}

private function updateTimeDisplay(time:String):void {
  if (duration)
    time += " / "+ duration;

  timeDisplay.text = time;
}

private function formatSeconds(time:Number):String {
  var minutes:int = time / 60;
  var seconds:int = int(time) % 60;

  return String(minutes+":"+(seconds<10 ? "0" : "")+seconds);
}
```

With OSMF, you get all the functionality with less code when compared with rolling your own NetStream-based video player. You also get the benefit of leveraging code written by video experts. If you need all of the functionality it provides, you can't go wrong by building your video player on top of OSMF. When run, this OSMF-based video player looks and behaves exactly like the one shown in Figure 8–11.

VideoRecorder Example

The final example of this chapter will be the video analog of the SoundRecorder that was presented earlier. The VideoRecorder application will use the Android camera interface to capture a video file and then allow the user to immediately play it back in the Flex application. The source code for this example can be found in the VideoRecorder sample application located in the examples/chapter-08 directory of the book's source code.

You may recall from Chapter 7 that the CameraUI class can be used for capturing video and images using the native Android camera interface.

This example will use an OSMF `MediaPlayer` to play the captured video. Listing 8–36 shows the initialization code for the `CameraUI` class and the `MediaPlayer` classes.

Listing 8–36. *Initializing the* `CameraUI` *and* `MediaPlayer` *Classes*

```
import flash.media.CameraUI;
import org.osmf.elements.VideoElement;
import org.osmf.events.DisplayObjectEvent;
import org.osmf.events.MediaElementEvent;
import org.osmf.events.TimeEvent;
import org.osmf.media.MediaPlayer;
import org.osmf.media.URLResource;
import org.osmf.net.NetLoader;

private var cameraUI:CameraUI;
private var player:MediaPlayer;
private var duration:String;

private function onInitialize():void {
  if (CameraUI.isSupported) {
    cameraUI = new CameraUI();
    cameraUI.addEventListener(MediaEvent.COMPLETE, onCaptureComplete);

    player = new MediaPlayer();

    player.addEventListener(DisplayObjectEvent.MEDIA_SIZE_CHANGE, onSize);
    player.addEventListener(TimeEvent.CURRENT_TIME_CHANGE, onTimeChange);
    player.addEventListener(TimeEvent.DURATION_CHANGE, onDurationChange);
    player.addEventListener(TimeEvent.COMPLETE, onVideoComplete);

    player.currentTimeUpdateInterval = 1000;
    player.autoPlay = false;
  }

  captureButton.visible = CameraUI.isSupported;
}
```

As always, we check to ensure that the `CameraUI` class is supported on the device. If so, a new `CameraUI` instance is created and a handler for its `complete` event is added. You learned in Chapter 7 that the `CameraUI` triggers this event when the image or video capture is successfully completed. Next we create our `MediaPlayer` and attach the usual event listeners. Note that the `autoPlay` property is set to `false` since we will want to start playback manually in this application.

Listing 8–37 shows the code that initiates the video capture with the native Android interface, as well as the handler that gets notified when the capture is completed successfully.

Listing 8–37. *Starting and Completing the Video Capture*

```
private function onCaptureImage():void {
  cameraUI.launch(MediaType.VIDEO);
}

private function onCaptureComplete(event:MediaEvent):void {
  player.media = new VideoElement(new URLResource(event.data.file.url));
  player.play();
```

```
    playBtn.selected = true;
    playBtn.visible = true;

  if (videoContainer.numChildren > 0)
    videoContainer.removeChildAt(0);

  videoContainer.addChild(player.displayObject);
}
```

When the user taps the button to start the capture, the onCaptureImage handler launches the native camera UI to capture a video file. If successful, the onCaptureComplete handler receives an event containing the MediaPromise as its data property. The MediaPromise contains a reference to the file in which the captured video was stored. We can use the file's URL to initialize a new VideoElement and assign it to the MediaPlayer's media property. Then we can start the video playing and adjust the properties of the playBtn to be consistent with the state of the application. If the videoContainer already has a displayObject added to it, we remove it and then add the player's new displayObject.

Most of the event handling code is the same as the OSMFVideoView code that was presented in the last section. There are two differences that are shown in Listing 8–38.

Listing 8–38. *A Slightly Different Take on the* MediaPlayer *Event Handling*

```
private function onSize(event:DisplayObjectEvent):void {
  if (player.displayObject == null)
    return;

  var scaleX:int = Math.floor(width / event.newWidth);
  var scaleY:int = Math.floor(height / event.newHeight);
  var scale:Number = Math.min(scaleX, scaleY);

  player.displayObject.width = event.newWidth * scale;
  player.displayObject.height = event.newHeight * scale;

  player.displayObject.x = (width - player.displayObject.width) / 2;
  player.displayObject.y = (height - player.displayObject.height) / 2;
}

private function onVideoComplete(event:TimeEvent):void{
  player.seek(0);
  playBtn.selected = false;
}
```

In this case, the onSize handler will try to scale the video size to be a closer match to the size of the display. Note the check to see if the player.displayObject is null. This can happen when switching from one captured video to the next. So we have to take care not to attempt to scale the displayObject when it doesn't exist. The other difference is in the onVideoComplete handler. Since users may want to watch their captured video clips multiple times, we reset the video stream by repositioning the playhead back to the beginning and resetting the state of the play/pause button. Figure 8–12 shows the application running on an Android device.

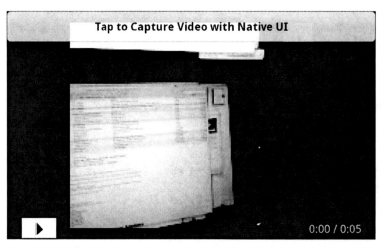

Figure 8–12. *The VideoRecorder example application after capturing a short video*

Summary

The ability to enjoy media on mobile devices will become more common as the devices continue to get more powerful. You now have the knowledge you need to utilize the power of the Flash media APIs in your own mobile applications. This chapter has covered a wide variety of topics having to do with playing various types of media on the Flash platform. In particular, you now know the following:

- How to embed and play sound effects using the SoundEffect class

- How to load MP3 files using the Sound class

- How to control the playback, volume, and panning of the sound using the SoundChannel and SoundTransform classes

- How to play dynamically generated or recorded sound

- How to write Flex mobile applications that are maintainable and testable

- How to write custom controls for Flex 4 Mobile applications

- How to play video using the Spark VideoPlayer component, the NetStream class, and the OSMF library

- How to interface with the CameraUI class to capture video and then play the captured video in an AIR for Android application

We will continue the theme of writing real-world Flex mobile applications in the next chapter by taking a look at some of the aspects of working in a team and utilizing a designer-developer workflow.

Chapter 9

The Designer-Developer Workflow

Whether you're a designer or developer, it's an exciting time to get into mobile development, a young industry that is full of potential and opportunity. But the mobile development industry does face the same challenges that other software development projects face, those of communication and workflow. Figure 9–1 pokes fun at communication and interpretation issues in a software project. The cartoon isn't a far cry from how many companies work. A project could have many actual requirements, yet most of the people involved will articulate only those requirements that concern or interest them.

| How the customer explained it. | How the designer designed it. | How the programmer wrote it. | What the customer really needed. |

Figure 9–1. *"How projects really work" from* www.projectcartoon.com[1] *licensed under Creative Commons Attribution 3.0 Unported License:* http://creativecommons.org/licenses/by/3.0/

---

[1] "How projects really work", http://www.projectcartoon.com, July 24, 2006

There are many places where the project can break down. A smart workflow can really help alleviate these pain points, so that what the client asked for is what the designer designs and what the developer executes. But first it is essential to understand the roles of the designer and developer, as well as the tools they use.

The Visual Designer's Role

The role of the designer is to understand the needs of the client, translate those to the application, and create visual designs for it. The designer discusses with the client how the application should work, how the GUI works to accomplish user stories, and why it works that way. This is a two-way street, as the client's input is taken into account as well. The designer also adjusts the visual design for the developer's needs. Sometimes the developer can foresee technical challenges that the designer isn't aware of, in which case they can and should collaborate on ways to solve the problem. Sometimes the collaboration is just clarification of how things work. Other times it can lead to a compromise between design and technical limitations.

> *"Design is the conscious and intuitive effort to impose meaningful order."*
>
> —Victor Papanek, designer and educator

Starting in Adobe Device Central

Adobe Device Central simplifies the creation of content for mobile phones, tablets, and consumer electronic devices. It allows both designers and developers to plan, preview, and test mobile experiences. You can access the latest device profiles through the dynamically updated online device library and simulate display conditions like backlight timeout and sunlight reflections in the context of device skins to tune designs for real-world conditions.

> **Tip** For more information, see `www.adobe.com/products/devicecentral.html`

Using Device Central

Adobe Device Central CS5.5 is integrated with most design programs, including Photoshop, Illustrator, Fireworks, and Flash, enabling you to leverage handset data and work more productively from inception to final launch of your mobile project.

Creating a New Document from Device Central

Device Central CS5.5 is a good place to start when embarking on a new mobile project. When you launch Device Central, a welcome screen appears (see Figure 9–2).

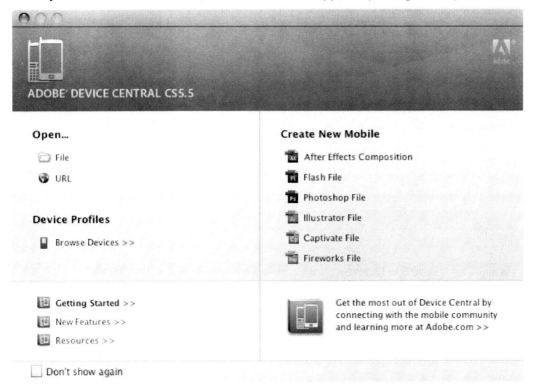

Figure 9–2. *Launching a new Fireworks document from Device Central CS5; the Captivate and Fireworks file formats have been added since Device Central CS4.*

1. Click the file type you want to create from the column on the right (see Figure 9–3) to start a new project. The message in the center states, "To start, please select device(s) in the 'Text Devices' panel."

2. Click the Browse button, located in the upper right corner. This will display a list of devices to create and test against (see Figure 9–3).

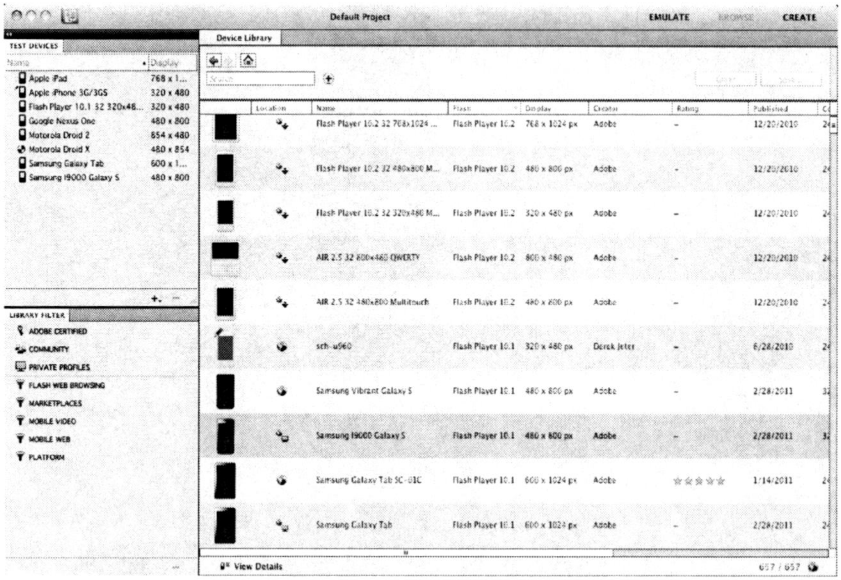

Figure 9–3. *Browse devices in the device library and sort by name, display creator rating or search for a specific device.*

3. Select the device to test against, and drag it to the Test Device panel.

4. Double-click the device name to view the device details (see Figure 9–4).

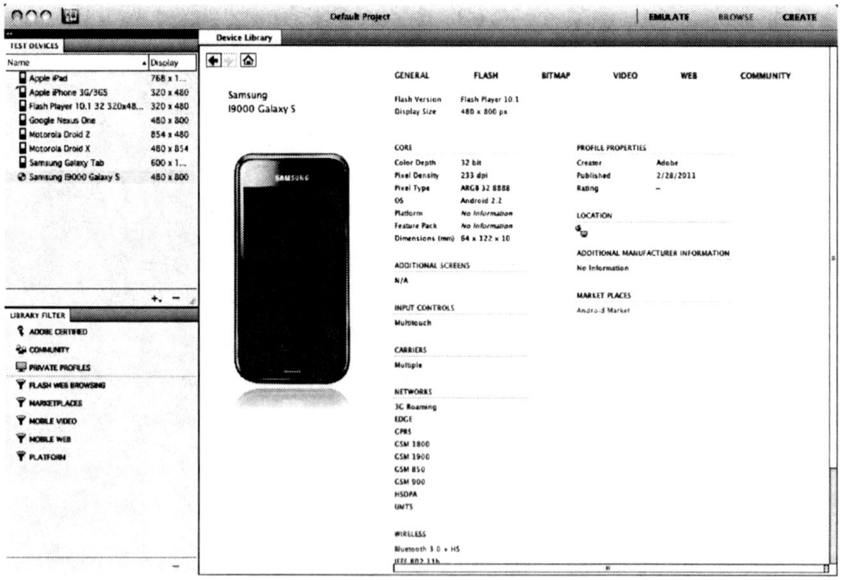

Figure 9–4. *Click and drag the device to the Test Devices panel to add it to the devices to test against*

5. Once you're ready to create a new file based on the selected profile,
double-click the profile from the Test Devices listed on the left side.
Then, click Create in the upper right-hand corner (see Figure 9–5).

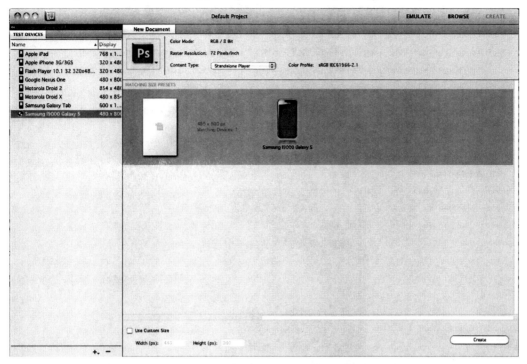

Figure 9–5. *Double-click the device profile from the Test Devices panel. Click Create in the upper right to create a new document based on that profile.*

The new document is automatically set to the correct display size and screen orientation
for your target device. Now you're ready to create your mobile design. It cannot be
overstated how helpful Device Central is when it comes to profiling devices and
simulating how content will look. This helps speed the design workflow and sure does
beat buying many different devices.

In terms of organization and productivity, one popular Fireworks feature is the ability to
create multiple pages with varying dimensions, screen orientations, and even document
resolutions, all in a single file. This means that you can easily work on portrait and
landscape layouts at the same time, which is really handy when targeting multitouch
devices and using the accelerometer. You can even save application icons alongside
your main content in the same file. No Adobe product except Fireworks does this.

Previewing Content in Device Central

When designing for mobile devices, there are points in the process where you may want
to preview your work in the context of an actual handset. The quickest and easiest way
to do this is to launch a preview from within Photoshop, Illustrator, Flash, or Fireworks.

1. In Photoshop, select File ➤ Save for Web & Devices…

2. In the lower left corner, select "Device Central…"

3. You will now be able to see how your design might look on various devices.

4. As you view your work in Device Central, you can change device skins by double-clicking different device profiles from the Test Devices panel.

5. You can also adjust the lighting or reflections using the Display panel in Device Central to test your content under different lighting conditions (see Figure 9–6).

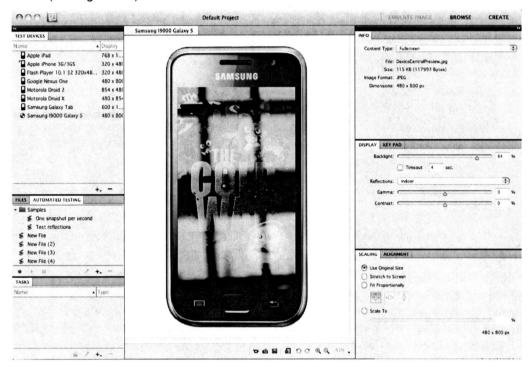

Figure 9–6. *Previewing a design on a Samsung Galaxy S in Device Central, with Indoor Reflections selected*

Creating Custom Profiles

There are several reasons you may want to create custom device profiles:

- You notice discrepancies between what is displayed in the Emulation workspace on the desktop and what you see on an actual device.

- You want to modify the device skin for presentation purposes (for example, to remove or add an operator logo).

- You manufacture devices and need to create a new profile (once the device ships, the custom profile can be distributed to the community).

The first step in creating custom profiles is making a copy of an existing device profile to use as a template. I recommend picking something as similar as possible to the custom profile you want to make. The more similarities between the original profile and your custom one, the less work you'll have to do in editing individual data points later.

1. In Device Central, click Browse (in the upper right-hand corner) so that you are in the Browse workspace.

2. If you've moved your panels, you can always restore the default by choosing **Window ➤ Workspace ➤ Reset Browse**.

3. Right-click the Flash Player 10.1 32 320×480 Multitouch profile, and select Create Editable Copy (see Figure 9–7).

4. Type a new name for the profile—for example, type "My_Multitouch_320x480"—and click OK.

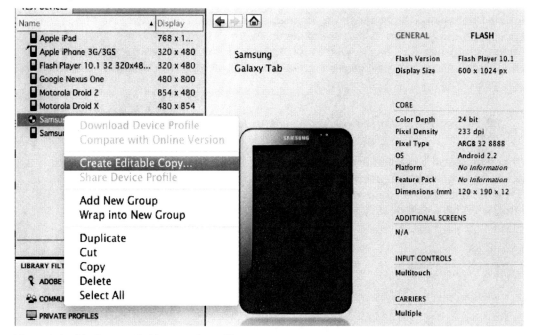

Figure 9–7. *Creating an editable copy of a profile*

Note that if you plan to share your custom profiles with others, you should give them names that are both unique and descriptive. Also, fill out all of the fields as completely as possible. This is an obvious best practice to help grow an accurate and complete dataset for the mutual benefit of the entire community.

On the right, you should now see a circle with a pencil just above the device skin, indicating the profile is now editable. Similarly, when you hover the pointer over any of the attributes, such as Input Controls or Languages, the same pencil icon appears. If an attribute does not display a pencil icon on hover, it is not editable.

Next, you can edit the device profiles directly from Device Central CS5:

1. Hover the pointer over Languages; the pencil icon appears, indicating this attribute is editable.

2. Click Languages and select the languages you want to display.

3. Click the check mark to confirm your selection.

The languages you selected should now be displayed in your custom profile.

Repeat these steps to edit all of your custom device profile information right from within Device Central. This easy and direct method of editing profile data from the interface is a real time-saver and a vast improvement over earlier versions.

Adobe Photoshop

Adobe Photoshop CS5 has a strong focus on photography but is also used to create application designs, due to its extreme flexibility for design creation and image editing. Adobe Photoshop CS5 has breakthrough capabilities for superior image selections, image retouching, and realistic painting, and a wide range of workflow and performance enhancements.

> **TIP:** For more information, see `www.adobe.com/products/photoshop.html`

Once the design is created in Photoshop (Figure 9–8), the next step in the workflow would be to bring these graphics into Flash Professional or Flash Builder for further development. This can be done by exporting each image separately, or importing the Photoshop file (`.psd`) directly into Flash Professional.

Figure 9–8. *An app design created in Adobe Photoshop CS5, complete with a shape layer, text, and smart objects, just to name a few*

Photoshop to Flash Professional Workflow

One exciting feature introduced in Flash Professional CS3 is the ability to import PSD files (Figure 9–9). On import, Flash Professional gives you the ability to determine how you want to import each layer. For instance, you can import a text layer as editable text in Flash Professional. Shape layers can be converted to editable shapes in Flash Professional as well. Even movie clips can be created from raster graphics, complete with instance names. Layers in Photoshop can appear as layers in Flash Professional, complete with layer effects that are still editable. Even the position of items can be maintained. The final result is a complete design in Flash Professional, ready to be animated and further developed for mobile.

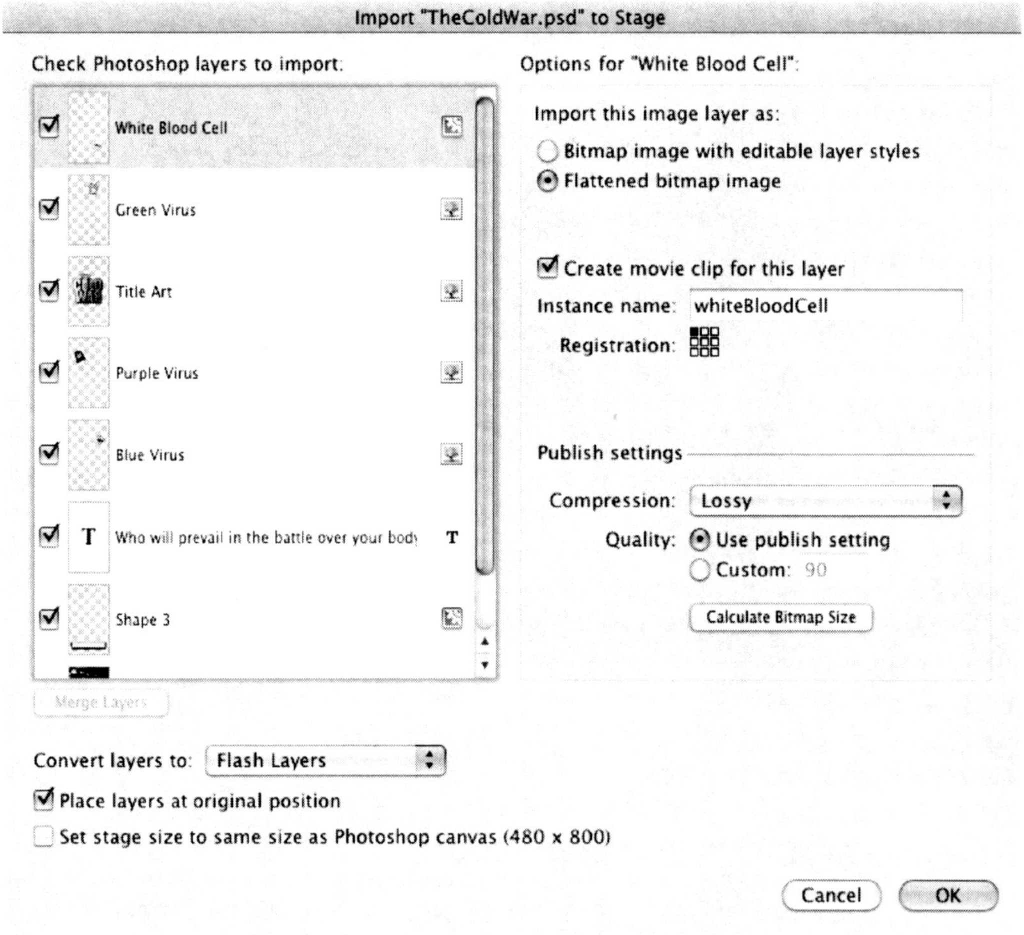

Figure 9–9. *The original Photoshop file, imported into Flash Professional; each layer can be imported differently, maintaining text, shape layers, and even layer effects.*

Although importing a Photoshop file is extremely easy and helpful, you do have to watch out for a couple of things. Be aware of the larger file size when importing many layers, and consider consolidating them. For instance, if you have multiple graphics on different layers that make up the background, consider merging those layers in Photoshop before it is imported. Also, consider drawing vector elements in Flash rather than importing them. This will give you more control when editing. If it helps, you can even import one graphic from Photoshop to serve as a guide while creating all parts as vector elements in Flash Professional.

If a Photoshop file is fairly complex, with multiple layers that make up the background, consider consolidating those layers into one background layer. The general rule is that if the graphic doesn't move, see if you can merge it with other graphics.

Photoshop to Flash Builder Workflow

Flash Builder doesn't import a Photoshop file the way Flash Professional does. Instead, separate images need to be exported from Photoshop. This is most effectively done by separating each element into its own Photoshop file and exporting the appropriate file type (Figure 9–10).

Figure 9–10. *Individual graphics in separate PSD files ready to be exported as a PNG, JPG, or GIF. Be sure to keep the original PSD file in case changes need to be made later.*

In Photoshop, the best way to export graphics is using the **Save for Web and Devices** option under the **File** menu. This gives you the ability to select the format you want to export as well as see its quality (Figure 9–11). In Flash Builder, you can then import the appropriate file type, regardless of whether it's a JPG, GID, PNG, SWF, or FXG.

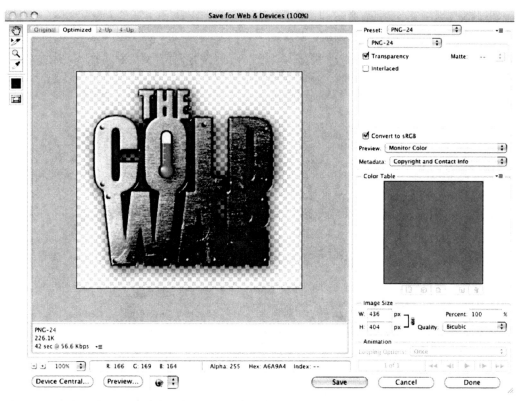

Figure 9–11. *Exporting a graphic from Photoshop using File ➤ Save for Web and Devices*

Graphic File Formats

There are basically four different file types you can use in Flash apps. The one you choose depends on the content of the graphic.

PNG-24 (Portable Network Graphics, 24-Bit Depth)

PNG-24 is probably one of the most popular graphic file types for rich graphics because it allows for varying levels of transparency and 24-bit color. There is also a PNG-8, which doesn't allow for transparency, but the file size is even smaller since the color depth is 8-bit (256 colors).

GIF (Graphics Interchange Format)

GIF is an 8-bit file format allowing for as many as 256 colors, which keeps the file size small. Because of the limited number of colors, GIFs are suitable for sharp-edged line art and flat colors, such as logos. Conversely, the format is not used for photography or images with gradients. GIFs can be used to store low-color sprite data for games. GIFs can be used for small animations as well, since they can contain multiple frames. GIF files can also have transparency, but not varying levels of transparency like a PNG-24 file. Every pixel in a GIF is either opaque or transparent.

JPEG (Joint Photographic Experts Group)

JPG files are commonly used for photographic images. This format has lossy compression, which means images can be compressed, leading to smaller file size, but this may cause some loss of image quality. Compressing images to JPG is a fine balance of maintaining image quality while keeping the file size small.

FXG (Flash XML Graphics)

The XML-based graphics interchange format for the Adobe Flash Platform enables designers to deliver more editable, workable content to developers for web, interactive, and RIA projects. FXG is used as a graphics interchange format for cross-application file support. It is XML-based and can contain images, text, and vector data. Flash Professional, Fireworks, and Illustrator can all create FXG files. These files can then be used in Flash Professional or Flash Builder (see Figure 9–12).

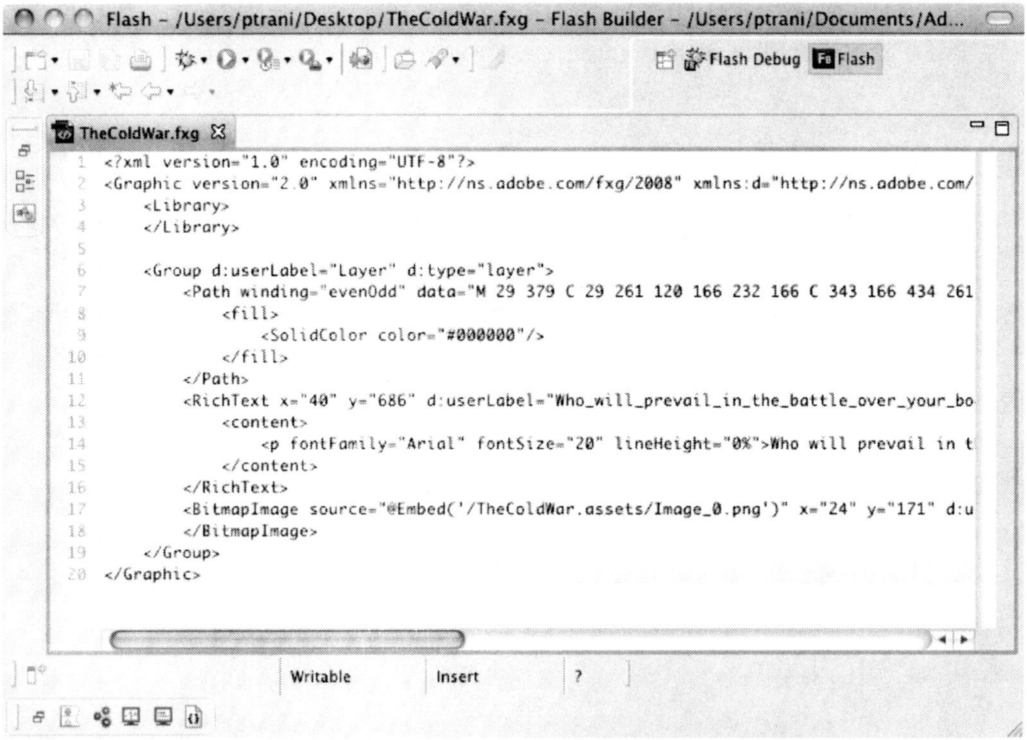

Figure 9–12. *An FXG file open in Flash Builder that contains vector, text, and bitmap data*

All these file formats can be created from most image editing programs. The program used depends largely on what the designer is most comfortable with, but if we take a more objective look, you'll notice that each program has its own particular strengths when it comes to mobile Flash development. The FXG format, for instance, is flexible, exposing the various text and vector graphic elements to the developer in Flash Builder. The PNG-24 file format is great when the designer needs pixel-perfect graphics with varying levels of transparency. The JPG format is great if it's a photo with a variety of colors and shades and when transparency isn't needed. Lastly, GIF is great for really flat graphics, like logos.

Adobe Illustrator

Adobe Illustrator helps designers create vector artwork for virtually any project. Illustrator has sophisticated drawing tools, natural brushes, and a host of time-savers built in when it comes to vector image editing. Illustrator CS5 allows users to create and align vector objects precisely on the file's pixel grid for clean, sharp raster graphics. Users can also take advantage of raster effects, such as drop shadows, blurs, and textures, and maintain their appearance across media, since the imagery is resolution-independent. This makes Illustrator a great place to start creating graphics regardless of the output.

> **TIP:** For more information, see `www.adobe.com/products/illustrator.html`

Illustrator to Flash Professional Workflow

With Illustrator you can create mobile designs and convert the individual graphics to movie clip symbols. Each instance of a symbol can have an instance name, just like in Flash. The movie clip symbol instances can be copied and pasted into Flash Professional. Flash maintains the movie clips and even the instance names (see Figure 9–13).

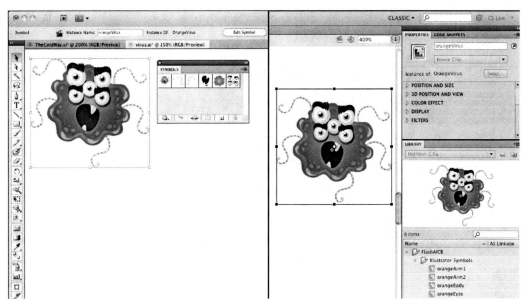

Figure 9–13. *In Illustrator (left), you can create movie clip symbols that can be copied and pasted directly into Flash Professional (right). Symbols and instance names are maintained.*

Adobe Fireworks

Adobe Fireworks CS5 software provides the tools you need to create highly optimized graphics for the Web or virtually any device. Fireworks allows you to create, import, and edit both vector and bitmap images.

Fireworks to Flash Builder Workflow

Once graphics are created in Fireworks (see Figure 9–14), they can be exported in most popular graphic formats, including FXG and MXML, specifically for Flash Builder. Exporting in the XML-based FXG format helps ensure rich application designs are converted precisely for Adobe Flash Builder. Both FXG and MXML are XML-based formats that can contain vector graphics and text that can be opened and edited in Flash Builder (see Figure 9–15). Bitmap-based images are referenced externally.

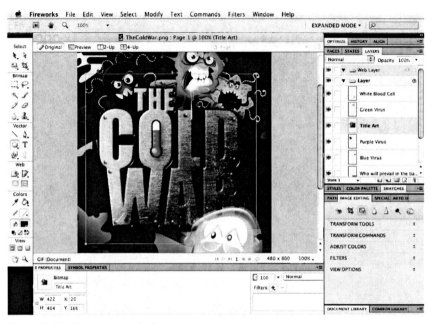

Figure 9–14. *Screen design in Fireworks*

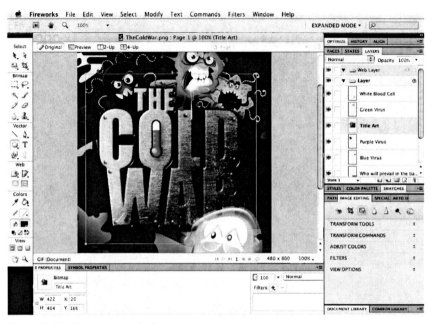

Figure 9–15. *FXG- and MXML-created files open in Flash Builder; note the reference to text on line 12 as well as the text label properties on lines 5–7. Bitmap images are external from the file.*

TIP: For more information, see www.adobe.com/products/fireworks.html

The Developer's Role

From a technical perspective, the developer is expected to be able to translate designs and technical specifications at the most basic level into an actual functioning application. Good developers differ from their more average colleagues in many ways. Some of the important ones are as follows:

- *Developing understanding*: Nearly anyone can blindly follow the instructions laid out for them, but good developers make it a point to understand what they're doing so that they can identify potential issues and opportunities for improvement at every turn.

- *Mastery of structures and application architecture*: In software development, there isn't any one "right" way to do things since the same problem can often be solved dozens of ways. However, there are usually some ways that are "more right" than others. Mastering well-known data structures and application architectures means that the problem is solved in the most straightforward manner and the application is architected in the most flexible and efficient way possible.

- *Specialization*: Specialization demonstrates the will to keep learning and to grow, which helps to differentiate a developer from the pack. A special mastery of mobile development techniques makes the developer a valuable employee and resource to any company.

The Developer's Toolbox

Developers have a limited toolbox. They are expected to know the development environment (including compiler and debugger) for the language or languages they've chosen, as well as a handful of common tools that every member of a development team needs to use. These tools are typically integrated into one platform that functions as both a compiler and debugger. This is typically the same tool that was used to learn the language, so learning a development environment isn't typically a big challenge. The following development environments are commonly used for mobile Flash development.

Adobe Flash Professional

Adobe Flash Professional CS5.5 is the leading authoring environment for producing expressive interactive content and is the one tool that both designers and developers share. ActionScript is the coding language that is used and can be written inside the binary FLA file format, which can contain graphics, sounds, fonts, animations, and sometimes video that the designer has added. Code snippets were introduced in Flash Professional CS5 and can be used to speed development. ActionScript can also be written in external ActionScript files (.as), which is routinely done for the Document class and other object classes. Often it depends on the project type to determine where

ActionScript will be written. For smaller projects, writing ActionScript in the FLA is fine. For larger projects, many developers prefer external ActionScript files to help organize their code.

Flash Professional CS5.5 includes on-stage symbol rasterization to improve rendering performance of complex vector objects on mobile devices. Also, more than 20 new code snippets have been added, including ones for creating mobile and AIR applications. Source-level debugging is possible on Adobe AIR–enabled devices that are connected with a USB cable, running content directly on the device.

> **TIP:** For more information, see `www.adobe.com/products/flash.html`

Flash Professional Workflow

The designer would often either create graphics in Flash Professional or import them from other sources. The FLA could be used as a prototype in meetings to show the client how the final application will work, and/or it can be used as the final source. The net result is as follows (see Figure 9–16).

- The client requests an application.
- The designer creates an initial design.
- The designer gives the developer an FLA or graphic files.
- The developer programs the design and incorporates graphics from the designer's FLA, or imports the designer's graphic files.
- The client requests changes.
- If the design changes, the designer sends new graphic files.
- The developer updates the application with new graphics/animations.

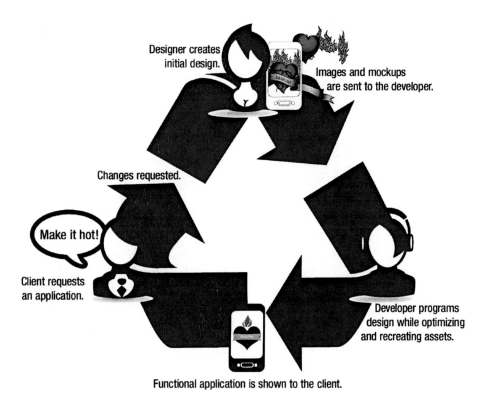

Designer creates initial design.

Images and mockups are sent to the developer.

Changes requested.

Make it hot!

Client requests an application.

Developer programs design while optimizing and recreating assets.

Functional application is shown to the client.

Figure 9–16. *A typical client, designer, developer workflow*

Flash Builder 4.5

Adobe Flash Builder 4.5 (formerly Adobe Flex Builder) is an Eclipse-based development tool for rapidly building expressive mobile, web, and desktop applications using ActionScript and the open source Flex framework. Flash Builder 4.5 allows developers to build stand-alone Flex/ActionScript applications for one or more mobile platforms (Android, BlackBerry, or iOS). Design and code views support mobile development using mobile-ready components. Test mobile applications on the desktop using a mobile Adobe AIR runtime emulator, or test on locally connected mobile devices using a one-click process to package, deploy, and launch. Developers can deploy, package, and sign required resources as platform-specific installer files for upload to a mobile application distribution site or store.

Flash Builder Workflow

Flash Builder can import many popular graphic file formats (see Figure 9–17). The content should determine what type of file will be used. For photography, JPG can be used. If there is animation, an SWF file would be needed. The file format that probably has the most flexibility is FXG. It is an XML-based format that exposes a lot of the content, enabling the developer to edit further or enable dynamic changes if needed.

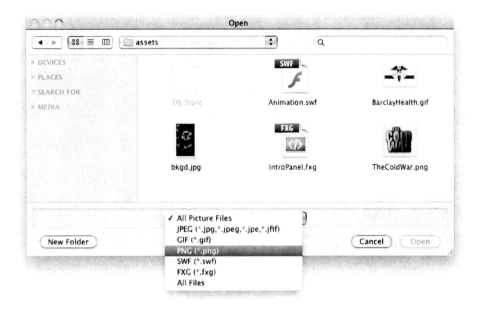

Figure 9–17. *Importing a graphic file into Flash Builder*

When using Flash Builder with the Flex framework, things are slightly different from the FLA workflow. First off, there is no FLA. Flex is just like traditional web development. All of your files are in a folder, and it's up to the developer to organize them and check all of them into source control (if one is being used). The code is also exposed and organized in appropriate folders, either as MXML (Flex framework) files or AS (ActionScript) files. As such, designers currently have no way to easily play in their own design "sandbox," like they could using their own FLA with Flash Professional. This has both pros and cons. The pros are that no designer can edit what a developer has done. The con is the designer cannot check out his or her design. It is up to the developer's skillset and preference to determine whether a Flash Builder or a Flash Professional workflow will be used.

Summary

A great workflow can really make the difference between a project succeeding and a project failing. You can have the best designers and developers on a project, but if they can't effectively work together and exchange ideas and assets, all could easily be lost. What the designer envisioned might not be what the developer executed, and what the project manager explained might not have been what was originally asked for in the first place. You can easily see where a project can break down in many places. A good workflow can alleviate many pain points in a process and can easily determine whether a project is a failure.

Chapter 10

Performance Tuning

There is an industry perception that Flash technology is slow. This has been reinforced by negative statements in the media, such as Apple CEO Steve Jobs's "Thoughts on Flash,"[1] where he stated that "Flash has not performed well on mobile devices."

While it is possible to write slow-performing applications in Flash or any other mobile technology, with the right tools and techniques you can also create fast, responsive applications. Just like native applications, Flash technology lets you take advantage of hardware-accelerated video playback and GPU-accelerated rendering. Proper use of these techniques can significantly speed up your application's performance and reduce the drain on the battery.

It is also very easy to fall into the trap of taking existing content optimized for desktop use and misusing it for mobile applications. Mobile devices have smaller screens, slower processors, less memory, and often slower or unreliable network connectivity. If you build your application with these constraints in mind and test often on your target mobile device, you will have much better results.

In this chapter, you will learn how the Flash runtime works in enough detail to understand the critical factors that constrain your application performance. We will then dig into several different performance-sensitive areas, including images, media, and text. In this process, we will go over new APIs in ActionScript and Flex that were specifically introduced to optimize mobile content that you should take advantage of.

There will always be poorly written Flash applications for the detractors to point out as examples of why Flash is not fit for mobile. However, by following the advice and guidelines in this chapter, you will ensure that your application is not one of them.

---

[1] Apple, "Thoughts on Flash," www.apple.com/hotnews/thoughts-on-flash/, April 2011

Mobile Performance Tuning Basics

Performance tuning mobile applications is not that much different than desktop applications, and breaks down into the same three fundamental considerations:

- Execution time
- Memory usage
- Application size

Execution time is CPU cycles spent by your application on processing prior to each frame being displayed. This could be application logic that you wrote to prepare or update the content, network I/O where your application is waiting on a response from an external server, or time spent in the underlying Flash runtime for validation or rendering of graphics.

Memory is the amount of device RAM that you are using while your application is running. This will typically grow over the duration of your application's execution until it hits a steady state where no additional objects are being created or the number of new objects roughly equals the number of freed objects. Continual growth of memory might indicate a memory leak where resources are not being freed or invisible/offscreen objects are not dereferenced.

Mobile devices add an additional level of complexity, with memory limitations both on the main system and on the GPU. Garbage collection also factors into this, because the memory in use will often be double what is actually needed as the collector copies over live objects to free unused memory.

Application size is an important consideration as well, because it affects both the initial download of your application from Android Market and its startup performance. Compiled ActionScript is actually quite compact, so static assets, such as images and video that you embed in your project, usually dominate the size of the application.

All of these factors are important in determining the overall performance of your application. However, what matters more than the absolute measures of execution time, memory, and application size is performance as perceived by your end users.

Perceived vs. Actual Performance

If you have written an application that is in widespread use, you have probably experienced user dissatisfaction with performance. For every user that complains about slow performance, there are tens or hundreds who give up or stop using the application instead of reporting an issue.

This correlation between slow application performance and low usage and user satisfaction has been substantiated by research done by John Hoxmeier and Chris

DiCesare at Colorado State University.[2] Through testing with a control group of 100 students, they proved the following hypotheses:

- Satisfaction decreases as response time increases

- Dissatisfaction leads to discontinued use

- Ease of use decreases as satisfaction decreases

Though they were testing with a web-based application, these findings are highly analogous to what you will experience with a rich client application built on the Flash platform. In this study, responses that took six seconds or less were perceived as being powerful and fast enough, while responses that took nine seconds or more were rated highly unfavorably.

> **NOTE:** In this study, they also disproved the hypothesis that expert users were more likely to tolerate slower response times, so don't assume that this research does not apply to your application.

So how fast does your application need to be in order to satisfy users? According to Ben Shneiderman,[3] you should stay within the following bounds:

- *Typing, cursor motion, mouse selection*: 50–150 milliseconds

- *Simple frequent tasks*: 1 second

- *Common tasks*: 2–4 seconds

- *Complex tasks*: 8–12 seconds

In addition, giving users feedback about long-running tasks with a progress bar or a spinning wait icon makes a huge difference to their willingness to wait. Beyond the 15-second mark, this is absolutely crucial to ensure the user will wait or come back after context switching.

So what does this mean for your Flash application?

Flash applications typically make use of animations and transitions to improve the user experience. If you plan to make use of these, they need to have relatively high frame rates in order to give the user the impression that the application is responding quickly. The goal for these should be around 24 frames per second or roughly 42 milliseconds, which is the minimum frame rate for users to perceive animation as being smooth. We talk more about how you can tune rendering performance to hit this in the next section.

---

[2]John A. Hoxmeier and Chris DiCesare, "System Response Time and User Satisfaction: An Experimental Study of Browser-Based Applications." *AMCIS 2000 Proceedings* (2000). Paper 347.

[3] Ben Shneiderman, "Response time and display rate in human performance with computers." *Computing Surveys* 16 (1984), p. 265–285.

For frequent tasks, such as showing details, submitting forms, or drag-and-drop, you should target under one second of response time. Flash applications have a distinct advantage over web applications in performing these operations since they can give the user immediate feedback while executing tasks in the background to retrieve or send data.

Common tasks, such as loading a new page or navigating via a tab or link can take longer, but should be accompanied by an indeterminate progress indicator to let the user know that activity is happening. In addition, judicious use of transition animations can make the loading seem to occur faster than it actually does.

Complex tasks, such as searching or populating a large list of data, can take longer, but should either be bounded to complete in less than twelve seconds or provide a progress bar that indicates how long the task will take to complete. Often it is possible to display intermediate results, such as partial search results or the first few pages of data. This will allow the user to continue using the application while additional data is loaded in the background, dramatically changing the perceived wait time.

Tuning Graphics Performance

At its core, the Flash runtime is a frame-based animation engine that processes retained mode graphics. Even if you are building applications using higher-level frameworks such as Flex, it is helpful to understand the rendering fundamentals of the Flash Player so that you can optimize your processing and content for optimal performance.

The heartbeat of the Flash engine is the frames-per-second setting, which controls how many frames get drawn onscreen each second. While performance bottlenecks may cause the number of frames per second to get reduced, there will never be more than this number of frames processed.

Many graphics toolkits use what is called immediate mode rendering to draw to screen. In immediate mode rendering, the application implements a callback where it has to redraw the contents of the screen each clock cycle. While this is conceptually simple and close to what the hardware implements, it leaves the job of saving state and providing continuity for animations up to the application developer.

Flash uses retained mode graphics where you instead build up a display list of all the objects that will be rendered on the screen, and let the framework take care of rendering and blitting the final graphics each clock cycle. This is better suited to animation and graphics applications, but can be more costly in resources based on the size and complexity of the display list.

The Elastic Racetrack

Ted Patrick came up with a very useful conceptual model for how the Flash Player handles rendering, which he called the Elastic Racetrack.[4] Shown in Figure 10–1, this model splits the work in each frame between code execution and rendering.

Flash Player Elastic Racetrack

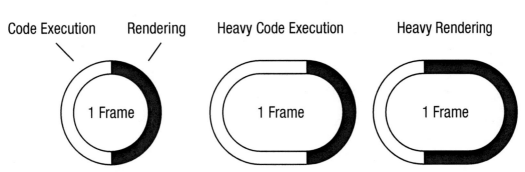

Figure 10–1. *The Flash Player Elastic Racetrack*

Code execution is the time spent running any ActionScript associated with that frame, including event handlers that get fired for user input, the `Timer`, and `ENTER_FRAME` events. Rendering includes processing done by the Flash Player to prepare the display list, composite images, and blit the graphics to the screen. To keep a steady frame rate, the total duration of these two activities cannot exceed the time slice allocated for that frame.

So how much time do you have to execute all your logic? Table 10–1 lists some common frame rates and how many milliseconds you have to process both code execution and rendering.

Table 10–1. *Processing Time for Different Frame Rates*

Target Frame Rate	Milliseconds per Frame
16fps	62.5ms
24fps	41.67ms
30fps	33.33ms
60fps	16.67ms

---

[4] Ted Patrick, "Flash Player Mental Model - The Elastic Racetrack," http://ted.onflash.org/2005/07/flash-player-mental-model-elastic.php, July 2005

The default frame rate for the Flash Player is 24fps; anything lower than this is noticeably choppy or laggy to the user. However, users can easily perceive frame rate differences up to 60fps, especially in tasks where there is a large amount of motion or scrolling. Shooting for frame rates above 60fps is usually not worthwhile, especially considering that most LCDs are capped at a refresh rate of 60hz and some devices have their max frame rate capped at 60.

When trying to diagnose a slow frame rate, the first step is to determine whether you are constrained by long code execution or slow rendering. Code execution is the easier of the two to profile since it is under your control, and if it approaches or exceeds the total frame length for your target frame rate, this is where you will want to start your optimization.

Reducing Code Execution Time

If your code execution time takes slightly longer than a single frame cycle, you may be able to get enough performance by optimizing your code. This will vary based on whether you are doing pure ActionScript or building on Flex. Also, if you are doing a complex or long-running operation, a different approach may be needed.

Some common ActionScript code performance best practices that are worth investigating include the following:

- *Prefer Vectors over Arrays*: The Vector datatype is highly optimized and much faster than doing basic list operations using Arrays. In some cases, such as large, sparse lists, Arrays will perform better, but this a rare exception.

- *Specify strong types wherever possible*: ActionScript is dynamically typed, allowing you to leave off explicit type information. However, when provided, type information can allow the compiler to generate more efficient code.

- *Keep constructors light*: The just-in-time (JIT) compiler does not optimize code in variable initializers or constructors, forcing the code to run in interpreted mode. In general, object construction is expensive and should be deferred until the elements become visible onscreen.

- *Use binding judiciously*: Binding introduces an extra level of overhead that makes sense for updating the UI, but should be avoided elsewhere.

- *Regex expressions are costly*: Use regex expressions sparingly and for validating data. If you need to search, `String.indexOf` is an order of magnitude faster.

If you are writing a Flex application, you will want to look into the following in addition:

▓ *Minimize nesting of groups and containers*: Measurement and layout of large object graphs can be very expensive. By keeping your containment as flat as possible, you will speed up your application. This is particularly important when building grid or list renderers that will be reused repeatedly.

▓ *Prefer groups over containers*: The new Spark graphics library was redesigned with performance in mind. As a result, groups are very lightweight in comparison with containers and should be used for layout instead.

If code execution is still the bottleneck after tuning your code, you may want to look into splitting up the workload over multiple frames. For example, if you are doing a hit detection algorithm, it may not be possible to check all the objects within a single frame. However, if you can group objects by region and process them incrementally, the work can be spread over multiple frames, increasing your application's rendering speed.

Speeding Up Rendering

When running on the CPU, Flash uses a highly optimized retained mode software renderer for drawing graphics to the screen. To render each frame, it goes through the list of all the objects in your DisplayList to figure out what is visible and needs to be drawn.

The software renderer scans line by line through the update region, calculating the value of each pixel by looking at the ordering, position, and opacity of each element in the DisplayList. Figure 10–2 contains a sample graphic created in Flash with several layers of text and graphics composited to create an image.

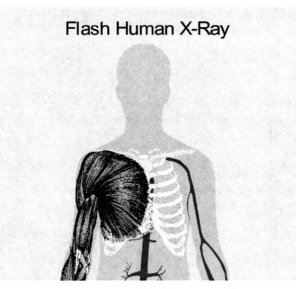

Figure 10–2. *Sample Flash graphic of internal organs[5]*

When placed in a Stage, this scene would have a DisplayList similar to that shown in Figure 10–3.

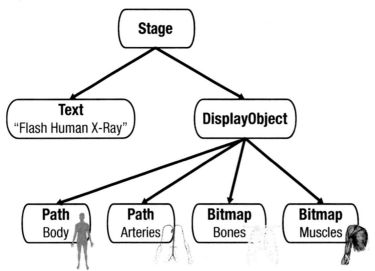

Figure 10–3. *DisplayList for the sample Flash organ graphic*

---

[5] Graphics based on public domain organ library: Mikael Häggström, "Internal Organs," http://commons.wikimedia.org/wiki/File:Internal_organs.png

During the rendering phase, Flash would use this DisplayList to determine how to draw each pixel on the screen. Since the graphics are opaque and the nesting is only three levels deep, this would render very quickly onscreen. As the complexity of your DisplayList goes up, you need to pay careful attention to the type of objects used in your application, and the effects applied to them.

Some of the ways that you can improve your application rendering performance include the following:

- *Keep your DisplayList small*: A well-pruned DisplayList will help the Flash renderer to save memory and execution time scanning the hierarchy. If objects are no longer in use, make sure to remove them for their parent. Otherwise you can hide and show individual elements by changing their visibility on the fly.

- *Use appropriate object types*: A Shape or Bitmap is the smallest object in the DisplayList, consuming only 236 bytes. Sprites are more heavyweight with features for interaction and event handling that takes 414 bytes. MovieClips are the most expensive objects in the scene at 440 bytes and additional overhead to support animation. To speed up rendering, you should choose the least complex object type that meets your needs.

- *Avoid alpha, masking, filters, and blends*: The Flash rendering engine cannot make certain optimizations if you use these features, which slows down the rendering performance. Rather than using alpha to hide and show objects, use the visibility flag instead. Masking is very expensive, and can often be substituted with simple cutouts or layering of the scene. Blend modes are particularly expensive and should be avoided whenever possible.

If you are developing a Flex-based application, you will want to pay careful attention to your use of UIComponents, GraphicElements, and FXG. Table 10–2 lists the trade-offs of using these different object types.

Table 10–2. *Usage and limitations for different Flex object types*

Object Type	Examples	Impact	Limitations
UIComponent	Button, Label, ...	Heavyweight	No limitations—allows full input, events, and platform features
GraphicsElement	Rect, Ellipse, ...	Lightweight	Cannot receive input and events, does not receive focus, no styles and properties
FXG	Rect, Ellipse, Path, ...	Ultralight	Graphics only, and must be defined in a separate file, and cannot be manipulated at runtime

UIComponents are the most complex object types in Flex and can significantly impact your rendering performance, especially if used extensively within a table or list renderer. GraphicsElements and FXG are both very lightweight components that the renderer can do significant optimization of. FXG has a slight performance edge since it is compiled down to graphics when the application is built, as opposed to GraphicsElements, which need to be processed at runtime.

A common mistake in mobile development is to develop exclusively in the desktop emulator and wait until the application is almost complete to start testing on device. If you wait until you have an extremely complex DisplayList, it will be very difficult to figure out which elements are contributing to the slowdown. On the other hand, if you are testing regularly as you build out the application, it will be very easy to diagnose which changes affect the performance the most.

Scene Bitmap Caching

Another technique that you can use to speed up rendering performance at the expense of memory is scene bitmap caching. Flash has built-in support via the cacheAsBitmap and cacheAsBitmapMatrix properties to easily capture and substitute static images in place of a completed scene hierarchy. This is particularly important on mobile devices where vector graphics operations are much slower and can significantly impact your performance.

cacheAsBitmap

cacheAsBitmap is a boolean property of DisplayObject, and by extension all the visual elements you use in Flash and Flex including Sprites and UIComponents have access to this variable. When set to true, each time the DisplayObject or one of its children changes, it will take a snapshot of the current state and save it to an offscreen buffer. Then for future rendering operations it will redraw off the saved offscreen buffer, which can be orders of magnitude faster for a complicated portion of the scene.

To enable cacheAsBitmap on a DisplayObject, you would do the following:

```
cacheAsBitmap = true;
```

Flex UIComponents have a cache policy that will automatically enable cacheAsBitmap based on a heuristic. You can override this behavior and force cacheAsBitmap to be enabled by doing the following:

```
cachePolicy = UIComponentCachePolicy.ON;
```

Turning on cacheAsBitmap is an important technique when you have complex graphics that change infrequently, such as a vector-rendered background. Even though the background is static, other elements that move around it can trigger an update when they overlap and obscure portions of it. Also, simple translations, such as scrolling the background, will cause an expensive redraw operation.

To figure out what portions of the screen are being repainted on each frame redraw by your application, you can enable showRedrawRegions with the following code:

```
flash.profiler.showRedrawRegions(true);
```

This will draw red rectangles around the screen areas that are being actively updated, and can be turned on and off programmatically. Figure 10–4 shows an example of a CheckBox control that lets you toggle redraw regions on and off. The control has recently been clicked, so it has a red rectangle drawn around it.

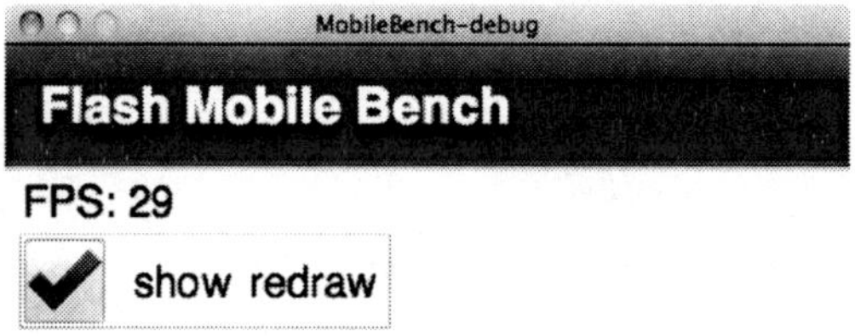

Figure 10–4. *Example of the redraw region debugging feature*

This option is available only in the debug player, so it will work in the AIR Debug Launcher while testing your application, but will not work when deployed in a runtime player, such as on a mobile device. Figure 10–4 also demonstrates a very simple frames-per-second monitor that can be used to benchmark your Flex application performance while under development. The full code for both of these is shown in the upcoming section on building the Flash Mobile Bench application.

While cacheAsBitmap is a very powerful tool for optimizing the redraw of your application, it is a double-edged sword if not used properly. A full-size screen buffer is kept and refreshed for each DisplayObject with cacheAsBitmap set to true, which can consume a lot of device memory or exhaust the limited GPU memory if you are running in graphics accelerated mode.

Also, if you have an object that updates frequently or has a transform applied, then cacheAsBitmap will simply slow down your application with unnecessary buffering operations. Fortunately, for the transformation case there is an improved version of cacheAsBitmap, called cacheAsBitmapMatrix, that you can take advantage of.

cacheAsBitmapMatrix

cacheAsBitmapMatrix is also a property on DisplayObject, and works together with cacheAsBitmap. For cacheAsBitmapMatrix to have any effect, cacheAsBitmap must also be turned on.

As mentioned previously, cacheAsBitmap does not work when a transformation, such as a rotation or a skew, is applied to the object. The reason for this is that applying such a transformation to a saved Bitmap produces scaling artifacts that would degrade the appearance of the final image. Therefore, if you would like to have caching applied to objects with a transform applied, Flash requires that you also specify a transformation matrix for the Bitmap that is stored in the cacheAsBitmapMatrix property.

For most purposes, setting cacheAsBitmapMatrix to the identify matrix will do what you expect. The offscreen Bitmap will be saved in the untransformed position, and any subsequent transforms on the DisplayObject will be applied to that Bitmap. The following code shows how to set cacheAsBitmapMatrix to the identify transform:

```
cacheAsBitmap = true;
cacheAsBitmapMatrix = new Matrix();
```

If you were doing the same on a Flex UIComponent utilizing a cachePolicy, you would do the following:

```
cachePolicy = UIComponentCachePolicy.ON;
cacheAsBitmapMatrix = new Matrix();
```

> **NOTE:** If you plan on setting cacheAsBitmapMatrix on multiple objects, you can reuse the same matrix to get rid of the cost of the matrix creation.

The downside to this is that the final image may show some slight aliasing, especially if the image is enlarged or straight lines are rotated. To account for this, you can specify a transform matrix that scales the image up prior to buffering it. Similarly, if you know that the final graphic will always be rendered at a reduced size, you can specify a transform matrix that scales down the buffered image to save on memory usage.

If you are using cacheAsBitmapMatrix to scale the image size down, you need to be careful that you never show the DisplayObject at the original size. Figure 10–5 shows an example of what happens if you set a cache matrix that reduces and rotates the image first, and then try to render the object at its original size.

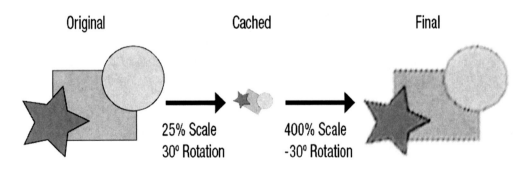

Figure 10–5. *Demonstration of the effect of* cacheAsBitmapMatrix *on image quality when misapplied*

Notice that the final image has quite a bit of aliasing from being scaled up. Even though you are displaying it with a one-to-one transform from the original, Flash will upscale the cached version, resulting in a low-fidelity image.

The optimal use of `cacheAsBitmapMatrix` is to set it slightly larger than the expected transform so you have enough pixel information to produce high-quality transformed images.

Flash Mobile Bench

Flash Mobile Bench is a simple application that lets you test the effect of different settings on the performance of your deployed mobile application.

The functionality that it lets you test includes the following:

- Addition of a large number of shapes to the display list

- Animation speed of a simple x/y translation

- Animation speed of a simple clockwise rotation

- Impact of `cacheAsBitmap` on performance

- Impact of `cacheAsBitmapMatrix` on performance

- Impact of the automatic Flex cache heuristic on performance

It also includes a simple FPS monitoring widget that you can reuse in your own applications.

In order to stress the capabilities of the device this application is running on, the first thing we had to do was increase the frame rate from the default of 24fps to something much more aggressive. Based on testing on a few devices, we found 240fps to be a ceiling limit that lots of platforms hit, and chose this as the target frame rate setting. Remember that this is a benchmark application testing theoretical performance, but in most cases you will not want to have the frame rate set this high, because you may be processing more frames than the hardware is able to display.

To change the frame rate, there is a property called `frameRate` on the `Application` class. Listing 10–1 demonstrates how you can set this in your Flex mobile application.

Listing 10–1. *Flash Mobile Bench* ViewNavigatorApplication (MobileBench.mxml)

```
<?xml version="1.0" encoding="utf-8"?>
<s:ViewNavigatorApplication xmlns:fx="http://ns.adobe.com/mxml/2009"
  xmlns:s="library://ns.adobe.com/flex/spark"
  firstView="views.MobileBenchHomeView"
  frameRate="240">
</s:ViewNavigatorApplication>
```

This follows the `ViewNavigatorApplication` pattern for building Flex mobile applications with a single `View` called `MobileBenchHomeView`. The layout for this `View` is done in MXML and shown in Listing 10–2.

Listing 10–2. *Flash Mobile Bench* View Code for Layout (MobileBenchHomeView.mxml)

```
<?xml version="1.0" encoding="utf-8"?>
<s:View xmlns:fx="http://ns.adobe.com/mxml/2009"
    xmlns:s="library://ns.adobe.com/flex/spark"
    title="Flash Mobile Bench" initialize="init()">
```

```
<fx:Script>
 <![CDATA[
   …
 ]]>
</fx:Script>
<s:VGroup top="10" left="10" right="10">
 <s:Label id="fps"/>
 <s:CheckBox id="redraw" label="show redraw"
            click="{flash.profiler.showRedrawRegions(redraw.selected)}"/>
 <s:HGroup verticalAlign="middle" gap="20">
   <s:Label text="Cache:"/>
   <s:VGroup>
     <s:RadioButton label="Off" click="cacheOff()"/>
     <s:RadioButton label="Auto" click="cacheAuto()"/>
   </s:VGroup>
   <s:VGroup>
     <s:RadioButton label="Bitmap" click="cacheAsBitmapX()"/>
     <s:RadioButton label="Matrix" click="cacheAsBitmapMatrixX()"/>
   </s:VGroup>
 </s:HGroup>
 <s:TileGroup id="tiles" width="100%">
   <s:Button label="Generate Rects" click="generateSquares()"/>
   <s:Button label="Generate Circles" click="generateCircles()"/>
   <s:Button label="Start Moving" click="moving = true"/>
   <s:Button label="Stop Moving" click="moving = false"/>
   <s:Button label="Start Rotating" click="rotating = true"/>
   <s:Button id="stop" label="Stop Rotating" click="rotating=false"/>
 </s:TileGroup>
</s:VGroup>
<s:Group id="bounds" left="20" top="{stop.y + tiles.y + stop.height + 20}">
 <s:Group id="shapeGroup" transformX="{tiles.width/2 - 10}"
          transformY="{(height - bounds.y)/2 - 10}"/>
</s:Group>
</s:View>
```

This creates the basic UI for the application, including a place to populate the FPS setting, radio buttons for selecting the cache policy, and buttons for adding GraphicsElements and starting and stopping the animations.

There is also an extra check box to show redraw regions. This control can be dropped into your own applications as-is, and can help you to minimize the size of the redraw region in order to optimize render performance. Remember that this feature works only in the AIR Debug Launcher, so you can't use it in the device runtime.

Other than the UI label, the code for the FPS monitor is fairly stand-alone. It consists of an event listener that is tied to the ENTER_FRAME event, and some bookkeeping variables to keep track of the average frame rate. The code for this is shown in Listing 10–3.

Listing 10–3. *ActionScript Imports, Initialization, and Code for the FPS Handler*

```
import flash.profiler.showRedrawRegions;
import flash.utils.getTimer;
import mx.core.UIComponentCachePolicy;
import mx.graphics.SolidColor;
import mx.graphics.SolidColorStroke;
import spark.components.Group;
import spark.primitives.Ellipse;
```

```
import spark.primitives.Rect;
import spark.primitives.supportClasses.FilledElement;

private function init():void {
  addEventListener(Event.ENTER_FRAME, calculateFPS);
  addEventListener(Event.ENTER_FRAME, animateShapes);
}

// FPS handler

private var lastTime:int = getTimer();
private var frameAvg:Number = 0;
private var lastFPSUpdate:int = getTimer();

private function calculateFPS(e:Event):void {
  var currentTime:int = getTimer();
  var duration:int = currentTime - lastTime;
  var weight:Number = (duration + 10) / 1000;
  frameAvg = frameAvg * (1 - weight) + duration * weight;
  lastTime = currentTime;
  if (currentTime - lastFPSUpdate > 200) {
    fps.text = "FPS: " + Math.round(1000.0 / frameAvg).toString();
    lastFPSUpdate = currentTime;
  }
}
```

The algorithm used for calculating the frame rate is tuned for the following characteristics:

- *Refresh no more than five times per second*: Refreshing the counter too frequently makes it difficult to read and can impact your performance negatively. This condition is enforced by the lastFPSUpdate comparison against a 200ms threshold.

- *Weight slow frames higher*: As the frame rate decreases, the number of events goes down. This requires each frame to be weighted higher to avoid lag in the reading. The weight variable accomplishes this up to the threshold of 1000ms (1 second).

- *Give a minimum weight to fast frames*: As the frame rate goes up, the weighting approaches zero. Therefore, a minimum weight of 1% is allocated to prevent the reading from lagging at the other extreme.

Something else to note in this algorithm is the use of integer and floating point arithmetic. The former is faster and preferred where possible (such as calculating the duration), while the latter is more accurate, and required for keeping a precise average (frameAvg).

The next critical section of code is the population of GraphicsElements into the scene. The code in Listing 10–4 accomplishes this.

Listing 10–4. *ActionScript Code for Creation of* `GraphicsElements`

```
[Bindable]
private var shapes:Vector.<FilledElement> = new Vector.<FilledElement>();

private function populateRandomShape(shape:FilledElement):void {
  shape.width = shape.height = Math.random() * 20 + 20;
  shape.x = Math.random() * (tiles.width - 20) - shape.width/2;
  shape.y = Math.random() * (height - bounds.y - 20) - shape.width/2;
  shape.fill = new SolidColor(0xFFFFFF * Math.random());
  shape.stroke = new SolidColorStroke(0xFFFFFF * Math.random());
  shapes.push(shape);
  shapeGroup.addElement(shape);
}

private function generateCircles():void {
  for (var i:int=0; i<100; i++) {
    populateRandomShape(new Ellipse());
  }
}

private function generateSquares():void {
  for (var i:int=0; i<100; i++) {
    populateRandomShape(new Rect());
  }
}
```

All the attributes of the shapes are randomized, from the color of the fill and stroke to the size and location. The overlapping logic between the `Rect` and `Ellipse` creation is also abstracted out into a common function to maximize code reuse.

To animate the shapes, we use the code found in Listing 10–5.

Listing 10–5. *ActionScript Code for Animation of the* `Rect` *and* `Ellipse` *Shapes*

```
private var moving:Boolean;
private var rotating:Boolean;
private var directionCounter:int;

private function animateShapes(e:Event):void {
  if (moving) {
    shapeGroup.x += 1 - ((directionCounter + 200) / 400) % 2;
    shapeGroup.y += 1 - (directionCounter / 200) % 2;
    directionCounter++;
  }
  if (rotating) {
    shapeGroup.rotation += 1;
  }
}
```

Rather than using the Flex animation classes, we have chosen to do it via a simple `ENTER_FRAME` event listener. This gives you the flexibility to extend the harness to modify the variables on the shape classes that are not first-class properties.

Finally, the code to modify the `cacheAsBitmap` settings is shown in Listing 10–6.

Listing 10–6. *Application Descriptor Tag for Setting the renderMode (addition in bold)*

```
private var identityMatrix:Matrix = new Matrix();

private function cacheOff():void {
  shapeGroup.cachePolicy = UIComponentCachePolicy.OFF;
}

private function cacheAuto():void {
  shapeGroup.cachePolicy = UIComponentCachePolicy.AUTO;
}

private function cacheAsBitmapX():void {
  shapeGroup.cachePolicy = UIComponentCachePolicy.ON;
  shapeGroup.cacheAsBitmapMatrix = null;
}

private function cacheAsBitmapMatrixX():void {
  shapeGroup.cachePolicy = UIComponentCachePolicy.ON;
  shapeGroup.cacheAsBitmapMatrix = identityMatrix;
}
```

This code should look very familiar after reading the previous section. Even though we have only one instance of an object to apply the cacheAsBitmapMatrix on, we follow the best practice of reusing a common identity matrix to avoid extra memory and garbage collection overhead.

Upon running Flash Mobile Bench, you will immediately see the FPS counter max out on your given device. Click the buttons to add some shapes to the scene, set the cache to your desired setting, and see how your device performs. Figure 10–6 shows the Flash Mobile Bench application running on a Motorola Droid 2 with 300 circles rendered using cacheAsBitmapMatrix.

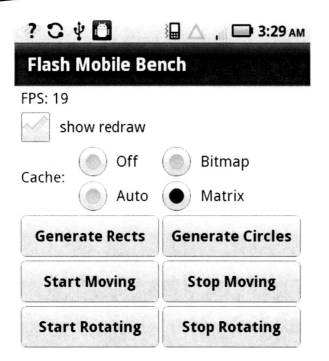

FPS: 19

show redraw

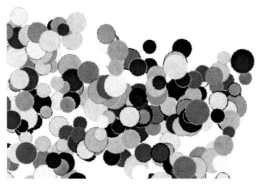

Figure 10–6. *Flash Mobile Bench running on a Motorola Droid 2*

How does the performance of your device compare?

GPU Rendering

One of the other techniques that is currently available only for mobile devices is offloading rendering to the graphics processing unit (GPU). While the GPU is a highly constrained chip, which cannot do everything a normal CPU is capable of, it excels at doing graphics and rendering calculations that take several orders of magnitude longer on the CPU. At the same time, the GPU produces less battery drain, allowing the mobile device to cycle down the CPU to conserve battery life.

The default setting for Flash mobile projects is to have a renderMode of "auto", which defaults to cpu at present. You can explicitly change this to gpu rendering to see if you get significant gains in performance for your application. To change the renderMode in Flash Professional, open the AIR for Android Settings dialog and choose GPU from the render mode drop-down, as shown in Figure 10–7.

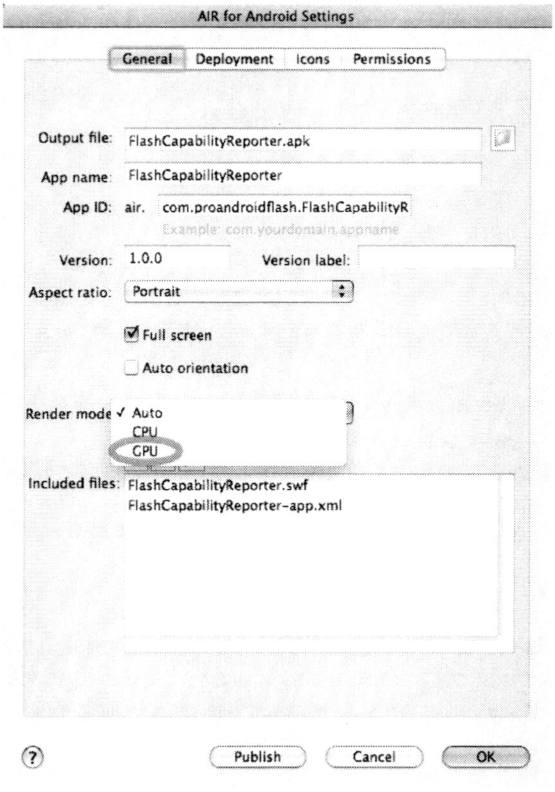

Figure 10–7. *GPU render mode setting in Flash Professional*

To change the renderMode in a Flash Builder project, you will need to edit the application descriptor file and add in an additional renderMode tag under initialWindow, as shown in Listing 10–7.

Listing 10–7. *Application Descriptor Tag for Setting the renderMode (Addition in Bold)*

```
<application>
  …
  <initialWindow>
    <renderMode>gpu</renderMode>
    …
  </initialWindow>
</application>
```

The results you get from gpu mode will vary greatly based on the application features you are using and the hardware you are running on. In some cases, you will find that your application actually runs slower in gpu mode than it does in cpu mode. Table 10–3 lists some empirical results from running Flash Mobile Bench on a Motorola Droid 2 with 100 circles and 100 squares on different cache and gpu modes.

Table 10–3. *Performance of CPU and GPU Compared on a Motorola Droid 2*

	CPU	GPU
Cache disabled	9fps	8fps
Cache as bitmap (auto)	9fps	4fps
Cache as bitmap matrix	18fps	17fps
Idle	220fps	150fps

As you can see from the results with this scenario on this particular device, the GPU provided no advantage, and was significantly slower in the case where cacheAsBitmap was enabled without a matrix set.

This underscores the importance of testing with different devices before you commit to design decisions in your application. In this particular example, the reduced performance was most likely due to write-back overhead of the GPU sending data back to the CPU. Most GPU devices are optimized for receiving data from the CPU in order to write it to the screen quickly. Sending data back in the other direction for processing is prohibitively expensive on some devices.

This is changing quickly, however, with new chipsets such as the Intel Integra features on the Motorola ATRIX and XOOM, which have optimized pipelines for bidirectional communication. Also, the Flash team is working on an optimized render pipeline that will reduce the need for write-backs to the CPU by doing more work on the processor. For more information about the performance improvements being done by the Flash team, see the "Future of Flash Performance" section later in this chapter.

Performant Item Renderers

Performance is best tuned in the context of a critical application area, which will be noticeable by users. For Flex mobile applications, organizing content by lists is extremely common, yet presents a significant performance challenge.

Since scrolling lists involve animation, it is very noticeable if the frame rate drops during interactions. At the same time, any performance issues in the item renderer code are magnified by the fact that the renderer is reused for each individual list cell.

To demonstrate these concepts, we will build out a simple example that shows a list of all the Adobe User Groups and navigates to the group web site when an item is clicked.

Listing 10–8 shows the basic View code for creating a Flex list and wiring up a click event handler that will open a browser page. We are also making use of the FPSComponent developed earlier to keep track of the speed of our application while developing.

Listing 10–8. *Adobe User Group Application* View *Class*

```
<?xml version="1.0" encoding="utf-8"?>
<s:View xmlns:fx="http://ns.adobe.com/mxml/2009"
    xmlns:s="library://ns.adobe.com/flex/spark"
    xmlns:renderers="renderers.*" xmlns:profile="profile.*"
    title="Adobe User Groups (Original)">
  <fx:Script>
    <![CDATA[
      import flash.net.navigateToURL;
      private function clickHandler(event:MouseEvent):void {
        navigateToURL(new URLRequest(event.currentTarget.selectedItem.url));
      }
    ]]>
  </fx:Script>
  <s:VGroup width="100%" height="100%">
    <profile:FPSDisplay/>
    <s:List width="100%" height="100%" dataProvider="{data}"
          click="clickHandler(event)">
      <s:itemRenderer>
        <fx:Component>
          <renderers:UserGroupRendererOriginal/>
        </fx:Component>
      </s:itemRenderer>
    </s:List>
  </s:VGroup>
</s:View>
```

> **TIP:** For mobile applications, always use the itemRenderer property rather than the itemRendererFunction property. The latter results in the creation of multiple instances of the item renderer and will negatively impact performance.

This class references a UserGroupRenderer that will display the list items. The creation of this renderer involves combining the following components:

- An image component for the user group logo

- Two text fields for displaying the user group name and description

- A horizontal line to separate different visual elements

Listing 10–9 shows a straightforward implementation of an ItemRenderer that meets these requirements.

Listing 10–9. *Unoptimized ItemRenderer Code*

```
<?xml version="1.0" encoding="utf-8"?>
<s:View xmlns:fx="http://ns.adobe.com/mxml/2009"
    xmlns:s="library://ns.adobe.com/flex/spark"
    xmlns:renderers="renderers.*" xmlns:profile="profile.*"
    title="Adobe User Groups (Original)">
  <fx:Script>
    <![CDATA[
      import flash.net.navigateToURL;
      private function clickHandler(event:MouseEvent):void {
        navigateToURL(new URLRequest(event.currentTarget.selectedItem.url));
      }
    ]]>
  </fx:Script>
  <s:VGroup width="100%" height="100%">
    <profile:FPSDisplay/>
    <s:List width="100%" height="100%" dataProvider="{data}"
          click="clickHandler(event)">
      <s:itemRenderer>
        <fx:Component>
          <renderers:UserGroupRendererOriginal/>
        </fx:Component>
      </s:itemRenderer>
    </s:List>
  </s:VGroup>
</s:View>
```

Upon running this example, we have a very functional scrolling list, as shown in Figure 10–8.

? ⟳ ⊞ 🤖 ⚡   📱 △ ⊪ ▭ 3:01 PM

Adobe User Groups (Original)

FPS: 220

Flash on Devices
San Francisco Community focusing on the Flash
Platform utlization on mobile, tablets, TV, and
large screens

SilvaFUG
Silicon Valley Flex User Group (SilvaFUG)

Adobe Mobile and Devices Usergroup UK
Creating Rich Content with Adobe Flash Lite for
Mobiles and other non desktop devices

D-Flex
Dallas Adobe Flex User Group

Seattle Flash User Group
To Motivate and Inspire all Flash Users

| Original | Image | Text | Cache | Built-in |

Figure 10–8. *Adobe User Group list using a custom* `ItemRenderer`

While the functionality and appearance are both fine, the performance of this
implementation is less than ideal. For normal scrolling, the frame rate drops to around
18fps, and when doing long throws of the list by swiping across the screen you get only
7fps. At these speeds, the scrolling is visually distracting and gives the impression that
the entire application is slow.

Flex Image Classes

Flash provides several different image classes that provide different functionality and have very different performance characteristics. Using the right image class for your application needs can make a huge difference in performance.

The available image classes in increasing order of performance are as follows:

- `mx.controls.Image`: This is the original Flex image component. It is now obsolete and should not be used for mobile applications.

- `spark.components.Image`: This replaced the previous image class and should be used anywhere styling, progress indicators, or other advanced features are required.

- `flash.display.Bitmap`: This is the core Flash image component. It has limited features, and is the highest performance way to display images onscreen.

For the original version of the `ItemRenderer`, we used the Flex Image class. While this was not a bad choice, we are also making no use of the advanced features of this class, so we can improve performance by using a `Bitmap` instead.

Also, a new feature that was added in Flex 4.5 is the `ContentCache` class. When set as the contentLoader on a `Bitmap`, it caches images that were fetched remotely, significantly speeding up the performance of scrolling where the same image is displayed multiple times.

Listing 10–10 shows an updated version of the item renderer class that incorporates these changes to improve performance.

Listing 10–10. `ItemRenderer` *Code with Optimizations for Images (Changes in Bold)*

```
<?xml version="1.0" encoding="utf-8"?>
<s:ItemRenderer xmlns:fx="http://ns.adobe.com/mxml/2009"
        xmlns:s="library://ns.adobe.com/flex/spark">
  <fx:Style>
    .descriptionStyle {
      fontSize: 15;
      color: #606060;
    }
  </fx:Style>
  <fx:Script>
    <![CDATA[
      import spark.core.ContentCache;
      static private const cache:ContentCache = new ContentCache();
    ]]>
  </fx:Script>
  <s:Line left="0" right="0" bottom="0">
    <s:stroke><s:SolidColorStroke color="gray"/></s:stroke>
  </s:Line>
  <s:HGroup left="15" right="15" top="12" bottom="12" gap="10" verticalAlign="middle">
    <s:BitmapImage source="{data.logo}" contentLoader="{cache}"/>
    <s:VGroup width="100%" gap="5">
```

```
        <s:RichText width="100%" text="{data.groupName}"/>
        <s:RichText width="100%" text="{data.description}" styleName="descriptionStyle"/>
      </s:VGroup>
    </s:HGroup>
</s:ItemRenderer>
```

With these additional improvements, we have increased the frame rate to 19fps for scrolling and 12fps for throws. The latter is over a 70% improvement for only a few lines of code and no loss of functionality.

Text Component Performance

One of the most notable performance differences that you will notice between desktop and mobile is the performance of text. When you are able to use text components and styles that map to device fonts, you will get optimal performance. However, using custom fonts or components that give you precise text control and anti-aliasing has a significant performance penalty.

With the release of Flash Player 10, Adobe introduced a new low-level text engine called the Flash Text Engine (FTE) and a framework built on top of it called the Text Layout Framework (TLF). TLF has significant advantages over the previous text engine (commonly referred to as Classic Text), such as the ability to support bidirectional text and print-quality typography. However, this comes with a significant performance penalty for mobile applications.

The optimal settings for Flash Player to get high-performance text display is to set the text engine to "Classic Text" and turn off anti-aliasing by choosing "Use device fonts" in the Text Properties pane, as shown in Figure 10–9.

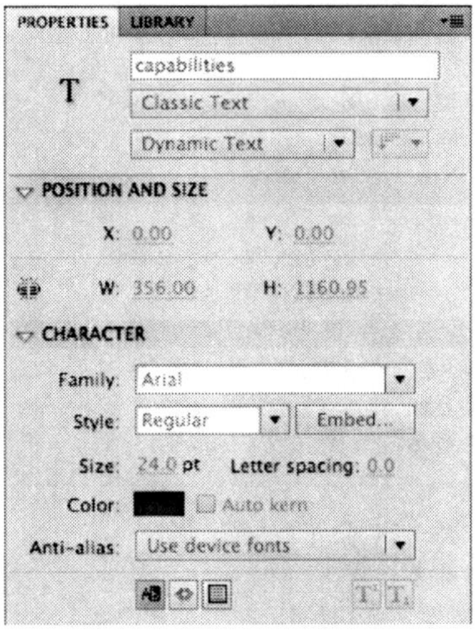

Figure 10–9. *Flash Professional optimal mobile text settings*

For Flex applications, you have a wide array of different Text components that make use of everything from Classic Text to TLF, and have varying performance characteristics as a result.

The available Text components are shown in Table 10–4, along with the text framework they are built on and mobile performance characteristics.

Table 10–4. *Text component comparison by framework, performance, and usage*

	Text Framework	Performance	Usage
MX Text	Classic Text	Poor	Not recommended for mobile use, replaced by Spark equivalent (see ahead)
MX Label	Classic Text	Poor	Not recommended for mobile use, replaced by Spark equivalent (see ahead)
RichEditableText	TLF	Poor	Use only where bidirectional text or other TLF features are required for an editable field
RichText	TLF	Poor	Use only where bidirectional text or other TLF features are required
Label	FTE	Good	Improved text performance since it avoids TLF; should be used wherever a single line of uneditable text is needed
TextInput	FTE	Best	Mobile optimized component that should be used wherever single-line text input is required
TextArea	FTE	Best	Mobile optimized component that should be used wherever multiline text input is required
StyleableTextField	FTE	Best	The underlying text component used in the TextInput and TextArea controls (accessible only from ActionScript); should be used anywhere performance is critical (such as item renderers)

For mobile applications, you will get the best performance by using the Label, TextInput, and TextArea components, and you should use them whenever possible. Since they don't support bidirectional text and other advanced features and styling, you may still have certain instances where you will need to use RichEditableText or RichText.

Since we do not require any advanced text features for the User Group List application, we can replace the use of RichText with Label. The updated code for this is shown in Listing 10–11.

Listing 10–11. *ItemRenderer Code with Optimizations for Text (Changes in Bold)*

```
<?xml version="1.0" encoding="utf-8"?>
<s:ItemRenderer xmlns:fx="http://ns.adobe.com/mxml/2009"
        xmlns:s="library://ns.adobe.com/flex/spark">
  <fx:Style>
    .descriptionStyle {
      fontSize: 15;
      color: #606060;
    }
  </fx:Style>
  <fx:Script>
    <![CDATA[
      import spark.core.ContentCache;
      static private const cache:ContentCache = new ContentCache();
    ]]>
  </fx:Script>
  <s:Line left="0" right="0" bottom="0">
    <s:stroke><s:SolidColorStroke color="gray"/></s:stroke>
  </s:Line>
  <s:HGroup left="15" right="15" top="12" bottom="12" gap="10" verticalAlign="middle">
    <s:BitmapImage source="{data.logo}" contentLoader="{cache}"/>
    <s:VGroup width="100%" gap="5">
      <s:Label width="100%" text="{data.groupName}"/>
      <s:Label width="100%" text="{data.description}" styleName="descriptionStyle"/>
    </s:VGroup>
  </s:HGroup>
</s:ItemRenderer>
```

After this change, the scrolling speed is 20fps and the throw speed is 18fps, which is a significant improvement. We could have achieved even higher speeds by using a StyleableTextField, which is exactly what the Flash team has done for their built-in components.

Built-In Item Renderers

In the past few sections, we have taken the performance of our custom item renderer from completely unacceptable speeds below 10fps, up to around 20fps on our test device. We could continue to optimize the renderer by doing some of the following additional changes:

- Use cacheAsBitmap to save recent cell images.
- Rewrite in ActionScript to take advantage of the StyleableTextField.
- Remove groups and use absolute layout.

However, there is already a component available that has these optimizations included and can be used right out of the box.

The Flex team provides a default implementation of a `LabelItemRenderer` and `IconItemRenderer` that you can use and extend. These classes already have quite a lot of functionality included in them that you can take advantage of, including support for styles, icons, and decorators. They are also highly tuned, taking advantage of all the best practices discussed throughout this chapter.

Listing 10–12 shows the code changes you would make to substitute the built-in `IconItemRenderer` for our custom item renderer.

Listing 10–12. *View Code Making Use of the Built-In* `IconItemRenderer`

```
<?xml version="1.0" encoding="utf-8"?>
<s:View xmlns:fx="http://ns.adobe.com/mxml/2009"
    xmlns:s="library://ns.adobe.com/flex/spark"
    xmlns:views="views.*"
    title="Adobe User Groups (Built-in)" xmlns:profile="profile.*">
  <fx:Script>
    <![CDATA[
      import flash.net.navigateToURL;
      private function clickHandler(event:MouseEvent):void {
        navigateToURL(new URLRequest(event.currentTarget.selectedItem.url));
      }
    ]]>
  </fx:Script>
  <fx:Style>
    .descriptionStyle {
      fontSize: 15;
      color: #606060;
    }
  </fx:Style>
  <s:VGroup width="100%" height="100%">
    <profile:FPSDisplay/>
    <s:List width="100%" height="100%" dataProvider="{data}"
        click="clickHandler(event)">
      <s:itemRenderer>
        <fx:Component>
          <s:IconItemRenderer labelField="groupName"
                    fontSize="25"
                    messageField="description"
                    messageStyleName="descriptionStyle"
                    iconField="logo"/>
        </fx:Component>
      </s:itemRenderer>
    </s:List>
  </s:VGroup>
</s:View>
```

The results of running this code are extremely close to our original item renderer, as shown in Figure 10–10. If you compare the images side by side, you will notice subtle differences in the text due to the use of the `StyleableTextComponent`, but there are no significant differences that would affect the usability of the application.

Figure 10–10. *Adobe User Group list using the built-in* `IconItemRenderer`

The resulting performance of using the built-in component is 24fps for scrolling and 27fps for throws on a Motorola Droid 2. This exceeds the default frame rate of Flex applications, and demonstrates that you can build featureful and performant applications in Flash with very little code.

Performance Monitoring APIs and Tools

The best-kept secret to building performant mobile applications is to test performance early and often. By identifying performance issues as you build out your application, you will be able to quickly identify performance-critical sections of code and tune them as you go along.

Having the right tools to get feedback on performance makes this job much easier. This section highlights several tools that are freely available, or you may already have on your system, that you can start taking advantage of today.

Hi-ReS! Stats

Getting real-time feedback on the frame rate, memory usage, and overall performance of your application is critical to ensure that you do not introduce regressions in performance during development. While you can roll your own performance measurements, if you are not careful, you could be skewing your results by slowing down your application with your own instrumentation.

Fortunately, an infamous web hacker, who goes by the name Mr. Doob, created an open source statistics widget that you can easily incorporate in your project. You can download the source from the following URL: `https://github.com/mrdoob/Hi-ReS-Stats`.

Mr. Doob's Hi-ReS! Stats gives you the following instrumentation:

- *Frames per second*: This shows the current FPS plus the target FPS set by in the player (higher is better).

- *Frame duration*: The inverse of frames per second, this lets you know how many milliseconds it is taking to render a frame (lower is better).

- *Memory usage*: The current amount of memory in use by the application (in megabytes)

- *Peak memory usage*: The highest memory usage threshold that this application has hit (also in megabytes)

To add Hi-ReS! Stats to an ActionScript project, you can use the following code:

```
import net.hires.debug.Stats;
addChild(newStats());
```

Since it is a pure ActionScript component, you need to do a little more work to add it to a Flex project, which can be done as follows:

```
import mx.core.IVisualElementContainer;
import mx.core.UIComponent;
import net.hires.debug.Stats;
private function addStats(parent:IVisualElementContainer):void {
  var comp:UIComponent = new UIComponent();
  parent.addElement(comp);
```

```
    comp.addChild(new Stats());
}
```

Then, to attach this to a View, simply invoke it from the `initialize` method with a self reference:

```
<s:View … initialize="addStats(this)"> … </View>
```

Below the statistics, a graph of these values is plotted, giving you an idea of how your application is trending. You can also increase or decrease the application frame rate by clicking the top or bottom of the readout. Figure 10–11 shows an enlarged version of the Hi-ReS! Stats UI.

Figure 10–11. *Enlarged screen capture of Hi-ReS! Stats*

PerformanceTest v2 Beta

Once you have identified that you have a performance issue, it can be very tricky to track down the root cause and make sure that once you have fixed it, the behavior does not regress with future changes.

Grant Skinner has taken a scientific approach to the problem with PerformanceTest, giving you pure ActionScript APIs to time methods, profile memory usage, and create reproducible performance test scenarios. Sample output from running the PerformanceTest tool is shown in Figure 10–12.

```
[MethodTest name='SampleError' error=1063 time=-1.0 min=-1 max=-1 deviation=0.000 memory=0]
[TestSuite name='Bitwise' tareTime=1 time=-1]
    [MethodTest name='math' time=577.0 min=531 max=674 deviation=0.248 memory=5303]
    [MethodTest name='bitwise' time=2.8 min=2 max=4 deviation=0.727 memory=0]
[TestSuite name='CollectionIteration' tareTime=2 time=-1]
    [MethodTest name='Array' time=9.5 min=9 max=10 deviation=0.105 memory=816]
    [MethodTest name='Vector' time=2.3 min=2 max=3 deviation=0.444 memory=0]
    [MethodTest name='linked list' time=0.8 min=0 max=1 deviation=0.000 memory=0]
    [MethodTest name='Dictionary' time=35.3 min=34 max=38 deviation=0.113 memory=789]
    [MethodTest name='Object w/uint keys' time=52.3 min=45 max=69 deviation=0.459 memory=749]
[MethodTest name='SampleTest' time=36.4 min=36 max=37 deviation=0.027 memory=760]
<TestCollection>
  <MethodTest name="SampleError" time="-1.0" min="-1" max="-1" deviation="0.000" memory="0"
retainedMemory="0">
    <error id="1063" name="ArgumentError" message="Error #1063: Argument count mismatch on
Math$/floor(). Expected 1, got 2."/>
  </MethodTest>
```

Figure 10–12. *Output from running the PerformanceTest tool*

Since the output is in XML, you can easily integrate this with other tools or reporting, including TDD frameworks for doing performance testing as you write code. For more information on PerformanceTest v2, see the following URL:

http://gskinner.com/blog/archives/2010/02/performancetest.html.

Flash Builder Profiler

For heap and memory analysis, one of the best available tools is the profiler built into Flash Professional. The Flash Builder profiler gives you a real-time graph of your memory usage, allows you to take heap snapshots and compare them against a baseline, and can capture method-level performance timings for your application.

While this does not currently work when running directly on a mobile device, it can be used to profile your mobile application when running in the AIR Debug Launcher. To launch your application in the profiler, select **Profile** from the **Run** menu. Upon execution, you will see a real-time view of your application, as shown in Figure 10–13.

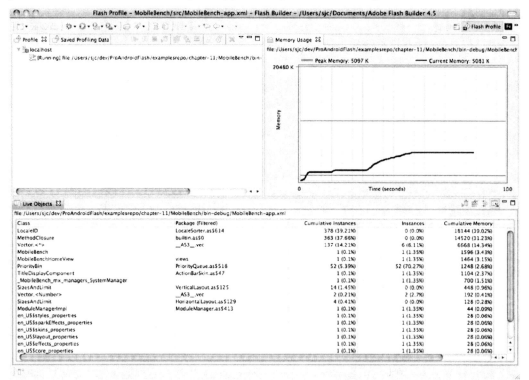

Figure 10–13. *Flash Builder profiler running against a Flash mobile project in debug mode*

The Future of Flash Performance

The Flash runtime team at Adobe is continually looking for new ways to improve the performance of Flash applications on the desktop and mobile. This includes performance enhancements in the Flash and AIR runtimes that are transparent to your application as well as new APIs and features that will let you do things more efficiently from within your application.

> **CAUTION:** All of the improvements and changes in this section have been proposed for the Flash roadmap, but are not committed features. The final implementation may vary significantly from what is discussed.

Faster Garbage Collection

As the size of your application grows, garbage collection pauses take an increasingly large toll on the responsiveness of your application. While the amortized cost of garbage collection is very low given all the benefits it provides, the occasional hit caused by a full memory sweep can be devastating to the perceived performance of your application.

Since Flash Player 8, the Flash runtime has made use of a mark and sweep garbage collector. The way that mark and sweep garbage collectors work is that they pause the application before traversing from the root objects through all the active references, marking live objects as shown in Figure 10–14. Objects that are not marked in this phase are marked for deletion in the sweep phase of the algorithm. The final step is to de-allocate the freed memory, which is not guaranteed to happen immediately.

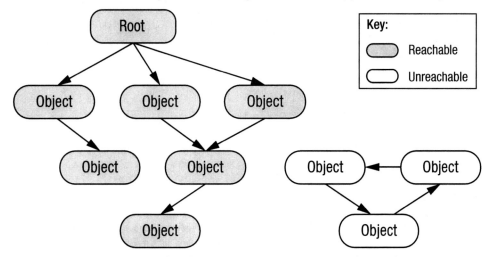

Figure 10–14. *Visual representation of the mark and sweep garbage collection algorithm*

The benefit of the mark and sweep algorithm is that there is very little bookkeeping involved, and it is reasonably fast to execute. However, as the size of the heap grows, so does the duration of the garbage collection pause. This can wreak havoc on animations or other timing-critical operations that will seemingly hang while the collection takes place.

The Flash runtime team is looking at several improvements to the garbage collection algorithms that would benefit performance:

- Incremental GC
- GC hint API
- Generational garbage collection

Incremental garbage collection would allow the garbage collector to split the mark and sweep work over several frames. In this scenario, the total cost of garbage collection will be slightly higher; however, the impact on any particular frame duration is minimized, allowing the application to sustain a high frame rate during collection.

The garbage collector is fairly naïve about when to trigger collections to take place, and invariably will choose the worst possible times to mark and sweep. A GC hint API would let the developer give hints to the garbage collector about performance-critical moments when a garbage collection would be undesirable. If memory is low enough, a garbage collection may still get triggered, but this will help prevent spurious garbage collections from slowing down the application at the wrong moment.

While it is not very well known, the converse is already possible. Flash already has a mechanism to manually trigger a garbage collection to occur. To trigger a garbage collection cycle to happen immediately, you need to call the `System.gc()` method twice, once to force a mark and a second time to force a sweep, as shown in Listing 10–13.

Listing 10–13. *Code to Force a Garbage Collection (Duplicate Call Intentional)*

```
flash.system.System.gc();
flash.system.System.gc();
```

> **TIP:** Previously this API was available only from AIR and worked only while running in debug mode, but it is now fully supported in all modes.

While mark and sweep collectors are fairly efficient and easy to implement, they are poorly suited for interactive applications and have a tendency to thrash on newly created objects. In practice, long-lived objects need collection fairly infrequently, while newly created objects are frequently discarded. Generational garbage collectors recognize this trend and group objects into different generations based on their age. This makes it possible to trigger a collection on younger generations more frequently, allowing for the reclamation of larger amounts of memory for less work.

Having an efficient generational garbage collector would make a huge difference in the usage pattern of ActionScript, getting rid of the need for excessive object pooling and caching strategies that are commonly used today to increase performance.

Faster ActionScript Performance

The Flash applications that you write and even the libraries in the platform itself are written using ActionScript, so incremental improvements in ActionScript performance can have a huge effect on real-world performance.

Some of the improvements that the Flash team is looking into that will benefit all applications include the following:

- Just-in-time (JIT) compiler optimizations

- Float numeric type

Flash makes use of what is known as a just-in-time (JIT) compiler to optimize Flash bytecodes on the fly. The JIT compiler translates performance-critical code sections into machine code that can be run directly on the device for higher performance. At the same time, it has information about the code execution path that it can take advantage of to perform optimizations that speed up the application.

Some of the new JIT optimizations that are planned include the following:

- *Type-based optimizations*: ActionScript is a dynamic language, and as such type information is optional. In places where the type is either explicitly specified or can be implicitly discovered by inspecting the call chain, more efficient machine code can be generated.

- *Numeric optimizations*: Currently in the Flash runtime all numeric operations, including overloaded operators like addition and multiplication, work on numeric objects rather than primitive numbers and integers. As a result, the code that gets generated includes extra instructions to check the type of number and fetch the value out of the object, which can be very expensive in tight loops. By inspecting the code to determine where primitive values can be substituted, the performance of these operations can be dramatically improved.

- *Nullability*: ActionScript is a null-safe language, which is very convenient for UI programming, but means that a lot of extra checks are generated to short-circuit calls that would otherwise dereference null pointers. This is even the case for variables that are initialized on creation and are never set to null. In these cases, the JIT has enough information to safely skip the null checks, reducing the amount of branching in the generated code.

The net result of these JIT optimizations is that with no changes to your application code, you will benefit from faster performance. In general, the more CPU-bound your application is, the greater the benefit you will receive.

In addition, the Flash team has proposed the addition of an explicit float numeric type and matching Vector.<float>. By definition, the Number type in Flash is a 64-bit precision value, and changing the semantics of this would break backward compatibility with existing applications. However, many mobile devices have optimized hardware for doing floating point arithmetic on 32-bit values. By giving programmers the choice of specifying the precision of numeric values, they can decide to trade off accuracy for performance where it makes sense.

Concurrency

Modern computers have multiple processors and cores that can be used to do operations in parallel for higher efficiency. This trend has also extended to mobile applications, where modern devices such as the Motorola ATRIX are able to pack dual-core processors in a very small package. This means that to make full use of the hardware your application needs to be able to execute code in parallel on multiple threads.

Even where multiple processors are not available, it is still a useful abstraction to think about code executing in parallel on multiple threads. This allows you to incrementally work on long-running tasks without affecting operations that need frequent updates, like the rendering pipeline.

Many built-in Flash operations are already multithreaded behind the scenes and can make effective use of multiple cores. This includes the networking code, which executes the I/O operations in the background, and Stage Video, which makes use of native code running in a different thread. By using these APIs, you are implicitly taking advantage of parallelism.

To allow you to take advantage of explicit threading, the Flash team is considering two different mechanisms for exposing this to the developer:

- *SWF delegation*: Code is compiled to two different SWF files that are independent. To spawn off a new thread, you would use the worker API from your main SWF file to create a new instance of the child SWF.

- *Entrypoint class*: Multithreaded code is separated into a different class using a code annotation to specify that it is a unique application entry point.

In both of these scenarios, a shared-nothing concurrency model is used. This means that you cannot access variables or change state between the code executing in different threads, except by using explicit message passing. The advantage of a shared-nothing model is that it prevents race conditions, deadlocks, and other threading issues that are very difficult to diagnose.

By having an explicit concurrency mechanism built into the platform, your application will benefit from more efficient use of multi-core processors and can avoid pauses in animation and rendering while CPU-intensive operations are being executed.

Threaded Render Pipeline

The Flash rendering pipeline is single-threaded today, which means that it cannot take advantage of multiple cores on newer mobile devices, such as the Motorola ATRIX. This is particularly problematic when rendering graphics and video, which end up being processed sequentially, as shown in Figure 10–15.

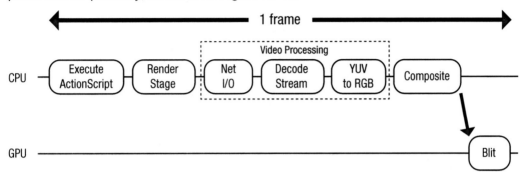

Figure 10–15. *Single-threaded render pipeline*

When the ActionScript code execution takes longer than expected, this can cause video frames to get dropped. Flash will compensate by skipping stage rendering and prioritizing video processing on the subsequent frame. The result is that your video and animation performance both suffer significant degradation while one of your processors remains idle.

The threaded render pipeline offloads video processing to a second CPU, allowing video to run smoothly regardless of delays in ActionScript execution or stage rendering. This makes optimal use of the available resources on a multi-core system, as shown in Figure 10–16.

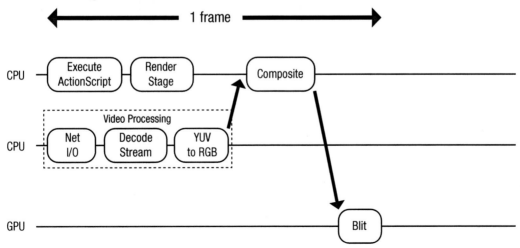

Figure 10–16. *Multithreaded render pipeline*

We can take this a step further by leveraging Stage Video to offload video decoding and compositing to the graphics processor, which gives you the optimized render pipeline shown in Figure 10–17.

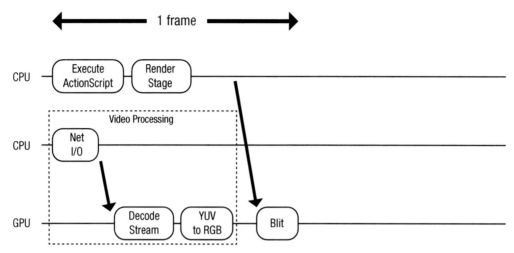

Figure 10–17. *Multithreaded render pipeline with Stage Video*

The net result is that you are able to do more processing in your ActionScript code without impacting either your frame rate or video playback.

Stage3D

One of the other items on the Flash roadmap that has received considerable attention is Stage3D. The code name for this technology is Molehill, and it is of particular interest to game developers who need a cross-platform 3D library that is very close to the underlying graphics hardware. Some of the applications that Stage3D makes possible are shown in Figure 10–18.

Figure 10–18. *Molehill demos from Away3D (top and bottom-right) and Adobe Max (bottom-left)*

These examples were built using a third-party 3D toolkit called Away3D on top of a pre-release version of Stage3D. Some other toolkits that you can expect to take advantage of Stage3D include Alternative3D, Flare3D, Sophie3D, Unity, Yogurt3D, and M2D.

Besides being useful to game developers, Stage3D also opens up the possibility of having a highly optimized 2D UI toolkit. As discussed earlier with the GPU acceleration support, graphics processors can do many operations much faster than the CPU can, while consuming less power and saving battery life. By completely offloading the UI toolkit to the graphics processor, the CPU can be dedicated to application and business logic, leaving the display list management, compositing, and rendering to the GPU via the existing 3D scenegraph.

Summary

As you have learned in this chapter, building high-performance Flex applications with advanced graphics, high frame rate, and smooth animation is attainable by following some mobile tuning best practices. Some of the specific areas in which you have gained performance tuning knowledge include the following:

- Speeding up graphics rendering
- Caching portions of the scenegraph as `Bitmaps`
- Building high-performance item renderers
- Optimal use of Text and Item components

In addition, you also learned about future improvements in the Flash runtime and graphics processing capabilities that you will be able to take advantage of in the future with no code changes.

All of these performance tuning techniques also apply to our final topic, which is extending the reach of your Flash and Flex applications to tablet, TV, and beyond.

Chapter 11

Beyond Mobile: Tablets and TV

Google and Adobe are working hard to extend the reach of the Android platform and the AIR runtime, respectively. Android has expanded onto tablets like the Motorola XOOM and the Samsung Galaxy Tab, and even into your living room with Google TV. This opens still more potential platforms for your AIR for Android applications! In addition, Research In Motion, known for its BlackBerry phones, has released its own tablet, called the PlayBook. The PlayBook is fully Flash-compatible and therefore provides yet another opportunity for your Flex and Flash applications to reach a new audience.

This chapter will look at some of the special considerations that are required to take your mobile application and move it to the larger screens of tablets and TVs.

Scaling the Screen

With a larger screen comes more freedom in the design of your interfaces. With more freedom comes more responsibility. Tablet users expect your application to make good use of the extra space that the larger screen provides. Figure 11–1 shows the MusicPlayer application from Chapter 8 running on a Motorola XOOM with a 10.1-inch screen. While the application is usable, the combination of the low pixel density and the large screen leads to small, stretched-out controls and a lot of wasted space. We can, and will, do better.

The motivation to do so comes from the fact that the Android tablet space is exploding since the introduction of Android 3.0, a version of Android specifically made for the larger screens of tablets and TVs. In addition to the existing Android 2.2 tablets—the Dell Streak and Samsung Galaxy Tab—there are now the Motorola XOOM and the Samsung Galaxy Tab 10.1, both of which run the latest versions of Honeycomb (the code name for Android 3.x). In addition, Toshiba, Sony, ASUS, and Amazon are all expected to release Honeycomb tablets in 2011.

Clearly this is a market segment that any application developer will want to take seriously. Applications that have been modified specifically to support these larger tablet screens will have a considerable advantage over those that haven't.

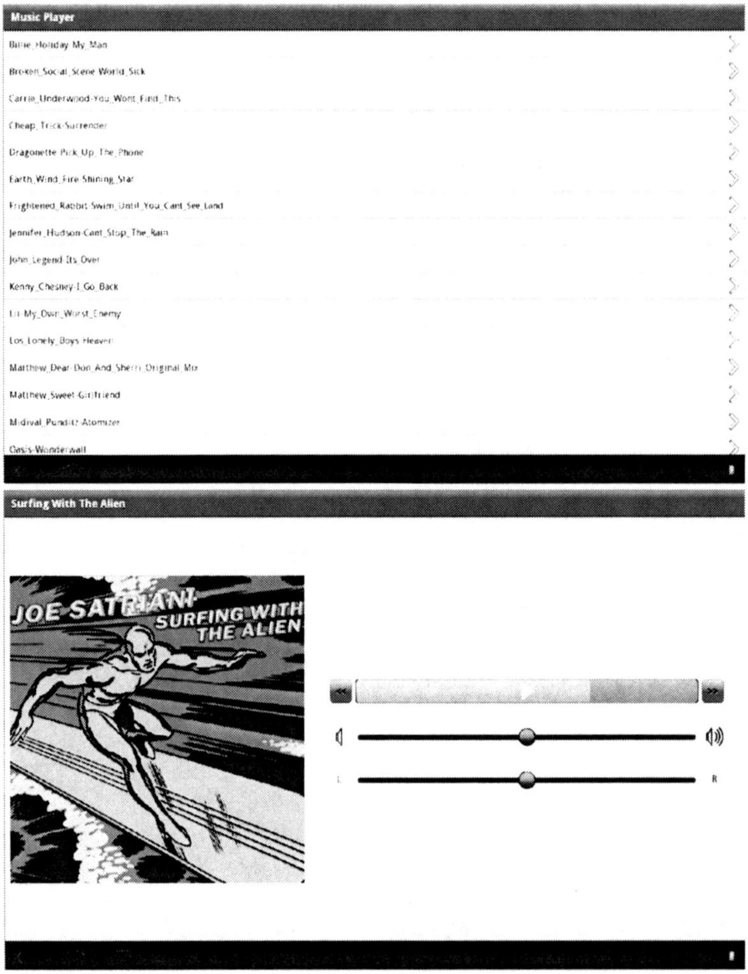

Figure 11-1. *The MusicPlayer application running on a Motorola XOOM tablet*

The first step is to familiarize you with the hardware. Most tablets have more powerful processors and more memory than the average smartphone. Table 11-1 shows a comparison of the displays of the popular Android tablets currently on the market. The table shows that most tablets are around 160 dpi, with larger, higher-resolution screens. With the combination of more powerful processors and large screens, you might be tempted to assume that your application will run faster than it does on a phone. This is not a good assumption to make, especially if your application is graphics-bound rather than CPU-bound. Unless they take advantage of hardware acceleration, graphically intense applications will often run slower on tablets due to the larger number of pixel calculations that must be done for the larger screens. As always, run performance tests and optimize as required.

Table 11–1. *Display Specifications of Some Popular Android Tablets*

Device	Screen Size	Resolution	Pixel Density
Motorola XOOM	10.1 inches	1280x800	160 dpi
Samsung Galaxy Tab 10.1	10.1 inches	1280x800	160 dpi
LG G-Slate	8.9 inches	1280x768	168 dpi
HTC Flyer[1]	7 inches	1024x600	170 dpi
Samsung Galaxy Tab 7	7 inches	1024x600	170 dpi

Whenever you are considering moving your application to a new platform, you should always take the time to study existing applications to determine what design patterns and conventions are in use. Figure 11–2 shows some existing Android tablet applications. From the upper left and proceeding clockwise, we see: Flixster, Newsr and TweetComb by Locomo Labs,[2] and Google's Movie Studio. What common patterns and conventions do you see?

Notice how, especially in landscape orientation (as shown), the applications all make use of the extra screen space to show multiple views? Unlike similar phone applications, Flixster and Newsr show their master and details view together on one screen rather than having to transition to a separate details view. TweetComb takes advantage of the extra space to show multiple columns of tweets, while Movie Studio gives you larger, easier-to-use controls. Also note the inclusion of more actions in the title bar (the `ActionBar` in a Flex application). We can make similar modifications to our MusicPlayer application and thereby transform it to a full-blown tablet interface, similar to those pictured in Figure 11–2.

When thinking about modifications that can be made to the tablet version of the MusicPlayer, one thing that comes immediately to mind is to use the extra space in the SongView to display the additional metadata that there simply wasn't room for on the phone version of the application. This sort of simple modification is an ideal candidate for the first technique that we will examine for extending your application to a new screen: state-based customization.

---

[1] Technically, the HTC Flyer runs Android 2.3 (code name Gingerbread) instead of Android 3.x, but your AIR for Android programs will run on Gingerbread as well.

[2] `http://locomolabs.com/`

Figure 11–2. *Popular applications running on an Android tablet*

State-Based Customization

We have already shown how to customize your application's UI layout using the
landscape and portrait View states. This technique takes that idea and expands upon
it. Instead of just portrait and landscape, you would define the four combinations of
state that you need to support each orientation for phones and tablets. Therefore your
hypothetical MXML code would look something like Listing 11–1.

Listing 11–1. *A First Cut at Adding Separate States for Phone and Tablet*

```
<s:states>
  <s:State name="portraitPhone"/>
  <s:State name="landscapePhone"/>
  <s:State name="portraitTablet"/>
  <s:State name="landscapeTablet"/>
</s:states>

<s:Group width="100%" height="100%">
  <s:layout.landscapePhone>
    <s:HorizontalLayout verticalAlign="middle" paddingLeft="10"/>
  </s:layout.landscapePhone>

  <s:layout.landscapeTablet>
    <s:HorizontalLayout verticalAlign="middle" paddingLeft="10"/>
  </s:layout.landscapeTablet>

  <s:layout.portraitPhone>
```

```
    <s:VerticalLayout horizontalAlign="center" paddingTop="10"/>
  </s:layout.portraitPhone>

  <s:layout.portraitTablet>
    <s:VerticalLayout horizontalAlign="center" paddingTop="10"/>
  </s:layout.portraitTablet>

  <s:Group width.portraitPhone="{height*0.4}" height.portraitPhone="{height*0.4}"
            width.landscapePhone="{width*0.4}"
            height.landscapePhone="{width*0.4}"
            width.portraitTablet="{height*0.3}"
            height.portraitTablet="{height*0.3}"
            width.landscapeTablet="{width*0.3}"
            height.landscapeTablet="{width*0.3}">
    <!-- And so on… -->
  </s:Group>
```

We now have four states in our View: a landscape and a portrait version for a phone and a tablet. These are each enumerated in the `<s:states>` section using the `<s:State>` element. Once the states are defined, you can use Flex's state-specific attribute declarations, such as `width.portraitPhone`, to customize the layouts, spacing, and even the visibility of any component in your View's user interface. As an example, the `Group` defined in our hypothetical code listing includes a customized `width` and `height` for each of our possible states.

As you can see, the major drawback of this technique is the proliferation of state-specific attribute declarations. You now need four of everything! Luckily there is a way to mitigate this problem.

Using State Groups

State groups are a way to assign multiple states—a group of states—to just one state declaration. Take the following state declaration:

```
<s:State name="portraitPhone" stateGroups="portrait,phone"/>
```

This says that when we set the `currentState` of our View to be `portraitPhone`, we will activate any attribute declarations we have that are modified by the `portraitPhone`, `portrait`, or `phone` states. This allows us to define MXML attributes using combinations of these states:

- `attributeName.portraitPhone`: This will apply only to phones in portrait orientation.

- `attributeName.portrait`: This will apply to phones or tablets in portrait orientation.

- `attributeName.phone`: This will apply to phones in landscape or portrait orientation.

This gives you much more flexibility in declaring your attributes and eliminates a lot of code duplication. Now that we no longer have the standard landscape and portrait states defined, Flex will no longer automatically set our View state. This is something we will take care of manually by overriding the getCurrentViewState method to return one of our new states based on the size and current orientation of the screen, as shown in Listing 11–2.

Listing 11–2. *Returning Customized View States*

```
override public function getCurrentViewState():String {
  var isPortrait:Boolean = height > width;
  var isTablet:Boolean = … // A calculation based on screen size or resolution.

  var newState:String = (isPortrait ? "portrait" : "landscape") +
          (isTablet ? "Tablet" : "Phone");

  return hasState(newState) ? newState : currentState;
}
```

The new state is determined by two Boolean variables. The isPortrait variable is determined easily by comparing the View's width and height. The isTablet variable is a little more complex. You can use the resolution of the screen by testing to see if the x or y dimension is larger than 960, which is the largest resolution currently in use on a phone. A more reliable method is to use the screen resolution and pixel density to determine the physical size of the screen. Then you can assume that anything over 5.5 inches is a tablet device. An example of this calculation is shown in the onViewActivate function in Listing 11–4.

Now we can get back to the idea of adding more information from the song's metadata to the UI. There are four things that would be nice to add to the tablet interface: the album's title, the artist's name, the year the album was published, and the genres to which the album belongs. We already have albumTitle and artistName defined as properties in the SongViewModel class. This means we just need to add the year and genres properties. Listing 11–3 shows the code to accomplish this.

Listing 11–3. *Adding year and genre Properties to the SongViewModel*

```
package viewmodels
{
  [Bindable]
  public class SongViewModel extends EventDispatcher {
    public var albumCover:BitmapData;
    public var albumTitle:String = "";
    public var songTitle:String = "";
    public var artistName:String = "";
    public var year:String = "";
    public var genres:String = "";

    // …

    /**
     * Called when the song's metadata has been loaded by the Metaphile
     * library.
     */
    private function onMetaData(metaData:IMetaData):void {
      var songFile:MusicEntry = songList[currentIndex];
      var id3:ID3Data = ID3Data(metaData);
```

```
      artistName = id3.performer ? id3.performer.text : "Unknown";
      albumTitle = id3.albumTitle ? id3.albumTitle.text : "Album by " +
          artistName;
      songTitle = id3.songTitle ? id3.songTitle.text : songFile.name;
      year = id3.year ? id3.year.text : "Unknown";
      genres = id3.genres ? id3.genres.text : "Unknown";

      if (id3.image) {
        var loader:Loader = new Loader();
        loader.contentLoaderInfo.addEventListener(Event.COMPLETE,
                                        onLoadComplete)
        loader.loadBytes(id3.image);
      } else {
        albumCover = null;
      }
    }

  // …
  }
}
```

The code highlighted in bold shows the changes that need to be made: declare new bindable variables to hold the year and genres strings and then load them from the ID3Data returned by the Metaphile library.

Our attention now turns to the question of how to add this information to our interface. Figure 11–3 shows two mockups for the new interface, one in landscape orientation and one in portrait orientation. The phone interface will stay exactly the same, but when we detect that we're running on a tablet, we will make the following changes:

- The song title in the ActionBar will be replaced with the album title.

- In portrait orientation, the four new pieces of metadata will be placed between the album cover and the playback controls.

- In landscape orientation, the new metadata will be placed on the left side of the screen with the album cover in the middle and the playback controls on the right side.

The new song information appears in different places depending on the orientation of the device, but that can be easily implemented using our custom state names and the includeIn property of the components.

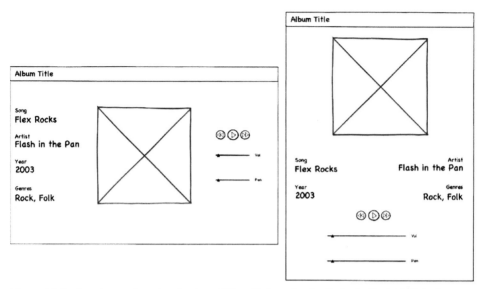

Figure 11–3. *A design mockup showing the additional information to display in the tablet interface*

The code in Listing 11–4 shows the first modifications that will need to be made to the original View code to achieve the new design shown in Figure 11–3.

Listing 11–4. *The Beginning of the Modified SongView MXML*

```
<?xml version="1.0" encoding="utf-8"?>
<s:View xmlns:fx="http://ns.adobe.com/mxml/2009"
        xmlns:s="library://ns.adobe.com/flex/spark"
        xmlns:assets="assets.*"
        xmlns:views="views.*"
        initialize="onInitialize()"
        viewActivate="onViewActivate()"
        viewDeactivate="onViewDeactivate()"
        resize="onResize()"
        title="{isTablet ? model.albumTitle : model.songTitle}">

    <s:states>
      <s:State name="portraitPhone" stateGroups="portrait,phone"/>
      <s:State name="landscapePhone" stateGroups="landscape,phone"/>
      <s:State name="portraitTablet" stateGroups="portrait,tablet"/>
      <s:State name="landscapeTablet" stateGroups="landscape,tablet"/>
    </s:states>

    <fx:Script>
      <![CDATA[
        import viewmodels.SongViewModel;

        [Bindable]
        private var isTablet:Boolean;

        [Bindable]
        private var model:SongViewModel;

        override public function getCurrentViewState():String {
```

```
            var isPortrait:Boolean = height > width;
            var newState:String = (isPortrait ? "portrait" : "landscape") +
                (isTablet ? "Tablet" : "Phone");

            return hasState(newState) ? newState : currentState;
        }

        private function onViewActivate():void {
            var w:Number = Capabilities.screenResolutionX/Capabilities.screenDPI;
            var h:Number = Capabilities.screenResolutionY/Capabilities.screenDPI;
            isTablet = Math.max(w, h) > 5.5;

            setCurrentState(getCurrentViewState());
        }

        private function onResize():void {
            setCurrentState(getCurrentViewState());
        }

        private function onInitialize():void { /* same as before */ }
        private function onViewDeactivate():void { /* same as before */ }
        private function onSongEnded(event:Event):void { /* same as before */ }
    ]]>
</fx:Script>
```

The View's title attribute uses a binding to the isTablet variable to determine whether to display the song title or the album title in the ActionBar. Remember that on the smaller phone screens we display the song title in the ActionBar's title area to avoid overcrowding the SongView interface. If a larger tablet screen is being used, it makes more sense to put the album title in the ActionBar and change the song information when moving from one song to the next.

Each of our states has been defined with its associated state groups as described previously in this section. The overridden getCurrentViewState function that appears at the top of the <fx:Script> section is responsible for determining which state the View should be in based upon screen size and orientation. If the View's height is greater than its width, then the device is marked as being in portrait orientation. Otherwise we know we are in landscape mode. Using this information along with the isTablet flag, the function builds and returns a string that describes the current state of the View.

The isTablet flag is set in the handler for the View's viewActivate event. When the View becomes active, the onViewActivate handler calculates the width and height of the device's screen in inches. If either of these dimensions is over 5.5 inches, then we can assume that the application is running on a tablet device. The function then calls our overridden getCurrentViewState method to get the initial state for the View and passes the result to the setCurrentState function.

We also attach a handler to the View's resize event to detect orientation changes. The onResize handler will set the current state of the View by calling our getCurrentViewState function and using the returned value to set the current View state.

> **NOTE:** Overriding the `getCurrentViewState` function to provide custom states does have the drawback that it makes Flash Builder's design view virtually useless.

It is time to put this state management code to use in our MXML declarations. Listing 11–5 shows the root `Group` container along with the group of labels that make up the song information section in the landscape orientation.

Listing 11–5. *The* `View`*'s Root Container* `Group` *and the Landscape Metadata Display*

```
<s:Group width="100%" height="100%">
  <s:layout.portrait>
    <s:VerticalLayout paddingTop="10" horizontalAlign="center"/>
  </s:layout.portrait>

  <s:layout.landscape>
    <s:HorizontalLayout verticalAlign="middle" paddingLeft="10"/>
  </s:layout.landscape>

  <s:VGroup width="30%" horizontalCenter="0" gap="20" paddingTop="40"
          paddingBottom="40" includeIn="landscapeTablet">
    <s:VGroup width="100%">
      <s:Label styleName="albumInfoLabel" text="Song"/>
      <s:Label styleName="albumInfo" text="{model.songTitle}"
            maxWidth="{width*.3}" maxDisplayedLines="1"/>
    </s:VGroup>
    <!-- repeated for artist, year, and genres -->
  </s:VGroup>

  <s:Group width.portrait="{height*0.4}" height.portrait="{height*0.4}"
          width.landscape="{width*0.4}" height.landscape="{width*0.4}">
    <s:BitmapImage width="100%" height="100%" source="{model.albumCover}"
              visible="{model.albumCover != null}"/>
    <assets:DefaultAlbum id="placeHolder" width="100%" height="100%"
                    visible="{!model.albumCover}" />
  </s:Group>
```

As in Chapter 8, we use a `VerticalLayout` for the root `Group` when in portrait mode and a `HorizontalLayout` in landscape mode. Thanks to the state groups that were declared previously, these layouts will be used for both the phone and tablet versions of the interface. The first child of the root `Group` container is the `VGroup` that contains the song information—recall from the mockup that it is on the far left of the screen—for the landscape version of the interface. Furthermore, this group should appear only on tablet displays. That is the reason for using the fully specified `landscapeTablet` state in its `includeIn` attribute. The next `Group` is the container for the album cover image. Since the previous `VGroup` is included only in the `landscapeTablet` state, the album cover `Group` will appear first in the layout on phones in any orientation and on tablets in portrait mode.

Listing 11–6 shows the portrait mode version of the song information display along with the rest of the controls.

Listing 11–6. *The Portrait Song Information Group and the Playback Controls*

```
<s:VGroup width="80%" horizontalCenter="0" gap="40" paddingTop="40"
          paddingBottom="40" includeIn="portraitTablet">
    <s:HGroup width="100%">
      <s:VGroup width="50%">
        <s:Label styleName="albumInfoLabel" text="Song"/>
        <s:Label styleName="albumInfo" text="{model.songTitle}"
                 maxWidth="{width*.4}" maxDisplayedLines="1"/>
      </s:VGroup>
      <s:VGroup horizontalAlign="right" width="50%">
        <s:Label styleName="albumInfoLabel" text="Artist"/>
        <s:Label styleName="albumInfo" text="{model.artistName}"
                 maxWidth="{width*.4}" maxDisplayedLines="1"/>
      </s:VGroup>
    </s:HGroup>
    <!-- repeated for year and genres -->
  </s:VGroup>

  <s:VGroup horizontalAlign="center" paddingTop="20" gap="40"
            width.portrait="100%" width.landscape="50%">
    <s:HGroup width="90%">
      <s:Button label="&lt;&lt;" height="40" click="model.previousSong()"/>
      <views:ProgressButton id="progressButton" width="100%" height="40"
                            click="model.onPlayPause()"
                            percentComplete="@{model.percentComplete}"
                            skinClass="views.ProgressButtonSkin"/>
      <s:Button label="&gt;&gt;" height="40" click="model.nextSong()"/>
    </s:HGroup>

    <s:HGroup verticalAlign="middle" width="90%">
      <assets:VolLow id="volLow" width="32" height="32"/>
      <s:HSlider width="100%" maximum="1.0" minimum="0.0" stepSize="0.01"
                 snapInterval="0.01" value="@{model.volume}" showDataTip="false"/>
      <assets:VolHigh id="volHigh" width="32" height="32"/>
    </s:HGroup>

    <s:HGroup verticalAlign="middle" width="90%" >
      <s:Label text="L" width="32" height="32" verticalAlign="middle"
               textAlign="center"/>
      <s:HSlider width="100%" maximum="1.0" minimum="-1.0" stepSize="0.01"
                 snapInterval="0.01" value="@{model.pan}" showDataTip="false"/>
      <s:Label text="R" width="32" height="32" verticalAlign="middle"
               textAlign="center"/>
    </s:HGroup>
  </s:VGroup>
  </s:Group>
</s:View>
```

In portrait mode, the song information VGroup is displayed between the album cover and the playback controls—hence its placement at this point in the MXML file with its includeIn attribute specifying the portraitTablet state.

As a finishing touch, we have added a little CSS styling in the ViewNavigatorApplication MXML file for the song information Label components. We now arrive at the application shown in Figure 11–4. Our application is now capable of adapting itself to run on the smallest and the largest of mobile devices. This is a simple example of the customization that is possible through the judicious use of states. The code for this application can be found in the MusicPlayerWithStates project located in the examples/chapter-11 directory of the book's sample code.

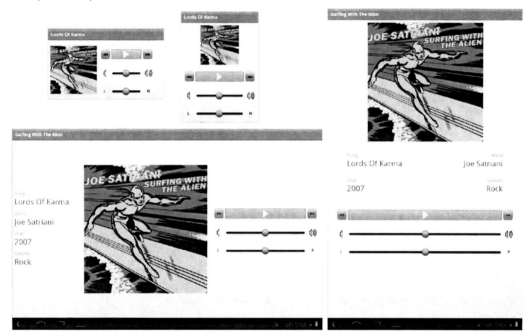

Figure 11–4. *The MusicPlayerWithStates application running on both small and large screens*

The main advantage of this state-based customization technique is that it allows you to keep all of your application code in one project. That makes it easier to maintain the code and simplifies the build process. The disadvantages become evident, however, when you consider what needs to be done when you want to start supporting other platforms. If you want to expand your market to include the iPhone, iPad, and PlayBook, then you will need to start performing UI tweaks to accommodate all of the different conventions in use for these platforms. You will suddenly be facing a combinatorial explosion of states. You will also run into problems if your interfaces for the different device classes or platforms start to diverge from each other too much. States will take you only so far before you have a long, difficult-to-read, and difficult-to-maintain MXML file.

If you find yourself in this position, you can turn to the second option for interface customization: project-based customization.

Project-Based Customization

The idea behind project-based customization is to put all of your application's shared code into a library project and then create separate projects that implement the customized user interface of each different platform or device class (phone vs. tablet, for example) that you target. Creating a separate project for each version of your application that is meant for a different class of device or a different platform affords you the ultimate flexibility in configuring your interface. This kind of setup is very common for projects that span two or more of web, desktop, phones, tablets, and TV. To avoid unnecessary code duplication, a library project is created to contain all shared source files and graphical assets.

Let's pretend that our designers have taken a look at some of the applications shown in Figure 11–2 and have decided to try a new look for our music player. They have come up with a new approach to the tablet interface in landscape mode that looks something like Figure 11–5. They want to move the song information to the right side of the screen, place the playback controls under the album cover, and add a list of songs to the left side of the screen. Selecting a song from the list should skip to that song. The list's selection highlight should always reflect the song that is currently playing. We'll also pretend that we've started hearing whispers from marketing about expanding to support other mobile platforms. Put all that together, and we will decide that it is time we opt for full customization ability by splitting our code base into separate projects with one common library project that the rest will share.

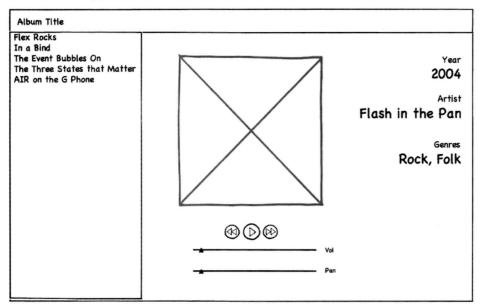

Figure 11–5. *A new interface prototype for MusicPlayer running on a tablet in landscape mode*

Creating the Library Project

The first thing to do is to create the shared library project. In Flash Builder 4.5 (or above), use the application menu and click **File ➤ New ➤ Flex Library Project**. Flash Builder will display the dialog box shown in Figure 11–6.

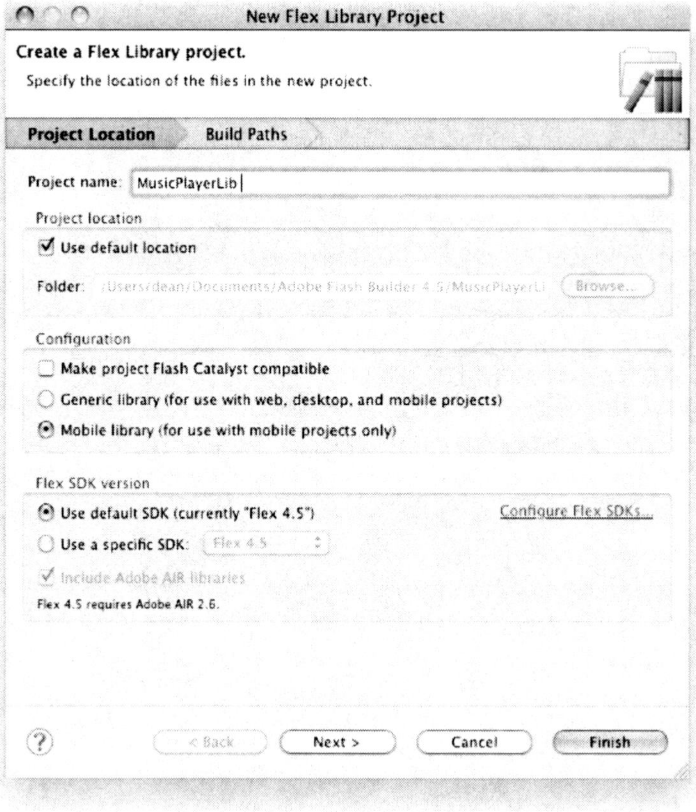

Figure 11–6. *Creating a new library project in Flash Builder 4.5*

You must specify a name for the library project (such as MusicPlayerLib) as we did in Figure 11–6. Since we are not concerned with supporting web and desktop in this project (yet!), we also selected the "Mobile library" option in the Configuration section.

We know our presentation models will be placed into this project. We also know that one of them depends on the Metaphile library. Therefore we will have to add the Metaphile.swc file to this project in order for it to compile. We created a libs directory and placed Metaphile.swc inside. We then added the libs directory to the build path by right-clicking the project and selecting Properties. The project's Properties dialog will be displayed, and it will look something like the one shown in Figure 11–7. Click Flex Library Build Path, and click the "Add SWC Folder..." button. Type the directory name "libs" into the text field of the dialog that comes up, and click OK. Your dialog should now look like the one in Figure 11–7, which shows that the Metaphile.swc file has been added to your build path.

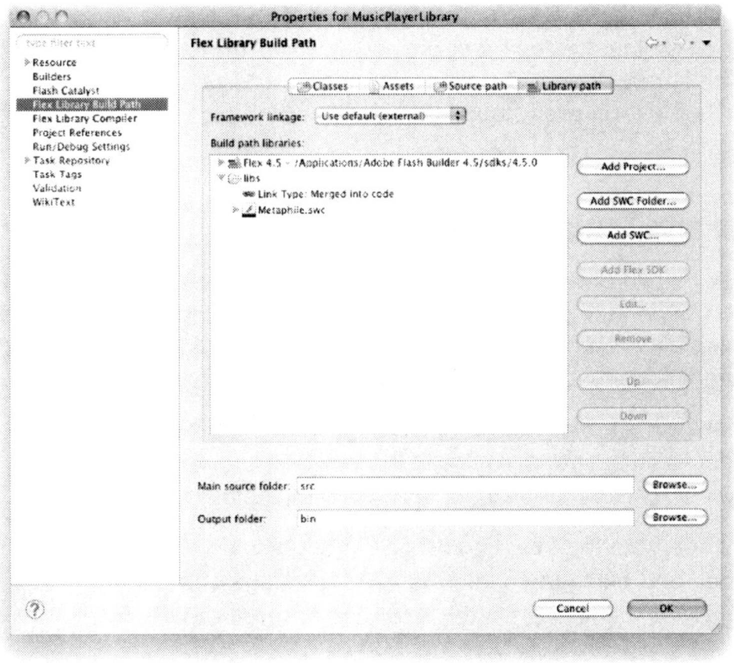

Figure 11–7. *Adding the* Metaphile.swc *file to our library project*

The final step in creating our library project is to replicate the necessary package structure from the original MusicPlayer application and copy the source code and graphical assets into the correct locations. Table 11–2 shows the packages that have been added and the files that go inside each package.

Table 11–2. *The Packages and Files That Go into the Shared Library Project*

Package	Files
assets	Play.fxg
	Pause.fxg
components	ProgressButton.as
	ProgressButtonSkin.mxml
models	MusicEntry.as
services	LocalMusicService.as
	MusicService.as
viewmodels	SongListViewModel.as
	SongViewModel.as

Notice that we have taken the custom ProgressButton control from the views package in the original MusicPlayer project and placed it into a new components package in the shared library project. The library project should now compile, and we are ready to create the new projects that we will use to build the versions of the application that will run on phones and tablets.

Creating the Phone and Tablet Projects

We will create a new Flex mobile project by using the application menu and clicking **File ➤ New ➤ Flex Mobile Project**. When the New Flex Mobile Project dialog appears, name the project MusicPlayerPhone, click the Next button, select a View-Based Application, and click Finish. The following steps must be performed to populate the new project:

1. Copy the graphical assets from the assets package in the original MusicPlayer project to an assets package in the new project. This includes the splash screen, volume icons, and the default album cover.

2. Copy the source code from the views package of the original MusicPlayer project, and place them into the views package of the new project. This will include the SongListView.mxml and SongView.mxml files.

3. Modify the code in SongView.mxml to take into account the new package for the ProgressButton control.

4. Copy the code from the main ViewNavigatorApplication MXML file in the original project's default package to the new project's main MXML file.

5. Add the MusicPlayerLib project to this project's build path by right-clicking the project and selecting Properties, clicking Flex Build Path, clicking the Add Project... button, and selecting the MusicPlayerLib project.

The new project should now compile and run, with the result looking exactly like the original MusicPlayer from Chapter 8. If you have any questions, you can review the source code in the MusicPlayerPhone project found in the examples/chapter-11 directory of the sample code for this book. By repeating these steps to create a MusicPlayerTablet project, you will be ready to start on the new custom tablet interface for the MusicPlayer application.

But before we get started, this is a good time to introduce you to Eclipse's Working Sets feature, if you don't already know it. Defining a working set will allow you to limit the number of projects listed in the Package Explorer to just the ones you are working on at any given time. And once you have working sets defined, you can easily switch between them. You access the Working Sets feature by using the View Menu to the right of the Package Explorer tab. The icon for the View Menu is the upside-down triangle. Figure 11–8 shows its location.

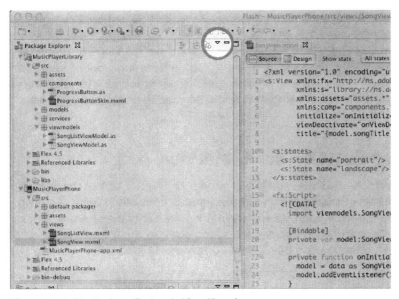

Figure 11–8. *The Package Explorer's View Menu icon*

You define a new working set by clicking the View Menu icon and choosing the "Select Working Set…" option. The Select Working Set dialog box will be displayed. Clicking the New button will display the New Working Set dialog box. Select Resource as your working set type, and click Next. In the final dialog box, type a name for your working set and select the projects that you want to be a part of the working set. Then click Finish. Figure 11–9 shows this sequence of dialog boxes.

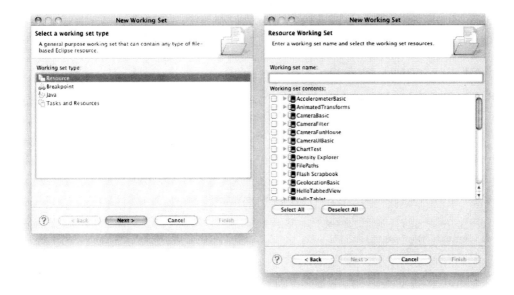

Figure 11–9. *Creating a new working set*

To select a working set, click the View Menu and Select Working Set again. The working sets you have defined will appear in the list. Select the check box next to the working set you want to activate, and click OK. Once you have selected a working set, its name will appear directly on the View Menu, allowing you to switch between working sets with only two clicks. When your Package Explorer view starts to get crowded with all of the different projects you are working on, being able to quickly define and switch between working sets is a huge benefit.

Implementing the Custom Tablet Interface

In the new SongView interface, the list of songs will appear on the left side of the screen. The current selection in the list should reflect the song that is currently playing. Tapping a new entry in the list should switch to that song. What we are describing here is two bindings: one between the song list in the model and the items in the list, and another between the list's current selection and the current song index in the model.

We shall start with the modifications that need to be made to the model. A new songList ArrayCollection will be created to serve as the source of the binding for the List in the UI. We will also need to make the model's currentIndex variable bindable to serve as the source of the List's selectedIndex property, as well as settable so that a new list selection will cause the model to take action to play a new song. Listing 11–7 shows the first of these changes to the model.

Listing 11–7. *Changes to the* SongViewModel *Because Six Pages with No Code Is Just Too Long!*

```
[Bindable]
public class SongViewModel extends EventDispatcher {
    // Some variables removed for brevity…

    public var year:String = "";
    public var genres:String = "";
    public var songList:ArrayCollection;

    private var _currentIndex:Number = 0;

    /** A collection of MusicEntry objects. */
    private var musicEntries:ArrayCollection;

    public function SongViewModel(entries:ArrayCollection, index:Number) {
        this.musicEntries = entries;
        this.currentIndex = index;

        timer = new Timer(500, 0);
        timer.addEventListener(TimerEvent.TIMER, onTimer);

        loadCurrentSong();
        filterEntriesBySongs();
    }

    /**
     * Takes all songs in musicEntries and puts them in songList.
     */
```

```
    private function filterEntriesBySongs():void {
      songList = new ArrayCollection();

      for (var i:int = 0; i<musicEntries.length; ++i) {
        var entry:MusicEntry = MusicEntry(musicEntries.getItemAt(i));
        if (entry.isSong)
          songList.addItem(entry);
      }
    }
```

In Listing 11–7, we have added the new ArrayCollection named songList and renamed the currentIndex variable to _currentIndex to indicate that it will now have public get and set functions associated with it. The songList collection is initialized in the filterEntriesBySong function that is called at the end of the class's constructor. This function loops through the musicEntries collection and copies each song entry to the songList collection.

Listing 11–8 shows the code in the model class that provides access to the currentIndex property and handles playing the song that corresponds to the currentIndex. The currentIndex's get function provides the View with access to the property's value. The set function stores the new value and calls the playSongAtCurrentIndex function.

Listing 11–8. *The SongViewModel Code Relating to Playing the Song at the Current Index*

```
    public function get currentIndex():Number {
      return _currentIndex;
    }

    public function set currentIndex(value:Number):void {
      _currentIndex = value;
      playSongAtCurrentIndex();
    }

    /**
      * Jump to the beginning of the next song in the list.  Will wrap to
      * the beginning of the song list if needed.
      */
    public function nextSong():void {
      incrementCurrentSongIndex();
      playSongAtCurrentIndex();
    }

    /**
      * Moves the play position back to the beginning of the current song
      * unless we are within 3 seconds of the beginning already.  In that
      * case, we jump back to the beginning of the previous song.  Will
      * wrap to the end of the song list if needed.
      */
    public function previousSong():void {
      if (channel && channel.position < 3000) {
        decrementCurrentSongIndex();
        playSongAtCurrentIndex();
      } else {
        percentComplete = 0;
```

```
      }
    }

    /**
     * Will load and play the song indicated by the currentIndex variable.
     */
    public function playSongAtCurrentIndex():void {
      loadCurrentSong();

      if (isPlaying) {
        pauseSong();
        playSong();
      } else {
        percentComplete = 0;
      }
    }
```

The playSongAtCurrentIndex function loads the song into memory and, if the model is in "play" mode, stops the current song and causes this new song to play. If the model is paused, then the percentComplete variable is just reset, so that playback will resume from the start of the song the next time the model's onPlayPause function is called. We have also gone back to the model's previousSong and nextSong functions and changed them to use the new playSongAtCurrentIndex function in order to eliminate unnecessary code duplication. Clean as you go!

Switching to the view, we know that the portrait mode UI should stay the same while we add the song list to the left side of the screen in landscape mode. At the same time, the song information migrates from the left side of the screen in the last incarnation of the interface to the right side of the screen in the latest design. Since we no longer need the extra states, this being a tablet-specific UI now, the beginning of the MXML file is now back to its original form with the exception that the ActionBar displays the album title rather than the song title as it does on the phone interface. All of the extra state declarations and the functions to set and get the View states are gone.

We need to add the declaration for the List as the first child of our View's root Group container and make sure it is included only in the landscape state. We will also enclose the album cover, portrait mode song information, and playback controls into one VGroup now, since those sections always appear as a vertical group in both the portrait and landscape states. Finally, a VGroup of labels will be added to the landscape state to show the song information on the right side of the screen in that orientation. Listing 11–9 shows these changes to the SongView MXML file.

Listing 11–9. *Changes to the SongView MXML to Support the New Landscape Interface Design*

```
<s:Group width="100%" height="100%">
    <s:layout.portrait>
      <s:VerticalLayout paddingTop="10" horizontalAlign="center"/>
    </s:layout.portrait>

    <s:layout.landscape>
      <s:HorizontalLayout verticalAlign="top"/>
    </s:layout.landscape>
```

```
<s:List id="songList" styleName="songList" includeIn="landscape" width="30%"
        height="100%" dataProvider="{model.songList}" labelField="name"
        selectedIndex="{model.currentIndex}"
        change="model.currentIndex = songList.selectedIndex"/>

<s:VGroup horizontalAlign="center" width.portrait="100%"
          width.landscape="40%" paddingTop="20 ">
  <s:Group width.portrait="{height*0.4}" height.portrait="{height*0.4}"
          width.landscape="{width*0.35}" height.landscape="{width*0.35}">
    <s:BitmapImage width="100%" height="100%" source="{model.albumCover}"
                   visible="{model.albumCover != null}"/>

    <assets:DefaultAlbum id="placeHolder" width="100%" height="100%"
                         visible="{!model.albumCover}" />
  </s:Group>

  <!-- The groups defining the portrait mode song info and controls are unchanged --
>
</s:VGroup>

<s:VGroup width="30%" gap="60" includeIn="landscape" paddingRight="10"
          paddingTop="20">
  <s:VGroup width="100%" horizontalAlign="right">
    <s:Label styleName="albumInfoLabel" text="Song"/>
    <s:Label styleName="albumInfo" text="{model.songTitle}"
             maxWidth="{width*.3}" maxDisplayedLines="2"/>
  </s:VGroup>
  <!-- Repeated for the other song information items -->
</s:VGroup>
```

The List uses the model's new songList as its dataProvider and uses it to display the song names. Its selectedIndex property is bound to the model's currentIndex property to ensure that whichever song is currently playing is also the one highlighted in the list. Whenever the List's selection changes, the new selectedIndex is used to set the model's currentIndex property. This allows the user to tap an item in the list to change the song that is currently playing.

After implementing these changes, the application now appears as in Figure 11–10. The figure shows the application running in landscape orientation on the Motorola XOOM and showing off the new song list on the left side of the screen. The image on the right side of the figure shows the application running in portrait mode on a Samsung Galaxy Tab. Rotating the tablet from portrait to landscape will cause the song list to appear seamlessly. And, of course, we have our original phone version of the interface tucked safely away in the MusicPlayerPhone project, which remains unaffected by these new features in the tablet version. The updates to the SongViewModel in the shared library will be present in the phone version, of course, but they remain unused in that application and therefore have no effect.

In some ways, having separate projects for each platform simplifies the build process, especially once you start dealing with multiple platforms, because you can have one application XML descriptor file per project instead of swapping them in and out at build time.

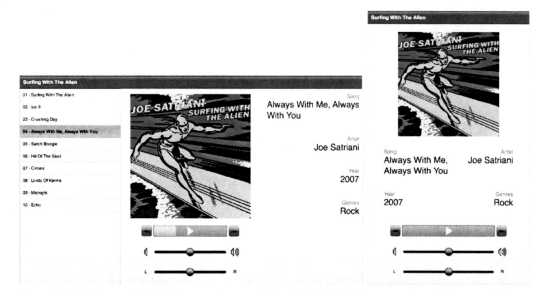

Figure 11–10. *The new tablet interface running on a Motorola XOOM in landscape mode and a Samsung Galaxy Tab in portrait mode*

Transitioning to TV

This is an exciting time to be a part of the Adobe Flash ecosystem. In addition to the web, desktop, and Android platforms, AIR is also becoming a viable programming environment for iOS devices, BlackBerry tablets, and even television sets, Blu-ray players, and set-top boxes! It is the one environment that truly lets you leverage your existing programming and design skills across all the screens of your life—even the *big* screens.

At Google I/O in May of 2011, Google announced that it was bringing Android 3.1, the so-called Honeycomb release, to its Google TV platform. With this update, the Android market will become available to Google TV users. With a few restrictions, your existing AIR for Android applications should port fairly easily to the Google TV platform. In addition, all new Google TV devices sold at retail will include the Android debugger, which means that you should be able to run and test your applications right on the Google TV in your living room.

Another path to the living room lies in the AIR for TV platform from Adobe. This is a runtime for TVs, set-top boxes, and Blu-ray players. It is currently in pre-release and runs on AIR 2.5. One thing to be aware of when developing for TV platforms is that they typically lie on the low end of the CPU horsepower spectrum. The CPUs found in TVs are often significantly slower than even those found in your average smartphone. This does not necessarily mean that your AIR for TV applications will be slow, but it does mean that you should pay attention to performance. Many of the tips given in Chapter 10 will also apply to TV platforms. Given the slower CPUs commonly found in TVs, you should pay particular attention to the advice given in the "Reducing Code Execution Time" section of that chapter.

Adobe AIR for TV is expected to make its debut in Samsung's Smart TV platform that, at the time of this writing, was expected to ship in 2011.

There are some things that you need to keep in mind should you decide to develop for one of these TV platforms. First, the input method is different for a TV. Even if TVs had touchscreens, nobody wants to constantly get up and walk to the TV to touch the screen in order to interact with their applications. Therefore TVs will likely use small touchpads or directional button pads for navigation and interaction. Secondly, as Google reminds us, TVs are really a "10 foot experience." The screens are larger, so the controls and fonts should be larger too. Tackling TV will almost certainly require a fresh design pass for your application.

Porting to PlayBook

Although Research In Motion is a newcomer to the tablet market, the BlackBerry PlayBook is an interesting entry. The PlayBook comes in a small form factor, measuring just 7.6 inches wide and 5.4 inches tall, which makes it an extremely portable device. It features a 7-inch touchscreen, a 1-GHz dual-core processor, and 1 GB of RAM. It is paired with the QNX Neutrino real-time operating system. This microkernel architecture-based OS is known for its use in mission-critical systems.

One thing to like about the PlayBook is that it is very developer-friendly. It offers developers a choice of no less than four environments in which to develop their applications: native C/C++, Java, HTML5 and related technologies, and (of course) Adobe AIR. Furthermore, AIR is not a second-class citizen on this platform. AIR apps can take advantage of hardware acceleration for video and graphics. Although the usual Flash platform components are present, there are special packages available to AIR programmers that give ActionScript programs the ability to use native, high-performance QNX components in their user interfaces. AIR applications can even access the platform's native notification features. In short, AIR programs are very well supported and integrate nicely into the platform. The only real drawback to the tablet is that since it is a brand-new platform, its market penetration is fairly low.

So as a Flash/Flex/AIR developer, how can you jump into this new market? A good place to start is the BlackBerry Tablet OS SDK for Adobe Air Development Resources web site.[3] From there you will find links to the "Getting Started Guide"[4] and steps for installing the development environment. You will first need to download and unzip the SDK installer program. The installer will create a new PlayBook directory in the sdks directory of your current Flash Builder 4.5 installation. This directory will contain everything you need to develop PlayBook applications. The PlayBook simulator is a

---

[3] http://us.blackberry.com/developers/tablet/adobe.jsp

[4] http://docs.blackberry.com/en/developers/deliverables/25068/

VMware-compatible virtual machine image that runs a PlayBook runtime environment right on your Windows, Mac, or Linux desktop. This image is included with the PlayBook SDK files that get placed in your Flash Builder installation directory. Just open this VM image in VMware, and the PlayBook environment will boot up. When it starts, it will ask for a password. Type in "playbook" and you should see the PlayBook UI appear.

You create a new project for your PlayBook application in Flash Builder 4.5 by selecting **File ➤ New ➤ ActionScript Mobile Project** from the application's menu. You use the default SDK, and select BlackBerry Tablet OS as the target platform.

> **NOTE:** At the time of this writing, official BlackBerry Tablet OS support is expected to ship in a Flash Builder update in the summer of 2011. That may change the way you create a mobile application project for this platform.

You can run and test your AIR applications right in the simulator on your desktop. You will just need to create a run configuration for your project in Flash Builder using the IP address of the PlayBook environment running in the virtual machine. You can get the PlayBook's IP address by clicking the icon of the person with a gear on his chest, located at the top right of the PlayBook screen. The "Getting Started Guide" just mentioned provides simple and easy-to-follow instructions for all of these steps, which will allow you to get started developing on the simulator in under an hour.

That is enough of a preamble; Listing 11–10 shows what a simple Hello World program looks like for the BlackBerry PlayBook.

Listing 11–10. *A Hello World ActionScript Program for the BlackBerry PlayBook*

```
import flash.display.Bitmap;
import flash.display.GradientType;
import flash.display.Graphics;
import flash.display.SpreadMethod;
import flash.display.Sprite;
import flash.events.MouseEvent;
import flash.geom.Matrix;
import flash.text.TextFormat;
import qnx.ui.buttons.LabelButton;
import qnx.ui.text.Label;

[SWF(width="1024", height="600", frameRate="30")]
public class PlayBookHelloWorld extends Sprite
{
  [Embed(source="splash.png")]
  private var imageClass:Class;

  public function PlayBookHelloWorld()
  {
    var bitmap:Bitmap = new imageClass();
    bitmap.x = 10;
    bitmap.y = 10;

    var goodByeButton:LabelButton = new LabelButton();
    goodByeButton.label = "Good Bye";
```

```
        goodByeButton.x = stage.stageWidth - goodByeButton.width;
        goodByeButton.y = stage.stageHeight - goodByeButton.height;
        goodByeButton.addEventListener(MouseEvent.CLICK, onClick);

        var myFormat:TextFormat = new TextFormat();
        myFormat.color = 0xf0f0f0;
        myFormat.size = 48;
        myFormat.italic = true;

        var label:Label = new Label();
        label.text = "Hello Pro Android Flash!";
        label.x = bitmap.width + 20;
        label.y = 10;
        label.width = stage.stageWidth - bitmap.width - 10;
        label.height = 100;
        label.format = myFormat;

        addChild(createBackground());
        addChild(bitmap);
        addChild(goodByeButton);
        addChild(label);

        stage.nativeWindow.visible = true;
    }

    private function onClick(event:MouseEvent):void{
        stage.nativeWindow.close();
    }

    private function createBackground():Sprite {
        var type:String = GradientType.LINEAR;
        var colors:Array = [ 0x808080, 0x404040 ];
        var alphas:Array = [ 1, 1 ];
        var ratios:Array = [ 0, 255 ];
        var spread:String = SpreadMethod.PAD;

        var matrix:Matrix = new Matrix();
        matrix.createGradientBox( 100, 100, (90 * Math.PI/180), 0, 0 );

        var sprite:Sprite = new Sprite();
        var g:Graphics = sprite.graphics;
        g.beginGradientFill( type, colors, alphas, ratios, matrix, spread );
        g.drawRect( 0, 0, 1024, 600 );

        return sprite;
    }
}
```

As you can see, it looks pretty much like any other Flash program. We have used a couple of the basic QNX controls just to show what it looks like to include them in your program. They have a very familiar API to anyone that is used to Flash programming. Figure 11–11 shows what the PlayBook environment and the Hello World program look like when running in the simulator.

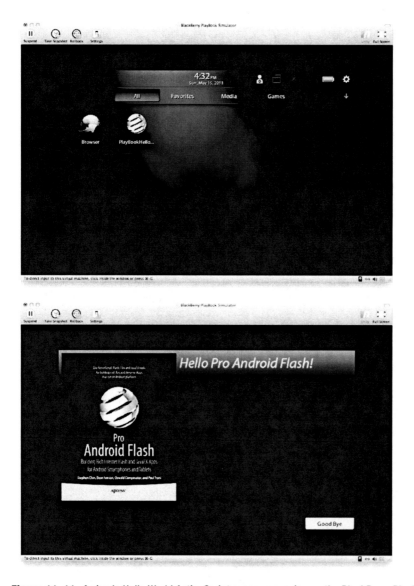

Figure 11–11. *A simple Hello World ActionScript program running on the BlackBerry PlayBook simulator*

You will need a "debug token" if you want to run your applications on actual PlayBook hardware. Getting such a token is free, but you will need to register with the PlayBook development program. You will also need to apply for a key to sign your applications if you wish to eventually deploy them into the BlackBerry app store.

If you do decide to port your Android applications to the PlayBook, you should follow the same advice we used previously when porting from phone to tablet: get to know your target platform. For example, the PlayBook does not have a hardware Back button; so, much like the iPhone or iPad, there is usually a Back button at the top left corner of most application screens. As always, a good way to get to know your target platform is to study the platform's popular applications. There is a Facebook app and plenty of pre-installed applications for you to look at on the PlayBook.

Investigating iOS

Android and iPhone devices are currently dominating the smartphone market in terms of worldwide popularity. This makes Apple's iOS attractive as a potential target when porting your applications to other platforms. But when you add the fact that Apple's iPad is the undisputed king of the tablet market, the decision suddenly becomes a very obvious one.

Getting Apple's development environment set up is somewhat similar to the process required for the PlayBook, although with Apple there is no free option for testing your software on an actual device. You will have to join its developer program[5] (currently $99USD per year) to have the ability to run and test your application on real hardware.

Once you have your membership and development key in hand, however, writing ActionScript-based applications for iOS is pretty much the same as it is for Android and PlayBook.

> **NOTE:** Like the PlayBook, at the time of this writing, updated support for iOS development with Flash Builder is expected in the summer of 2011.

Once again you will need to spend some time familiarizing yourself with the common design patterns employed on this platform. For example, just like the PlayBook, iOS devices do not have hardware Back buttons. Fortunately, the good folks on Adobe's platform teams have made life somewhat easier for developers in this respect. The `defaultButtonAppearance`-style property of the `ActionBar` can be set to "beveled" to approximate the look of the native iOS `ActionBar` buttons. In addition, titles in the `ActionBar` tend to be centered rather than right-aligned as they are on Android. The `ActionBar`'s `titleAlign` property can be set to "center" to achieve this effect in your AIR application. See Listing 3-8 in Chapter 3 for an example of using these styles in your application.

You can even apply these styles dynamically at runtime by using the `@media (os-platform:"ios")` CSS selector or by making sure that `Capabilities.cpuArchitecture` returns the string "ARM" and that `Capabilities.os` returns a string containing the term "iPhone".

---

[5] http://developer.apple.com/programs/ios/

Summary

This chapter has shown you how to take your mobile AIR applications and adapt them to Android tablets, TVs, and even Apple and BlackBerry devices. You have learned the following:

- How to use states and state groups to customize your interface for different devices while maintaining a single code base

- How to split your application into multiple projects that include shared library code as well as fully customized UIs for each of the different platforms that you want to target

- What options you have for expanding your reach onto TV screens and some of the things you will need to consider when doing so

- How to get up and running with the BlackBerry PlayBook development environment for Adobe AIR

- Some tricks for porting your Android applications to Apple's iOS platform

You made it! Welcome to the end of the book! We hope you have enjoyed reading it as much as we enjoyed writing it. And if you've learned a thing or two to make your life easier as an AIR for Android developer, then that makes the journey worthwhile. These are exciting times in the technology world. This modern world of smartphones, tablet computers, smart TVs, and incredibly fast wireless bandwidth is opening up new opportunities and new challenges for software developers all over the world. Good luck and good programming!

Index

H

CPSIA information can be obtained at www.ICGtesting.com
Printed in the USA
237896LV00005B/65-228/P